The New Political Economy of D

The New Political Economy of Development

Globalization, Imperialism, Hegemony

Ray Kiely

First published 2007 by
PALGRAVE MACMILLAN
Houndmills, Basingstoke, Hampshire RG21 6XS and
175 Fifth Avenue, New York, NY 10010
Companies and representatives throughout the world

PALGRAVE MACMILLAN is the global academic imprint of the Palgrave Macmillan division of St. Martin's Press, LLC and of Palgrave Macmillan Ltd. Macmillan® is a registered trademark in the United States, United Kingdom and other countries. Palgrave is a registered trademark in the European Union and other countries.

ISBN-13: 978–1–4039–9996–2   hardback
ISBN-10: 1–4039–9996–1   hardback
ISBN-13: 978–1–4039–9997–9   paperback
ISBN-10: 1–4039–9997–X   paperback

This book is printed on paper suitable for recycling and made from fully managed and sustained forest sources.

A catalogue record for this book is available from the British Library.

A catalog record for this book is available from the Library of Congress.

10 9 8 7 6 5 4 3 2 1
16 15 14 13 12 11 10 09 08 07

Printed and bound in Great Britain by CPD (Wales) Ltd, Ebbw Vale

Contents

Acknowledgements

Thanks to a number of friends and colleagues from various institutions for comments on drafts, discussion, reference sources, support, and even the occasional debate. These include Liam Campling, Denis Cattell, Stephen Chan, Alex Colas, Chris Cramer, Susie Jacobs, Paul Kennedy, Jens Lerche, Iain Pirie, Alfredo Saad-Filho, Rick Saull, Subir Sinha and Andy Storey. Thanks at Palgrave Macmillan to Steven Kennedy, first for periodically asking me to undertake a project for which I was initially less than enthusiastic, but that I actually enjoyed doing more than any of my previous books, and secondly, for his useful comments throughout. Thanks also to the anonymous reviewers of the original proposal, and of a first draft, even if I did write a somewhat harsh response to one of them. These comments were particularly valuable in forcing me to make my own positions more explicit. Many thanks, as always, to my partner Emma, and son Will, and now to my daughter Ella, who was born while I was writing this book, and to whom it is dedicated.

Chapter 1

Introduction

If the 1990s was the decade of globalization, then the post-2001 world is one dominated by the return of imperialism to the social sciences. While much of the debate of the 1990s assumed either a declining or a newly benign US hegemony in a post-Cold War world, debates since 2001 have more explicitly returned to older questions of relations between states and the question of power. This has been most obvious in the context of the open unilateralism of the Bush administration in the United States, but it has also drawn attention to the need not only for greater reflection on the post-9/11 world, but also to re-examine the questions of US hegemony and imperialism in the so-called decade of globalization. In short, three key concepts in the social sciences – globalization, imperialism and hegemony – have come under renewed scrutiny since 2001, to help us understand the world both *before* and *after* the terrorist attacks on 11 September. This suggests less that we need to regard the 1990s as the decade of globalization and post-2001 as the era of renewed imperialism; rather, we need to better understand both the continuities as well as discontinuities, pre- and post-9/11. In other words, what does imperialism mean today and in the globalization decade of the 1990s, and what does globalization mean both before and after 2001? And how does this relate to the question of the role of the US state as the primary state in the international order, and the related but narrower question of US hegemony?

This book addresses these crucial questions of international (and transnational) relations. But it does so by specifically relating these questions to that of development. What does development mean in an era of globalization? What is the relationship between imperialism and development? And is US hegemony a force that promotes development in the former Third World? Or, put slightly differently, how is development promoted and what kind of development does the US support in the developing world (and how is this challenged and supported in the latter)? Moreover, does the development of East Asia, and specifically China, constitute a challenge to US primacy and/or hegemony? What are the similarities and differences, continuities and changes, which have

1

occurred since 2001? Perhaps above all, what is the relationship between neo-liberalism on the one hand, and globalization, imperialism and US hegemony on the other? And how have issues of security combined with the question of development, both prior to, and after September 2001?

This book is therefore concerned not only with international relations, but more specifically with international political economy, and even more precisely, the international political economy of development. It addresses a wide variety of key issues and debates, including: historical structures of capitalist development; post-war development in the Third World; the end of the Bretton Woods era and rise of neo-liberalism; theories of globalization and imperialism; global governance and development; development, poverty and inequality in the context of global capital flows; state formation and restructuring in the developing world, including 'rogue' and 'failed' states; the shift from the Washington to post-Washington consensus; the relationship between development and security; regional 'challenges' to US hegemony; Islamist, post-development, anti-globalization and progressive alternatives to neo-liberal globalization (including in Latin America). The chapters that follow address these issues in some considerable depth. In the rest of this opening chapter, however, the four key concepts addressed so far – globalization, imperialism, hegemony and development – are briefly discussed, as a prelude to the more detailed expositions and discussions of later chapters. The chapter then outlines three positions on these four concepts, which implicitly (and explicitly) run through the specific topics that follow. Finally, a brief summary of later chapters is provided. But first, we need to define and discuss the four key concepts addressed so far, and show how they relate to each other.

Defining Globalization

'Globalization' emerged as the new buzzword in the social sciences, and indeed entered mainstream political discourse, in the 1990s. As we will see in later chapters, despite its increased use, there was something of a lack of clarity over what it actually meant. Some saw globalization as something that referred to a new period in history (Appadurai 1996; Held et al. 1999), while others regarded it as a new way of understanding, or a new methodology for interpreting, older periods of history, as well as the present (Gills and Thompson 2006). Related to these points, there was considerable debate about whether globalization was an established fact, to which we all had to respond. This interpretation was often allied to the idea that globalization was a political project, a way of responding to the fact of globalization (Giddens 2000). Others argued that globalization was largely an ideological myth, used in an attempt to justify the political project of extending pro-globalization policies (Hay and Watson 1999; 2003). Much of this debate reflected disputes about how globalization was to be measured, and the extent to which these measurements added up to the existence of a new era of globalization (Castells 1996; Hirst and Thompson 1999). Other, more normative debates, not unrelated but certainly not the same as this debate, focused on the extent to which globalization was or was not desirable, and more precisely, what aspects were to be supported and what deserved rejection (Bello 2003; Appelbaum and Robinson 2005).

This bewildering array of debates in part reflected the lack of precision in much of the globalization debate, an issue examined in depth in Chapter 5. Having said that, what more or less all protagonists in the debate agreed on was that there were a number of processes, flows, relationships and values that could not be reduced to, and in some ways extended or even transcended, the nation-state (Scholte 2005a). Thus, flows of capital were not exclusively tied to a particular nation-state. This, of course, was not necessarily new, as there had been important capital flows prior to the current era of globalization, which was usually said to start in the 1970s or 1980s. But it was also clear that the current era was in some respects novel – the massive increase in direct and portfolio foreign investment in the 1990s, for instance – but at the same time it forced us to reflect back on earlier periods of international, and perhaps global, history (Went 2002). Similarly, the rise of human rights discourses since 1948, and perhaps especially since the end of the Cold War, did in some ways force us to think more critically about the relationship between state sovereignty and individual human rights (Archibugi 2003). This allowed us to think through changes in the international order since 1991, but also to think again about earlier histories of ethical political philosophy. In particular, the idea that there are universal human rights which transcend particular territorial states can be rooted in cosmopolitan political philosophy, which dates back at least to Immanuel Kant (1983) in the eighteenth century.

Debates over globalization therefore reflected both the changing realities of social and political territorial space, and the (supposedly) new ways of thinking about this space (Scholte 2005a). In terms of the former, this reflected the rise of institutions of global governance that were not confined to particular nation-states (Held and McGrew 2002), the rise of movements of capital, commodities and people from one territory to others (Dicken 2003; Cohen 2006), and the rise of cosmopolitan human values (Beck 2006), and of problems that transcended nation-states, such as global warming (Lipschutz 2004). Much of the literature on globalization – both mainstream and critical – was therefore concerned with moving beyond the idea that social and other relations were contained within particular territorial units, and above all the nation-state. Globalization therefore represented a challenge to 'state-centrism' (Sklair 2001).

But there was an irony in the timing of this challenge. This was because for much of the world, and specifically the post-colonial or what used to be called the Third World (see Chapter 3), state sovereignty was a relatively new phenomenon (Kiely 2005b). Thus, some theorists of globalization talked of the transformation or even the death of the nation-state, at a moment when some territories had only just won independence and sovereign statehood (Rosenberg 2005). This reflected in part a great deal of Eurocentrism in talk of globalization (Slater 2004), where the idea that events in one territory were affected by events in another was regarded as historically novel. For much of the post-colonial world, this was far from being a new experience, but was part of a much older history of colonialism (F. Cooper 2004). Equally, in much of the literature (mainstream and critical), this historical amnesia was often accompanied by an approach that 'flattened out' the reconstruction of territorial space, so that all nation-states were being transformed in similar ways (Robinson 2004), or even transcended (Hardt and Negri 2000). In one respect – the increased globalization of neo-liberalism – this was true, but as we will see, this had very different – and highly unequal – effects in different parts of the world (Kiely 2004a). Much talk about globalization therefore had little to say about the developing world. Even worse, in its neo-liberal (including 'third way' and neo-conservative) form, much of the new discourse was hopelessly optimistic about the opportunities, and naive about the constraints, that globalization was said to present for the developing world (see, for instance, World Bank 2002a). These issues are addressed in depth in Chapters 5 through to 8.

But equally, the discourse of globalization tended to assume away any need for causal explanation (see Rosenberg 2000). Certainly, in suggesting that globalization entailed a transformation of all states, much of the literature downplayed the ways in which nation-states have always been influenced by relations that transcended nation-states. But in terms of understanding the current world order, what was equally downplayed was the role that some states – and dominant social and political actors within these states – had played in promoting globalization (Panitch 1994). For instance, the free movement of capital was promoted by nation-states. Similarly, the creation of new institutions of global governance was essentially carried out by states, and these states were the institutions' main representatives. The concept of globalization thus too easily set up a dichotomy between the state sovereignty of the past (when it was far from universalized) and the globalization of the present (when it was states that had played a key role in carrying out 'globalizing processes'). Moreover, at its worst, globalization theory tended towards the circular argument that globalization can be explained by globalization (see Chapter 5).

As will become clear in the chapters that follow, globalization does usefully capture some of the recent changes in the international order. At the same time, it tends to over-estimate these real, but limited, changes. But perhaps more important, it tends to ignore the continued importance of the nation-state system, and the hierarchies within this order. Certainly it is true that sovereignty has been more or less universalized, but the power of individual states within the international system of nation-states is very unequal. This reflects not only blatant institutional inequality, such as unequal voting rights at the International Monetary Fund (IMF), World Bank, and United Nations Security Council, but also the bargaining power of states at ostensibly more democratic institutions such as the World Trade Organization (see Chapter 6). But equally, the 'transnational' social relations that are related to, but not identical with, the nation-state are hierarchical and unequal. Some territories have far higher rates of capital accumulation than others, and the flows of foreign investment in the international order are very unequal, in both their direction and their effects (see Chapter 7).

Thus, the book does take globalization seriously, and accepts that it does in part 'capture' some important contemporary processes in the international order. In particular I will suggest that neo-liberal globalization has become increasingly generalized (but this has had uneven and unequal effects), and with it the growing importance of competitiveness as something that influences and even determines state behaviour. I will also suggest that cosmopolitan ideas should be taken seriously, not least as a (limited but necessary) challenge to neo-liberalism and US hegemony. But central to the argument that follows are the following qualifications: first, that these changes do not mean the transcendence of the nation-state system; second, that this nation-state system is hierarchical; third, that globalizing processes are in part the creation of nation-states (and capitalist interests in such states), and of some nation-states more than others; fourth, that contemporary globalization does not mean the end of uneven and unequal development, but rather its intensification. These qualifications therefore suggest that hierarchy, unevenness and inequality need to be taken very seriously – and therefore, we need to examine the return of an old concept, that of imperialism.

Defining Imperialism

Only a few years ago, the idea that imperialism would become a renewed source of inquiry in the social sciences seemed unthinkable (see Chibber 2004a). As I have already suggested, the main reason why it has become so prevalent once again is the unilateralist, militarist response of the Bush II administration in the US to the terrorist attacks in 2001. The naked displays of overwhelming US military power in Afghanistan and Iraq, as well as more belligerent US policy towards other states, and uni-lateralist policies in terms of the environment, international justice, arms control and so on, all suggest that the optimism of liberal views of glob-alization in the 1990s was misplaced.

The return of imperialism has generally taken two forms. First, there is the critical approach, which is mainly (but not exclusively) produced by radical and especially Marxist literature (Callinicos 2003; Harvey 2003; Mann 2003). But secondly, there has also been a boom in litera-ture broadly supportive of a new, US-led imperialism, particularly in dealing with so-called 'rogue' and 'failed' states in the developing world. Much of this is associated with neo-conservative and other right-wing think-tanks, sometimes linked to the Bush II administration (Kaplan and Kristol 2003). However, there is also a revived interest from some would-be radicals and liberals who support a benign US imperialism, which is said to be enforcing cosmopolitan human rights in the interna-tional order (Cushman 2005; Ignatieff 2005; Kamm 2005).

These issues are discussed further below and in later chapters, but first we need a working definition of imperialism. Standard definitions usually refer to the domination of one territory over another, and so this is often associated with colonialism. If this is a useful definition then it is clear that the utility of the concept of imperialism is limited, because we live in a world of sovereign states. On the other hand, classical Marxist accounts of imperialism argued that the domination of one nation or territory by another did not necessarily have to take place through direct territorial acquisition, but could be through other (eco-nomic, military, political) forms of control. In other words, colonialism was only one form of domination among others. Thus, in the early twen-tieth century, Marxist thinkers such as Lenin (1975), Bukharin (1973) and Hilferding (1981) argued that a new form of capitalist imperialism had emerged, which was characterized by the increased concentration and centralization of capital, and an increase in capital export overseas. While this capital export could be associated with colonialism, it could also lead to the development of new, semi-colonies that were formally independent but economically dependent. The precise details of these (problematic) arguments are discussed further in Chapters 2 and 5, but what is clear is that the Marxist tradition usefully reminds us that different forms of domination do not preclude the fact of imperialism existing in a post-colonial era of universalized state sovereignty.

What is therefore needed is a theory of capitalist imperialism which is sensitive to the different forms taken in specific historical periods. Capitalist imperialism thus refers to the subordination of some territories and nation-states to other territories, which arises out of the uneven development of international capitalist accumulation and the associated hierarchies of the international nation-state system. This may involve economic, political or military domination, or (more likely) a combination of these things. For reasons outlined in later chapters, it will be suggested that there are substantial differences between the era of classical imperialism before 1914 (or 1939) and contemporary imperialism. Briefly, in terms of the relationship between dominant and dominated states, the current era of US-led imperialism is one characterized by US primacy in international organizations, both in military strength and (more contentiously) in the strength and centrality of the US economy as against other economies (not least those of other developed capitalist countries). Indeed, while it is far from being the only agent, the US state has certainly been the principal agent of globalization. None of this means that such primacy is without its tensions, contradictions and potential weaknesses, nor indeed that it is uncontested, but it is also clear that the US remains the main state power in the international and global order. Indeed, the US's self-defined right to by-pass international rules when it is deemed necessary, clearly sets the US apart from all other nation-states in the current international order, an exception that has become highly visible since 2001 (Agamben 2005), but which also existed before then.

Whether or not such primacy is a force for good is an issue discussed below and throughout the book. But clearly, the question of primacy is closely linked to the question of hegemony.

Defining Hegemony

Hegemony is a concept used in much of the critical social sciences, but in international relations at least it has historically been associated with realist theories of international relations. Realist theories argued that international relations are essentially relations between nation-states, each of which is primarily concerned with issues of security and self-preservation (Waltz 1979). In a world of anarchy, which is characterized as one in which there is no overall authority in relations between states, realist theory is mainly concerned with describing (rather than analysing) the ways in which international order is achieved. This can occur through a number of means, but one way relevant to our discussion is through the emergence of a hegemonic power. Hegemony is basically seen as the ability to make and enforce rules in the international order, an ability which itself is secured by the possession of sufficient material resources to enforce rules on others (Keohane 1984). In the era of globalization, much of the literature assumed that US state hegemony was in decline, and being replaced by some form of transnational hegemony, in which states were just one form of power among others.

This view of hegemony tended to mirror closely much of the mainstream and critical globalization debate, in that an era of state sovereignty and US hegemony was said to be in decline, and replaced by an era of globalization and transnational hegemony (Robinson 2004). This view not only under-estimated the continued importance of state and US power, but also downplayed the ways in which US hegemony was secured through means other than hard, military power. This led to a more subtle understanding of hegemony, in part derived from the work of Marxist theorist Antonio Gramsci (1971), which focused on the ways in which dominant states secured their primary position in practice. This of course was in part through force and coercion, but it was also through the use of powers of persuasion and the construction of consent. Liberal advocates of US hegemony called this 'soft power' (Nye 2005), while neo-Gramscians tended to focus on ideological constructions of US hegemony (Cox 1987).

As we will see, these views are not unimportant. But they need to be supplemented by a greater focus on the ways in which hegemony is constructed both materially and ideologically, and on the contradictions that emerge out of these processes. What this means, as will become clear, is that hegemony is constructed through ideological processes which themselves cannot be separated from concrete forms of class and state formation in different parts of the world. Chapter 9 develops this theme in detail, where it is suggested that dominant classes and state actors in many parts of the world have actively bought into a US-led, neo-liberal international order, and that there are concrete benefits to be gained from doing so. Of course not everybody benefits, but it is mistaken to assume that dominant classes in the other developed countries, and in much of the developing world, reject a US-led neo-liberal order. On the other hand, they may well reject aspects of that order, and it could be argued that since 2001, US hegemony has been partially eroded by the naked unilateralism and militarism of US foreign policy. But at the same time, this does not mean that ruling classes and state elites in the rest of the world reject neo-liberal capitalism wholesale. In contrast to much of the literature on US hegemony, the position taken in this book is that US hegemony has actually intensified, and not declined in the post-Cold War, neo-liberal order. Having said that, there has been some erosion of US hegemony, as opposed to dominance, since 2001, but this largely amounts to a challenge that accepts the basic, neo-liberal parameters of US hegemony, as opposed to an outright rejection.

In this account then, US hegemony is closely linked to neo-liberalism. Briefly, neo-liberalism can be regarded both as an ideology propagated by advocates of free market economics, but also as the dominant form of capital accumulation in the modern world. US hegemony has played a crucial role in promoting neo-liberalism as both ideology and the current form of capital accumulation, in that it has led the way in promoting the shift from fixed to floating exchange rates, the elimination of capital controls, and the liberalization of trade and investment rules. This has become the hegemonic form of social rule in the world today because, with the exception of East Asia, dominant classes in other countries have largely accepted the need for such policies. Indeed, even in East Asia, this is changing. This suggests then that hegemony should not be regarded as a simplistic zero-sum game, in which one nation-state or region increases its powers of consent or coercion at the expense of another. As will become clear, US hegemony has important sources of strength and weakness, but these must be analysed in terms of cooperative as well as conflictual relations with other states and regions.

None of this means of course that neo-liberal or US hegemony goes unchallenged, but it does mean that such challenges occur from social and political movements committed to far more radical social and political change, who are unconvinced that neo-liberalism is the most efficient or just way of satisfying people's needs throughout the world. And this point leads us on to the question of development.

Defining Development

Defining development is not perhaps as straightforward as it may first appear. Any standard account must accept that 'development' usually referred to something that primarily took place in what used to be called the Third World, particularly in the context of the period after 1945. 'Development' thus usually refers to something that occurs in the developing world, describing the processes by which poorer countries catch up with richer, developed, countries. One of the more important historical reflections on the idea of development has challenged the assumptions that development is a post-1945 creation that applies largely to the developed world. Cowen and Shenton (1996) suggest that although not used so explicitly before 1945, the idea of development has its roots in

older debates about modernity and progress that stretch back at least to
the eighteenth century. Insofar as their approach applies to current
debates, they also make an important distinction between immanent and
intentional development. The former is essentially defined as the spon-
taneous development of capitalism, based on development of the productive forces (technologies) which is rooted in the competition between
capitals. Intentional development, on the other hand, is defined as deliberate action designed to control the contradictions and problems that
arise out of immanent development. This action is located in the activities of various agencies, including states and civil society organizations.

These definitions usefully distinguish different understandings of
development, something that is increasingly important in the context of
the increased turn away from social theory, historical sociology and even
radical political economy in much that now passes for development
studies. Indeed, some critics have regretfully suggested that development
studies has effectively made its peace with any critical account, not only
of capitalism, but even of neo-liberal capitalism (Payne 2004; 2005).

On the other hand, there are some problems with the distinction made
between immanent and intentional development. In particular, in sepa-
rating the immanent development of the market from the intentional
development of the state, Cowen and Shenton come perilously close to
repeating the fallacies of neo-liberalism, which assumes that states and
markets can be separated in this way. As those influenced by Marx
(1976) and Polanyi (1944), and any number of classical sociologists
contend, the idea that 'natural' markets can be so easily separated from
'political' states, is highly problematic. It is a fallacy repeated by much
of the literature on globalization, which assumes that the fact of globalization (or the natural market) has an impact on states, but it is a strange
separation to be made by two writers who owe considerable allegiance
to Marxist thought. Indeed, as we will see in Chapters 2 and 5, the idea
that there are separate economic and political spheres is one that is
rooted in capitalist social relations, and Marxists interrogate the ways
that this separation is rooted in these historically specific relations
(Wood 2002). They do not take such a separation for granted.

These abstract points have important implications for understanding
post-war development, and the shift away from the developmental to
neo-liberal states. For while it is true that development has a history
prior to 1945, it is also true that it emerged as a far more prominent idea
in the context of the emergence of newly independent sovereign states in
the years after 1945 (Hewitt 2000). The former colonies, and poorer
countries in Latin America, committed themselves to a consciously
directed process of capitalist development (Kambhampati 2004). The
main strategy for promoting catch up with the developed world – in

other words, development – was import-substitution industrialization (ISI). Under ISI, states directed processes of industrial development, usually along capitalist lines (even when socialist ideas influenced state leaders). As Chapter 3 shows, this was done through a process of state fostering of industries, through subsidies, tariffs and import controls designed to protect domestic producers (whether locally or foreign owned) from competition from cheaper imports from overseas (Kiely 1998). In this way, intentional and immanent development was combined. Such a strategy was hardly exclusive to the Third World after 1945, as the developed countries protected themselves from foreign competition in the pre-1914 period (see Chapter 2).

Crucially for the argument that follows, this era of post-war development has been increasingly eroded since the shift away from neo-Keynesian, state-directed capitalist development, to one based on neo-liberalism (Toye 1987; Leys 1996; Kiely 2005a). This shift occurred in the developing world from the early 1980s, with the onset of the debt crisis (see Chapter 4). This crisis laid the foundation for a new set of policies designed to increase global competitiveness, including trade and investment liberalization, and in an increasing number of cases in the 1990s, the removal of controls on the movement of money capital. While much of this was externally enforced in the 1980s, by the 1990s there was considerable support for policies designed to increase competitiveness among powerful groups within the developing world – which, as we have seen, reflected growing neo-liberal hegemony in the international order.

By the turn of the twentieth century, there was considerable support for the idea that globalization provided the best way forward for the development of the former Third World. Considerable evidence was presented to suggest a decrease in global poverty, and the rise of China, the most populous country on Earth, seemingly backed up these claims. The mainstream development debate had supposedly moved on from neo-liberalism to one where a taken-for-granted globalization, combined with domestic institutional changes in poorer countries, provided the basis for sustainable development in the poorer countries. In practice however, the parameters for this globalization had been set by the neo-liberalism of the 1980s, and in most respects represented a continuation of this era.

This begged the question of the relationship between neo-liberal globalization and development. For it was also clear that in terms of social questions such as poverty, inequality and participation in social and political life, development was a genuinely global issue that applied to the so-called developed as well as developing countries (Sen 1999). But equally, it was far from clear that, like the East Asian miracles that pre-dated it, China had become a success story (itself an issue of contention) through the adoption of neo-liberal or 'globalization friendly' policies. In short, the rise of China reflected a much older debate about the ways in which developed capitalist countries had actually achieved developed status. The likes of Germany, the United States and France had achieved catch-up with Britain through the adoption of protectionist policies – in contemporary language, they had adopted markedly 'globalization unfriendly' policies, just as the first-tier East Asian newly industrializing countries did later in the 1960s through to the 1980s (Chang 2002). What is equally clear in the current era of neo-liberal globalization, is that these kinds of policies are increasingly undermined by the rise of neo-liberalism as a new form of social rule – and indeed, this may be accepted by dominant actors in the developing world, but for them it is also increasingly irrelevant. Moreover, as we will see, China's rise is quite ambiguous in terms of these debates, but we will also see that its own miracle has implications for other developing countries, not all of which are necessarily as positive as 'pro-globalization' advocates suggest. For all these reasons then, the case made for neo-liberal globalization as an opportunity for renewed development has its problems, as Chapters 7 and 9 contend. Seen in this light, attempts by the hegemonic power to police the neo-liberal international order, and incorporate 'failed' and 'rogue' states into that order through development, are problematic at best, and counter-productive at worst (see Chapter 8). The relationship between globalization and development is therefore one that is full of contradictions, which reflect the continued realities of a US-led, imperialist international order.

What should be clear by now then, is that all of the definitions discussed so far – of globalization, imperialism, hegemony and development – relate in some way to each other. What is perhaps less clear, although we have already hinted at some of the different contentions, is the *politics* of each position. Indeed, I have already suggested that at its worst, the concept of globalization essentially depoliticizes highly contentious, and therefore highly political issues. While imperialism and hegemony are perhaps more explicitly political issues, it is also the case that it is perfectly possible to recognize that these exist, but completely disagree on the implications of their existence – as we will see, some may regard imperialism and US hegemony as benign, and some may see them as malign. Often (but not always) the divide reflects a particular position taken on the relationship between one or more of the concepts and how they relate to development. Thus, those that see US hegemony and globalization (and even maybe imperialism) as benign, tend to argue that they are also good for the development of the South, or former Third World. Others argue that US hegemony is bad, precisely because it promotes a form of globalization that hinders development in the South.

What I am suggesting, then, is that we not only need to define the concepts, but we need to identify *particular positions* on globalization, imperialism, hegemony and development. Indeed, it could be argued that these positions also influence how the concepts are defined. In the substantive chapters that follow, specific debates are examined. However, these debates and political positions can broadly be categorized into one of the three positions I now plan to outline. This is not always the case, and I identify some qualifications below. But broadly speaking, these accounts correspond to at least one of the arguments in each chapter, and usually two or three of the arguments. They are not necessarily entirely mutually exclusive, and nor is there one single version of each argument, and undoubtedly something is lost in the detail in presenting them in this way. But this presentation is also useful, as it will help the reader to make links from the specific arguments in each chapter to the wider, general assumptions about globalization, imperialism, hegemony and development. These three accounts come under three headings: (i) globalization as a win–win situation; (ii) globalization as a zero-sum game; (iii) globalization as uneven development. In each case, these positions also make particular arguments about imperialism, hegemony and development.

Globalization as a Win–Win Situation: Diffusing Development

This argument is most closely associated with neo-liberalism (and the 'third way' and post-Washington consensus), and it closely parallels the liberal imperialism that is discussed in the next chapter. The basic argument made is that everyone can win from globalization provided that each state adopts the correct policies. This involves increasing integration into the international economy, so that each country specializes in exercising its comparative advantage – that is, each country specializes in producing those goods or services that it can produce most efficiently. If each country specializes in this way, then one country can exchange the surplus of those goods it produces most efficiently, for the surplus of another country's comparative advantage. Thus, both output in each country and world output are maximized.

The theory of comparative advantage is derived from the work of the nineteenth-century classical economist David Ricardo. This theory attempted to develop Adam Smith's observation that a country should not produce a good that it could buy more cheaply from abroad. Ricardo developed this argument further with the suggestion, based on a two-sector/two country model, that even in cases where one country has an initial absolute advantage in both goods, each country would benefit by specializing in producing one good and exchanging with the surplus produced by the good in which the other country had a relative advantage. In his famous hypothetical example, Portugal had an advantage in both wine and cloth production over England, as it used 90 labour hours in making wine (compared with England's 120) and 80 hours in making cloth (compared with 100 hours in England). Even though Portugal had an absolute advantage in both, it still made sense to specialize in wine production, leaving England to specialize in cloth. This was because it was *relatively* better than England in wine production and so should concentrate on in that sector, leaving England to concentrate on cloth, and leaving each to trade their surplus wine and cloth with each other. In the process both would be better off through such specialization (Ricardo 1981: 133–41). Any trade deficit in one country will have the effect of leading to a fall in export prices relative to its import prices, which would increase the competitiveness of exports (and increase export values) while simultaneously increasing import prices (and thus the exports of trade-surplus countries). Adjustment will therefore be automatic, and although there may be some short-term difficulties, in the long run markets will clear and full employment will be restored. This theory was further developed on the basis of the idea of comparative factor advantages, so that the relative abundance of a particular factor of production (land, labour or capital) will generate low costs and therefore specialization based on one or more of these factors. Thus, according to this 'Hecksher–Ohlin model', labour-abundant economies will specialize in labour-intensive production, until at same point factor endowment prices will be equalized across the world (Ohlin 1933).

Ricardo argued that this scenario rested on three preconditions, which were full employment, capital immobility and similar capacities to produce goods for the world market. Full employment would be guaranteed as markets cleared, so that effective supply is always effective demand. Ricardo also argued that if capital were mobile, and could easily move from one country to another, then the result would not be towards equalization and equilibrium in the world economy, but rather towards uneven development. Trade occurred precisely because investment was immobile, but if this was not the case, then (to return to his example) capital would move to Portugal in search of higher profits, thus leading to expansion in Portugal and contraction in England. In this scenario, given the lower costs of production in one particular location, investment would tend to concentrate in that region, thus lowering costs and increasing competitive advantage, even when wages increased, as these could be more then compensated for by improvements in technology and hence productivity increases. And this in turn would mean that countries would not have similar capacities to produce goods for the world market. This is a picture closer to the third position outlined below.

Clearly, in the era of contemporary globalization, at least one of these assumptions no longer holds, which is capital immobility. This is particularly true because reduced transportation and communications costs have made capital more mobile. However, neo-liberals argue that this should not matter and indeed it can work to the advantage of developing countries. This is because capital can move from high-cost areas to take advantage of lower costs in the poorer countries. Provided the correct (open) policies are pursued, developing countries can exercise their (competitive) advantage because they have lower costs. This is reinforced by the return of smaller-scale businesses, which are both 'leaner' and more efficient than large and cumbersome companies. Although this will initially mean that they concentrate in labour-intensive sectors, the increase in investment will provide the funds to allow them to upgrade into more capital-intensive sectors (Balassa 1989). This is sometimes associated with the 'flying geese' model, in which Japan and first-tier newly industrializing countries (NICs) in East Asia upgrade to higher-value production, shedding their lower-value, labour intensive sectors, and thus allowing the next tier of NICs to concentrate production in these sectors.

Contemporary advocates of (neo-liberal) globalization are thus upbeat about the potential for development and convergence between rich and poor countries. Globalization constitutes an opportunity for the latter, provided that they adopt the right policies, which effectively means ones that encourage specialization. In practice this means trade and investment liberalization, with the prospect of financial liberalization in the future. Some evidence is provided to back up these claims, and many advocates of globalization – and not just those committed to neo-liberalism – argue that this current period is a return to earlier periods of globalization, such as that from the 1880s to 1913 (Sachs and Warner 1995; Desai 2002). In this account, globalization is said to promote convergence between countries, but this was interrupted by the years of relatively closed economies, from 1914 to 1945 (or 1982). Some limitations are identified, including the double standards of First World protectionism, but the hope is that current commitments (above all, through the World Trade Organization) will encourage liberalization in those sectors too.

Although neo-liberals often claim hostility to the state, they also argue that for globalization to continue in this way, there needs to be a benevolent hegemonic power. The United States is regarded as such a power by most advocates of globalization (Lal 2004), although there is some concern about the increased unilateralist direction taken since 2001 (Kaldor 2003). Some parallels are made with the benevolent hegemony of British liberal imperialism from the mid-nineteenth century, with its commitment to the expansion of free trade throughout the international economy. In this scenario, the US plays the role of benevolent hegemon, policing rogue and failed states that challenge the commitment to openness generated by states incorporated into the international community. This incorporation expands the liberal zone of peace, in which commercial relations between states replace older relations based on war. This is because international openness expands interdependence so that each state has a vested interest in not waging war on other states (Kant 1983; Cobden 1903). This is reinforced by growing financial and productive integration (Giddens 1999; Friedman 2005a, 2005b), of which the latter at least is part of the contemporary era of globalization, with the result that liberal states do not go to war with each other, something that is reinforced by the accountability of governments in an era of growing liberal democracy (Doyle 1983; Russett 1990). Liberal internationalism committed to neo-liberal expansion is thus progressive, but it requires considerable leadership from a progressive hegemonic state. For some advocates of this point of view, the more openly unilateralist administrations such as that of George W. Bush are regarded as liberal internationalist, even if some advocates of liberal expansion are concerned at the means by which that particular administration was committed to such ends. This is because globalization represents new challenges, particularly in terms of global terror networks committed to fundamentalist resistance to the progressive globalization of liberal internationalism.

There are considerable differences between US hegemony and the British hegemony which preceded it. The latter was committed to formal colonization, while the former since 1945 has supported the expansion of sovereign states. Although there are one or two contemporary thinkers who come close to advocating a return to colonialism as well as Empire (Ferguson 2003, 2004; Cooper 2002; Boot 2003), most prefer the US (or in Cooper's case, an alternative hegemonic power) to exercise hegemony by less formal means. The key similarity, however, is support for the expansion of liberal openness.

Globalization as a Zero-Sum Game: Development as Underdevelopment

This approach is almost diametrically opposed to the broad position outlined above. Again there are considerable variations in this view, but it is united around the idea that globalization is largely a malign force, which represents either a return to, or a new form of, imperialism. Taking its cue from neo-Marxist theories of underdevelopment, dependency and the world system, this view argues that globalization represents the interests of the powerful, and these are overwhelmingly concentrated in the western world. Globalization is best theorized as capitalist globalization, in which some parts of the world grow at the expense of other parts. Greater global integration through trade, investment and financial liberalization does not lead to global convergence, but instead intensifies the gap between the powerful and powerless in the world order. Rich countries, companies and people develop at the expense of poorer parts of the world in what amounts to a zero-sum game. In the 1960s, this was associated with the view that the development of the rich world occurred through the exploitation of the poor world, and that therefore development and underdevelopment were two sides of the same coin (Frank 1969a and 1969b). Contemporary globalization thus represents new wine in old bottles, as the rich get richer and the poor get poorer. Changes have occurred in recent years, and the old international division of labour has given rise to a new division in which the global South is integrated into the world economy increasingly as a producer of manufacturing goods rather than the primary goods of the colonial era, but the basic division between core and periphery (and perhaps semi-periphery) has not changed (Wallerstein 1974; Frobel et al. 1980).

In terms of hegemony, some writers – who may not ally themselves entirely with the arguments of underdevelopment theory, even if they share much of its methodology (see Chapter 5) – link US hegemony to the continuation of capitalist imperialism. In this approach, capitalist economic competition gives rise to military competition between competitive capitalist states, which ultimately leads to war (Lenin 1975; Bukharin 1973). For some classical Marxists, events since 2001 confirm the continued relevance of this theory of inter-imperialist rivalry (Callinicos 2002a; 2005). Capitalist competition is thus bound to lead to war, and recent conflicts are essentially caused by continued rivalries between the core capitalist states, or are premised on the view that the United States must discipline any potential challengers to its hegemonic status. Interventions in Afghanistan and Iraq are therefore less about humanitarian intervention against rogue states, and more about US power. This may be rooted in economic interests such as oil, but also in strategies designed to deter potential geopolitical challenges to US power (Gowan 1999; 2002). The two are of course not mutually exclusive and the war in Iraq could be regarded as a lesson to China in US power, and an attempt to gain exclusive control of Iraqi oil, also at the expense of China.

In the return to imperialism thesis, globalization is ultimately an ideology designed to protect powerful imperialist interests. Reference to the international community, responsible behaviour by states, and human rights observations are mere rhetoric, which hides the real motives of expanding either US and/or capitalist hegemony, neither of which meets the developmental needs of poorer nations.

Globalization as Uneven Development

This view is closest to the position taken in the rest of the book. It certainly does not reject the second position entirely, but suggests that the developmental implications of contemporary globalization are not well theorized by either of the positions outlined above. Moreover, this view also attempts to forge a position on hegemony and imperialism somewhere between these two contending schools of thought. Perhaps above all else, it highlights the contradictions, as well as the power relations, in the contemporary global economy.

In terms of development, this position rejects the view that globalization is a straightforward zero-sum game in which some regions grow simply at the expense of other regions. Capitalist expansion is a dynamic but also an uneven process, and in contrast to the neo-liberal (and pro-globalization) positions, this unevenness is not seen as a result of market imperfections, but is in fact a product of the way competitive markets work in the real world. Thus, to return to Ricardo's preconditions (above), clearly full employment, capital immobility and potentially equal structures of production do not exist. The update of the Hecksher–Ohlin model which suggests that capital mobility can work to the advantage of poorer countries, as they have lower labour costs, ignores the fact that costs can be decreased through technological innovation and productivity increases, while market share and profits can be accumulated through the generation of rents, as Ricardo himself suggested. Rents can be defined as 'a situation where the parties who control a particular set of resources are able to gain from scarcity by insulating themselves from competition. This is achieved by taking advantage of, or by creating barriers to the entry of competitors' (Kaplinsky 2005a: 62).

These arguments therefore point to a different understanding of competition. Rather than the 'level playing field' assumed by current advocates of globalization as well as earlier neo-liberal claims for the world economy, this approach views competition as an inherently unequal process, above all driven by producers in their search for rents, oligopolistic profits, and increasing returns to scale (Kaldor 1972). This is done through the development of economies of scale and scope, investment in Research and Development and thus new technology, and capturing markets in new and therefore relatively uncompetitive sectors. The market leaders therefore have a competitive advantage over new entrants to national and international markets, and while this can never be absolute, it can certainly tilt the playing field in favour of established producers (and, as we will see, retailers and buyers). Moreover, suppliers, credit and infrastructure may also develop in close proximity to these market leaders, thus further facilitating spatial agglomeration in favoured locations. The market leaders and their state representatives are therefore in a position to take advantage of intensified competition, and therefore have a vested interest in greater openness through trade and investment liberalization.

For developing countries, it therefore does not follow that liberalization represents a straightforward opportunity. Orthodox theory argues that free trade will lead to equilibrium because trade surpluses for an initially competitive country will lead to capital flowing in to invest in that country's currency (for which there will be high demand due to the trade surplus), which in turn will lead to increased prices, including in the export sector. In the poor, deficit country, capital outflow will lead to falling prices, which will increase export competitiveness. But in fact what is more likely to happen is that countries with a trade surplus will benefit from an inflow of money, as the availability of credit would cheapen the costs of borrowing, thus stimulating further investment. At the same time the deficit country will see an increase in the cost of borrowing, thus undermining investment further. This may be offset by the attraction of high interest rates, but this is likely to lead to investment in financial speculation more than production – a common occurrence in the current era of globalized financial flows. In other words, free trade may intensify imbalances in production and trade across countries, thus intensifying uneven development and undermining the prospects for sustained capital accumulation and development in poorer countries (Shaikh 1979–80; Darity and Davis 2005). The precise forms of uneven development – including deficits in core countries, particularly the US – are considered in detail in the chapters that follow.

At the same time, capitalism has become more open and transnational in recent years, and one manifestation of this globalization is the rise of manufacturing in what used to be called the periphery. This has in part been facilitated by the reduction in transport and communications costs, as well as by state policies designed to attract investment through increased openness. However, with the partial exception of East Asia, no region from the former periphery has enjoyed any significant success in breaking into those dynamic, high-value-added sectors where above-average profits or rents can be generated. This is because the barriers to entry in these sectors are so high, so that competitive advantage tends to remain concentrated in the developed world, along with significant concentration in the form of high-value trade and investment (Amsden 2001; Nolan 2003).

This phenomenon constitutes a massive problem for the approaches outlined in the previous two sections. Neo-liberals and advocates of contemporary globalization argue that, provided the right policies are adopted, convergence will occur through specialization and/or capital relocation from richer to poorer areas. For underdevelopment and dependency theorists, capital relocates from core to periphery in order to 'super-exploit' labour in the latter. For theorists of the new imperialism, the export of capital to the periphery is necessary so that capital can take advantage of new, profitable opportunities and thus avoid recessions in the centres of capital accumulation. But the approach suggested here is that there is a significant tendency towards the concentration and centralization of capital, as capital is attracted to existing areas of capital accumulation. These points applied equally to the supposed period of earlier globalization, where capital investment and trade tended to be between the colonial powers and where colonialism failed to modernize the colonies. But in some respects, in an era of enhanced mobility and the globalization of production, this has become all the more apparent in recent years. Moreover, contrary to the claims made by new trade theory (see below), these are not 'market imperfections' that can be overcome by strategic trade policy led by states otherwise committed to orthodox free trade policies (Krugman 1986). In fact, these inequalities are intrinsic to the uneven development of international capitalism (Shaikh 2005).

At the same time, there has been some significant relocation in lower-value production, including the production of component parts as well as finished goods. And it is in these labour-intensive sectors that competition is most acute, not least because of the rise of China and its growing competitive advantage in those sectors, which has led to something close to a race to the bottom. This discussion points to the potential revival and update of the theory of unequal terms of trade, developed in the context of the post-war case for industrial development by Hans Singer (1950) and Raul Prebisch (1959). Briefly, this thesis challenged the assumptions of orthodox trade theory in the 1950s by suggesting that the lower prices that resulted in productivity improvements among manufacturing producers was more than offset by the disadvantages faced by primary-goods producers. This was first because of the lower income elasticity of demand for primary goods, which meant that as incomes increased, a declining share of income would be spent on these, rather than manufactured goods. In addition, primary producers suffered from low barriers to entry and therefore intensive competition, the threat of synthetic substitutes, and comparatively low costs due to full employment (and trade unions winning wage increases) in the high-cost developed countries as opposed to high unemployment, which served to keep wages down in the developing world. It was this argument about falling net barter terms of trade for primary goods as against manufactured goods that served to rationalize the case for industrialization strategies in the developing world, as Chapter 3 will show. But later chapters will also show that a similar scenario applies to the current era of globalization, and the terms of trade between different kinds of manufactured goods. Thus, much of the developing world continues to face adverse barter terms of trade, because these areas specialize in manufacturing goods where competition is intense, demand has reached certain limits (and global overcapacity is common) and costs continue to be low due to the existence of a large and global reserve army of labour. This leads to intense competition and falling prices among developing countries, even as unemployment, flexible labour markets and government legislation have undermined trade union power (and real wage increases) in the developed world. This is in part because of the impact of competition from countries with lower wages – a race to the bottom (discussed below) – but equally it is because of the wider political defeats of organized labour since the 1970s and 1980s, with the effect that real wages have declined in favour of capital, not least in non-tradeable sectors not subject to foreign competition.

These developments suggest that globalization should be regarded as a new era of international capitalism, an argument usefully made by theorists of transnational capitalism. They contend that as capital becomes more transnational, so US (economic) hegemony further declines (Burbach 2004; Robinson 2004). Washington thus represents the interests of a transnational, rather than US, hegemony. This argument is thus very different from the idea that the world can still be characterized as imperialist. But in one respect, it shares the view of the second perspective outlined above, in that they both highlight the ways in which the periphery (insofar as it still exists) remains dependent on foreign capital, technology and markets, and employment is based on the 'super-exploitation' of the labour force in the developing world (Klein 2000). Indeed, the era of globalization is associated with the increased mobility of capital, which has further facilitated such super-exploitation, and led to a race to the bottom in which capital can easily flow from place to place, thus undermining the power of labour in both the North and the South (Burbach and Robinson 1999). Thus, in this respect, like the neo-liberals, the transnational capitalism view accepts that there is a tendency towards global convergence between different nations and regions in the world economy, but unlike neo-liberals, argues that this has led to a levelling down, rather than the levelling up envisaged by the latter. In this way, theories of transnational capitalism do not fall easily into one of the three categories outlined above, but actually encapsulate elements of both the second and third approaches.

In my view, while the transnational capital theory usefully points to a greater integration of global capitalism in recent years, it also under-estimates the continued importance of nation-states in the world order, and particularly the hegemonic role of the United States. For it is above all that particular state that has promoted increased global integration, through the trade, investment and financial liberalization associated with contemporary economic globalization. On the other hand, it is important to understand that these policies have enjoyed substantial backing from dominant social groups in different parts of the world, particularly but not exclusively in the core capitalist countries. For this reason the idea that the current era is based on inter-imperialist rivalries is mistaken, and there is considerable evidence of high degrees of cooperation between core powers. Even if there is also economic competition and some disagreements on military strategy, this does not amount to anything like a return to inter-imperialist rivalries.

This in part reflects the increased global interdependence that is central to theories of transnational capitalism. However, these theories downplay continued hierarchies based on both capital flows and state power in the international state system. In other words, they lack an adequate theory of uneven development of the kind that is central to the third position outlined above, and developed throughout this book. The US remains the hegemonic state, even if its economic prominence is not what it was in the period after 1945. In particular it is the US that takes the lead (albeit selectively) in promoting increased openness (as opposed to the relatively closed policies of core states except Britain before 1914). As a significant market leader in many sectors, this has the effect of boosting many US companies, even if this also has some contradictory effects within the United States. Moreover, the US also benefits from its central role as the main source of international finance, which allows it to enjoy certain privileges over its competitors, including the ability to live beyond its means as it runs trade deficits financed by capital inflows into the US from abroad. These arguments are developed further in Chapters 5 and 9.

Ultimately, the US's hegemonic power is backed by its military force. The liberal internationalist advocacy of the benign hegemon is undermined by the continued selectivity and double standards practised by US administrations in dealings with rogue states. But equally, the argument that military hegemony easily promotes economic hegemony is unconvincing. This is because military actions have limitations in terms of disciplining weak powers as well as potential competitors like China, but also because the US's commitment to international openness means that securing supplies of certain raw materials (like oil) cannot generate total control of what amounts to a global industry. In other words, military power has its limits, especially in an era of enhanced global integration. This is not so much an argument that favours the liberal position on 'democratic peace' (above), but one that shows the limits of hard power in a more open world, whatever the fantasies of some neo-conservative and other hawks in the United States. US military power should therefore be seen as one that plays a policing role, attempting to expand the perceived liberal zone of peace by undermining rogue states (even if alliances are also made with some authoritarian states). The hope then is that intervention can lead to the development of growth and prosperity based on liberal democracies and market economies for all. But this is a forlorn hope, first because it assumes that liberal states are natural, waiting to be liberated from 'rogue' and 'evil' elements in particular societies. Moreover, given that this involves the promotion of neo-liberal policies – which undermine the potential to generate the development of cutting-edge sectors within these economies – the potential for such high growth and prosperity is undermined, not least by the very same US state that promotes these policies. In these respects (and leaving aside the specifics of regional geopolitics such as the Israel–Palestine conflict), recent attempts to promote development (growth, prosperity) to increase security (liberal expansion of the zone of peace) are full of contradictions.

This brief outline of perspectives on globalization, imperialism, hegemony and development will be expanded and developed in the chapters that follow, both generally and in relation to specific issues and topics. The three-fold division does have its limits. For example, as already noted, the theories of transnational capitalism and imperialism cross over into both the second and third of the three major perspectives offered, and are themselves the subject of an intense debate over hegemony and international capitalism, as Chapter 5 will show. Similarly, and somewhat paradoxically, many versions of contemporary social democracy accept some of the contentions made for international trade by the third perspective, but believe that state intervention can shape comparative advantage so that the international economic order increasingly comes to be characterized by the first position outlined above. As will be seen in Chapter 8, this social democratic position accepts that there are economies of scale and thus imperfect competition, but argues that these can be resolved by appropriate institutional change and state policies, which can promote balanced trade, growth and development. Some other issues, such as the related questions of global governance, global civil society and cosmopolitanism, do not neatly fit into any of the three approaches outlined in this chapter. Certainly there is distrust of the state and some commitment to liberal democratic peace, but equally most contemporary cosmopolitans do not endorse neo-liberalism, or the unilateral methods of some US administrations in expanding the liberal order. But the discussion above does illuminate the extended discussion of these issues in Chapter 6, as the argument made there is that cosmopolitanism (at least in its liberal form) is weak in terms of its optimism concerning institutional change, its under-estimation of neo-liberal capitalism, and the realities of uneven development in the international order.

A further theory which receives only a small amount of attention in this book is perhaps the dominant theory in international relations, that of realism. As we have seen, this theory says little about forms of power other than state power, and while power cannot be separated from the state, it also cannot be reduced to it. Equally, realist theory is less a theory than a *description* of international relations – the rise and fall of hegemonic powers, and indeed the power of states in relation to other states, is barely analysed, but merely described. Indeed, not only does too much study of international relations focus on the most powerful states, but the discipline sometimes appears to be designed for that purpose (Phillips 2005: 2). Ironically then, the state-centrism of realist theory is hindered above all by the fact that it does not have an adequate theory of the state.

This leads me to my final point. The purpose of this book is to examine the relationship between international political economy and development. Implicit – but sometimes explicit – in what follows is a challenge to the Eurocentrism of much of what passes for international relations. In this sense globalization can also be seen as a methodology, based on the notion that too much of international relations and international political economy has excluded the question of development and developing countries from its concerns (Phillips 2005: 2–4; Taylor 2005). This is not to embrace any simplistic notion of the specificity of the study of development, or of what used to be called the 'Third World', but it is to suggest that any notion of universality in international relations, international political economy, or globalization, must not take the developed countries as the norm. Equally, the study of development should not assume away the existence of the highly unequal international political and economic order, as so much of 'development studies' today tends to do, so that the broad ambition of that once stimulating area of study is lost (Payne 2004; 2005). This book therefore embraces a universalism that is sensitive to differences in the world order, not necessarily in the sense of embracing cultural relativism, but in the much wider sense of recognizing social and historical diversity, and social, economic and political power, in the international order.

The Structure of the Book

As its title suggests, this book is about the relationship between globalization, imperialism, hegemony and development. The book treats globalization as something that in some respects is historically novel, which applies particularly (though not exclusively) to the last twenty-five years, while at the same time suggesting that there are considerable continuities as well as differences between the current era and earlier periods in the international economy. Each chapter reviews particular debates which relate to specific areas of contention within the wider globalization 'paradigm', and each can be read in its own right as a contribution to these particular debates. These include three historical chapters (2 to 4) on earlier periods, and on the origins, of contemporary globalization, and how these related to the (implicit or explicit) question of 'development'. Chapter 5 then considers globalization theory and theories of globalization, and also gives considerable treatment to the relationship between globalization, neo-liberalism, US hegemony and capitalism. Chapter 6 addresses the question of cosmopolitanism and how this relates to issues of global governance, using the United Nations, humanitarian military intervention, the World Trade Organization (WTO) and global civil society as case studies. Both these chapters focus on these broad questions, but relate them in particular to the subject of development and developing countries. Chapter 7 then examines the relationship between poverty, inequality and globalization, and does so by examining the evidence for and against the claim that these have increased or decreased in recent years, before moving on to consider the wider question of the nature and direction of capital flows in the contemporary global economy. Once again the matter of development is central, and it is argued in this chapter that 'North–South' inequalities persist, albeit in more complex forms than those associated with older theories of dependency. This chapter is followed in Chapter 8 by a consideration of the role of the nation-state in the era of globalization, with a particular focus on the restructuring of the nation-state, and how this issue relates to the question of the developmental state, the Washington and post-Washington consensus, and restructuring rogue and failed states through military intervention. Chapter 9 addresses in further detail the question of US hegemony by examining potential challenges from East Asia and Europe, both generally and with specific focus on development, which is then used to reconsider the specific nature of contemporary hegemony in the context of higher degrees of global integration. Finally, the question of political alternatives 'from below' is considered in Chapter 10, which examines aspects of 'political Islam' and 'fundamentalism', before moving on to consider alternatives to 'actually existing globalization'.

Each chapter therefore constitutes a specific topic and debate, and can be read in its own right. However, considerable reference is made throughout to other chapters, and this relates to the question of certain running themes which pervade the book, in terms of both structure and argument. Obviously, questions of globalization, neo-liberalism, hegemony and, above all, development are central to most, if not all, of the chapters. But it will, hopefully, become clear to the reader that there are certain commonalities which connect the argument throughout the book, even if these are applied to specific topics in their respective chapters. These general issues are addressed throughout, and we return to them in summary form in the concluding chapter, which (together with Chapter 10) revisits the debates outlined and introduced in this opening chapter.

Chapter 2

Capitalist Expansion and Imperialism

In order to provide a clear understanding of contemporary globalization, we first need some historical perspective. A crucial theme of this book is the capitalist nature of contemporary globalization. Therefore, it is necessary to explain the origins of capitalism and the development of an international capitalist system. This is an enormous task and this chapter can only provide the outlines of an explanation.[1] The focus of the chapter is on the origins and development of capitalism, including a brief periodization of international capitalist development, looking at mercantile expansion (around 1500 to 1840), free trade imperialism (Europe-wide, 1850–80; specific to Britain, 1840–1914), and classical imperialism (1880–1914, and 1918–45). Central to the arguments that follow in later chapters is an examination of the historical legacy of this expansion, and an investigation of three fallacies about the nineteenth century, which have been repeated in current debates over the nature of contemporary globalization.

The Origins of Capitalist Development

Capitalism is often defined as the expansion of production for the market. This is a definition that unites both neo-liberals and some radicals. In this definition, there is an implicit view that capitalism represents a form of quantitative progress, in which there is a gradual development away from production for use, and towards production for exchange. At a certain point this develops to such a degree that market competition comes to dominate economic behaviour. At this point radicals and neo-liberals depart, the former arguing that market exchange is inherently unequal and exploitative (Sweezy 1976), the latter suggesting that it represents the most advanced social and political order (Bauer 1991).

Marxists reject this definition of capitalism, or at least regard it as unsatisfactorily incomplete (Marx 1976: 873–904). They instead argue that capitalism cannot be defined simply as quantitative expansion,

27

because it represents a qualitatively new system of production and exchange. According to this approach, trade and the market have existed throughout history, but in capitalist society they take on a new, disciplinary form. In pre-capitalist societies, production for the market exists, but this is simply a mechanism to exchange a variety of goods, or for merchants to make profits through buying cheap and selling more expensively. In these examples the market represents an opportunity for diversifying consumption or merchant profit. For the direct producers in such societies, there is no compulsion to diversify production, or improve production methods. It is probably true that production methods improved through experience, the development of skills, and basic technologies, which all reflect the fact that human beings want to improve their quality of life, including increasing output. However, such improvements tended to be on a relatively small scale and often came at the cost of harder and longer work. In capitalist society, on the other hand, the market takes on a new disciplinary form, forcing producers to develop the most efficient methods of production, or else face the prospect of being put out of business. This is because the production of goods for the market is generalized, so that all (or most) goods are now bought and sold through the market.

Crucially, however, Marxists argue that this does not simply represent quantitative expansion and the generalization of market opportunity, but rather it reflects a set of social processes that give rise to the generalisation of production for the market – or commodity production. Most specifically, producers are deprived of access to the means to produce goods for direct use, and they are deprived of this access because they are forced from their means of livelihood. In agrarian England, where capitalism first developed, this occurred through a long process of forcing people off the land. This reflected earlier processes of peasant differentiation in which land was increasingly concentrated in the hands of wealthy tenant farmers, who bought the leases for the land from less productive and therefore uncompetitive producers, a process which intensified with the enclosures, which further forced direct producers from the land (Brenner 1976; 1982). These developments laid the grounds for the development of agrarian and then industrial capitalism, because they meant that the separation of the producers from the means of production simultaneously generalized production for the market. The direct producers could no longer produce for direct use because they no longer had access to land, their means of livelihood. They therefore searched for work on the large farms and in towns, in order to earn a wage. This wage was then used to gain access to the means of livelihood, but now this was through the buying of goods in the market. The generalization of commodity production therefore pre-supposed a social, class division between the owners of the means of production, and those who sold their capacity to labour in order to gain access to goods through the development of a wage – the working class.

At the same time, faced with the prospect of being out-competed by competitors through the cheapening of goods sold in the market, the owners of the means of production – the capitalists – had to find ways to lower prices. One way was to invest in new technologies that increased the productivity of labour, which laid the grounds for an unprecedented accumulation of capital and the development of the productive forces, including new technologies.

This brief account of the origins and development of capitalism has been subject to a number of criticisms. Some have questioned the 'uniqueness' of North-West Europe and especially England in the seventeenth century. This debate has been revived through the development of 'new global history', much of which suggests that Europe was at a level of development similar to parts of Asia up until as late as the eighteenth century (Pomeranz 2000). Some have even argued that Europe was behind Asia, and that this historical fact will re-occur in the twenty-first century (Frank 1998). These arguments are problematic however, and most evidence points to an earlier divergence that can be explained through the development of capitalist social relations in parts of Europe, particularly England (Allen 1992; Wrigley 1994). Contrary to the claims made by some 'global historians', this does not constitute a Eurocentric argument, but rather an explanation for the historical fact that Europe did at some date develop at a faster rate than the rest of the world. At times, these historians come close to arguing that recognizing this historical fact is a Eurocentric argument (see, for instance, Blaut 1993; Hobson 2004). This is ironic given that they too recognize that divergence did take place at some point, but also because this account fails to recognize the historical specificity of capitalism (Wood 2002).

Having said that, what the account of capitalism presented above fails to do is to relate these developments to a theory of 'the international'. In this respect, the new global historians have a valid argument, and they rightly criticize a tendency to theorize 'capitalism in one country' (McCauley 2001). However, the rest of this chapter will suggest that this account of capitalism can provide a theory of the international, and an account of how this has developed through a number of periods (Rosenberg 1994; Teschke 2003). In doing so, it will explicitly draw on – and where necessary, criticize – the arguments of the new global historians. It will also give some brief attention to the views of 'liberal historians' (Landes 1998; Ferguson 2003) who argue that capitalism and colonialism were progressive developments in history.

Periodizing International Capitalist Development

This section outlines three periods of international capitalist development: the mercantile era, the free trade era, and the era of classical imperialism. As will become clear, these three periods do not neatly follow from each other, and the second period only really applies to the (briefly) hegemonic power of the time, Britain. Moreover, this period of free trade crosses over into the era of classical imperialism, when Britain continued to adopt free trade policies, which were quite unlike the policies adopted by other imperialist powers.

Mercantile expansion

Given the definition of capitalism outlined above, it should be clear that the expansion of merchant *capital* does not in itself constitute *capitalist* expansion. Indeed, as many of the new global historians have pointed out, there have been many periods in history in which trade across localities and regions has expanded (Rodney 1972; Abu-Lughold 1989; Frank 1998). But mercantile expansion is important in that, from the seventeenth century at least, it coincided with the development of capitalism in Europe. Indeed, for under-development and world systems theories, it was precisely this expansion that *caused* the development of capitalism in the core (European) countries (Williams 1987; Frank 1969; Rodney 1972; Wallerstein 1974). The new global historians have qualified this argument, suggesting that there were a number of possible causes, like abundant raw materials such as coal (Pomeranz 2000), but they also argue that Europe's contact with the New World was central to the industrial development of the former (Blaut 1993; Frank 1998).

The problem with this argument is that it implicitly rests on a definition of capitalism that reduces it to the expansion of trade. As a result, there is nothing distinctive about capitalist trade, and therefore there is no explanation for why there is a tendency to develop the productive forces in one part of the world – Europe – but not (or not at the same level) in other parts of the world. In other words, trade may take place between different regions, but only under capitalist social relations is there a compulsion to invest in productivity-enhancing technologies. The effect of trade in different parts of the world will therefore depend in part on the social relations in those different parts of the world. Certainly there was colonial plunder, but this was only turned into capitalist investment in those countries where capitalist social relations were most developed. Thus, England's plunder of the New World was at times used to facilitate further investment, but this was not the case for Spain, where capitalist social relations developed at a later date. Even if we leave aside the social relations of production that led to re-investment, the evidence suggests that trade relations between Europe and the New World were not so central that they can be considered the real engine of growth for the former. In 1700, Britain exported only about 8.4 per cent of its national product, and by 1801, this had increased to only 15.7 per cent. Moreover, colonial trade was only a small proportion of total foreign trade (Bairoch 1993; Engerman 1994). Britain was dependent on the New World for some products, particularly sugar, timber and cotton. However, as Britain industrialized it shifted its dependence on sugar and timber to Europe (Duchesne 2001/2). Cotton was more crucial because Britain was totally dependent on imported raw materials, and the cotton and textiles industry was central to the industrial revolution. However, in 1770 the industry accounted for only 1 per cent of total industrial production, and by 1841 it still accounted for only 7 per cent of Gross National Product (O'Brien 1991: 302). Moreover, prices paid for these New World products were actually *above* world market prices, which again suggests that it was not trade itself that promoted the development of the core and the underdevelopment of the periphery. Rather, it was the different ways that different parts of the world responded to international trade, and this was a product of very different social relations of production (Brenner 1977). This suggests that assigning causality to trade – be it development or underdevelopment – is problematic, an argument to which we will return throughout the book.

It should be clear then that the development of international trade through networks of merchant capital cannot explain the rise of capitalism. However, while international trade was not the engine of growth that fuelled the industrial revolution, neither was it irrelevant. In the period from 1688 to 1815, exports from Britain increased, and the Americas, Africa and Asia became major markets for British manufactured goods, at a time when its European markets temporarily fell (Solow and Engerman 1987: 9–10). This development led to all kinds of favourable spin-offs, including new ports, networks of merchant activity, new supplies of food and raw materials, and markets for British manufacturers. But perhaps more important than this was the way in which the colonial encounter helped to forge the development of British hegemony, not least through the further development of a fiscal–military state and dominant naval and sea power. In other words, the development of state power was intimately connected with colonialism (O'Brien 1999).

However, most important of all is the point that while colonization, trade and plunder cannot be identified as the main causal factors behind the industrial revolutions in Europe, the fact remains that such contact had devastating effects for the periphery. This included contact with

European diseases, the mass murder of indigenous populations, and the expansion of systems of forced labour such as slavery. These practices undermine the argument that the eighteenth-century empire was a progressive development for the periphery. Moreover, even if we only focus on the narrower question of economic development, similar conclusions can be reached. If we return to the definition of capitalism outlined above, and link the development of the productive forces to historically specific class relations, then we can see that European contact with the periphery did not lead to 'development' for the latter. Instead, the nascent capitalist powers of Europe drew on existing systems of forced labour such as slavery. There were of course indigenous merchants and landowners who benefited from the triangular trade. West African slave traders were happy to buy European goods in return for slaves, while New World landowners bought European goods in return for the products of various systems of forced labour. Already then, an international division of labour was in place which served the interests of powerful indigenous classes in the periphery, and at the same time hindered capitalist development along European lines.

Free trade imperialism

Nineteenth-century free trade imperialism applied only to Britain, the hegemonic power of the time. Following earlier criticism by Adam Smith, after 1815 a number of prominent economists criticized the costs of Empire (Ward 1983). This was often linked to the idea that free trade between nations would increase wealth, through countries exercising their respective comparative advantages, and that greater commercial interdependence would facilitate peace between nations. The former argument was linked to David Ricardo's theory of comparative advantage, which, as we saw in the introductory chapter, suggested that specialization and free trade could increase world output, and therefore any countries that entered the world market could mutually benefit from trade. Ricardo said that this argument held even when one country held an initial advantage in, say, two goods over another country. This country could forgo production in that good which had the higher opportunity cost, and specialize in the good in which it had a lower opportunity cost, and thus through specialization could exchange the surplus of the good in which it had a comparative advantage for another country's surplus. This would work for the benefit of both countries, although as we have also seen, Ricardo (1981) suggested that this applied only under certain conditions, including full employment, similar levels of production, and capital immobility, an argument that tended to be ignored by later proponents.

The latter argument was often made by free trade's principal advocate in the nineteenth century, Richard Cobden (1903), who argued that free trade could lead to the replacement of the mercantilist international relations of war with a new form of international relations based on mutually beneficial commerce and therefore peace. In this respect the movement towards free trade was linked to earlier ideas of cosmopolitanism and the promotion of the universal interest of all humanity (Kant 1983). We will see in later chapters that this argument was revived under US hegemony after 1945, and is closely associated with the globalization debates of the 1990s and beyond.

But on the other hand, there was also a recognition that the universal interest was not incompatible with British interests. With Britain the workshop of the world, it was argued that there was little need for direct colonial rule. Britain's productive and competitive supremacy was such that it could out-compete other powers in a 'level playing field' of open access to markets. At the same time, Britain's links to its colonies actually became less significant, and its trade with other capitalist powers increased. From 1790 to 1860 the share of British exports to imperial markets fell by about 50 per cent. From 1860 to 1913, the percentage of imports from the Empire rose from 20 to 36 per cent, but much of this came from the white settler dominions such as Canada and Australia, rather than the colonies of the periphery (O'Brien 1999: 64). Moreover, Britain's trade with its colonies was unusually high, and the figures for other European powers were much lower (Barratt-Brown 1970).

The growing marginalization of the colonies did not mean the end of an imperialist relationship between colonizer and colonized. The increase in exports to the periphery, particularly after the onset of the industrial revolution, led to widespread de-industrialization. While Europe and the United States protected themselves through imposing high tariffs on British imports, India was not allowed to pursue such a policy. When the colonial government in India imposed very low tariffs in 1859, Britain reciprocated. African and Middle Eastern countries, although starting from lower levels of industrialization, suffered similar fates. In Latin America, independence initially made things worse as British pressure opened up Latin America's markets to cheap imports from European – and especially British – producers, a policy supported by the dominant landowning classes in the region and enforced through a series of 'unequal treaties' from the early to mid-nineteenth centuries. In Latin America at least, from the end of the nineteenth century, tariffs were imposed in order to protect local producers from foreign competition, a course of action unavailable to the formal colonies, and indeed China, which also entered a number of unequal treaties with Britain from the 1840s, a policy enforced by the 'gunboat diplomacy' of the

British (Semmel 1970). This violent enforcement of 'liberal' free trade thus undermines the basic contentions of the 'liberal peace' thesis associated with Cobden (Barkawi 2006: ch. 2).

Thus, the idea that free trade represented the interests of all countries in the world, and that growth and prosperity could be secured for all so long as each exercised its comparative advantage, ignores the force involved in incorporating different parts of the world into the international economy. Moreover, it also ignores the very different growth experiences of different regions, and the ways in which some parts of the world shifted away from free trade in order to promote what later came to be called development. For a brief period in the mid-nineteenth century, Britain successfully convinced other European countries that free trade represented their interests – for instance, the Anglo-French (Cobden–Chevalier) treaty of 1860 liberalized French trade, and tariffs in Germany tended to go down from the 1850s to 1870s. Between 1861 and 1866, almost all European countries entered into what became known as the network of 'Cobden treaties', named after Britain's foremost advocate of free trade (Bairoch 1993: 22–4). But by the late 1870s and early 1880s (and earlier in the US), there was a marked shift back towards protectionism. For these new challengers to British hegemony, free trade ultimately represented British interests. It was these same protectionist countries – in western Europe and the United States – that most effectively caught up and overtook Britain, a development that has some important parallels with the emergence of the East Asian newly industrializing countries in the late twentieth century.[2] It was also these same countries in Europe and the United States that promoted a new period of imperialist expansion in the late nineteenth century.

The era of imperialism

From 1870 to 1900, a few core states added 10 million square miles of territory and around 150 million people – one-tenth of the world's population – to their already existing colonial empires. By 1900, 90 per cent of the African continent was in European hands, and by 1913 the European colonies controlled 11 times the amount of land and 18 times the number of people that were directly ruled within the European states themselves (Cohen 1973; O'Brien 1997). This colonization process was carried out by just a handful of core states: Britain, which increased its territories by 4 million square miles; France, which had an increase of 3.5 million square miles; Germany, Belgium, Italy (1 million); United States and Japan (100,000 each); and Portugal (300,000) (Hobsbawm 1987: 59). In the context of this new era of colonial expansion and the build-up to the First World War, Marxists attempted to develop a theory

of capitalist imperialism. These theories linked the rivalry between imperialist powers before 1914 to what they perceived to be a new stage of
capitalism. Thus, Lenin argued that imperialism had five characteristics:
concentration of capital, which led to monopoly; the merger of bank and
industrial capital (financial capital); the export of capital; the formation
of trusts and cartels; and the territorial division of the world (Lenin
1975). Monopoly was for Lenin a key characteristic and this was linked
to the concentration of production, seizure of raw materials, the rise of
national banks and colonial policy. This tendency towards monopoly did
not mean the end of competition but rather its intensification. Bukharin
(1973) further developed this contention, arguing that the world
economy was dominated by competing blocs of nationally organized
capital.

Lenin was certainly right to point to increased territorial expansion,
capital export and inter-imperialist rivalry. But his account of the
(causal) links between them is largely unconvincing. Britain did not have
close links between industry and finance, and the British state maintained its commitment to free trade. Indeed, British colonial acquisition
was intended to defend free trade against the more exclusive trade policies of its rivals, and British finance played a prominent role in financing
competitors. Moreover, there was no close link between foreign investment and colonial expansion. The proportion of investment in the
Empire increased from 36 per cent in 1860–70, to 47 per cent by
1901–10, and then declined slightly to 46 per cent from 1911–1913.
However, the Dominions and India (that is, existing colonies) accounted
for most of this investment. The proportion of total investment in Africa
(excluding South Africa) stood at only 2.5 per cent in 1913. From
1900–1913, the US accounted for 20 per cent, Latin America around 22
per cent, and Europe 6 per cent of British foreign investment. In terms of
British exports, the Empire accounted for 34 per cent from 1881–1890,
34 per cent (1901–10) and 36 per cent (1911–13), but again the
Dominions (18 per cent in 1911–13) and India (11.5 per cent in
1911–13) were far more important than Africa (2 per cent). On the eve
of war, Europe (36 per cent), South America (12 per cent) and the US
(9 per cent) were also more important (Barratt-Brown 1970: 110).

In the case of other imperialist powers, trade *between* these countries
was more important than trade with the colonies. In 1913, 68 per cent
of France's trade was with other 'Northern' countries, while the figure
for Germany was 53 per cent, the US 74 per cent, and other western
European countries 70 per cent. As a whole, in the period from 1880 to
1938, only 17 per cent of total developed world exports went to the
periphery, and of these, only half went to the colonies (Bairoch 1993:
72–3).

These shares took place in the context of growing international trade, which from 1870 to 1913 grew at an annual average of 3.5 per cent (Bairoch and Kozul-Wright 1996: 8). This fact is used by some writers to support the idea that this was a period of early globalization, characterized by open trade and high rates of growth (Sachs and Warner 1995; Desai 2002), and is usually linked to an optimistic thesis about the developmental potential of globalization in the early twenty-first century, discussed in Chapter 7. Thus, Lindert and Williamson (2001: 18) argue that pre-First World War globalization 'looks like a force equalizing average incomes between participating countries', implying that late nineteenth-century globalization was a progressive force so long as countries were prepared to adopt policies that could reap the benefits. The idea that globalization can be a marginalizing force is thus discounted from the outset, and the divergence between countries is assumed to be the product of insufficient globalization, a weak argument that we will return to in due course. Even leaving this aside for the moment, the fact is that the evidence for an open economy in the nineteenth century is unconvincing. In 1913, average tariff rates were high in all the advanced capitalist countries except Britain, which had a free trade policy of open access and therefore zero tariff rates. In contrast, average tariffs on manufactured goods in Austria–Hungary were 18–20 per cent, in France 20 per cent, in Germany 13 per cent, in Sweden 20–25 per cent, and in the United States 44 per cent (Bairoch and Kozul-Wright 1996: 8).

If Marxist theories of imperialism – especially those associated with Lenin and Bukharin – suggest that there is a close connection between monopoly capital, capital export, and colonial expansion, then the figures above seriously undermine this argument (Warren 1980). But this argument is perhaps one that may not have been made by Lenin and Bukharin, and rather it is one taken up by their later followers (Brewer 1990). Certainly Lenin barely mentioned the scramble for Africa and he explicitly rejected the argument that colonialism and imperialism were one and the same. In this respect, Lenin was concerned less with explaining how the world had been divided, and more 'to show the disastrous effects of competition between various blocs of capital upon a world *already divided up*' (Etherington 1984: 135). Bukharin also drew out the contradiction involved in the practice of each state protecting its own state (and colonies) through tariffs, while simultaneously demanding the right to sell freely in other territories. Britain did attempt to continue a policy of business as usual, and promoted free trade, but, with the development of new industrial rivals who themselves were expanding their empires, the context had changed and there was clearly a new era of inter-imperialist rivalry.[3] It was this conflict that, for Lenin and Bukharin, made war necessary. Indeed, this era of protectionism was closely linked to territorial expansion, as, Britain apart, the colonial powers exercised protectionist policies designed to secure the raw materials and markets of their newly acquired territories. As Rudolf Hilferding (cited in Hobsbawm 1987: 72), another classical Marxist theorist of imperialism put it, 'tariff and expansion became the common demand of the ruling class'. In this respect at least, the views of Lenin and Bukharin, as well as Hilferding, were convincing.

Having said that, both Lenin and Bukharin link imperialism – including the export of capital to the colonies and semi-colonies – to the necessity of renewed capital accumulation, suggesting that this opened up new fields for surplus capital in search of new profits. Certainly the new imperialist wave of the late nineteenth century took place in the context of the prolonged recession from 1873 to 1896, but this does not mean that this recession was overcome by exporting capital to the colonies and semi-colonies. Lenin's own evidence showed that most capital was exported to other core countries, which supposedly suffered from an excess of surplus profits. This suggests that the new era of imperialism was the product not of a stagnant, decaying capitalism in the core countries, but rather of a new era of capitalist expansion, even if this was one that started in a recessionary phase (Olle and Schoeller 1982).

If this is the case, then this leads us back to the question of the impact of such expansion on the colonies and semi-colonies. For if it was a new era of expansion, did this lead to the promotion of capitalist development in the poorer areas, and therefore did it lead to progressive liberal modernization? This is the question asked by 'liberal' apologists for Empire (Ferguson 2003: Lal 2004) as well as some Marxists who not only argued that capitalism was progressive compared with pre-capitalist modes of production, but who also suggested that such expansion promoted capitalism in the periphery (Warren 1980). Paradoxically, the figures above undermine not only the so-called Leninist position on imperialism, but also the idea that imperialism was a modernizing force, for as we have seen, most capital investment and trade stayed in the already developed regions. This both reflected and exacerbated an unequal international division of labour which was 'suited to the requirements of the chief centres of modern industry' and which 'converts one part of the globe into a chiefly agricultural field of production, for supplying the other part which remains a chiefly industrial field' (Marx 1976: 520). What then of the capital investment that did go to the colonies?

Much of this was invested in secure, low-risk ventures such as transport and infrastructure, and this in turn was used to secure important raw materials that were used as inputs for the new wave of industrial expansion, or were luxuries consumed by the wealthy in the developed world. This included rubber from West Africa, Latin America and Malaya, tin from Asia and South America, gold and diamonds from southern Africa and copper from Chile and Peru. Oil became increasingly important in the early twentieth century, and although the US was the major supplier, there were also important sources from within the developing world. Much of the production of these and other goods was carried out by peasant or forced labour, with the result that (apart from appalling work conditions) the colonies essentially rested on relatively stagnant production, in which the producers were vulnerable to fluctuations in market prices and/or the systems of taxation imposed by colonial states (Phillips 1987; Nzula et al. 1979).

These developments also left longer-term political and economic legacies. Colonial states often not only reinforced but actually intensified precolonial social hierarchies, magnifying previously fluid and changeable social divisions. This policy was carried out in order to ensure that minority colonial rule could be more easily controlled by the colonial power, and so access to land or political office was often determined by 'race', 'tribe' or ethnicity (Mamdani 1996; 2001). Previously fluid social categories such as Hutu and Tutsi, and Tamil and Sinhalese, were thus fixed, and the colonial power consciously favoured one social group over another, a legacy that persists in various forms to this day.[4] Economically, the effect was to leave the colonies marginalized through their dependence on the export of one or two primary commodities, almost all of which were sold to the metropolitan countries, while European and other core states tended to invest and trade with each other far more than with their colonies (see above). This meant that the colonies and semi-colonies were far more dependent on the metropoles than the metropoles were on the colonies. This fact did not reflect the burden of the colonial powers as many imperialists (then and now) contend, but rather reflected the fact that colonialism effectively marginalized the developing world, or, at the very least, the incorporation of the developing world into the world economy was done in a way that promoted inequality. This point applied also to the semi-colonies in Latin America, whose landowning elites were (at least for a while) happy to import manufactured goods and export primary goods. Developing countries thus faced a 'Catch-22' situation – in times of boom (such as 1900–13), they earned income from exporting products to the developed world, but not at a sufficiently high level to effectively develop the 'national economy', and in times of crisis they particularly suffered from the lack of demand in the developed world. This situation was particularly acute in the war years (1914–18) and in the depression of the 1930s (O'Brien 1997). Along with the war effort of colonial peoples, these developments were important in promoting anti-colonial and labour rebellion, especially in the 1930s, and were also important in the promotion of a more developmental colonialism which promoted some industries and more investment in welfare colonialism (Kiely 1996: ch. 2).

One result of this unequal international division of labour was an increase in divergence in income between the rich world and the poor. In 1950, when colonialism began to end, average incomes were at most 10–20 per cent higher than they were in 1800, while in the developed world, they were more than 500 per cent higher. Moreover, in some parts of the developed world, they were 1000 per cent higher, while in parts of the Third World, they were actually lower than they had been in 1800 (Bairoch 1993: 95).

Conclusions: Three Fallacies and the Legacy of Imperialism

This chapter has provided a brief overview of international capitalist expansion from around 1700 to 1945. The discussion has implicitly pointed out three fallacies which I want to more explicitly emphasize in this conclusion. These fallacies are important for the discussion that follows in later chapters, and not least for understanding contemporary globalization and/or US imperialism, and how these relate to the question of development. The three fallacies are:

(i)   that capitalist expansion and imperialism led to the progressive diffusion of capitalism to other parts of the world, and thereby enabled the periphery to catch up once it was incorporated into the world economy;

(ii)   that the late nineteenth century was an era of globalization based on a relatively open world economy, and which therefore led to a sustained economic growth that was only interrupted by war and the 1930s depression;

(iii)   that the late nineteenth-century imperialism was a product of the need for 'surplus capital' to expand into the colonies/developing world in order to find new outlets for capital accumulation.

The first two fallacies are associated with liberal apologies for Empire, imperialism and (as we will see) globalization.[5] The first argument can be linked to the idea that colonialism integrated the developing world into the world economy and therefore secured the conditions for economic growth, through specialization and the exercise of comparative advantage. It is also associated with the idea that the liberal empire (mainly associated with Britain) was more advanced than the rest of the world, and therefore the civilizer, or (more politely) the teacher, of the backward world. The second argument then follows from the first, as it is associated with the argument that the (alleged) progressive opening of the international economy promoted economic growth for all partici-pants in the world economy. These arguments are essentially the same (although the post-colonial context is different) as those made by liberal apologists for globalization in the early twenty-first century, as Chapters 5 and 7 will show. On the other hand, the third argument, which con-tends that capitalist expansion into the periphery was a necessity, is very similar to (some) early twenty-first century Marxist critiques of 'the new imperialism' (Harvey 2003), which will also be discussed in later chap-ters, particularly 5, 6 and 9.

What should be clear from this chapter is that each of these con-tentions, at least as applied to the nineteenth and early twentieth cen-turies, is unconvincing. There was capitalist expansion, and indeed eco-nomic growth throughout the world, but it was uneven and hardly promoted convergence between countries specializing in their respective comparative advantages. Instead, there was unequal and uneven devel-opment, which in turn encouraged high rates of protection and colonial expansion by the new rivals to Britain. This uneven development of the world economy in some respects confirms the views of classical Marxists on imperialism, but on closer inspection this too is a fallacy. Ironically, it is a fallacy for one basic reason, which itself can be used to undermine the liberal case for Empire and imperialism, namely that most capital did not flow from the core to the periphery, but tended to concentrate in the core regions of capital accumulation. The periphery was thus incorpo-rated into the international economy, but in a way that reinforced its peripheral status (O'Brien 2006). This left a legacy in the periphery of racialized state structures, poverty, and dependence on the export of one or two primary goods.

The colonial legacy is certainly not the sole explanation for 'disap-pointing' development indicators in the post-colonial era, but it is cer-tainly not irrelevant.[6] This will become clear in Chapters 3 and 8, which examine post-war development and the relationship between the nation-state and development. It also left a legacy for 'developing countries' of unequal incorporation into the world economy, and 'it is no exaggera-tion to say that the opening up of those economies was one of the major reasons for their lack of development in the nineteenth century. In fact, the term non-development is an understatement since it led to a process of de-industrialization and to structural changes that made later devel-opment more difficult' (Bairoch 1993: 171). This is not an argument that favours the idea that the colonial powers deliberately underdeveloped the colonies and semi-colonies. No matter how small, there was some economic growth in the periphery, and we cannot know for sure what would have happened had the colonies not been colonized. For these reasons we can accept the view that underdevelopment is a myth. But equally it is clear that the economic, social and political record of imperialism is hardly impressive, and so the idea that liberal imperialism led to modernization is equally problematic.[7] What this chapter has argued is that the creation of the nineteenth-century international economy was one that strongly favoured established producers in the core, many of whom actually pursued protectionist policies in order to achieve core status. In other words, the legacy was a deeply unequal international division of labour. How this affected the emergence and record of post-1945 'development' is the subject of the next chapter.

Chapter 3

Post-1945 Capitalism and Development

The post-1945 period saw the emergence of the 'discourse of development' (Escobar 1995), which set out a framework for understanding the problems of poverty and underdevelopment in the 'Third World' and developed strategies to alleviate these problems. The *content* of post-war development emerged in a particular *context*, which was above all characterized by US hegemony, the Cold War and the end of Empire. This chapter will therefore examine both the context and the content of post-war development. It will first examine the nature of the post-1945 international economic order, whose foundation was laid at Bretton Woods, New Hampshire, in 1944. This will involve an examination of the nature of 'US-led multilateralism', the development of new international institutions, the selective promotion of free trade, and the regulation of international finance after 1945. In addition, it will include an examination of the impact and influence of the Soviet Union and the communist 'expansion' on the capitalist world in this period. The chapter will then move on to examine the post-war boom and the generalized development of mass production in the 'core' countries. Finally, and in more detail, the chapter will examine the promotion of development in what came to be called the 'Third World', with particular attention paid to import-substitution industrialization, modernization, and 'non-alignment'. The strengths and weaknesses of this development strategy will also be addressed, partly through a short examination of some case studies. The shift to neo-liberalism, an issue taken up in detail in the next chapter, is also touched on.

The Post-war International Settlement: Bretton Woods and the Cold War

The settlement at Bretton Woods in 1944 was intended to avoid the instability of the 1930s, which had paved the way for the Great Depression, which in turn had helped the Nazis to come to power in

Germany in 1932–3. Bretton Woods was based on an uneasy compromise between orthodox and Keynesian economic theory. In an effort to avoid the competitive devaluations of the 1930s, the delegates at Bretton Woods agreed that there was a need for an international currency that could provide stability and therefore promote international trade, which had collapsed in the 1930s. The British representative, John Maynard Keynes, argued for an international currency, the bancor. He argued that this currency could be used to redistribute finance automatically from countries that had a surplus in traded goods, to those that had a deficit. Keynes justified this mechanism by arguing that it would enable countries to maintain buying power in the world economy, and so they could continue to participate in international trade and buy the exports of surplus countries. An international clearing union would act as the agent of redistribution, transferring savings from surplus to deficit countries, and thereby maintaining effective demand in the world economy. This clearing union would act for the good of the system as a whole, but Keynes also argued that there was no conflict between the systemic good and the interests of specific countries. This was so for two reasons: deficit countries would avoid having to make cuts to their economies to restore balance of payments equilibrium, while surplus countries would continue to enjoy the benefits of sustained markets in the deficit countries, which would not exist if cuts had to be made to these economies.

However, the United States and its chief delegate, Harry Dexter White, rejected these proposals. The bancor was never introduced, and instead, the dollar became the international currency or means of payment. The 'dollar-gold standard' was introduced, whereby the prices of national currencies were fixed against the price of the dollar, and the dollar was in turn priced against gold (at $35 an ounce). This appeared to be a reasonable solution because the US was by far the most powerful economy in the world, and the rest of the world faced a shortage of foreign exchange. At this time, the US controlled 70 per cent of the world's financial assets and produced about half of total world output. Orthodox trade theory assumed that adjustment would automatically occur as, faced with higher costs, capital would leave the US and flow to lower-cost countries, thus relieving them of foreign currency shortages and in the longer run allowing them to buy US and other goods. But in fact US reserves increased in the immediate post-war era, and the US ran balance of trade surpluses until 1971. This meant that US companies could not run at full capacity unless overseas buyers were found. It also meant that the post-war economies of Europe and Japan could not immediately finance post-war reconstruction, which meant that political instability would continue. This was all the more dangerous in the context of communist revolution in Yugoslavia and (in 1949) China.

Communist parties were also very popular in Europe and Japan and there was a real fear of communist expansion. This threat was intensified by economic instability, which in turn was caused by a shortage of internationally acceptable money available in Europe and Japan. In terms of the economy then, there was a world-wide shortage of dollars.

The US resolved this problem – and held back communist expansion – by running balance of payments deficits, which meant that dollars flooded into Europe and Japan to finance post-war recovery. This was carried out initially through Marshall Aid to Europe, and later through very high rates of military spending in Korea (the 1950s) and Vietnam (the 1960s), as well as increasing rates of direct foreign investment by US transnational companies. In this way, the dollar shortage was averted between 1950 and 1958, and the foreign exchange component of world reserves increased by nearly $7 billion (Glyn et al. 1990: 69–70). This system benefited some of the US's potential competitors, as we will see. But, in the short to medium term, it also benefited the US, because of the international role of the dollar. Because this currency was both the US's national currency and the main international currency, the US could run balance of payments deficits on its overseas accounts without having to deflate its economy. Instead, the US could simply print more dollars to finance deficits. At the same time, in order to ensure that there were not significant and rapid shifts in the movement of money, most countries placed controls on the free movement of financial capital (Helleiner 1994).

It was hoped that under this post-war order of regulated liberalism, international trade stability would be maintained through the dollar–gold exchange system. Some countries would of course face short-term balance of payments difficulties, and at Bretton Woods it was agreed that a new organization, the International Monetary Fund (IMF), would provide short-term finance to ensure that such countries made the required adjustments necessary to restore economic stability. Keynes's argument that such stability should be maintained through countries with a surplus financing the payments difficulties of those with a deficit was rejected (see above), and so deficit countries would face the burden of readjusting their economies to ensure that deficits could be turned into surpluses. This was to become a major issue of contention from the late 1970s and early 1980s, when many developing countries faced massive deficits. Specific controversies did arise earlier, but not on the same level. Indeed, given that post-war reconstruction was financed by Marshall Aid, and given the growing significance of foreign investment, loans and aid in the developing world (see below), the IMF was not a particularly significant financier in the 1950s and 1960s.

The World Bank was also established at Bretton Woods as an agency that directly carried out programmes of development assistance or aid.

This role increased in importance with the establishment of the International Development Association within the World Bank in 1960. Aid is essentially a loan to a country at concessional or zero rates of interest. Critics of aid point to the conditions usually attached to it, an issue addressed in the context of neo-liberalism in the next chapter. But even before the resurgence of neo-liberalism, aid had its critics on both political left and right, the former regarding it as a form of imperialism designed to keep the developing countries in a dependent relationship, the latter arguing that it interfered with the efficiencies associated with the free market (Hayter 1971; Bauer 1971). While neither of these positions was completely convincing, there were certainly problems associated with aid. Much of the aid dispensed by developed-world governments was tied to the purchase of donor goods, and so was effectively a way of subsidizing domestic industries of the rich countries. Bilateral aid (from government to government) was also clearly influenced by strategic factors, and key Cold War allies were often the main recipients, irrespective of the needs of the poor in developing countries. Indeed, aid could be military as well as economic.

Despite these deficiencies, it was envisaged that the Bretton Woods agreement, which was designed to promote financial stability, which would in turn ensure free trade in goods and services, would thus avoid the growing protectionism that characterized the 1930s. The General Agreement on Tariffs and Trade (GATT) was established in 1947, in which various periodical rounds of meetings proposed tariff reduction and various other means of liberalizing international trade. It was an informal organization dominated by developed countries, and the majority of developing countries never signed up to the GATT. At the same time, this movement towards free trade was selective and managed in such a way that states could continue to protect some economic sectors from foreign competition, and particularly that from developing countries. This was theoretically designed to allow late developers some room for manoeuvre in developing new sectors through protectionist policies. As Gibbon and Ponte (2005: 46–7) suggest, in principle,

> GATT accepted developing countries' own definitions of their problems in relation to the international trading system. That is, development was seen in term of overcoming specific structural problems, notably those of industrializing within an already established pattern of international specialization and of managing economies where the balance of payments position was heavily dependent on the price of primary commodities.

In practice, then, this gave some room for protectionist domestic policies combined with assistance at the international level. There were limitations to these policies, including protectionist policies in the advanced countries implemented through the subsidizing of agriculture and introducing quotas on the imports of light manufacturing goods, particularly clothing. These measures particularly discriminated against exports from developing countries (see further below). But at the same time, the developing world did enjoy some 'special and differential treatment', which allowed for the principles of preferential access to developed countries' markets and some protection from foreign competition (Bello 2005: ch. 5). These included international commodity agreements, such as those involving cocoa (1972 onwards), coffee (1962 onwards), sugar (1954 onwards) and natural rubber (1980 onwards), although these ran somewhat erratically and suffered from non-cooperation on the part of producers and consumers, before, with the exception of natural rubber, petering out in the 1980s. There were also Generalized Systems of Preferences for certain commodities, but in practice these had only a limited impact on market access for primary producers, although they benefited some industrializing countries in East Asia (Gibbon and Ponte 2005: 50–1).

The idea of these and other preferential agreements, such as Lomé (discussed in Chapter 9), was to guarantee market access for developing countries' exports without insisting that they reciprocate, and to provide price support in instances of export earning shortfalls, as well as aid. The GATT system and the wider post-war international economic order had its limitations in providing effective support mechanisms, as aid was often tied, price support schemes failed to stop many commodity prices from falling, and preferential access was often limited particularly for manufacturing exports (which further locked some countries into primary exports). Nevertheless, for all their faults, some space for development was allowed, and the preferential systems now in place have been considerably watered down. This is discussed further in the context of structural adjustment (Chapter 4), the World Trade Organization (Chapter 6), and the European Union (Chapter 9).

Ultimate backing for the post-war system was provided by the military power of the United States, which spent enormous amounts of money and had large military bases overseas. This presence was justified by the need to protect the 'free world' from the supposed threat of communist expansion. US hegemony was therefore secured by both its economic and its military strength. However, and this is central to the arguments that follow, the US was a different kind of hegemonic power from its predecessors. As Panitch and Gindin (2005b: 106; also Wood 2003: 137–42) suggest, 'Something more historically distinctive was emerging than just the rise of a new power or the international extension of American capital: the American state was now acting as a self-conscious agent in the making of a truly global capitalism, overseeing the drive to universalize the law of value through the restructuring both of states themselves and of inter-state relationships.' In this new system of hegemony, the US was able to exert pressure on states through economic means, but it was also prepared to intervene militarily if necessary. Sometimes this was direct, as in the cases of (among others) Korea, Vietnam, and Guatemala, and sometimes it was through proxies such as in Chile and Nicaragua (Saull 2001: ch. 7). At the same time, the conflict between the US and the Soviet Union did provide Third World states with some bargaining power, and there were attempts to promote independence from both superpowers, through non-alignment, from 1955 onwards. In practice however, this was limited and most countries were effectively allied to one or the other superpower, even if these alliances sometimes shifted quickly from one superpower to another (Hoogvelt 1982; Halliday 1989: 21–2). But the existence of the communist alternative was important, and was central to understanding the post-war order. The usual argument made by most theorists of globalization is that 1945 was the highpoint of US hegemony and that this has declined in the era of globalization (Chapter 5). What is being argued here is that the communist alternative meant that, despite the US's 'preponderance of material resources' (Keohane 1984: 32) at the end of the war, there were strong limits to US hegemony. This was not only because of the direct challenge from Communism, but because this challenge had led the US to some forms of compromise at Bretton Woods. These were not as great as Keynes wanted, and this had implications for the later, post-Bretton Woods era, as we will see in the next chapter. But, although the US was clearly the hegemonic power, there were still some limits on this power.

In other words, the compromises at Bretton Woods, particularly over free trade and capital controls, were regarded as temporary, short-term measures, to be replaced at a later date (Panitch and Gindin 2004; Konings 2005). This is not to say that the US planned the turn away from Bretton Woods in the early 1970s, and that it was the contradictions of that system which culminated in its demise. But it is to challenge the standard globalization story of US strength simply giving way to decline in the era of globalization. We return to these questions in later chapters, but first we need to examine further the post-war years.

The Post-war Boom

The period from the late 1940s to the late 1960s was the so-called Golden Age of capitalism. The developed capitalist countries experienced high rates of growth in output and consumption, almost full employment, and varying but generally substantial welfare rights. A virtuous circle emerged in which high rates of profit facilitated high rates of capital accumulation, which in turn led to unprecedented economic growth, high productivity, high wages and expanding demand. Annual growth rates from 1950 to 1973 averaged 2.2 per cent (USA), 2.5 per cent (UK), 4.1 per cent (France), 5 per cent (Germany) and a massive 8.4 per cent for Japan (Glyn et al. 1990: 47).

This period from around 1947 to 1973 has been described as the era of 'high Fordism' (Harvey 1989: ch. 8), in which unprecedented rates of economic growth were facilitated by the extension of mass production systems to more and more sectors in the economies of the 'advanced' countries. These were initially financed by US balance of payments deficits, which, as we have seen, were consistently run from 1952. This system of Fordism drew on highly capital-intensive machinery, a rigid division of labour and specialization within the workplace, and massive production runs on specific products, which facilitated economies of scale whereby unit costs declined as production batches increased. The Fordist system also promoted the development of mass consumption of relatively standardized products. Although many sectors did not develop Fordist techniques, it was still quite widely diffused, particularly in the leading economic sectors such as car production, electronics, and light engineering. High rates of accumulation in these sectors were reinforced by the availability of low-cost primary products, particularly oil, which became the major raw material fuelling the post-war boom. From 1940 to 1974, the proportion of oil in the world's energy supply increased from 21 per cent to over 67 per cent. Before the oil price rises of 1973–4, oil prices were very low, with crude prices as low as $1.8 a barrel for much of the post-war era (Itoh 1990: 90–1).

The development of neo-Keynesian policies that maintained demand and therefore full employment, and of welfare states throughout the advanced capitalist world, were acceptable to capital so long as high rates of profit, accumulation and investment were maintained. Indeed, such arrangements even functioned effectively for capital in that demand for the products in the consumer goods sectors remained high. At the same time, poverty levels remained high, and within the labour market there was significant social differentiation. In particular, the expansion of labour forces due to rural–urban migration, increased female participation, and international migration provided a crucial source of cheap labour for capital, but also opened up a division between a relatively privileged core labour force, and those in less privileged positions in the labour market. But the boom was still important in opening up gains for labour, while at the same time trade unions generally accepted managerial controls within the workplace, and a de-politicization of demands beyond it. There was thus a trade-off between Fordist managerialism and thus continued hierarchy within the workplace on the one hand, and concessions such as high wages, more consumer goods, and increased social protection on the other (Panitch 1981; Burawoy 1983).

Development and the 'Third World'

Post-war development was heavily influenced by all these factors. The Cold War, the international economic order, and the post-war boom stimulated – and hindered – development. A further central factor was the beginning of the end of European and Japanese empires. This was partly a product of the defeat of some colonial powers, such as Japan, which ensured that it could not hold on to its empire in Asia. It was also a product of the rise of anti-colonial movements that demanded independence. Independence was thus granted to (among others) the Philippines (1946), India and Pakistan (1947), Morocco (1956), Ghana (1957), Malaysia (1957), Nigeria (1960), Algeria (1962), Trinidad and Tobago (1962), Kenya (1963), Botswana (1966), Angola and Mozambique (1975) and Zimbabwe (1980). The US (itself a lesser colonial power) supported independence provided that postcolonial leaders were not too radical, and it did so because it saw itself as the leader of a new post-war liberal order of sovereign states, which in the long run would promote a free international economic order. There was thus a close connection between market expansion and the prevention of communist expansion.

Post-war development was thus closely connected to the Cold War. For its Western proponents, development simultaneously resolved two closely connected problems. First, there was the problem of the poverty and underdevelopment of the (former) colonies, and secondly, there was the problem of alleviating the attraction of communism. One major reason for the attraction of the second problem was the existence of the first problem. The United States thus simultaneously supported national liberation for the colonies, provided these were anti-communist, and promoted 'development' for the ex-colonies. In the words of President Truman in 1949:

> More than half the people of the world are living in conditions approaching misery. Their food is inadequate, they are victims of disease. Their economic life is primitive and stagnant. Their poverty is a handicap and a threat both to them and to more prosperous areas. For the first time in history humanity possesses the knowledge and the skill to relieve the suffering of these people. ... I believe that we should make available to peace loving peoples the benefits of our store

of technical knowledge in order to help them realize their aspirations for a better life. . . . What we envisage is a program of development based on the concepts of democratic fair dealing. We must embark on a bold new program for making the benefits of our scientific advances and industrial progress available for the improvement and growth of underdeveloped countries. The old imperialism – exploitation for foreign profit – has no place in our plans. What we envisage is a program of development based on the concepts of democratic fair dealing. Greater production is the key to prosperity and peace. And the key to greater production is a wider and vigorous application of modern scientific and technical knowledge.   (cited in Sachs 1992: 1)

In this way, development came to be associated with the idea of a Third World. Although this initially referred to a non-aligned third path between the capitalist First World and communist Second World, the connection to poverty and underdevelopment was equally crucial. As Peter Worsley (1984: 40) suggested, 'What the Third World originally was, then, is clear: it was the non-aligned world. It was also a world of poor countries. Their poverty was the outcome of a more fundamental identity: that they had all been colonized.'

This idea of development was linked to more academic ideas of progressive social change, such as Rostow's five-stage model of social development. He argued that all societies – which he assumed to be nation-states – pass through five similar stages in their development. These were defined as traditional society, preconditions for take-off, take-off, drive to maturity, and the age of mass consumption. Take-off was the critical phase, and Rostow (1960: 40) defined this as 'a period when the scale of productive economic activity reaches a critical level and produces changes which lead to massive and progressive structural transformation in economies and societies'. He therefore saw American society – the age of mass consumption – as the end goal of development. He was certainly hopelessly optimistic about the degree of consensus that existed in the United States in the 1950s, and the ease with which developing countries could catch up with the developed ones (Kiely 1995: ch. 3). What Rostow hoped was that contact with the advanced countries, through aid, trade and investment, would help to facilitate development. This was not only good for the Third World in that it would alleviate poverty, but also it would help to prevent the spread of communism. Indeed, Rostow's book was sub-titled *A Non-Communist Manifesto*.

In practice, most of the new Third World states rejected, or ignored, the open politicizing of works like Rostow. The leaders of these states were generally suspicious of 'the West', not least because of the recent colonial past. But at the same time, these leaders also accepted the need to promote development policies and attempt to catch up with the developed countries. This was not quite the model outlined by Rostow's modernization theory, but it was also not a total rejection of it. For the new states, modernization would come about through the promotion of pro-industrialization policies, which would reduce dependence on primary commodity exports and manufactured imports, and thus reduce their subordinate and dependent position in the international economy (Prebisch 1959). In developing industrial capacity, the peripheral status that was a legacy of colonialism would be overturned. Although there was a great deal of rhetoric that suggested a commitment to socialist oriented development strategies, most countries attempted to develop along capitalist lines, albeit with considerable levels of state intervention. The basic development strategy adopted was known as import-substitution industrialization (ISI). The rationale for this strategy was thus rooted less in modernization theory, and more in the structuralist economics associated with the likes of Raul Prebsich and Hans Singer (1950), who both argued that there was a need for industrialization in order to overcome the colonial and semi-colonial legacies of specialization in the export of a few primary commodities. In other words, industrialization was necessary in order to alleviate the structured inequalities – including unequal net barter terms of trade (see Chapter 1) – that were created in the eighteenth and nineteenth centuries. Despite these important differences, both modernization theory and structuralism agreed on the requisite development strategy of ISI, and at least one prominent development economist clearly linked the two approaches (Lewis 1954).

This strategy had actually been utilized in independent Latin America in the 1930s, but it became more or less generalized in the post-war era. Import-substitution industrialization was based on three key ideas:

(i)   the promotion of a domestic industrial base that would, initially at least, produce goods for the home market;
(ii)   reduction in the dependence of expensive manufactured imports, and relatively cheap primary product exports;
(iii) the protection of new domestic industries through tariffs or import controls.

Industrial development would be promoted through offering incentives to investors, such as tax breaks and subsidies, as well as protection from foreign competition. In the longer term, once these industries had sufficiently developed, they could break into export markets and effectively compete with the established industries in the developed world.

ISI strategies were not exactly the same in each country and there were significant variations as well as similarities. Thus, Brazil carried out a policy of enforced ISI in the 1930s, which was essentially a response to the falling demand for Brazilian exports in the prolonged depression. After the war, a more conscious ISI strategy was promoted, particularly under President Kubitschek (1956–60). Systems of protection were introduced such as the law of similars, which limited the import of items that were either regarded as luxuries or were already produced in Brazil. The state also invested in new sectors such as steel and oil-refining, and in new infrastructural projects such as hydroelectricity. The private sector was also given incentives to invest, such as tax breaks. The Brazilian state was happy to attract foreign investment, which was justified by the employment and linkages that such investment would bring to the Brazilian economy. In the mid-1950s, direct foreign investment increased from $52 million in 1954 to $139 million in 1956. Transnational investment was particularly high in the automobile, chemicals and machinery sectors, as well as in light manufacturing and consumer goods. In this period, manufacturing output soared, and it replaced agriculture as the main sector in terms of value added to production (Kiely 1998: 85–90).

In the 1960s, there were increased social and political tensions which culminated in a military coup in 1964. From the late 1960s to the early 1970s, the Brazilian economy once again grew rapidly, with annual growth rates from 1968 to 1974 averaging 10 per cent a year. There was also in this period some breakthrough into export markets, but the focus remained on the domestic market. After the slowdown in world economic growth and the oil price rises of 1973–4, the Brazilian economy faced a number of difficulties, and increasingly borrowed money to finance continued growth and development. This was sustained until 1982, when interest rates soared and Brazil threatened to default on its debt repayment. At this point, Brazilian ISI strategy came to a halt, and there began a shift towards neo-liberal policies, which are discussed in the next chapter.

India also carried out an ISI strategy. This was planned from the time of independence in 1947, but it was from 1951, with the implementation of the first 5 Year Plan, that ISI really developed. The state played a leading role in industrial investment and in addition granted licences to the private sector to develop new industries. The state tended to concentrate on developing heavy industries, such as steel and machine-tool production. The private sector enjoyed state protection from foreign competition, and tended to concentrate on the consumer goods sector. However, unlike Brazil, the state restricted foreign investment and instead encouraged domestic capital investment. There was a suspicion that foreign investment would increase foreign control of the Indian economy, and thus colonialism would be replaced by neo-colonialism.

On the other hand, despite a great deal of socialist rhetoric, the private sector did play a leading role in the economy, accounting for as much as 80 per cent of the output of organized industry by 1966. Industrial production almost trebled from 1950 to 1964, and from 1951 to 1969 there was a 70 per cent rise in the consumer goods sector, a 400 per cent rise in intermediate goods output, and a 1000 per cent increase in the capital goods sector (Vanaik 1990: 28–9). However, growth slowed down from the mid-1960s, but then increased in agriculture through the diffusion of Green Revolution technologies, which increased output. In industry, growth continued but was generally slow and production costs were high, until the sharp upturn in the 1980s, an issue discussed in later chapters.

ISI strategies were therefore in some respects developmental. They were intended to allow developing countries the opportunity that had not been granted to them during the nineteenth century. That is, they were intended to develop industry, and with it sustained economic growth through high productivity and dynamic linkages to the rest of the economy, and thus reduce dependence on a few primary goods exports. As we saw in the previous chapter, colonialism and (in the case of Latin America) the vested interests of rich landowners had made this policy impossible for the periphery. It is also the case that ISI was developmental for the poorest countries. From 1950 to 1975, income per person in the developing world grew by an average of 3 per cent a year, including high rates of 3.4 per cent a year for the 1960s, which was higher than growth rates for the advanced countries in their years of take-off (Glyn et al. 1990: 41–2). Measured in constant (1960) prices, average GNP for all developing countries increased from $338 billion in 1950 to $1280 billion in 1980 (Bairoch 1993: 95). Although uneven, unequal and subject to regional variation, there were also significant improvements in living standards such as life expectancy, which increased from 35–40 years for all developing countries in 1950 to 56 years by 1980 (Todaro 1989: 195). Crucially, as should by now be clear, the post-war order did provide a favourable context for development to take place, not least because that GATT agreements allowed for some flexibility in terms of trade restrictions (see above). In some respects then, the post-war order can be characterized as one that, limited as it may have been, was 'development friendly' (Arrighi 1994).

On the other hand, the benefits of development were unevenly and unequally distributed. Successes in East Asia contrasted with much more limited progress in parts of Africa and South Asia, and increases in output in these places barely kept pace with increases in population. Figures produced by the International Labour Organization (ILO) in 1972 estimated that 39 per cent of the population in developing countries were 'destitute' and 67 per cent were 'seriously poor' (cited in Kitching 1982: 70). The economic record was also problematic. ISI strategies placed great financial burdens on states and they faced ongoing budget deficits. These were often accompanied by trade deficits, which resulted from an increase in the dependence on the import of machinery that was necessary to develop new industries. Thus, the displacement of dependence on the import of consumer goods often came at the expense of a new dependence on capital goods. The development of new industries was not sufficient to absorb the migration of labour from countryside to town, and so there developed massive informal sectors, living in squalid conditions in new shanty-towns. Moreover, even those who did get employment were often subject to authoritarian state controls, which were deemed necessary by states desperate to receive investment. These economic and social inefficiencies were central to the neo-liberal turn in development in the 1980s.

There were of course other explanations for the 'failure' of development. Underdevelopment and (some) dependency theories argued that the problems were not 'internal' to Third World societies, but were in fact a function of the continued hierarchies of the international economic order. Writers such as Frank (1969a, 1969b), Rodney (1972) and Amin (1975) thus applied their analyses of world capitalism from the sixteenth century (and earlier), and argued that development in the core was still promoting underdevelopment in the periphery. They agreed with Prebisch's analysis insofar as he emphasized structured inequalities in the international economy, but Frank and Amin in particular went further, and argued that Prebisch's proposed solution of ISI was actually part of the problem. This was because ISI was insufficiently radical, and did not propose delinking from the world economy (Amin et al. 1982). Instead, ISI strategies continued to support trade with, and investment and aid from, the developed countries. This led to new processes of surplus extraction from the periphery to the core. The mechanisms through which this process supposedly occurred were not altogether clear, and some Marxists argued that capital investment in the periphery was progressive as it developed the productive forces (Warren 1973). Ironically, leaving aside their differences over the impact of foreign investment, both this Marxist view and underdevelopment theory exaggerated the extent to which capital was actually relocating to the periphery, a problem that applied equally to neo-liberalism, as we will see. But for our present purposes, underdevelopment theory could not clearly explain the mechanisms of surplus transfer from periphery to core. Related to this point, nor could it explain why – in terms of trade at least – one of the more integrated regions of the world economy, East Asia, was experiencing rapid levels of economic growth.

Neo-liberals used the success of the East Asian miracle economies as validation of their theories. Indeed, they argued that there was a causal link between trade openness and economic growth in East Asia, an argument that continues to be used by those who suggest that globalization is good for development. This does not mean, of course, that the rise of East Asia explains the rise of neo-liberalism: first, because the idea that East Asia was a haven of neo-liberal policies is unconvincing (see below), but secondly, because the rise of neo-liberalism (and globalization) cannot be reduced to the realm of ideas, but is linked to the concrete material changes that occurred in the international order in the 1960s and 1970s, issues addressed in Chapters 4 and 5. Having said that, the East Asian miracle did provide important ideological support for neo-liberalism, and therefore some immediate consideration of this theory is required, before fuller consideration is given in later chapters.

The central neo-liberal argument is quite simple: it is that the international division of labour that emerged in the nineteenth century is not a problem. For neo-liberals, the problem was with the ISI strategies developed by Third World states. In attempting to develop new sectors that were protected from competition, ISI had prevented countries from developing through the exercise of their respective comparative advantages. It was no surprise that the new industries developed in India and Brazil were costly and inefficient, precisely because state protection discouraged any attempt to become efficient. For neo-liberals, this was in sharp contrast to the successful development experiences of East Asian countries like South Korea. The argument that South Korea was a neo-liberal model of development thus deserves some attention.

The developmental performance of South Korea has in many respects been a resounding success. From 1960 to the early 1990s, the four first-tier newly industrializing countries in East Asia (South Korea, Taiwan, Hong Kong and Singapore), together with three other high performers (Malaysia, Thailand and Indonesia), grew more rapidly than all other countries in the world economy (World Bank 1993: 2). While growth rates fell for many developing countries in the 1970s and especially the 1980s, growth continued at high levels in East Asia, averaging as much as 7 per cent a year (Wade 1990: 34). Moreover, as well as economic growth there were also important advances in social development. By the early 1990s, literacy rates had reached 97 per cent and life expectancy stood at 71, which contrasted with 82 per cent and 66 for Brazil, and 46 per cent and 53 for India. The number of people in poverty in East Asia in 1990 was just 5 per cent in the towns and 4 per cent in the countryside, compared with 38 per cent and 66 per cent for Brazil, and 38 per cent and 49 per cent for India (UNDP 1995: 76–7).

For much of the 1980s and early 1990s, neo-liberals argued that these miracle economies had followed neo-liberal policies. Protectionist ISI strategies were contrasted with competitive strategies of export-oriented industrialization, which focused on the world market rather than the protected domestic market, and which followed broadly free trade principles of openness to foreign trade and investment (Balassa 1981).

In the 1950s, South Korea essentially followed an ISI strategy. Industries were developed through protectionist measures, and the state carried out a land reform which redistributed land to the producers and therefore abolished the landowning class. This was designed to repel the attraction of communism, which had successfully developed in the North and led to partition in the late 1940s and early 1950s. Like Taiwan, South Korea was a major recipient of US aid, and this was designed to prevent the spread of communism from the North (or from China in the case of Taiwan). From 1946 to 1978, South Korea received almost as much economic aid from the US as the whole of Africa, and from 1955 to 1978, military aid to South Korea and Taiwan totalled $9 billion, compared with $3.2 billion for Africa and Latin America combined (Cumings 1987: 67). US aid to South Korea in the 1950s was equivalent to 75 per cent of fixed capital investment and 8 per cent of its GNP (Hart-Landsberg 1993: 44).

However, it was from the early 1960s that the miracle really took off, and it is from this point that neo-liberals claim that the correct policies were introduced. The contribution of manufacturing to GDP increased from 14 to 30 per cent, and the country successfully broke into export markets, exercising its comparative advantage in light manufacturing goods such as clothing, textiles, electrical machinery and telecommunications equipment. Neo-liberals argue that these successes were due to 'market friendly interventions' (World Bank 1993) such as the devaluation of the Korean currency, the won, in 1961 (and again in 1963 and 1971–2). Unlike ISI strategies, in which exchange rates were generally overvalued, this policy promoted exports, and thus avoided the difficulties of mainly focusing on the domestic market while remaining dependent on some imports.

For a brief period, the idea of an East Asian model was promoted. The shift away from the 'western model' supported by modernization theory (above) was replaced by an East Asian, neo-liberal model, at least until the financial crises that affected the region from 1997, discussed in Chapter 9. However, there are serious problems with such an analysis, not only because it is too optimistic about the prospects for replication by other late developers, but also because its analysis of East Asia itself is flawed. Above all, the idea that export promotion and import substitution are mutually exclusive strategies is mistaken. The state in South

Korea subsidized industries and protected them from foreign competition. The state planned industrial output and used its control of the credit system – the banks were nationalized in 1961 – to target selected industries. Import controls were used to favour the most successful exporting companies, so that they were granted access to import licences for certain goods and recovered losses made on the world market through protected sales in the home market. These policies were used extensively in the 1960s, and in the 1970s when the state directed a shift away from light and towards heavy industries, which was extended to the high-technology sector in the 1980s. Foreign capital was restricted by the state, and the export of domestic capital was subject to strong state controls (Amsden 1989; Kiely 1998: ch. 7). It was only from the 1980s and early 1990s, under pressure from an increasingly powerful private sector, that there was significant liberalization, including of the financial sector.

South Korea's strategy therefore hardly conformed to neo-liberal ideals. Much the same point can be made about Taiwan, which if anything was even more interventionist than the Korean state, carrying out similar policies in terms of industrial strategy, nationalizing finance and direct state investment (Wade 1990). A revised neo-liberal interpretation of the state, known as the 'post-Washington consensus', will be examined in Chapter 8. But for now the implication should be clear – South Korea (and others in East Asia) did not develop through open policies and the exercise of static comparative advantage. Indeed, even labour-intensive sectors such as clothing and textiles were protected from cheap, Japanese import competition (Amsden 1989: 66). This has two implications. First, if South Korea had exercised its static comparative advantage, then its main export would probably still be rice. Secondly, even low comparative costs are not sufficient to attract large amounts of capital, or to promote a comparative advantage in labour-intensive goods. The path to development may not therefore lie in adopting neo-liberal policies – certainly the East Asian miracle was not a neo-liberal model. Indeed, its success was partly brought about by adopting the developmental strategy which neo-liberals so deride. Whether or not this represents an alternative model of state-led developmentalism is a question discussed in later chapters, but again it needs to be emphasized that South Korea in the 1960s to 1980s was not a model of neo-liberalism.

Conclusion

This chapter has shown how the post-war international settlement led to a new liberal order, but one that provided sufficient space for advances for both labour in the developed world, and development in the Third World. While the former benefited from full employment and important welfare measures, the latter promoted industrial growth as the main way in which to achieve convergence, and 'catch up' with the already developed countries. The international economic order gave sufficient space for such policies through a complex system of preferences and exceptions for developing countries. This allowed for some (limited) guarantees on market access to the developed world in traditional commodities, but more important, it also ensured that protectionist, pro-industrialization policies could be adopted. In this era, most of the developing world experienced high rates of economic growth, and indeed important advances were made in terms of health, education and other social indicators. If this was an era of relatively high rates of growth and capital accumulation, it was also one where states directed economic activity in consciously 'developmental' ways. In other words, it was an era where intentional and immanent development were combined.

On the other hand, the social, economic and political advances made from the 1940s to the early 1980s were far from unproblematic. Poverty and global inequality remained very high, and the benefits of development were both uneven and unequal. In practice, much of Truman's statement was either rhetoric or a concrete attempt to de-politicize the issue of what later came to be known as the North–South divide. There was no Marshall Plan for the developing world; aid was often tied to strategic and commercial interests; and development was to be carried out through attracting capital investment, albeit with some state protection. In the context of underdeveloped infrastructures, skills and technology, this effectively meant that cheap and controlled labour was a major attraction for investment, alongside market access to heavily protected economies. It is certainly true that some economic and social advances were made in this period in the developing world, but these were uneven and unequal and, with very few exceptions, did not amount to anything like a 'catch-up' to developed-country status. For many, development remained a largely unfulfilled promise. Nevertheless, both the promise of development and the limited social advances that were made were real. However, by the late 1960s and early 1970s, the postwar order was in crisis, and this had profound implications, both for US hegemony and for development. This is the subject of the next chapter.

Chapter 4

The End of the Post-war Boom and Capitalist Restructuring

This chapter examines the breakdown of the post-1945 international order, the beginnings of what came to be known as globalization, and how this affected development. The chapter starts by outlining the reasons for the end of the post-war boom. This includes consideration of a number of closely related issues: the decline of US hegemony, the end of fixed exchange rates and the devaluation of the dollar, the rise of competitive rivalries, the slowdown in accumulation, the resurgence of resistance and the spread of the communist alternative. It then goes on to examine the crucial role of the United States in restructuring, paying particular attention to the Reagan years and the increase in interest rates, unemployment and debt burdens, as well as the uneven shift to new modes of accumulation, based on (limited) relocation, flexibility and the defeat of organized labour. Above all, the chapter focuses on the reconfiguration of development in the South after 1982, through the origins and development of the debt crisis, and the central role of the IMF in policing that crisis. In doing so, it looks at the broad policies implemented by indebted developing countries, and how these meant the effective erosion of the 'developmentalism' of the ISI period, as well as how adjustment policies in the 1980s laid the grounds for the movement towards policies designed to promote global competitiveness.

The End of the Post-war Boom

(i) The decline of the dollar

As we saw in the last chapter, the dollar played a crucial role in the post-war international order. It was not only the US's national currency, but it acted as an international currency too. This meant that its value relative to other currencies ultimately depended on the competitiveness of the United States economy. If the US economy became less competitive, US gold reserves would erode, and it would therefore have to devalue.

The dollar would no longer be as 'good as gold'. At the same time, in the immediate post-war period, the supply of international currency to the rest of the world depended on the US transferring dollars abroad, and thus the US running a balance of payments deficit was crucial to post-war recovery. But the US's decision to run ongoing balance of payments deficits had the effect of undermining the currency's value, and the dollar shortage of the 1940s had become a problem of too many dollars by the late 1960s. The US resolved the problem of dollar shortage by providing international credit from the 1940s, which facilitated the restoration of international trade through payments in dollars. But this policy was at the long-term cost of undermining US productive capacity and competitiveness. By the mid-1960s, the US had a constant trade deficit with its two main competitors, Japan and Germany. As a result, these countries no longer needed as many dollars to buy US goods, so dollars stockpiled in European banks. These dollars thus formed a new Eurocurrency market from the 1950s. These deposits fell outside the control of normal domestic banking regulations, and so banks that used Eurodollars could lend more cheaply, pay higher interest rates and still make more profits. In the early 1960s, some attempts were made to impose controls on the export of capital from the United States, but these were far from comprehensive, and the US government recognized that the Eurodollar market was in many respects a welcome development, as these markets facilitated the overseas expansion of US capital. This included the expansion of US banks that took advantage of the lack of controls over these dollars, a policy that was tolerated or even encouraged by the US state. It also included the expansion of US transnational companies (TNCs), which set up production sites in Europe in order to take advantage of market access and higher productivity, and which found the Eurodollar markets a cheap source of finance. This investment further encouraged the development of Fordism in Europe, and led to an intensification of the internationalization of capital flows, which increased further with the rise of European and Japanese foreign investment. From the 1950s onwards, an increasing proportion of TNC investment was in manufacturing, and it tended to be from advanced capitalist countries to other advanced capitalist countries, although a few richer Third World countries received substantial direct foreign investment (FDI), and used this investment to promote the ISI strategies discussed in the previous chapter. This internationalization of capital (in both production and finance) was cautiously welcomed by the US state. In terms of finance, the Eurocurrency market reinforced the role of the dollar as the main international currency, even if at the same time this reflected the undermining of the competitiveness of the US economy (Helleiner 1994: ch. 4).

The problem of the value of the dollar was intensified by the US's military commitments overseas, especially in Vietnam. The US's trade balance of $10 billion in 1947 had declined to $0.6 billion by 1968. The balance of payments was in constant deficit from 1950, and this increased to $19.8 billion in 1971, when the US ran a trade as well as payments deficit for the first time (Brett 1983: 173). Europe therefore held growing amounts of dollars, the value of which was being increasingly undermined, in exchange for their own output, while the US sustained consumption levels by printing more dollars, but at the cost of further undermining the US's competitive position. In the long run, the US economy might become so uncompetitive, its foreign exchange reserves would disappear and it would have to devalue. The basic problem then was that the supply of US dollars to the rest of the world depended on the US deficit, but the stability of the dollar depended on the US economy returning to surplus.

These problems cut across a number of competing, and largely incompatible interests. From the viewpoint of the US, the deficit guaranteed military supremacy, but also reflected a decline in US productive power located in the 'home economy', while at the same time guaranteeing expanded consumption without normal balance of payments constraints (because of the role of the dollar). From the viewpoint of the European powers, their surpluses meant that their foreign exchange reserves were constantly expanding, but these of course were mostly held in dollars. Devaluation would wipe out the value of some of these savings, but if the US deficit continued, there was the problem of growing inflation – existing side by side with slower rates of economic growth due to falling profit and declining productivity increases (see below). In either case, the problem manifested itself as a dollar glut in which excess dollars in the international economy were increasingly worthless.

The struggle between these competing interests culminated in the breakdown of key parts of the Bretton Woods agreement in the period 1971–3. The Nixon administration abandoned gold convertibility and allowed the dollar to float downwards in 1971. The United States could now continue to sustain a deficit and devalue while still sustaining high levels of imports and consumption. In effect, the size of the transfer of real resources from the surplus countries to the US increased. The US's competitors benefited from the continued expansion of the US market, but at the cost of an increasingly devalued dollar. This ending of dollar–gold convertibility was followed by devaluation of the dollar, and therefore the abandonment of the system of fixed exchange rates and its replacement by a 'managed floating' system from 1973.

The effect of these developments was to dis-embed financial capitalism from the embedded liberalism (Ruggie 1982) of the post-war agreement.

The Bretton Woods era was one characterized by fixed exchange rates and restrictions on the movement of (financial) capital, which allowed for expansionary monetary policy. In the immediate aftermath of the collapse of fixed exchange rates and dollar devaluation, it was hoped that these adjustments would restore a balanced equilibrium to the international economy, and that an automatic fall in the dollar would lead to an automatic increase in the competitiveness of US exports, thus restoring the US trade balance. However, the actual effect was to free financial capital from state regulation, which undermined any hope of restoring trade balance. The development of the Eurodollar market, and the end of fixed exchange rates, radically altered the context in which state monetary policy operated. Expansionist policies designed to maintain growth and employment could now put pressure on the exchange rate and foreign exchange reserves, as financial speculators would sell local currency in favour of safer foreign currencies. Any fall in reserves would have a deflationary effect on the economy, as France found to its cost after its short-lived attempt to revise neo-Keynesian policies in the early 1980s. The hope that currency falls would restore trade balance through an increase in export competitiveness was undermined by the fact that there now developed a serious discrepancy between trade and payments. High interest rates could encourage the movement of (financial) capital back into a country and therefore lead to an *increase* in the value of a currency, which would undermine export competitiveness and encourage cheap imports. We return to this problem below.

(ii) The slowdown in economic growth

The problem of US decline and the end of fixed exchange rates was exacerbated by the end of the boom and the movement towards recession in the mid-1970s. As the previous chapter showed, high growth rates in the 1950s and 1960s were the result of a virtuous circle of high profits, investment rates, productivity, state spending and demand, ultimately facilitated by the international role of the dollar. However, by the 1970s lower profits, investment rates, and productivity, combined with slower demand and pressures on state spending, to produce a crisis of high inflation and high unemployment. This coincided with the problem of the dollar glut and intensified competition between the core capitalist states.

This move to recession can be linked to the exhaustion of Fordist systems of production. Once the mechanized systems of production had been introduced to those sectors that could be reorganized on Fordist lines, productivity rates were bound to slow down. Increased productivity could then only occur through the reorganization of mechanized assembly lines and the intensification of management pressure on labour. Confident in the face of full employment, workers in the core countries resisted these pressures. The result was a gap between wage and productivity growth, which further fuelled inflation. In the context of economic slowdown, governments' attempts to spend their way out of recession simply served to intensify inflationary pressures. Major oil price increases in 1973–4 finally tipped the advanced capitalist countries into a major recession in 1974–5. There was a substantial slowdown in growth, and both inflation and unemployment increased. Unemployment rates increased from annual averages (1968–73) of 4.6 per cent (US), 1.2 per cent (Japan), 0.8 per cent (West Germany) and 2.4 per cent (UK), to (1974–9) 6.7 per cent (US), 1.9 per cent (Japan), 3.5 per cent (West Germany) and 4.2 per cent (UK) (Green and Sutcliffe 1987: 307–15). Average inflation rates increased from 1 per cent in Europe and nearly 4 per cent in the United States in 1961, to over 12 per cent in Europe and almost 10 per cent in the United States in 1975, and around 8 per cent in Europe and 11 per cent in the United States in 1980 (Harvey 1989: 148). It was clear then that the neo-Keynesian policies that had promoted the post-war boom had become part of the problem. These policies now exacerbated the problem of inflation in a context of slower productivity growth, falling profits, floating exchange rates and high levels of state spending.

The US State and Capitalist Restructuring

(i)   US hegemony and economic policy

The US attempted to overcome recession through expansionary policies in the 1970s. But by the late 1970s it was clear that these policies were no longer effective. From the mid- to late 1970s, the US ran record trade and current account deficits, and there was a run on the dollar led by Saudi Arabia. This reflected a crisis of confidence in the dollar, and therefore the international system that relied largely on this currency as a means of payment was under threat.

From 1979 onwards, and particularly from 1981 under President Reagan, there was a shift in policy in the United States, and control of inflation became the priority. This was to be achieved through increases in interest rates, which had enormous implications, both within the US and beyond. At the same time, this tight monetary policy of controlling inflation and sustaining the dollar through high interest rates was accompanied by a growing 'military Keynesianism' (Davis 1985), in which the US ran massive budget deficits to finance military spending in the renewed Cold War (Halliday 1983), and cut taxes for the rich at the same time. The US financed its trade and budget deficits by actively competing for capital investment from overseas, and this was attracted by high rates of interest. Capital was also attracted by high rates of return, not only because of high interest rates but because of the defeat inflicted on organized labour by these policies. Many employers drew up new contracts for workers in the early 1980s, and in 1982, 44 per cent of unionized workers took wage cuts or freezes. Cost of Living allowances were gradually eroded, and social welfare spending was cut in terms of both quantity and eligibility (Campbell 2005).

Thus, US restructuring in the early 1980s had the effect of simultaneously dealing with the three key problems identified in the 1970s, namely a crisis of profitability, of inflation and of a weakening dollar caused by ongoing deficits (Dumenil and Levy 2004). The US went from being the largest creditor nation in the 1950s to the largest debtor and foreign capital recipient by the 1980s. However, rather than undermining US hegemony, the deficits in some respects reflected a renewed hegemony. Certainly this was one that relied on cooperation from other states, particularly in the advanced capitalist world, but this was forthcoming. As we will see in later chapters, the US effectively used its financial role to reinforce its hegemony, successfully competing for capital flows and using the dollar as an effective tool against other advanced capitalist states, and indeed successfully restructured its domestic economy so that its competitive position was restored. Moreover, US capital had successfully penetrated other capitalist states and the increasing dominance of shareholder value (see below) led to the gradual dissemination of US corporate standards beyond its borders. US hegemony was thus restored, but in the context of a changed international economic order. The world had moved from one based on state-directed capitalist expansion, to one in which the neo-liberal idea of the domination of markets held sway (Arrighi 2003). These developments are crucial to understanding the era of globalization, as we will see.

(ii)   Capitalist restructuring

This shift in state policy was increasingly accompanied by new ways of increasing profitability in the core countries. This entailed a movement away from the rigidities of Fordism towards more flexible accumulation strategies (Harvey 1989: ch. 9). 'Flexibility' is a controversial term and has been used to refer to a number of different experiments in work organization that were increasingly carried out in the 1980s and 1990s. These were variously referred to as post-Fordism (Murray 1989), flexible specialization (Piore and Sabel 1984), neo-Fordism (Tomaney 1994) and Japanization (Womack et al. 1990). Some upbeat assessments saw flexibility as part and parcel of a process of re-skilling of workers and/or a new way forward for competitive, small firms, which had the effect of lowering entry barriers for late developers. These optimistic scenarios tended to over-generalize from the limited experiences of a minority of skilled workers in Japan (Womack et al. 1990), under-estimated the continued importance of economies of scale in new, successful industrial districts such as the Third Italy, or ignored the ways in which small firms remained in subordinate positions in relation to larger firms who subcontracted out low-value labour-intensive work to the former (Piore and Sabel 1984). The reality was that for most workers, flexibility effectively meant the increased intensification of work routines in an effort to increase productivity and restore profitability, and this had negative implications for progressive alternatives to neo-liberalism, as we will see in Chapter 8. Flexible labour was effectively disciplined by the effects of unemployment and so in many countries wage increases and welfare benefits grew less quickly than during the boom years, or in real terms were actually eroded. Capital increasingly used flexible, part-time work, which limited workers' rights and undermined their bargaining power. The use of subcontracting increased, including some limited relocation of capital to parts of the periphery. Service work also increased, but contrary to some optimistic visions that pervade the mainstream globalization literature, most of this work was for low wages, unskilled and insecure (Henwood 2003).

Central to the restructuring process was the movement towards financialization, which can be defined as the gradual elimination of controls on financial capital. This process was particularly significant in two areas. First, as finance was liberalized, there was a shift towards shareholder value as a strong influence on corporate behaviour (Grahl 2001). The growth of equity markets meant that companies could now raise capital in those markets. In practice however, equity is not a major financier for companies, and most finance is obtained from borrowing and retained earnings (Henwood 2003). However, in this new context share prices become major determinants of the credit ratings of these same companies, which are strongly influenced by share prices. Corporate behaviour thus became increasingly focused on improving share prices, a process reinforced by the growing practice in the 1980s and 1990s of payments to senior managers in the form of equity/stock options, which increased from 22 per cent of US chief executive officer salaries in 1979 to 63 per cent at the height of the stock market boom of 1995–9 (Crotty 2003: 274). Shareholder value thus comes to increasingly influence corporate behaviour, and this leads to an agenda which promotes reorganization and downsizing, and disposal of under-performing divisions.

Crucially, this development has wider implications, not least for those national capitalisms committed to different models from that of neo-liberalism. As Grahl (2001: 40–1) argues, financial globalization

> represents a new balance of forces between proprietors and managers, very much in favour of the former. And it is driven not only by the as yet very limited cross-border market in equities, but also by the global transformation of currency and debt markets in ways which universalize these pressures, even in economies where equity itself is traded predominantly among domestic agents. The visible effect is to reinforce, in the most powerful way, the familiar drive towards more complete and immediate market disciplines in other areas, in labour and output markets. Trade liberalization or labour market flexibilization alone would only sharpen pressures on some product markets, some categories of labour and so on. The shareholder value drive, in contrast, tends to eliminate the notion of a sheltered sector by imposing the same norms of cost, price and profit as prevail elsewhere.

These developments are crucial to understanding wider notions of state restructuring, particularly in the developed capitalist countries, as well as the relationship between developed states. In effect, and this became clear only from the 1990s onwards, Anglo-American systems of neo-liberalism became more competitive 'not because they arrive at better or more effective financial decisions in particular cases (there are good reasons to believe that they are often inferior to the traditional European systems in this respect) but because they can mobilise staggering amounts of monetary resources and deploy these resources on an immense scale' (Grahl 2005: 122; see also Lysandrou 2005: 781–3). In other words, one need not accept neo-liberal arguments for the efficiency of capital markets – indeed in many respects they are socially inefficient and also tend towards concentration as well as speculation, as we will see in later chapters – but clearly the scale and dynamism of such markets had implications, not only for the US, but for global capitalism and particular national capitalisms. For instance, in terms of international finance, the IMF classified only five out of nineteen advanced capitalist countries as having open capital markets in 1976, but by 1995, with Scandinavian countries the last to succumb, this classification applied to all advanced capitalist countries (Glyn 2006: 65). This internationalization in part reflects greater levels of domestic liberalization, which eventually reached levels which made restraints on overseas funds increasingly unviable. Moreover, even if there remain significant national variations in the sources of finance (see Chapter 8), the dominance of Anglo-American systems of finance serve to strongly influence corporate behaviour throughout the world (Harvey 2005: 32–4). It is perhaps above all in this respect that we can talk of a new era of global capitalism, even if this continues to take specifically national forms. As Williams (2000: 6) suggests, 'The result is a new form of financial competition of all against all whereby every quoted firm must compete as an investment to meet the same standard of financial performance.' These issues are discussed further in Chapters 8 and 9.

The second crucial development in financialization has implications for the developing world too, and is perhaps best understood by relating it to wider processes of adjustment there. This is undertaken in the next section.

Neo-liberalism and the Developing World

(i) The 1982 debt crisis: causes and consequences

Although their significance is sometimes exaggerated, combined with the wider long-term trajectory outlined above, the oil price rises of 1973–4 were very important. The immediate result of these price rises was that oil exporters needed to find an outlet for their windfall profits, and oil importers now faced potentially devastating import bills. The oil exporting countries deposited their windfalls in European banks (or European affiliates of US banks) and these petrodollars added to the already expanding Eurodollar market. Banks then loaned these dollars to a small number of countries, mainly located in Eastern Europe and Latin America. In the 1970s private bank lending became the major means by which some 'developing countries' gained access to capital, as opposed to official channels such as the IMF and World Bank, as was the case in the 1950s and 1960s.

Banks loaned money at low rates of interest and, in a competitive and unregulated climate, often committed enormous sums to particular Latin America states – by 1982, the nine largest US banks had committed over twice their combined capital basis to a handful of developing countries. Government debtors happily borrowed as interest rates were low, repayment periods were generally long term, and there were not the conditions that were usually attached to aid. However, with the change in US economic policy from the late 1970s (see above), interest rates increased rapidly and repayment periods generally became shorter. The London Interbank Offered Rate (LIBOR), which was usually used to set the basic rate of interest for loans to developing countries, increased from 9.2 per cent in 1978 to 16.63 per cent in 1981 (Corbridge 1993: 138). The effect of this increase on developing-country debtors was devastating. First, it added perhaps as much as $41 billion to their debt, based on average interest rates from 1961 to 1980. Secondly, high interest rates in the US attracted capital from all over the world, including from those countries that now faced an increase in their interest payment obligations. This combination of high interest rates and capital exports from the indebted countries completely changed the international context in which development operated. As Arrighi (1994: 323) states:

> From then on, it would no longer be First World bankers begging Third World states to borrow their overabundant capital; it would be Third world states begging First World bankers to grant them the credit needed to stay afloat in an increasingly integrated, competitive, and shrinking world market.

In 1982, Mexico defaulted on its foreign debt, and there was the threat of generalized non-payment spreading to other countries. There was thus a real danger that banks that had committed capital to Latin America could fail. This was the start of the debt crisis and with it, the shift to neo-liberal policies in the developing world. Banks faced the prospect of large-scale default, and so from their point of view what was needed was more money to be loaned to the high-debt countries, but now with some guarantee that these countries could meet their debt obligations. However, no single bank was prepared to take this responsibility, as there were no guarantees that all the other banks would follow.

One possible solution was for surplus countries to transfer money to the indebted countries at low or zero rates of interest, a position not unlike that advocated by Keynes at Bretton Woods (see previous chapter), and also supported by the Brandt reports of the early 1980s (Brandt 1980; 1983). This was also close to the position advocated by many developing countries in the mid-1970s, when they voted at the UN General Assembly for a New International Economic Order (NIEO). It was envisaged that this would be based on increased aid flows to the developing world, and an improvement in the quality of this assistance so that it would become increasingly detached from the strategic and commercial concerns of the developed countries. Similarly, developing countries called for private companies to increase investment in the developing world, but equally argued that multinational investors should be tied to codes of conduct. The rationale for this policy was that it would force multinational or transnational companies (TNCs) to draw on local suppliers, develop a local skills base, and limit the repatriation of profits or tax evasion. Finally, the NIEO envisaged compensation schemes for developing-country producers if commodity prices fell below a certain level, and/or guaranteed (and non-reciprocal) market access and prices to developed world markets (Hoogvelt 1982). In practice, these demands were largely ignored by the developed world, although there were some limited schemes such as Lomé, discussed in more detail in Chapter 9.

The problem with these proposals is that they rested on quite untenable assumptions about the likely behaviour of capital, both generally and in the specific conditions of the 1970s and early 1980s. Holders of capital had little interest in investing on such a sustained level in the developing world, and were even less interested in agreeing to restrictive codes of conduct. Moreover, these points were all the more central in the context of the crisis of the 1970s and the attempts by capital (and states) to boost accumulation, not through the neo-Keynesian demand stimulants proposed by the NIEO and Brandt, but by restoring profitability through supply-side measures. These included the strategies discussed above, such as the growing financialization of corporate strategy, and attempts to roll back wages (including the social wage). And in the developing world, restructuring involved ensuring that the obligations of debtors – and loans by creditors – were met. Thus, a policy of policing the debt crisis through the granting of limited access to new loans with conditions emerged. The key institution that carried out this task was the IMF, which effectively policed many indebted economies in the 1980s. Thus, despite its limited resources, the IMF became a highly visible institution throughout the developing world.

(ii) Policing the debt crisis and the rise of neo-liberalism in the developing world

To understand the role played by the IMF in the 1980s debt crisis, and indeed that of the World Bank, it is crucial to understand how the debt crisis was viewed by the core states, and the United States in particular. Countries that faced severe balance of payments deficits, and therefore faced difficulties in meeting their interest-payment obligations, were said to have adopted incorrect policies. Countries were therefore in debt, not because of the international economy, but because of the bad policies that they themselves had adopted. The neo-liberal assumption was that the bad policies were rooted in too much government intervention in these economies. For neo-liberals, just as inflation and the 1970s recession was caused by 'too much government', so too was the debt crisis of the 1980s. What was therefore needed was a set of policies that would encourage countries to readjust their economies, enabling them to earn foreign exchange to meet their debt obligations. Ironically, these policies were to be formulated by a public institution – the IMF – whose conditions served to ensure that lenders continued to receive debt payments from their borrowers. This was inconsistent as individuals and institutions – and both creditors and debtors – are said to be responsible for bad investment decisions, and so must pay the price in the marketplace. But this principle was only applied to the debtors and not the creditors, the latter of whom drew on (international) state intervention in order to secure their loans. As had been agreed at Bretton Woods, the burden of adjustment was placed solely in the hands of the debtor countries, rather than countries wikth a surplus, and therefore they had to make enormous policy changes, and move away from strategies of import-substitution industrialization, while the IMF protected powerful creditors.

In the short term, countries had to restore balance of payments equilibrium, and thus earn sufficient foreign exchange to meet interest-payment obligations. The IMF promoted policies such as currency devaluation (to make exports cheaper), reductions in state spending (to combat inflation), and wage cuts (to restore 'private sector incentives' and thus profitability). In terms of restoring trade balances, the strategy was a resounding success, and large debtors like Brazil and Mexico quickly moved from current account deficits to small surpluses in just two years (1982–4). But these results were achieved simply by a massive cut in imports. The debtors faced the problems of falling commodity prices and protectionist measures against some of their goods in the developed countries. Moreover, the debt itself adversely affected the potential for future investment because of the need to service the debt, lack of new loans from far more cautious banks, and the cutting of imported inputs that were used by the export sector. Cuts in state spending and wages generally had undesirable social consequences, such as falling demand and declines in living standards. This led to both negative growth and increased external debt in sub-Saharan Africa, the latter of which rose from US$6 billion in 1970 to US$134 billion by 1988, an amount equal to its total GNP, and three and a half times its total export earnings. At the same time, while many of the poorest countries relied on the export of one agricultural commodity for more than 40 per cent of their export earnings, the price of these commodities dropped by more than 40 per cent in the 1980s (Hewitt 2000: 303). In Latin America, debt servicing increased from an average of 1 per cent of GDP in 1972 to 5.4 per cent in 1983. At the same time, trade liberalization meant that imports increased for the wealthier classes as real wages and employment fell, not only for public sector workers, but increasingly for workers in manufacturing as the region de-industrialized in the face of overseas imports (Saad-Filho 2005). From 1980 to 1986, urban poverty in Latin America rose by an estimated 50 per cent, as average incomes fell, informal employment increased and social expenditure fell. In Mexico, for example, informal employment almost doubled between 1980 and 1987, while social spending fell to half its 1980 level over the same period (Davis 2006: 156–7). These outcomes were rationalized as necessary readjustments to the distortions of the ISI period, so that the medicine was not the problem, and short-term harm would lead to long-term benefit. The benefits were said to be realized by the 1990s, as we will see, leading to the upbeat assessments of globalization of the 1990s discussed in depth in Chapter 7. For the moment, a little more needs to be said about the 1980s.

IMF policies were principally concerned with short-term stabilization measures. Although the distinction is in practice largely meaningless, the World Bank was concerned with longer-term issues of development. The Bank also promoted neo-liberal policies which envisaged rolling back the state and promoting the free market. World Bank structural adjustment loans from the early 1980s were also associated with 'market friendly' conditions. The basic assumption of both the IMF and World Bank was that indebted countries had focused too much on states protecting domestic economies from the opportunities that global market forces could offer (World Bank 1981). Instead, they should exercise their comparative advantage, and produce the goods that they could produce most cheaply and efficiently. In practice this could only be discovered through principles of open competition and therefore trade policies should be liberalized. In addition, competition should be encouraged through privatization and deregulation of the state sector. In terms of the world economy, developing countries were therefore said to be (to use an argument commonly made in the 1990s) 'insufficiently globalized', and could best develop through embracing globalization through open, market-friendly, neo-liberal policies. The record of development was so poor in the 1980s that it came to be considered the lost decade. For the critics, neo-liberal policies exacerbated the problem (Simon 1995; Elson 1995). For its advocates, neo-liberal policies were not the problem but the solution, and they needed to be properly implemented, albeit in a more favourable institutional context, which included paying greater attention to the role of the state in development (World Bank 1992). However, in the era of modified neo-liberalism in the 1990s, the assumption was retained that once the right conditions were in place, growth and development would occur, as developing countries could embrace the opportunities presented by what came to be known in the 1990s as 'globalization' (World Bank 1994).

Indeed, in many respects this was a decade of great optimism regarding the prospects for development, as we will see. In part this optimism was linked to the second key area of financialization, the liberalization of capital accounts. This policy was increasingly implemented in the 1980s and 1990s, and was justified on the grounds that it would free up financial resources to enable the potential benefits of privatization to be delivered (McKinnon 1973; Shaw 1973). In particular, financial liberalization was seen as a way of drawing on both domestic and foreign savings for private investment. It was argued that stock markets in the developing world could raise money for investment, and once these markets rose, this would encourage foreign portfolio investment, thus further increasing savings and investments. This would include foreign finance converting to local currencies, thus stimulating investment and preserving exchange rate stability. As we will see, such funds did arrive, at least to some of the richer developing countries in Latin America (Chapter 7) and East Asia (Chapter 9), but did not have the effects envisaged by their advocates. Nevertheless, in the early 1990s there was a substantial increase in foreign capital flows to parts of the developing world, and this fuelled much of the optimism concerning both (neo-liberal) globalization and development.

For the moment, the detailed claims made for and against the effectiveness of neo-liberalism need not concern us. Later chapters – and particularly Chapters 7, 8 and 9 – will assess the relationship between neo-liberalism and development. However, given the arguments made in earlier chapters, it will come as no surprise that this assessment will be overwhelmingly negative, while at the same time it will also be suggested that there are good reasons why states adopt neo-liberal policies. In making these arguments, one negative assessment of neo-liberalism can usefully be made at this point. In the 1980s, the dominance of neo-liberalism meant that an increasing number of countries were adopting policies to ensure competitiveness in the world economy. This meant adopting policies that reduced domestic demand at home (through lower real wages, public sector cuts), and simultaneously exporting to other countries. The problem was that these other countries were themselves carrying out similar policies, and so this limited the market for the first country's exports. Thus, in the 1980s, 'the spread across the capitalist bloc of neo-liberal policies of keeping down wage increases below productivity growth and pushing down domestic costs has led to an unstable vicious circle of *"competitive austerity"*: each country reduces domestic demand and adopts an export-oriented strategy of dumping its surplus production, for which there are fewer consumers in its national economy given the decrease in workers' living standards and productivity gains all going to the capitalists, and the world market' (Albo 1994: 147).

For those developing countries dependent on the export of a small number of primary goods, this was even more problematic, as an increase in export volumes in the context of declining demand, while other developing countries were simultaneously dumping the same good onto the world market, meant that increasing export volumes was not necessarily accompanied by increased export values. Competitive austerity was thus in some respects self-defeating, for what made sense for one individual country was not necessarily good for the system as a whole. However, in practice this potential stagnation was averted by two related factors: first, in living beyond its means and massively increasing its trade deficit, the United States acted as a market of last resort; and secondly, in the context of financial liberalization, all kinds of financial instruments were employed to sustain demand in the context of lower world growth. These are issues which are central to understanding both the geopolitics and the economics of globalization, and they form a central part of the story in the chapters that follow.

Conclusion

This chapter has considered the breakdown of the post-war international order, and the emergence of neo-liberalism in the 1980s. This had its origins in the world recession of the 1970s, and capitalist restructuring, which attempted to restore profitability and sustained accumulation. The US state played a leading role in this restructuring, although other states (such as Chile after 1973 and Britain from 1976) also initiated adjustment programmes. In response to decline in the face of competition from other developed countries, US hegemony effectively changed its form, particularly with the Volcker shock of the early 1980s. For much of this period, there was talk of the decline of US hegemony (Kennedy 1988; Arrighi 1994), as well as of the nation-state (Ohmae 1995; Harris 2003), in the context of globalization. What has been implicit in this and the previous chapter is that this is not a convincing argument. Instead, as the next chapter will argue in detail, globalization has been associated with a change in the nature, but not with the erosion, of US hegemony. Certainly there are questions around the US's military role after the Cold War, and equally it is clear that the US state must rely on considerable cooperation from other states (even if many US [neo-]conservatives reject this belief). But this in part reflects the success of US hegemony after 1945, particularly in reconstructing global capitalism – and in some respects, reconstructing it in the US's own image. From now on, the US used its predominance in finance to compete aggressively for global capital, in a context where shareholder value would increasingly challenge and eventually dominate. This restructuring led to the erosion of the post-war 'social consensus' in the developed capitalist countries, and the movement away from full employment and the partial erosion of the welfare state. The shift was uneven, and varied from country to country, but as we will see it affected all countries in the developed world.

Although also varying across countries, in the developing world, the slowdown in economic growth and increase in interest rates led to the debt crisis of 1982, and the undermining of the post-war 'development consensus'. In its place, neo-liberal policies were implemented by many Third World states, after negotiations with the IMF and World Bank that granted access to, or the seal of approval for, new loans. Neo-liberals argued that adjustment policies were necessary in order to sustain development. Indeed, for them, the 'developmentalist' policies of the 1950s to the 1970s were the root cause of the problems faced by the Third World, and the solutions were to open economies up to competition and investment. This was the beginning of the end of the era of state-directed policies designed to promote convergence with the developed world. In its place, development was either coming to an end, or at least being redefined as the ability to compete effectively in the global economy. Protectionist, pro-industrial policies were increasingly marginalized, and replaced by liberalization policies designed to promote competitiveness. Its advocates argued that this was the best way to promote convergence with the developed world, as it would lead to specialization in those sectors where developing countries were most efficient, and an end to counter-productive, costly and inefficient protectionism.

We have seen that the actual record of these policies in the 1980s was far from impressive. However, their advocates argued that it was not the policies that were at fault, but the way in which they were implemented. This led to renewed debates around the role of the state in the late 1980s and 1990s, and a growing recognition of the need for institutional reform to accompany the new economic policies. Indeed by the 1990s, there was an increasingly optimistic agenda concerning not only the prospects for global capitalism, but how this would lead to development in the poorer countries. More critical accounts – including the position taken in this book – were sceptical concerning this new optimistic account of the relationship between globalization and development. In particular the argument was made that competitiveness did not lead to an unambiguous process of levelling up, but instead intensified uneven development, and with it situations where some nations, regions or localities won at the expense of others. In this context global inequality was bound to increase. This debate is examined in considerable depth in Chapter 7.

Nevertheless, the notion that there was no alternative to neo-liberalism, and, by the 1990s, globalization, was further reinforced by the collapse of Communism, which served to reinforce both neo-liberal ideology and neo-liberalism as a form of social rule, increasingly dominating the system of regulation of global capitalism in the late twentieth century. In terms of ideology, central to early 1990s optimism was the supposedly supportive framework of globalization, and so we first need to examine this concept in depth, and this is the subject of the next two chapters.

Chapter 5

Globalization and Contemporary Imperialism: Theoretical Debates

This chapter examines the broad globalization debates that came to dominate the social sciences – and mainstream political discourse – from the 1990s onwards. It starts by providing some basic definitions of globalization, before moving on to examine in more detail some of the contentions made by globalization theorists. This section also provides a critique of these approaches, and suggests that these tend to under-estimate the continued importance of some nation-states and the neo-liberal character of 'actually existing globalization'. This is linked to a lack of clarity over the precise status of globalization in these debates, and particularly whether the concept refers to a set of determined processes, or whether it itself determines such processes. In defending the former usage of the term 'globalization', the chapter then moves on to examine more critical, and broadly Marxist inspired, accounts of globalization as a new period of (transnational) capitalism. While there is much utility in this, it is also suggested that it under-estimates the continued centrality of nation-states, and particularly the US state. This issue is discussed in detail in the final section, both generally and with specific reference to debates over classical imperialism, the 'new imperialism', US hegemony and development.

Defining Globalization

Globalization replaced postmodernism as the main area for debate in the social sciences in the 1990s. This was generally seen as a welcome development, because a notoriously unclear and slippery idea (postmodernism) had been replaced by something that was both far more grounded and easy to define. Indeed, globalization entered mainstream political discourse, and became part of the vocabulary of politicians such as Tony Blair and Bill Clinton. When 'postmodernism' was used by cultural commentators, one had the suspicion that they did not really know what they were talking about. But is globalization easy to define and grounded in reality? When Tony Blair and Bill Clinton talked about globalization, did *they* know what they were talking about?

This is not simply a flippant question, for one of the most striking features of the globalization debate is the lack of agreement, and even lack of clarity, over its meaning and significance. Thus, what remains the best text on globalization starts by claiming that '(g)lobalization is an idea whose time has come', but then quickly moves on to suggest that 'there is, somewhat surprisingly, no cogent theory of globalization nor even a systematic analysis of its primary features' (Held et al. 1999: 1). Perhaps the most well known 'definition' is associated with Anthony Giddens (1991: 64), who defines it as 'the intensification of worldwide social relations which link distant localities in such a way that local happenings are shaped by events occurring many miles away and vice versa'. Held and his co-authors try to give a more concrete definition, defining globalization as '(a) process (or set of processes) which embodies a transformation in the spatial organization of social relations and transactions – assessed in terms of their extensity, velocity and impact – generating transcontinental or interregional flows and networks of activity, interaction, and the exercise of power' (Held et al. 1999: 16).

In these accounts then, globalization is defined as a set of social relations which have expanded beyond older territorial boundaries, with the result that interconnectedness is not only international, but somehow global. This theme is taken up by Jan Aart Scholte (2005a: 54–9), who is careful to distinguish globalization from internationalization, liberalization, universalization, and westernization and modernization. Internationalization is rejected because this is not new, and interconnections between countries have existed for hundreds of years. One thinks here of slavery and the slave trade, the rise and fall of empires, international trade, investment, cross-border migration, and so on. Liberalization is rejected because the idea of free trade is hardly novel, as we saw in Chapter 2. Universalization is rejected because this too is hardly novel. Scholte provides us with the examples of the spread of the human race and of world religions, which precede globalization by thousands of years. Finally, westernization is also rejected, because this is associated with previous eras of imperialism. Scholte argues that globalization must instead refer to something quite different from (though not necessarily unrelated to) these other concepts, and something that is historically novel. For Scholte (2005a: 59), globalization is best characterized as 'deterritorialization', which means 'the spread of transplanetary – and in recent times also more particularly supraterritorial – connections between people'. This refers to 'a shift in the nature of social space'. Interestingly, this more hesitant definition can be contrasted with the greater certainty of an earlier edition of his work, which argued that '(t)he proliferation and spread of supraterritorial . . . connections brings an end to what could be called "territorialism", that is, a situation where social geography is entirely territorial' (Scholte 2000: 46).

Whatever the reason for this partial retreat (see the discussion below), the fact is that Scholte's focus on space and 'supraterritoriality' remains highly abstract. Perhaps the best attempt to put some concrete flesh on these abstract bones is provided by Manuel Castells (2000a and 2000b; 1997). His work on the network society represents one of the most ambitious accounts of the state of the world in the late twentieth and early twenty-first centuries. Central to Castells's work is his argument that informational networks are crucial for understanding the rise of the global, information society. Informational networks lead to a culture of 'real virtuality' based on electronic media, particularly information technology and the internet. In this global economy, social division is based on those at the cutting edge of the supraterritorial 'space of flows', and those marginalized from such flows who are thus effectively confined to the 'space of places'. Castells thus links globalization to the rise of the post-industrial, network society, which among other things has undermined the centrality of the nation-state in understanding 'society'.

In these accounts then, globalization refers to the increasing interconnectedness of the world, and an increase in the speed and intensity of this interconnectedness. For mainstream globalization theory, this has reached such unprecedented levels that we need to re-think our conceptions of society, and in focusing on space, transnationality and supraterritoriality, move away from 'methodological territorialism' and 'methodological nationalism' (Urry 2002; Beck 2004). Globalization thus refers to the flows (people, capital, goods), networks (information, production), institutions (UN, WTO etc.), and challenges (environment, terrorism, poverty), that (supposedly) transcend territory, particularly the nation-state.

This is a contentious view and globalization theorists have recognized and incorporated dissenting views. In particular they have identified the debate in terms of that between hyper-globalists and global sceptics. These two positions are primarily concerned with the question of economic globalization. The hyper-globalist position argues that:

> economic globalization is bringing about a 'denationalization' of economies through the establishment of transnational networks of production, trade and finance. In this 'borderless' economy, national governments are relegated to little more than transmission belts for global capital, or, ultimately, simple intermediate institutions sandwiched between increasingly powerful local, regional and global mechanisms of governance.   (Held et al. 1999: 3)

The political implications of this erosion of state power are contested. Neo-liberals welcome this development on the grounds that the supremacy of market forces will lead to an efficient allocation of resources throughout the world economy (Ohmae 1995: Bhagwati 2004). Marxists, social democrats and other radicals generally regret that state power has been eroded, on the grounds that it undermines the space for winning concessions from the state and thus reinforces the power of an increasingly oppressive global capitalism (Frobel et al. 1980; Korten 1995).[1] On the other hand, the global sceptics claim that the evidence for capital flows shows that they are not historically unprecedented, and that there are similarities with the late nineteenth and early twentieth centuries, which in some respects were more globalized. One clear implication drawn for the argument is that given that capital flows are not as great as is sometimes claimed, the state retains considerable capacity to regulate international economic activity (Weiss 1998; Hirst and Thompson 1999), an issue also examined in detail in Chapter 8.

What has become the mainstream of contemporary globalization theory seeks to distance itself from both these perspectives, and does so by introducing a third perspective, that of global transformations, arguing that

> in comparison with the sceptical and hyperglobalist accounts, the transformationalists make no claims about the future trajectory of globalization; nor do they seek to evaluate the present in relation to some single, fixed ideal type 'globalized world', whether a global market or a global civilization. Rather, transformationalist accounts emphasize globalization as a long term historical process which is inscribed with contradictions and which is significantly shaped by conjunctural factors.   (Held et al. 1999: 7–8)

At the same time, this perspective also argues that

> at the dawn of a new millennium, globalization is a central driving force behind the rapid social, political and economic changes that are reshaping modern societies and world order ... contemporary processes of globalization are historically unprecedented such that governments and societies across the globe are having to adjust to a world in which there is no longer a clear distinction between international and domestic, external and internal affairs.   (Held et al. 1999: 7)

This statement sounds suspiciously like an endorsement of a version of the hyper-globalist position after all. True, it broadens the debate beyond economics, but it essentially assumes that global flows are historically unprecedented. This is necessary for the argument of the transformationalists, because if such flows are not unprecedented, then there can be no supraterritoriality. Put differently, the qualitative transformation of supraterritoriality identified by the transfomationalists rests on the assumption that the quantitative transformations identified by the hyperglobalists have actually taken place. The transformationalists do qualify their arguments, thus allowing some room for the empirical claims made by sceptics (see below). But more important for our argument here is the fact that not only do the transformationalists effectively endorse the hyper-globalists, but they take the argument one step further. The hyperglobalists argue that globalization refers to a number of outcomes, and particularly the idea that markets 'outgrow' states. But transformationalists not only borrow this argument for empirical verification, they then elevate globalization so that it becomes the *causal factor* rather than the *outcome* (Rosenberg 2000). Thus, in the quotation above, the claim is made that globalization is a 'central driving force' behind rapid social, economic, cultural and political change. The result is that globalization – defined as the expansion of space – becomes the causal factor that explains the changes that occurred in the 1990s.

Thus, the mainstream globalization theory associated with 'global transformationalists' uneasily combined empirical insight from the hyper-globalists in order to assert that important changes had occurred in the international order, and from the sceptics in order to recognize that there were limits to these changes, with a theory which gave causal primacy to time and space. The concrete changes associated with the 1990s (and earlier) were thus linked to the idea of globalization as the stretching of spatial relations. In this way, as Rosenberg points out, globalization became less something that needed to be explained and more something that did the explaining, and so 'the causal properties of particular social relations that were undergoing spatio-temporal expansion or compression were instead attributed to the expansion or compression itself' (Rosenberg 2005: 13; see also Rosenberg 2000; Hay and Watson 1999; Kiely 2005a: ch. 2; 2005b: ch. 2).

These abstract points can best be illustrated by drawing on the example of the relationship between the territorial state and wider transnational relations, and then relating these to an understanding of contemporary, 'actually existing globalization'. First then, we need to look at the issue of the nation-state and relate this to methodological territorialism and globalization. In arguing for the need for a new paradigm for the social sciences, Scholte contends that 'methodological territorialism reflected the social conditions of a particular epoch when bordered territorial units, separated by distance, formed far and away the overriding framework for macro-level social organization' (Scholte 1999a:

107). This argument ironically reproduces the fallacies of realist theories of international relations, which argue that the world is composed of sovereign nation-states all exercising their self-interest in an anarchic international order (Waltz 1979). Scholte thus sets up a rigid dualism between the realism of the past and the globalism of the present.[2] But is this a convincing account – either of the realist past or of the global present? The world has not been made up of nation-states, each mutually recognizing their sovereign right to exist, until relatively recently. The world until the 1950s and 1960s was made up of empires, and it does seem odd that globalization asserts the end of territorialism precisely when, for the first time in history, the nation-state is (almost) universalized (Kiely 2005b: ch. 3). Equally however, Scholte's (2000: 57) claim that 'the mercantile and industrial activity that dominated capitalism during this period [seventeenth to mid-twentieth century] . . . operated almost exclusively in territorial space', is highly problematic. This bewildering statement ignores Empire, slavery and the slave trade, other systems of forced labour, classical imperialism, conflict between the major powers, to name but a few. It is guilty of the charge made by Frederick Cooper (2004: 250) against another book on globalization, namely that it is 'bubbling with enthusiasm for the new without enough curiosity about the past to know whether it was new or not'.[3]

The question then is how to avoid the rigid demarcation of state and market, and territoriality and globality. This can be done through a historical analysis which shows how these 'separations' are historically and socially constituted, and this leads us back to an analysis of *capitalism.* In capitalist society, production is for the market. As we saw in Chapter 2, production for the market existed in pre-capitalist society, but it becomes generalized in capitalist society. And the basis for this generalization of commodity production is the separation of producers from the means of production. This process both creates a potential wage labour force, and at one and the same time it also means that goods must be produced for the market, precisely because the direct producers no longer have direct access to land, their means of livelihood. This leads to competition between capitals, expansion beyond territorial borders, and constant (but uneven) technological innovation as firms strive to stay ahead of their rivals in the competitive marketplace. In other words, this leads to what globalization theorists describe as supraterritoriality, time–space compression or 'the annihilation of space by time' (Marx 1973: 539). In other words, transnationality is present in capitalist social relations *from the outset.* But at the same time, this transnationality is not incompatible with state sovereignty and territoriality. In pre-capitalist societies, territorial expansion occurred in the context of social relations where there was no clear division between state and market, and politics and economics. Mutual recognition of fixed territorial boundaries did not therefore exist. However, in capitalist societies, the mutual recognition of fixed territorial boundaries (the sovereign state) co-exists with the private, economic sphere of the market. The existence of this market, and particularly the market for labour power, guarantees the extraction of surplus value. In feudal times, surplus products, goods and labour were guaranteed through political obligation. This was necessary because the producers had direct access to their means of livelihood (land). In capitalist society, the dull compulsion of economic relations ensures that workers enter the labour market in order to secure a wage that gives them access to their means of livelihood. Thus, this differentiation of the public state and private market constitutes the basic social relations of capitalism. This means that (capitalist) expansion can occur without the necessity of territorial expansion, and indeed the construction of separate public and private spheres guarantees this expansion. In this sense then, there is no longer the necessity of a territorial empire, but rather the emergence of the 'empire of civil society' (Rosenberg 1994). Thus, rather than seeing state and market, politics and economics, and territoriality and globality as dichotomies, we should instead see how they are internally related through the emergence of capitalist social relations.

There are two possible historical objections to this approach. First, it cannot account for the fact that capitalist society did not create geopolitical or international fragmentation, which pre-dates the emergence of capitalism. Secondly, it cannot account for the emergence of territorial empires in the late nineteenth century, which Lenin saw as the highest stage of capitalism (see Chapter 2). The first argument is undoubtedly true, and the mutual recognition of sovereign states in Europe is generally dated back to the Treaty of Westphalia of 1648. But this was a treaty between absolutist states in which capitalist social relations were not yet developed – indeed, England was not a signatory to the treaty. It was only later, when faced with the threat of British hegemony, that these states consciously developed capitalist social relations, in part to ensure that the resultant competition between (domestic) capitals would lead to the development of the productive forces, and thereby promote catch-up with the dominant capitalist power (Teschke 2003; Lacher 2003). In this way, sovereignty was transformed into a specifically capitalist sovereignty, based on the institutional separation of public state and private market.

These developments have implications for a response to the second objection. As was implied in Chapter 2, it is a mistake to theorize late nineteenth-century imperialism in terms of the functional necessity of capitalist expansion and the territorial acquisition of the periphery. Most capital exports actually went to other advanced capitalist countries. While there may have been some demand for particular raw materials, this alone does not explain the movement towards renewed colonization. For this reason, many historians argue that economic factors were not sufficient to explain the scramble for new colonies. However, as was suggested in Chapter 2, the new imperialism can be located in the context of uneven development, and the rise of competitors to British hegemony. As part of this process, Britain's competitors employed increasingly protectionist measures both at home through tariff protection, and abroad through territorial acquisition. Britain responded by also acquiring new territories, but did so in order to try to maintain an open world economy based on free trade. What this argument suggests then is that the new imperialism cannot be explained by some direct logic of capitalism, and that it was in part a contingent, particular process that was linked, but not reducible, to the expansion of international capitalism. It most certainly was not the highest stage of capitalism, but actually a stage of relatively early capitalist development (Wood 2003: 119–30). More relevant to our concerns here is how these points relate to the relationship between territoriality and transnationality, for together they suggest that it is true that capitalism 'did not invent the general fact of geopolitical fragmentation; but . . . perhaps uniquely, it has no intrinsic need to overcome it in order to expand its own reach or further its own development' (Rosenberg 2005: 25).

This argument therefore challenges the dichotomies set up by globalization theory. However, in fairness to Scholte, and to Held and his collaborators, they continually qualify the rigid dichotomy that they initially construct between territoriality and globality. Thus, Scholte (2000: 59; also 2005a: 75–8) argues that 'we should not replace territorialism with a globalist methodology that neglects territorial spaces'. Held and his co-authors (1999: 9) similarly claim that 'in arguing that globalization is transforming or reconstituting the power and authority of national governments, the transformationalists reject both the hyperglobalist rhetoric of the end of the sovereign nation-state and the sceptics claim that "nothing much has changed"'. But the problem with these more measured and balanced approaches to understanding globalization is that they remain purely descriptive. For there to be any explanatory power to the argument, the idea that globalization or supraterritoriality are 'driving forces' must be abandoned, and the social and political changes that have given rise to globalizing *processes and outcomes* must be considered. But this means abandoning the idea of globalization as representing a new paradigm. Indeed, Scholte effectively does this when he examines the causes of globalization, and locates them in the emergence of a number of 'institutionally separate' factors such as the capitalist economy, modern rationalization, and technological innovation (Scholte 2005a: 135–52). This of course does not explain how these factors became institutionally separate, but more important is the fact that Scholte in the end effectively abandons the idea of attributing causal significance to spatial relations, and ultimately sees these as being produced by social and political change. This, however, is at the cost of the earlier claims made for the causal significance of globalization.

Castells does try to derive the extension of spatial relations from other, determining factors, but he tends to do so in a way that gives undue prominence to information technologies. The result is that his analysis tends towards technological determinism, which is also sometimes present in Scholte's analysis (Castells 1996: 66; Scholte 2000: 49). Of course technological change is significant, but this is not the same as claiming that it is determinant or even of the greatest significance in accounting for social change, both recently and throughout history. The new information technologies essentially allow *existing* social processes and interaction to occur more quickly, rather than promoting completely new forms of activity (Golding 2000). Moreover, the idea of time–space compression is hardly new, as we saw with the quotations from Marx above. Thus, in the nineteenth century the shrinking effects of railways and the telegraph were prominent. Indeed, the telegraph – which 'shrank' communication with distant locations from weeks to minutes and seconds – was in some respects more revolutionary than the internet, which shrinks communications from seconds to fractions of seconds (Thrift 1996). For much of the early twentieth century there was little talk of a shrinking world, but that was not because of the absence of technological change, but rather because political cleavages meant that the world remained both divided and fragmented. Political and social change cannot therefore simply be derived from technological change, and the significance of current technological change may itself be exaggerated.

How then does this discussion relate to how we understand contemporary globalization? One response is to argue that globalization theory reifies the separation of state and markets, and thus fails to see that this historically constituted separation is part of the wider social relations of capitalism. This argument is acceptable as a starting point for an alternative account, but on its own, is insufficient. This is because it effectively amounts to an argument that capitalism is capitalism, as though capitalism should be seen as a never changing international order. But, as should be clear from Chapters 2 to 4, capitalism is a constantly changing international order, which suggests that we need to locate specific *periods* of capitalist development in order to better characterize a particular historical conjuncture. In doing so, there is no need to abandon the general theory of capitalism in order to move to a concrete

analysis of a particular period, but neither should the general theory substitute for such a concrete analysis (Rosenberg 2005: 29–40).

Some attempts to examine globalization as a particular period of capitalism are examined in the next section, but first a few more points need
to be made in relation to how the general theory relates to the particular
conjuncture of the 1990s. As we saw in Chapters 3 and 4, the post-war
period saw a movement from neo-Keynesian to neo-liberal capitalism.
The neo-Keynesian era was dominated by US hegemony, social democratic or developmentalist state management, the Cold War and decolonization. By the 1970s, this era had more or less exhausted itself, leading
to neo-liberal restructuring from the 1980s, and the collapse of communism in the 1980s and 1990s. This meant the breakdown of managed
social democratic capitalism in the First World, the collapse of communism in the Second, and the erosion of the developmental state in the
Third (see Chapters 8 and 9). Liberalization led to a massive opening up
of national economies through trade, investment and financial liberalization; the end of communism led to a shift in strategic alliances
between states, so that processes of (limited) democratization were
encouraged by the major powers in states that were previously authoritarian but also anti-communist, former allies of the Soviet Union joined
the western camp, and states increasingly entered into regional and international agreements in order to try to win some gains in the international order. As Rosenberg (2005: 51) points out, this led to precisely
those changes identified by the transformationalists and hyper-globalists:
expanding social space through the opening up of previously 'closed'
societies; the reconfiguration of geopolitical space through diplomatic
realignment; the blurring of international space through the creation and
reconstruction of international organizations; the unification of historical space through the dissolution of the three worlds; the merging of
inter-societal space through the deepening of transnational interconnections; and the compression of geographical space through the increased
use of information and communications technologies. But, as Rosenberg
(2005: 52) also points out, the problem for globalization theory was that
'these matters stood the other way about. It was the cascading social and
political change, precipitated by the conjunction of capitalist deregulation with the Soviet collapse, which was producing the spatial effects.'

In terms of the relationship between the state and transnationality, the
1980s and 1990s did not see a transformation of state sovereignty so
much as 'a (re)assertion of the abstracted form of capitalist sovereignty
. . . an attempted withdrawal, voluntary or otherwise, from the state's
historically evolved entanglements with civil society in the varying forms
of "First World' social democracy, "Second (and Third) World" state
socialism, and "Third World" patrimonial state capitalism' (Rosenberg

2005: 54). In other words, the 'separation' of politics and economics that characterizes capitalist social relations never went unchallenged, and social and political struggles, and military conflict, laid the basis for a more 'interventionist' state, in the forms of welfare and developmentalist capitalism, or state socialism. In terms of understanding globalization, *all* the protagonists in the debate are wrong. We have not witnessed the transformation of state sovereignty (the claim of the hypers and the transformationalists), but we have witnessed a fundamental shift in the nature of international capitalism, from the neo-Keynesianism of the 1950s to 1970s and 1980s, to the neo-liberal capitalism of the 1980s to the present (which thus challenges the views of the globalization sceptics).

Most globalization theorists do effectively abandon the inflated claims made for the significance of spatial relations, although as we will see in the next chapter, significant ambiguities are retained, particularly in relation to understanding global civil society. There are good political reasons for this movement away from spatial explanation, because the spatial outcomes identified by globalization theory have their roots in political and social change, which most of these theorists reject. In other words, globalization cannot be delinked from the neo-liberal turn of the 1980s and 1990s. Globalization theory is in danger of too easily ignoring or even accepting the political parameters established by the victory of neo-liberalism. These parameters can easily be accepted because globalization theory relies on spatial explanations which effectively sever the link between social actors and historical and political processes. In this way, globalization is said to be inevitable, but the 'explanation' ignores the ways in which agents of neo-liberalism have promoted globalization in the first place.

Indeed, unlike most globalization theorists, Anthony Giddens effectively endorses this neo-liberal project. The Third Way of the 1990s, associated with Giddens and endorsed by pro-globalization politicians like Blair and Clinton, was essentially a political project that attempted to depoliticize globalization. The Third Way uneasily moved from the assertion that globalization was inevitable to the argument that it was desirable. Thus, for example, social exclusion came to be defined as incorporating people into globalization, so that they could reap the benefits of flexible labour markets or participation in the world economy (Cameron and Palan 2004: ch. 6). The idea that globalization itself was inherently marginalizing or exploitative was thus rejected from the outset. As we will see in Chapter 7, this amounted to an argument that combined the claims of modernization theory of the 1960s with the neo-liberalism of the 1980s (Kiely 2005e). In the cases of Giddens, Blair and Clinton, not only was causality assumed to lie with globalization, but the assumption was made that this causality would have positive outcomes

(Kiely 2005a: chs 2 and 4). In this sense then, globalization theory quickly served the ideological needs of globalization as a political project. It is accepted that globalization has its 'bads' as well as 'goods', but just as the latter can be delivered by adopting technocratic policies that take neo-liberalism for granted, so the former can be regulated in managerial ways that take the politics out of globalization. For example, in referring to the globalization of terrorism, Tony Blair reduces the phenomenon to an amorphous mass, devoid of specific contexts and rendered fixable by technocratic diktat.

This section has argued that globalization does refer to important changes in the international order that occurred around the 1990s, even if some can be traced back to the 1970s and 1980s. However, mainstream globalization theory has too easily inflated the significance of these changes, or failed to locate them in the context of a longer-term history of capitalist social relations, and especially an adequate theorization of the relationship between territorial states and 'transnational' markets. In Giddens's case, this effectively led to an endorsement of a political project that accepted the politically created policies of neo-liberalism as inevitable, and ultimately desirable. These points suggest, then, that we need to have a better understanding of the globalization of the 1990s and beyond as a specific period of international capitalist development. The next section reviews and critiques some attempts to provide such an analysis.

Globalization, Transnational Capitalism and Empire

A number of different Marxist-inspired approaches have attempted to theorize the relationship between capitalism and contemporary globalization. This section will mainly focus on two of these: the theory of transnational capitalism, associated with Bill Robinson (2004), Jerry Harris (1998/9, 2003) and Leslie Sklair (2001; 2002), and the theory of globalization as Empire, associated with Michael Hardt and Toni Negri (2000; 2004). Some reference will also be made to related theories such as that of post-imperialism (Becker et al. 1987), as well as broader neo-Gramscian theories of international relations (Cox 1987; Gill 2003; Bieler and Morton 2004), which at least in part have inspired the theories of transnational capitalism.

The theory of transnational capitalism accepts the view that globalization represents 'an *epochal* shift' which is characterized as referring to 'fundamental worldwide changes in social structure that modify and even transform the very functioning of the system in which we live'

(Robinson 2004: 4). At first, this sounds similar to the claims made by both hyper-globalists and transformationalists, but Robinson then goes on to argue that globalization must be understood as the fourth period of international capitalism, following the earlier periods of primitive accumulation and mercantilism, competitive capitalism, and monopoly capitalism and imperialism. Drawing on the neo-Gramscian work of Robert Cox (1987; 1993), Stephen Gill (1990; 2003) and Kees van der Pijl (1998), Robinson (2004) argues that globalization has arisen as a product of the rise of transnational capital and a transnational capitalist class, and has been facilitated by the revolution in communications technologies and transportation, which has created a genuinely global, as opposed to international, economy. This global economy is characterized by capital mobility, globalized circuits of accumulation, and the fragmentation of production. Thus, globalization is distinguished from earlier periods of internationalization, which mainly related to trade and finance. Globalization thus mainly refers to new ways of organizing capitalist production beyond the territorial boundaries of the nation-state, and is therefore related to the post-Fordist restructuring briefly outlined in Chapter 4. This is reflected in increased direct foreign investment, including mergers and acquisitions between firms originating in different countries, the increased practice of subcontracting and outsourcing by companies to (local and foreign) suppliers, and the increase in trade between two or more subsidiaries of the same parent company. These issues are critically examined in detail in Chapter 7, but a few examples illustrate Robinson's argument. From 1996 to 2000, outsourcing by US firms increased from $100 billion to $345 billion, and was particularly common in call centres, graphic design, computer programming and accountancy (Robinson 2004: 18). Foreign direct investment grew from $57 billion in 1982 to $1.27 trillion in 2000, a rate of growth much faster than that of world production or investment (Robinson 2004: 23–4). Crossborder mergers and acquisitions grew from just 14 deals in 1980, to 9655 in 1999, and transnational companies grew in number from 7000 in 1970 to 60,000 by 2000 (Robinson 2004: 58, 55).

The full significance of these important changes – including their implications for development – is considered in Chapter 7. What interests us here is how these developments are related to the question of the state, and in particular the hegemonic US state. Robinson's argument is that a new transnational hegemony is emerging which cannot be reduced to the interests of dominant states. He argues that a new historic bloc has emerged, and that this transnational capitalist class is committed to the promotion of neo-liberal expansion throughout the world. This development cannot be explained by reference to US imperialism, or new inter-imperialist rivalries, but rather by the transnational interpenetration of all nation-states. Thus, 'local elites have sought, not a regional circuit of accumulation in rivalry with circuits elsewhere, but a complete *integration* into globalized circuits. . . . Capitalists with investments in the territory of the United States, for instance, carry passports from Germany, France, Saudi Arabia, Mexico, Japan, Brazil, Korea, and numerous other countries, and the US national state protects and promotes their investments' (Robinson 2004: 131).

Robinson accepts that competition and conflict persist, but this 'is less a case of national states using their power to win export markets for territorially based corporations than one of competition among transnational conglomerates seeking advantage over competitors through corporate dominance achieved via the global integration of production facilities and seeking the favor of a multiplicity of states' (Robinson 2004: 130). This argument is linked to the idea that the nation-state is 'neither retaining its primacy nor disappearing but becoming transformed and absorbed into a TNS [transnational state]' (Robinson 2002: 210).[4] Robinson recognizes that there is no transnational military apparatus of this nascent transnational state, but argues that the US military is operating not on behalf of the US state, but for transnational capital in general. Thus, '(t)he empire of capital is located in Washington' (Robinson 2002: 140).

This argument is similar to that of the theory of post-imperialism. This approach argues that 'global corporations function to promote the integration of diverse national interests on a new transnational basis' (Becker and Sklar 1987: 6). Central to the claim that we live in a post-imperialist era is the argument that transnational corporations do not 'underdevelop' the Third World, but offer access to capital, technology and markets. However, this does not necessarily mean that expansion of capitalism throughout the world is promoting global convergence, and the precise forms that development takes within particular nations and localities will vary. Becker and Sklar (1987: 13) therefore claim that

> *postimperialism is not a theory of economic development per se.* One can properly infer from it that the current global division between developed and less developed territories is fluid rather than fixed – but not that capitalism will develop the latter uniformly. On the contrary, there is every likelihood that capitalist development will continue to be uneven, as in the past, although the present national boundaries may cease to serve as adequate delineations of that unevenness.

This theory is therefore not the same as the return to the idea that imperialism is progressive, discussed in Chapter 2. Instead, more attention is paid to local manifestations of capitalist development, and how these are influenced by class formation, structure and organization. But in terms of the international economy, this theory is close to that of transnational capitalism in that the system of nation-states is said to be eroding as a result of the increasing domination of 'extra-territorial' capitalism.

This theme has also been developed in the work of Michael Hardt and Toni Negri, although they reject the idea that a transnational state has developed. Instead, they argue that the old imperialist order has been replaced by a deterritorialized apparatus of power, which they call 'Empire'. This new global order,

> can no longer be understood adequately in terms of imperialism as it was practiced by the modern powers, based primarily on the sovereignty of the nation-state extended over foreign territory. Instead, a 'network power', a new form of sovereignty, is now emerging, and it includes as its primary elements, or nodes, the dominant nation-states along with supranational institutions, major capitalist corporations, and other powers. This network power we claim is 'imperial' not 'imperialist'. (Hardt and Negri 2004: xii)

This is different from the old imperialist order, but also to some extent the post-war international order based on sovereign nation-states with the US as the hegemonic state. This new system of Empire is based on a three-tier pyramid, with the US state at the top, and other core nation-states (the G7) as junior partners within this top tier. The second tier is made up of transnational companies and the third tier comprises the UN General Assembly, and international non-government organizations (NGOs) (Hardt and Negri 2000: 309–11). The challenge to Empire comes from the transnational multitude, a 'multiple social subject whose constitution and action is based not on identity or unity (or, much less, indifference) but on what it has in common' (Hardt and Negri 2004: 100).

This rather vague idea of the multitude is considered further in Chapters 6 and 10, but more appropriate to our concerns here is how US hegemony, and the international system of sovereign states, are theorized, not only by Hardt and Negri, but by theories of transnational capitalism and post-imperialism. Perhaps what is common to all these theories is not so dissimilar from the problem of globalization theory, which is the tendency to set up too rigid a dichotomy between nation-state and global capital. For example, Burbach and Robinson (1999: 26) argue that a transnational state 'has been brought into existence to function as the collective authority for a global ruling class'. Thus, states are deemed to act solely on the basis of their functionality to the requirements of capitalism. The fact that states do perform certain functions for the reproduction of capitalism does not mean that states *always* act in this way, and that there are no contradictions between state and capital. The socio-historical 'separation' of economy and polity that characterizes capitalist social relations does not mean that 'unity' is re-established by analyses which assume that the latter simply acts for the needs of the former (Lacher 2005). We therefore need to understand that states act in their own right, and that such actions may be limited by the requirements of capitalism, but they also have implications for the expanded accumulation of capital.

These abstract points apply to the current era of globalization, and the role of the US state in this international order. It is undoubtedly the case that the world has become more open and globalized in recent years. However, rather than globalization occurring 'behind the backs' of nation-states, some nation-states have actually promoted globalization. The United States in particular has promoted increased liberalization in response to (perceived and real) discrimination against US companies by other nation-states, and in order to disproportionately benefit from free trade and liberal finance and investment regimes. As we saw in the previous chapter, one (possibly unintended) consequence of the liberalization of financial controls was that the US benefited through the international role of the dollar and the consequent capacity to run deficits that would be impossible for other states. The dichotomy between transnational capitalism, Empire and imperial rule on the one hand, and state, US hegemony and imperialism on the other, is overplayed by Robinson, Becker and Sklar, Hardt and Negri, and others. As Stokes (2005: 228) argues,

> when the US state acts it is because of the structural power of the US economy within world capitalism, with transnational outcomes primarily benefiting US capital through the US' preponderance of global market power. Thus, the US state acts to secure the generic global conditions for transnational capital accumulation less at the behest of a TCC (transnational capitalist class), but rather because, in so doing, the US state is, by default, acting in the generic interests of its national capital because of its high level of internationalization. In short, the US state is the first state among capitalist equals.

This reflects a weakness in most of the literature on globalization, which implicitly suggests not only a decline in the nation-state, but also a similar decline in US hegemony.

In other words, the increased globalization of capital does not mean that transnationality has led to the end of the nation-state. Nor has it ended an international nation-state system, which is based on sovereignty, but which is simultaneously a profoundly hierarchical nation-state system. To use the language of Castells, but to challenge his analysis, the 'space of places' remains central to understanding the 'space of flows'. These points of course became far more apparent with the emergence of the unilateralist Bush administration, and the aggressive foreign policy adopted by this administration made it clear that state power was far from a relic of a past of national capitalisms and/or imperialism.

Globalization, US Hegemony and the 'New imperialism'

This section draws on the argument so far, and (re-)introduces some theories that claim to better explain the current international order. Given the aggressive foreign policy of the United States, particularly (but not only) after 2001, some Marxists argue that the world remains imperialist. This imperialist world order is usually characterized as one based on US 'super-imperialism', or it is one based on inter-imperialist rivalries. However, these two theories are not incompatible as US super-imperialism is usually seen as a strategy by the US state designed to pre-empt the re-emergence of inter-imperialist rivalries. This section critically surveys these arguments, and suggests that those who advocate a return to classical theories of imperialism fail to adequately account for some very real changes in the international capitalist order since the 1970s, and indeed, since 1945. In criticizing these theories, I will suggest that the theories of transnational capitalism and Empire do point to some real changes that defenders of classical theories of imperialism tend to under-estimate. But at the same time, I will extend the argument made at the end of the previous section, and focus more closely on the relationship between the US state and international capitalism, both historically and in the era of globalization. In doing so, I will examine more closely the 'neoconservative' Bush administration, and how this relates to both US hegemony and international capitalism.

As we briefly saw in Chapter 2, classical Marxist theories of imperialism were not without their problems in terms of their analyses of the period preceding the First World War. None the less, some writers defend the usefulness of these theories for understanding the current international order. Central to these theories was the idea that inter-imperialist rivalries played an important part in colonial annexation and war. Some Marxists suggest that these rivalries have not disappeared, that intervention by the core powers in the wars in the periphery actually reflect continued inter-imperialist rivalry. This analysis influenced some Marxist understandings of the Cold War, which was regarded as a conflict between the 'liberal capitalism' of the US and its allies, against the 'state capitalism' of the Soviet Union and its allies. This problematic interpretation of the Cold War, and of the social relations that existed in the Soviet Union and elsewhere, need not concern us here.[5]

More relevant is the idea that inter-imperialist rivalries have continued since the end of the Cold War, and that these are between states that are undoubtedly capitalist. Thus, according to this theory, the 1991 Gulf War upheld US power against Germany and Japan. Similarly, the war over Kosovo in 1999 was less about humanitarian intervention and the disciplining of the repressive regime in Serbia, and more about military and economic expansion into central and eastern Europe, not least at the expense of Russia. The 2001 conflict in Afghanistan was about the exercise of US power against Russia, Iran and Europe. In all these cases then, and despite the rhetoric of humanitarian values and freedom, the wars were largely concerned with the exercise of state power (Rees 2000; 2001). This 'realist' analysis of state power is often augmented in the analysis by the assumption that the dominant regimes also need to exercise such power in order to sustain capitalist accumulation. This is sometimes related to the (Leninist) idea that surplus capital must search for new areas of capital accumulation, and must therefore exercise war in order to find new 'spatial fixes', and this may simultaneously involve the search for new, essential resources to sustain capital accumulation (Harvey 2003; Klare 2002; 2004). Thus, the 2003 conflict in Iraq was a war exercised by the US for guaranteed long-term oil supplies, which involved the defeat of rivals like France and Germany, as well as potential long-term rivals such as Russia and China (Morgan 2003). In some cases this war is even linked to the idea of a return to colonialism, in which the US constructs a puppet state in order to promote US interests in Iraq and the Middle East region (Ali 2004a).

This understanding of imperialism as inter-imperialist rivalry is not incompatible with the idea that the world is dominated by one super-imperialist state, the United States, which has successfully pre-empted the rise of competitors since the end of the Cold War. Thus, Peter Gowan (2001: 81) highlights 'the central fact of contemporary international relations', which is that the United States 'has acquired absolute military dominance over every other state or combination of states on the entire planet'. This indisputable fact is often linked to the more contentious claim that this military power is sufficient to secure the (economic) dominance of the US by preventing the rise of (economic) rivals to the US. Thus, Gowan (2002: 22) claims that 'US policies are tending to conflict with the collective interests of major capitalist centres,' while Harvey (2003: 85) argues that the invasion of Iraq constitutes 'an attempt to control the global oil spigot and hence the global economy through domination of the Middle East' *and* 'a powerful military bridgehead on the Eurasian land mass which, when taken together with its gathering alliances from Poland down through the Balkans, yields it a powerful geo-strategic position in Eurasia with at least the potential to disrupt any consolidation of Eurasian power'.[6] Thus, for these theorists of a new imperialism, inter-imperialist rivalries persist, or at least have the potential to return, and this ultimately guides the actions of the super-imperialist United States. Lenin and Bukharin thus remain indispensable guides for understanding contemporary international politics (Callinicos 2002a; 2003; 2005).

There is undoubtedly something in this analysis. There is plenty of evidence which suggests that US actions are often guided by the idea of preventing the rise of potential competitors. Unlike theories of transnational capitalism, this approach correctly focuses on the continued importance of the nation-state, and the dominant US state in the international order. But there are equally a number of serious weaknesses with this analysis. These relate to the question of cooperation between states, the growth of an increasingly integrated world market, the causes of war and conflict, and how these relate to an adequate theory of contemporary imperialism. The first point then is that relations between the major powers have changed substantially since 1945. There is far more cooperation between major states, which is reflected in the rise of international organizations and summits. This was in part facilitated by cooperation against the communist world, but even in the post-Cold War era the major capitalist states have continued to cooperate. As theories of transnational capitalism point out (see above), this has not meant the end of economic competition, but in the current international order there is little likelihood of this competition leading to military rivalry between the major nation-states. As we have seen, the theories of transnational capitalism contend that competition in the era of globalization only exists between companies and not between nation-states. This argument under-estimates continued rivalries between states, such as disagreements at the WTO (see next chapter) or even disagreement over war in Iraq in 2003. However, these disagreements do not add up to a return to inter-imperialist rivalry of the sort that existed prior to 1914 or 1939. Indeed, apart from the Iraq war of 2003, there was a high degree of cooperation between the most powerful capitalist states in the international order. This does not apply to all states, and US primacy may be linked in some respects to attempts to pre-empt the rise of China and Russia. The resurgence of inter-imperialist rivalries in these cases is therefore a more open question, but even here, military 'competition' reflects perceived future rivalries rather than ones that exist in the present order.[7]

As things stand then, we have an international order in which competition exists alongside high levels of cooperation between the major states, led by the United States. The US has certain advantages over other major states and the developing world (see below), but other states are happy to cooperate in this order provided some gains are made for all. This is not an argument that suggests that gains are distributed equally, but it is one that suggests that considerable gains are made by dominant actors in other states. To an extent this point applies to the developing world, but it is in relations with parts of the South that the contradictions of the international order are most acute. These issues are addressed in more detail below and in later chapters, but for the moment, the point that needs to be emphasized is that while capitalist competition exists in acute forms, contrary to Lenin and Bukharin and their contemporary followers, this does not *necessarily* lead to military competition.[8] In this respect at least, the most useful classical Marxist theory for understanding current reality is Kautsky's (2002) theory of ultra-imperialist cooperation between the core capitalist states.[9]

These points are reinforced by the changes in the nature of international capital since 1914. As we saw in Chapter 2, the main trend before the First World War was the concentration of capital on a national level, with colonial annexation facilitating market access, investment and raw materials. Today we have a far greater internationalization of capital, which was facilitated by US hegemony after 1945, but was subject to some compromise until the neo-liberal turn of the 1980s. The US has committed itself to a policy of integration through openness, an idea that has strong roots in the formation of the US nation (Smith 2005). This commitment to openness means that, in theory at least, capital can move from one part of the world to another. In practice, and for reasons discussed below and in Chapter 7, capital is not as mobile as this, and in fact most capital tends to flow between advanced capitalist countries.

This concentration of flows between core states is not so different from the pre-1914 era. What *is* novel, however, is the rise of manufacturing in the periphery and, most crucially, the fact that the capital that is invested in developing countries does not originate from one nation. This does not mean that capital is no longer tied to particular nation-states, but it does mean that the world cannot be divided into *exclusive* blocs. Economic competition has in many ways intensified, but in a context of increased openness, rather than the context of colonial monopoly and territorial acquisition that characterized the pre-1914 period (apart from the British Empire – see Chapter 2). In the current order then, power is exercised more by directly 'economic', rather than 'political' or military means (Green 2002; Went 2002). Thus, if we take the example of the Middle East and oil, the common argument made is that the US wants to secure access to, or control over, Middle East oil. At some level of generalization this may well be true, although this alone can hardly explain the decision to go to war with Iraq in 2003, not least because the US could have secured more diplomatic relations with its old ally Saddam Hussein, in order to secure Iraqi oil. Moreover, the question then becomes one of access, for whom? Is it for the US alone or its allies? Similarly, if it is about control of Iraqi oil to gain leverage over potential rivals then there is the question of how, in the context of a relatively open international oil market, exclusive access to Iraqi oil can secure such leverage.

Some of these factors may have influenced the decision to go to war and neo-conservative rationalizations of how the war may secure US hegemony (see below). However, this is not the same thing as assuming that this decision was a rational one, both on its own terms, and in assuming the longer-term interests of US capital. In other words, simplistic critiques of the 'war for oil' too often assume that there is a straightforward causality between oil on the one hand, and a war led by the United States for US capital on the other. As Bromley states,

> the form of control that the United States is now seeking to fashion is one that is open to the capital, commodities and trade of many states and firms. It cannot be seen as an economically exclusive strategy, as part of a predatory form of hegemony. Rather, the United States is seeking to use its military power to fashion a geopolitical order that provides the political underpinning for its preferred model of the world economy: that is, an increasingly open liberal international order.   (Bromley 2005: 253)

Given the planned preferential treatment given to US companies in post-war Iraq, the intentions of neo-conservatives partially challenged this idea, but it did not represent a return to the territorial monopoly system of the pre-1914 period, and so it was unlikely that in the long term non-US companies would be excluded from Iraq.

These points reflect one of the features of the contemporary world economy that mainstream globalization theory and theories of transnational capitalism correctly allude to, but do not satisfactorily theorize – namely, the wider and deeper integration of international capital. As we saw in Chapter 4, this is an issue that is closely related to the rise of neo-liberalism and the changing fortunes of US hegemony in the international order.[10] The end of one of the key features of the Bretton Woods post-war order in the early 1970s – the gold–dollar link and fixed exchange rates – was instigated by the United States in an effort to recover its competitive position in the world economy. In the 1970s, successive US governments pursued expansionary monetary policies and a relatively weak dollar, in order to both increase production at home and expand exports abroad. However, the policy led to inflation and potentially undermined the international role of the dollar. This led to a new era in the last two years of the Carter administration (1979–80), and especially under Ronald Reagan, when the money supply came under tighter control, alongside tax cuts for the rich and increased deregulation of capital investment. From 1982 onwards, there was a big increase in military spending and a marked intensification of Cold War hostilities. Increased military spending and tax cuts led to a big increase in the government's budget deficit. At the same time, the US benefited from the continued international demand for the dollar, the main international currency, which allowed it to run massive trade deficits that could be financed through attracting dollars back into the US. In the early 1980s, this was achieved through a policy of high interest rates, promoted by Chair of the Federal Reserve Paul Volcker, which led to the restructuring of US (and world) capitalism, and undermined full employment in the United States and development in the Third World (see Chapter 4).

In the 1990s, when the government budget became solvent and the trade deficit substantially declined, the latter began another upward surge, and this was financed through the selling of government debt securities (bonds), and facilitated by the promotion of liberalization of overseas financial markets, which could guarantee continued flows into the US economy, thus financing the ongoing deficit. After the arrival of the Bush administration in 2001, the Federal budget deficit grew from 1.8 per cent of GDP to an estimated 3.7 per cent in 2003, 4.3 per cent for 2004, and around 6 per cent for 2005, while the trade deficit grew from a record $435 billion in 2001, to new records of $489 billion by 2003 and $726 billion in 2005, the last figure amounting to 5.8 per cent of GDP (Brenner 2003; Monthly Review 2003: 8; Godley et al. 2005). It has been estimated that, if present trends persist, net income payments from abroad will also go into the red, and the US current account deficit will reach at least 8.5 per cent of GDP by 2010 (Godley et al. 2005). Since the 1990s, the US deficits have been financed by foreigners speculating in the stock market, buying real estate, acquiring firms or setting up new sites, and buying US Treasury bonds. Equity purchases fell by 83 per cent from 2000 to 2002 as share prices fell, and so there has been a sustained movement into buying government bonds. In 2001, 97 per cent of the US current account deficit was financed by foreign purchases of these bonds. From 1992 to 2001, the foreign share of US national debt increased from 17 per cent to 31 per cent (Monthly Review 2003: 11).

The US deficits reflect the increasing integration of international capital, and the dilemmas of cooperation in this increasingly interdependent world. The US remains the hegemonic power and in some respects other states are happy for this to occur. This is because the US incurs most of the costs of policing the international order, through its high military budget, which stood at $399 billion in 2004 – almost as large as that of the rest of the world combined, and 29 times as large as the combined spending of those identified as rogue states (Cuba, Iran, North Korea, Sudan, Syria, and Iraq and Libya before 2003) that comprised the 'axis of evil'.[11] Moreover, there are sound economic reasons why other states are not entirely opposed to the US deficits, and that is because they sustain reasonably high levels of growth in the US economy, which in turn serves to stimulate demand for capital seeking to sell goods in the US market. In this respect then, the US acts as a market of last resort for the rest of the world.

But at the same time, there are tensions within this system, which can be traced back to the problems of the Bretton Woods order. The continued increase in US deficits may serve to undermine the competitiveness of US capital, which in turn *may* undermine the international role of the dollar (though this will have an impact not only on the US but on all major states – see Chapter 9). Since 1982, US administrations have periodically switched between supporting a strong and a weak dollar. The problem with the weak-dollar policy is that it was likely to erode confidence in the dollar, a major means by which the US sustains its hegemonic position in the international order. One result would be that US deficits would have to be financed by other means. The rationale for such a policy is the belief that a weaker dollar would deal with the deficit problem through increasing exports and thus reducing the trade deficit, and would bring about economic growth and increased tax revenue to cover the budget deficit. In this way, both the US economy and the international economy could be restored to something approaching balanced growth and development. But there are problems with these expectations. It would take very high rates of growth in the US economy and in its export sector to erode the deficits. A weak dollar has the effect of increasing import prices and stimulating inflationary pressures, which in turn increases the pressure to raise interest rates and re-stimulate the dollar. But higher interest rates and a stronger dollar will have the knock-on effect of undermining economic growth, both in the domestic economy and in the export sector. These challenges have been central to the international economic concerns of US administrations since the 1980s. In practice, weak dollar policies have been periodically practised but eventually abandoned, at the cost of increasing trade imbalances in the world economy.

Whether or not these tensions will lead to the erosion of US hegemony need not concern us here, and it will be further examined in the context of regionalism in Chapter 9. It should however be pointed out that even if we take a narrow view of US hegemony, based on its preponderance of material resources, then the US has successfully managed to reverse its decline as against other rising powers since 1982. From 1983 to 2001, the rate of growth in the US was greater than in all the other G7 countries, and by the late 1990s the real GDP of the US was around 20 per cent higher than in all the other G7 countries, compared with approximate equality between the two in 1982 (Panitch and Gindin 2004: 28). This reflects a higher rate of growth in the US from 1984 to 2004 than in all other advanced capitalist countries, and a maintenance of its competitive position in cutting-edge sectors like aerospace, computers, communications equipment, and scientific instruments, at a time when Japan's and Germany's share have substantially declined (Cumings 1999; Panitch and Gindin 2005b: 113–14). There remains though the question of the deficits, and these are of more significance than Panitch and Gindin's otherwise suggestive account of contemporary US hegemony would lead us to believe. But as we will see in Chapter 9, these are best analysed in terms of a wider view of hegemony that moves beyond a simple account of productive resources, and recognizes the problems (and opportunities) of these deficits for *all* countries.

For the moment, we should emphasize that what these tensions do suggest is that increased openness and integration in the international economy is qualitatively different from what happened in the era of classical imperialism. Indeed, the neo-liberal era effectively started with the Reaganite switch to high interest rates in the early 1980s, and since then, the world economy has been characterized by delicate balancing acts based above all on movements in the main currencies, and designed to deal with the question of the US trade deficit in a way that could secure growth in all the major regions of the world economy. In particular, the Plaza Accord of 1985 led to a devaluation of the dollar, supported by the major states of the advanced capitalist world, but ten years later this policy was abandoned and the dollar's value increased in order to try to stimulate the economies of western Europe and Japan. But the attempt to stimulate simultaneous growth in all the major regions has been unsuccessful, and the world recessions of the early 1980s and early 1990s have also been accompanied by slow rates of growth and recession in one or more of the main regions in the world economy throughout the period. At the same time, economic tensions, particularly over trade, have existed side by side with this cooperation, but this has occurred in the context of managing and maintaining increased integration and greater openness.

It is in this context that the 'military imperialist' role of the United States should be situated. Certainly this is designed to maintain and promote US hegemony, but this has less to do with the 'accumulation needs' of US capital, and much more to do with the policing role of the United States in an increasingly integrated international economic order. Above all, it is an attempt to incorporate 'failed' or 'rogue' states into the liberal international order, or what is sometimes called the 'liberal' or 'democratic zone of peace' (Doyle 1983; Starr 1997; see further, Chapter 8). Those theorists who advocate a return to Leninist theories of imperialism effectively reduce both the conflicts and the authoritarian states that exist in parts of the periphery to theatres in which inter-imperialist rivalries are currently played out. While of course historical legacies of colonialism and the Cold War may well be important in these processes, they cannot be reduced to them, not least because in other former colonies no such conflicts exist. The general, historical explanations must therefore be accompanied by more specific, contingent explanations, and this is something almost entirely lacking in accounts advocating a return to Lenin. In this approach then, the idea of failed states is simply ideological, and functional to the imperialist aspirations of the United States and other major capitalist powers. But this is clearly not the case, even if it is true that these same powers are highly selective in whom they deem to be rogue or failed states. The reasons for 'state failure' are examined in more detail in Chapter 8, but what concerns us here is the relationship between greater integration and openness on the one hand, and attempts to incorporate these 'illiberal zones' into the liberal capitalist world.

For one major problem is that this incorporation is unlikely to happen. This is in part because war is likely to lead to both innocent deaths and nationalist reaction in cases of occupation, as Iraq has made clear. It is also in part because there is an unwarranted assumption that liberalism is the norm and that this can simply be imposed as a model that is bound to promote economic growth, prosperity and peace in the periphery. But equally, *it is questionable that openness in itself is conducive to the development of the periphery*. This is so for two reasons. First, financial liberalization can have the effect of undermining stability and increasing uncertainty in countries where productive investment is crucial to development. The use of hedge funds is certainly necessary to provide security against uncertainty in an era of floating exchange rates, but these same funds are then used to speculate in ways that intensify the uncertainty that they were meant to alleviate in the first place. Furthermore, such liberalization can encourage the outflow of capital away from the periphery and into the core, not least to the United States. This diversion of funds can undermine potential for investment, even if, by allowing the US to live beyond its means, it simultaneously acts to secure access to the US market for some producers in the developing world. Secondly, increased openness has included policies of trade and investment liberalization, and these too are not necessarily conducive to the development of poorer countries. This is a situation not dissimilar to the free trade imperialism of the mid-nineteenth century, discussed in Chapter 2, and reconsidered in detail in the context of the current world economy in

Chapter 7. But essentially, one likely effect of free trade is the reinforcement of some countries producing lower-value goods such as primary products or low-cost manufacturing, while others produce high-cost manufacturing and services. Free trade policies undermine the prospects for state policies that are designed to promote dynamic comparative advantages and shifting to higher-value production. Investment is potentially developmental, but the removal of state regulations designed to promote higher-value production and accrue beneficial spin-offs such as the use of local skilled labour and suppliers undermines the prospects of these benefits being realized.

The liberal assumption that incorporation can occur through the removal of rogue leaders and the promotion of neo-liberal policies of openness, therefore under-estimates the tensions that exist between neo-liberal policies, development and security. In some respects the economic policies promoted by international institutions (and to an extent, states in the developing world) undermine the prospects for development and thus increase insecurity. This does not mean, of course, that there is any simplistic correlation between military intervention and neo-liberal policies, but it does mean that there are enormous tensions between US hegemony and neo-liberalism on the one hand, and military intervention on the other. This can be seen most clearly through a brief consideration of the neo-conservative influence on US foreign policy in the era of George W. Bush.

The crude Leninist position assumes that the rise of neo-conservatism in the Bush administration somehow represents the needs of US capital (Callinicos 2003). This tends towards a highly functionalist account, reading off the specifics of policy making within the US government from the needs of a section of US capital. Contemporary neo-conservatism should instead be seen as a particular ideology, which has implications for capital accumulation but which cannot be taken to be as somehow functional to its needs.[12] Rather, the neo-conservative policy of the Bush administration should be regarded as an attempt to use military and unilateral means to Americanize the world. This is a strategy that combines hard, military power with an older liberal internationalism based on incorporating non-liberal states into the US-led 'international community'. On the one hand the Bush administration argued that it was 'time to reaffirm the essential role of American military strength' and that, given the existence of rogue states in the international order, the US retained the option of 'preemptive actions to counter a sufficient threat to our national security' (National Security Strategy 2002: 29, 15). On the other hand, US military power will serve the means of expanding liberal universalism, 'based on non-negotiable demands of human dignity, the rule of law, limits on the power of the state, respect for women and private property and free speech and equal justice and religious tolerance' (National Security Strategy 2002: iii).

While the former statements represent a break from the partial movement towards multilateralism in the 1990s, in that it is more openly unilateralist, the extent of this shift should not be exaggerated. The Clinton presidency was prepared to use force and marginalize the United Nations in the process of doing so, as the intervention in Kosovo made clear. Under Clinton, the United States also became increasingly wary of the World Trade Organization, particularly with the breakdown of talks at Seattle in late 1999. Moreover, the multilateral commitment to free trade was not regarded as being incompatible with US interests, a point discussed in depth in the next chapter. However, US neo-conservatives argued that the Clinton administration lacked a grand strategy, and was not prepared to use military force or employ unilateralist means to enhance US primacy (Project for the New American Century 1997). It was argued that US primacy alone was sufficient to guarantee the expansion of states allied to the US, and neo-conservatives often pointed to the collapse of communism to back up this claim. Furthermore, in the case of recalcitrant rogue states (such as Iraq), the case was made for military intervention (Project for the New American Century 1998). For neo-conservatives, in the post-Cold War world, there were potentially new dangers arising from competitor or rogue states, and these needed to be dealt with, if necessary by military power. This new world therefore needed an expansion of US primacy (Kagan and Kristol 2000).

The Bush administration essentially accepted the idea that US primacy and military power were sufficient to secure its hegemonic status, but even in Iraq it quickly became clear that military power alone was insufficient to achieve this goal. The limits of military power were all the more clear in cases of relations between other core capitalist states and emerging powers from within the developing world, such as China and India.[13] This again in part reflects the higher degree of global economic integration, which undermines any simplistic assertion of power based solely on military resources. But equally this military power was to be used to construct a world of liberal, sovereign states promoting neo-liberal policies. Berger (2006: 19) is thus right to argue that:

> Although the focus of the Bush administration after 11 September 2001 may have shifted, what has occurred is a reorientation, or a military deepening of, rather than a retreat from, the globalisation project as such.

However, the tensions associated with globalization under US hegemony have continued, and in a more acute form since 2001: first, between the unilateral means by which this was to be achieved and the perceived outcome of an expanding liberal order, with some neo-conservatives coming perilously close to embracing an older-style empire led by the US;[14] secondly, between continued US hegemony and this liberal core of states, which could presumably undermine US economic hegemony; and thirdly, in the way in which the US was prepared to compromise its policy by aligning with non-liberal states and allowing the policy of market expansion to effectively 'trump' the idea of expanding formal democracy into something far more substantive (Kiely 2005b: ch. 6). But equally, despite these differences over means, the endgame of globalization remained intact in the Bush years – indeed, the second and third of these tensions applied as much to the Clinton administration's endorsement of globalization as to Bush's unilateralism (Smith 2005).

In terms of development (and globalization), this has had a number of implications. Security remains a major part of development policy, but this is increasingly linked to the security of people in the core states as well as in the failed states of the periphery. For some commentators, the war on terror has led to an important break from development policy in the 1990s. Drawing on interviews with a number of development NGO workers, Duffield and Waddell (2004) suggest that the war on terror is a 'new Cold War', whereby aid is tied to political allegiance, and human rights, poverty reduction and UN peacekeeping are sidelined by the coercive policies of the US state and its allies. Like international relations in general, it is true that there has been a significant change in official development policy since 2001. However, like those same international relations, it would be a mistake to over-estimate the extent of this change.[15] Thus, George W. Bush's closest ally, Tony Blair, suggests that 'globalisation is not just economic. It is also a political and security phenomenon . . . we cannot turn our backs on conflicts and the violation of human rights in other countries if we want to be secure' (cited in Higott 2003: 16). This represents a partial shift from the upbeat messages associated with the globalization of the 1990s, but Blair has attempted to provide a coherent bridge between the era of Clinton and the era of Bush II, and he has done so by employing the language of globalization. While some harder conservatives in the Republican Party, such as Vice-President Cheney, emphasize continuity with the Cold War era, the 'democratic imperialist'[16] wing of the neo-conservative movement argue that US security concerns are inseparable from a (selective) commitment to liberal democratic expansion. Despite the hatred of Clinton, this is broadly compatible with the globalization of the 1990s, and Blair has linked the two eras by talking up the balance of risk[17] in international politics (see Runciman 2006). In other words, interconnectedness means that the suffering of populations in one part of the globe is bound to have consequences in other parts of the world, and globalization entails both risks as well as opportunities. As we saw above, security was hardly irrelevant to the concerns of development in the 1990s, and Bush's 'axis of evil' was essentially derived from the foreign policy of previous presidencies – above all, Clinton's focus on rogue and failed states.

More narrowly, the poverty reduction and governance agendas of the 1990s were still accompanied by neo-liberal policies, which had little positive effect on growth in the poorest countries and which promoted only speculative booms – followed by slumps – in the so-called emerging markets of Latin America and East Asia (these are discussed in Chapters 7 to 9). Thus, the neo-liberal Washington consensus of the 1980s was replaced by the neo-liberal post-Washington consensus of the 1990s, the latter of which focused more explicitly on institutional reforms that were designed to better implement the structural adjustment policies of the 1980s. These, however, had limited positive effects in terms of economic growth and security, and were increasingly challenged, most visibly by the rise of 'anti-globalization' protests, but equally by right-wing think-tanks that advocated a more aggressive linkage of security and economic policy. Thus, in 2000, the Meltzer Commission report in the United States criticized the World Bank's record on poverty reduction in the developing world, and the US began to take a more critical stance towards the World Trade Organization (see Chapter 6). This paved the way for a more unilateralist development policy, which explicitly linked security and development concerns and promoted more open US leadership. These tendencies grew after 2001, and the US administration increasingly advocated that larger amounts of aid should take the form of grants rather than loans. US Under-Secretary to the Treasury John Taylor argued in 2002 that 'grants can be tied more effectively to performance in a way that longer-term loans simply cannot. You have to keep delivering the service or you don't get the grant' (cited in Soederberg 2006a: 169). In 2002, President Bush announced a substantial increase in US aid and the development of the new Millennium Challenge Account. This planned to increase the amount of aid dispensed in the form of grants, and was tied to a 16-point list of criteria, which benefited those governments 'who rule justly, invest in their people, and encourage economic freedom'.[18] Certainly these practices represent something of a shift in aid policy, and above all they represent an attempt by the US to carry out a more pro-active policing role in the failed states of the periphery (see Chapter 8). But at the same time, the end goal of expanding liberal democracies that promote neo-liberal policies, in order to integrate them into the liberal zone of peace, is not so far removed from Clinton's strategy of engagement and enlargement.

Conclusion

This chapter has considered the claims of both mainstream globalization theory and classical Marxist arguments which suggest that we are still living in an era of imperialism. Both perspectives were rejected – globalization theory for its conflation of globalization as explanation and outcome, and classical theories of imperialism for failing to take adequate account of some crucial changes in the world economy since the period immediately before 1914. Theories of transnational capitalism were also examined, and these at least have attempted to combine an understanding of globalization as referring to a set of outcomes, with the recognition of important changes in the international order, above all increased global integration through the promotion of more open economies. But these theories also tend to under-estimate the continued centrality of the nation-state, and the hierarchical nature of both the international state system and global capital flows. A theory of imperialism therefore remains indispensable for understanding both the contemporary world order, and the place of the South in that order.

The alternative position proposed in this chapter suggested the need to situate contemporary imperialism in the context of cooperation as well as competition between the core nation-states, the promotion of a more open international economy, and the consequent greater integration or 'globalization' of capital. The United States remains the most powerful nation-state, and continues to enjoy considerable economic advantages over its competitors. It is also the main military power, and thus plays some role in policing the international order, even if this is neither sufficient nor necessary to maintain US economic hegemony. For the South, development is undermined by the (selective) commitment to 'universal' free trade and the contradictory role of finance in further facilitating the concentration of capital in the developed world – an argument developed further in Chapter 7. The US and other core capitalist states have attempted to expand the 'liberal core' of developed states, albeit in ways that are often self-serving, but greater openness actually serves to discourage such incorporation. Since 2001, this has involved the greater use of unilateral military power, but this has only served to further undermine the legitimacy of US hegemony. Moreover, the 'break' in US policy since 2001 hides real continuities based on the continued promotion of neo-liberal policies, as well as the movement towards unilateralism under the Clinton presidency. The next chapter elaborates on these themes through detailed consideration of the issue of global governance.

Chapter 6

Cosmopolitanism, Globalization and Global Governance

Developing some of the themes of the previous chapter, this chapter examines the debate over the relationship between globalization and the institutions of global governance. The main focus of the debate is over the relationship between global governance and the claims that these represent a partial movement towards the development of cosmopolitan systems of governance, which transcend the specific interests of nation-states. This debate is examined both analytically, and through reference to some of the key institutions of global governance. The chapter opens by examining the debate over cosmopolitanism, and how this relates to global governance. It then moves on to examine particular institutions of global governance. The first case examined is the United Nations and the international system of human rights, and its enforcement and justification through the doctrine of humanitarian intervention. The second case is that of the World Trade Organization, though some brief details of other institutions of global economic governance, such as the World Bank and International Monetary Fund, are also discussed. The relationship between these institutions and the nation-state is then examined, both generally and in relation to the question of US hegemony, which in turn is related to the question of civil society and power. In each of these discussions, but particularly in the final section, the claim that global civil society represents an agent of cosmopolitanism, which can provide the basis for a genuinely universal ethics in the global age, is discussed.

Cosmopolitanism and Global Governance

According to Archibugi and his collaborators, the debate over contemporary global governance is closely linked to three crucial changes in the late twentieth century. The first is the increase in the processes of globalization, discussed in the previous chapter. The second is the end of the Cold War, which has not ended conflict between states, but which has the potential 'for creating a more progressive, stable system of interstate relations' (Archibugi et al. 1995: 1–2). The third is the extension of the democratic ideal to an increasing number of states throughout the globe (Shaw 2000). Some commentators draw particular implications from these changes, and suggest that this new global era has 'enabled a more inclusive form of multilateralism than had been feasible in a politically and economically divided world' (Held and McGrew 2003: 8). This rather upbeat and optimistic assessment is usually qualified by a distinction between the reality of, and the potential for, genuinely multilateral and democratic global governance, not least in an international order dominated by an aggressive and unilateralist US foreign policy (Held 2004). The argument is still nevertheless made that changing international circumstances have at least provided hope for the forging of genuine global governance operating according to cosmopolitan political principles, which transcend the particular interests of nation-states. Above all, this means the development of a concept of global citizenship, in which people have some sense of global belonging, involvement and responsibility which is effectively enforced by both the nation-state system and the international institutions of global governance (Tomlinson 1999: ch. 6).

For Rosenau (1997), this post-Cold War, global era promotes a new and complex multilateralism, in which states have set up new transnational arrangements such as bilateral agreements and multilateral institutions in order to regulate events outside their own borders. This extension is in part a reality, as many former dictatorships have been replaced by democracies, even if these are in some respects limited. But equally, this movement is also in some respects aspirational, as political and social movements demand an increased political voice, both within and beyond nation-states. This development is thus not only a product of national struggles for democratization within nation-states, but it also reflects the emergence of organizations and institutions *beyond* them. According to Held and McGrew (2003: 7), the sovereign nation-state 'now lies at the intersection of a vast array of international regimes and organizations that have been established to manage whole areas of transnational activity . . . and collective policy problems'. As well as the rise of international organizations, summits and agreements, there has also been a massive increase in the number of international non-government organizations (NGOs). At the start of the twentieth century there were 37 international governmental organizations and 1760 international NGOs; by 1996, there were 1830 international governmental organizations and 38243 international NGOs (Held and McGrew 2003: 7). The rise of these organizations reflects the fact that some issues are genuinely global and transcend the nation-state. This is most obvious in the case of the environment. For those writers who are optimistic about the prospects for global governance, these developments are important because they mean that while the state system is still unequal and hierarchical, even the most powerful of states is in some senses subject to processes beyond its control. At the same time, this means that cooperation between states becomes a functional necessity, as national solutions are no longer adequate. Just as crucially, the rise of international NGOs reflects the rise of 'global civil society'(Kaldor 2003; Keane 2003),[1] made up of organizations and associations which are independent of nation-states and the profit-making activities of commercial corporations. The development of this 'space' beyond national states and global markets acts as a kind of countervailing power, pressuring governments to take action on issues related to human rights, arms limitation, the environment, debt, and so on. Thus, global civil society also ensures that (some) states move beyond their interest-maximizing behaviour of the past, and thus international relations increasingly comprise ethical considerations, rather than just the exercise of power.

This optimistic view is challenged by both realist and Marxist theorists of international relations. The realist perspective argues that global governance is simply an extension of state interests, and that the agendas of international institutions are always dominated by the interests of the most powerful states. International relations have always been dominated by interests and power, and it is naive to believe that the recent 'ethical turn' can be divorced from these questions of real politics (Krasner 1982; Gilpin 1987). Marxists (including neo-Gramscians) broadly accept this argument, but suggest that it should be extended so that state interests and power are linked to the wider question of capitalism. Realists tend to *describe* rather than *explain* the links between the dominant states – and the US state in particular – and wider questions of power (Cox 1987; Rosenberg 1994; Callinicos 2002a). For this reason, they do not have an adequate account of power in the international system, and indeed, insofar as they purport to describe rather than explain, they are complicit in the existing exercise of power. For Marxists then, the question of state power needs to be located within the context of international capitalism. As we saw in the last chapter, some Marxists suggest that this needs to be theorized in relation to a new, transnational capitalism, while others contend that a theory of imperialism remains indispensable for understanding the current international order.

These broad points were debated in the previous chapter, and so the rest of this chapter examines the cosmopolitan-realism–Marxism debate with particular reference to the question of global governance. The next section looks at the UN, universal rights and humanitarian intervention, while the section after that examines global economic governance with particular reference to the WTO.

The United Nations, Universal Rights and Humanitarian intervention

Two disastrous wars between self-interested states led to an attempt to reconstruct international relations after 1945. The League of Nations had failed as states continued to exercise their self interest – the US failed to join, the post-1918 international settlement was far from satisfactory, and the Nazis and their allies embarked on a new era of national expansion. After the Second World War, the UN system attempted to promote both genuine international cooperation, and the development of a system of international justice. This was above all promoted through the Universal Declaration of Human Rights of 1948. Most states signed this agreement, though there were exceptions. South Africa and Saudi Arabia both refused on grounds of race and religion, while the Soviet Union and its allies argued that the rights embodied in the agreement were too biased towards the interests of western, liberal capitalism (see below). Over time an increasing number of states, including the newly independent states of the Third World, came to sign the agreement, but the contents of the Declaration remain contentious.

The idea of universal rights is most clearly associated with the political philosophy of liberalism. The seventeenth-century philosopher John Locke (1994) argued that human rights were universal in that they applied to all of humanity (though he did make a number of qualifications). He argued that before the existence of the state, there was a condition of nature based on peaceful co-existence, whereby people engaged in commercial activity and exchange. However, he argued that a state was necessary to arbitrate in the case of disputes over property and exchange in the free market. Locke therefore argued in favour of a classical liberal, limited state, in which there would be minimal interference in the lives of individuals, thus allowing them to exercise their freedom through choices made in the free market. Central to Locke's conception were the natural rights to life, liberty and property. Rights theory has developed substantially since Locke's day, and has become increasingly associated with struggles for social advance, thus changing and perhaps even transforming the legacy of classical liberalism. Nevertheless, Locke's argument continues to provide the starting point for liberal theories of universal human rights.

Thus, Article 3 of the UN Declaration emphasized the right 'to life, liberty and security of person'. The Declaration also argues that 'recognition of the inherent dignity and of the equal and inalienable rights of all members of the human family is the foundation of freedom, justice and peace in the world'.[2] The Soviet Union and its allies failed to sign the Declaration because they argued that it was biased towards 'western', liberal rights. Of the 24 specific rights listed (in Articles 3–26), 18 were civil and political (individual) and only 6 were social and economic (collective). This division between individual and collective rights has dominated debates over rights, and was reflected in the creation of two International Covenants at the UN: the International Covenant on Civil and Political Rights (ICCPR) and the International Covenant on Economic, Social and Cultural Rights (ICESCR). These debates of course also reflected as well as exacerbated Cold War divisions.

These debates reflected wider argument over the nature of 'universal' human rights. There have basically been three areas of contention. The first argument made by critics is that there is no such thing as natural rights, and that therefore rights can only ever be established through states granting civil liberties to individuals.[3] In this argument, rights are historically specific and only exist within particular social and political communities. This is not necessarily an argument against the desirability of human rights, but has been made to suggest that the language of rights too easily ignores complex social and political realities.[4] We will return to this argument in the context of humanitarian intervention, below. The second objection is that claims to rights are too selective, and that their origins in western, individualist liberal thought means that social, economic and collective rights tend to be ignored. These include the 'positive rights' such as the right to a basic income, food, clothing and shelter. These are sometimes called positive rights because they entitle individuals to do certain things. Liberal freedoms, based on the right to exercise individual autonomy from the state, through ownership of private property, free speech and so on, do not guarantee these positive rights.[5] Many socialists have argued since the nineteenth century that the inequalities associated with ownership of private property – advocated by liberal rights theory – mean that those individual rights actually undermine collective rights (Marx 1978). These points lead to the third objection, which is that 'universal rights' are nothing of the sort, and that the claim to universalism is actually a claim made to justify western rights (and power) over other ideas about rights. This ignores not only the different social context identified by the first criticism, but also the very different cultural values that exist in the world order.

These critiques of liberal universalism are complicated further when we come to examine the international sphere, because this is made up of a world of (sovereign) nation-states. Therefore, individual rights may conflict with the right of nations to self-determination. For communitarian and realist perspectives, this right of self-determination effectively trumps the rights of individuals within those nations. Indeed, the claim to represent the universal good is used by the dominant states to expand their power. The claim to universalism is thus nothing more than the claim of the western powers to dominate the rest of the world. Critics argue that in a world of increased global interconnectedness, but where human rights abuses by states remain common, this argument is insufficient. Cosmopolitan perspectives argue that universal human rights should in some way be enforced because these rights are greater than the right of nations to self-determination. This latter position can in some respects be regarded as the political companion to the global transformationalist position outlined in the last chapter. The problem however is that this position too tends to under-estimate the questions of power and agency in the context of the real world of globalization. More specifically, the question is: Who should enforce cosmopolitan human rights? We therefore arrive back at the debate over global governance, outlined in the first section above.

Cosmopolitan theorists suggest that enhanced institutions of global governance should be the main enforcer of human rights. This has led to a particularly contentious debate over the issue of humanitarian intervention. When the UN was founded, the recognition of the sovereignty of states was incorporated into the UN Charter (Article 2(7)). However, there has been a gradual shift way from the idea that state sovereignty is paramount and towards the idea that individual rights are more important than state sovereignty. This has been true in particular since the end of the Cold War, and has been reinforced by other manifestations of contemporary globalization, such as the rise of the global media and communications, and of global civil society organizations, discussed further below.[6] Both the UN and other international organizations have promoted a far more interventionist position since the end of the Cold War, reflected for instance in the report by the International Commission on Intervention and State Sovereignty (ICISS 2001), which argued that when human rights abuses reach a certain threshold, 'the principle of nonintervention yields to the international responsibility to protect'. The case made for intervention is sometimes a legal one, and can involve drawing on the UN Charter (particularly Articles 1(3), 55 and 56), or the idea that there is a customary international law that binds states to behave in a particular way (Arend and Beck 1993). But it is the moral case which is usually made, and this rests on the argument that there are universal human rights which should be upheld by all states within the 'international community'.

This of course leads us back to the debates over rights discussed above, and the related questions of agency and motivation in cases of humanitarian intervention. Parekh (1997: 50) argues that for an intervention to count as properly humanitarian, it must be 'guided by the sentiment of humanity, compassion or fellow feeling'. Both realists and Marxists contend that a purely altruistic intervention will not occur, and that humanitarian intervention is therefore simply a rhetorical device designed to conceal self-interested motivations. Certainly even in cases sometimes deemed to be successful, such as the NATO intervention to protect Kosovars from Serb oppression in 1999, the motivations were not solely altruistic, and were partly driven by other interests as was briefly suggested in the previous chapter. For this reason, some argue that humanitarian intervention should be judged according to outcomes and consequences more than motivation (Brown 2002: ch. 8). But these factors too are difficult to quantify. Thus, ethnic cleansing briefly intensified after the NATO bombing of Serbia, and after the return of refugees to Kosovo, Serbs in the area also faced repression. This also raises questions concerning the *selectivity* of intervention, and the fact that some instances of repression are deemed to be fit for intervention while others are not. Indeed, some of these others are carried out by allies of the dominant powers that lead the humanitarian interventions, and critics point to the double standards of intervention against Serbia (and Afghanistan and Iraq), and non-intervention or even tacit support in cases such as Israel–Palestine and Russia–Chechnya, as well as support for regimes like those of Uzbekistan, Saudi Arabia and Colombia. The stock response to these arguments is that 'western double standards' are preferable to murderous regimes like those of the Taliban or Saddam Hussein. However, this argument sounds remarkably like a justification for the unquestioned exercise of western power, and ignores the wider consequences of these double standards for any movement towards the democratization of global governance. Thus, Michael Ignatieff (2003: 45–76; also Hitchens 2003) argues that some form of imperial rule is a regrettable necessity in the current international order. But this argument assumes that the US 'has exercised no agency in bringing about the state of affairs in which it now finds itself' (Rao 2004). Ignatieff is not unaware of these legacies, and indeed at times questions the motives of US empire-building. At the same time however, he remains hopeful of good outcomes, but does so by suggesting that these can then occur only by appealing to the good intentions that he earlier questioned (Ignatieff 2003: 24).

These critical points do not mean that the US and its allies should be condemned whatever policy they adopt, as some anti-imperialist Marxists tend to do. But it does mean that there needs to be much more scepticism about humanitarian intervention, particularly when such interventions draw on allies with questionable human rights records (Roth 2004). The argument that the US has a liberal democracy and a better domestic human rights record than those of rogue states, and that this gives the US a mandate to intervene in other countries, is similarly problematic as it again ignores the repressive ways in which the US has behaved – and continues to behave – in its relations with other states. Moreover, attempts from the outside to build new states are likely to lead to new attempts at nation-building, which is itself crucial to the construction of stable liberal democracy. However, this nation-building is likely to be *against* the intervening power, and not in support of it. As Rao (2004: 156) suggests, 'if democracy promotion is unlikely to be successful without a pre-existing sense of national identity, and if empire can do little to precipitate such an identity (except in a thoroughly antagonistic way), it is difficult to see how empire – however heavy – can accomplish the task of putting failing states back on their feet'.

The selective nature of human rights also reflects the liberal bias in the international human rights regime. Much more attention is paid to military intervention in the cases of failed or rogue states, in preference to the resolution of social and economic inequalities and injustice. According to UN figures, the developed countries spend as much as 25 times on defence as they spend on overseas aid. Every developed country spends more on defence than on aid, and Britain and especially the United States have the worst records in this respect (Elliott 2005). Thus, according to Thomas Pogge (2002: 2), only 1 per cent of world annual GDP (the equivalent of $312 billion) would be necessary to alleviate global extreme poverty. Of course the stock response to this is that there is no guarantee that this money would be spent on poverty reduction, and it could be wasted on corruption and so on. Therefore any increase in aid must be conditional on the adoption of policies that promote economic growth. These issues are discussed in Chapters 7 and 8, which will suggest that the (developmental) significance of corruption is exaggerated and that the polices favoured by the dominant states and international institutions are not necessarily conducive to growth or poverty reduction. But even if they were, there is still a question that needs to be addressed. For if the governments of Britain, the United States and other western powers are genuinely committed to resolving the problems of the developing world, then why are their priorities so overwhelmingly focused on military rather than non-military intervention? Indeed, even those sympathetic towards humanitarian military intervention have argued that too often it has been a 'short-term palliative that does little to address the underlying political causes of the violence and suffering' (Wheeler and Bellamy 2005: 571). The claim that with Afghanistan and Iraq, things will be different this time, and that the US and Britain are in it for the long haul, is unconvincing. This is because the foreign occupation has contributed enormously to the problem, and the neo-conservative optimism about liberation betrayed a naive faith in the belief that liberalism could quickly be imposed on these nation-states, and that this was simply held back by the presence of evil in the forms of the Taliban and Saddam Hussein (Gregory 2004; Kiely 2005b; Chan 2005; Bernstein 2006). This liberal imperialism failed to address any of the complexities of state formation and the emergence of rogue and failed states – an issue addressed in depth in Chapter 8.

It is for these reasons that many Marxists endorse a blanket opposition to any form of humanitarian intervention and any commitment to cosmopolitanism. This is because both the practice and the principle effectively endorse the primacy of the US state in the international arena. The institutions of global governance, including the United Nations, are dismissed as 'lightly disguised instruments of US policy' and a 'screen for American will' (Gowan 2002; Anderson 2003). The UN is too weak to challenge US primacy, as witnessed by the post-occupation acquiescence to the US invasion of Iraq in 2003. Cosmopolitanism is given equally short shrift because it justifies the erosion of state sovereignty in favour of expanding US power. Finally, the selective nature of intervention is alluded to by Callinicos (2003: 128–9), when he contrasts the priority given to wars against failed states with the lack of attention to wars in the poorest countries, such as the Democratic Republic of Congo.

As a critique of 'actually existing global governance'and 'actually existing cosmopolitanism', these points are largely convincing. However, as a blanket dismissal of any form of global governance and any commitment to cosmopolitanism they are not. Thus, Callinicos's critique of the priorities given by some governments to war rather than poverty alleviation is undoubtedly correct (see above). But his use of the example of the Democratic Republic of Congo is less convincing, because one suspects that any change in western policy towards that particular country would itself be condemned as imperialist – indeed, this was the basic 'anti-imperialist' position taken in response to changing 'western' policy towards the former Yugoslavia in the 1990s. What this suggests is that in remaining committed to outmoded theories of imperialism and anti-imperialism, these Marxists will always dismiss the actions of the most powerful states, and the existing institutions of global governance, *no matter what action these institutions take.* As we saw in the last chapter, this is because they remain committed to an analysis of imperialism in which the only agents in the international order are the dominant states. This neglects complex and difficult issues around human rights abuses within states, which are not resolved by simply defending state sovereignty, or indeed, no matter how significant, the various legacies of colonialism. In practice this means putting some flesh on the bones of cosmopolitanism, which too easily asserts solidarity and justice beyond state borders, but fails to specify the politics of this principle, either in the content of a cosmopolitan political programme or in the agencies that would begoing to put this into practice. Indeed, the ambiguity over what constitutes cosmopolitan principles was one reason why both supporters and opponents of the Iraq war in 2003 claimed allegiance to cosmopolitanism (Kiely 2004b). Crucially however, cosmopolitan principles can be used to challenge *both* human rights abuses within states *and* the exercise of domination by one state over others in the international order (Archibugi 2005). In contrast, it is unclear how appeals to state sovereignty or to 'anti-imperialist' forces automatically secure the progressive political outcomes that the anti-imperialist Marxists otherwise claim to endorse.

It bears repeating that this partial defence of cosmopolitanism is not made to endorse the claims made by some politicians that they are promoting freedom and democracy in the developing world. Indeed, the wars in Afghanistan and Iraq do not conform to Walzer's (1992) (questionable) criteria for a just war, which include just cause, right intention, proper authority, proportionality, and last resort, at least some of which were not met in either or both cases. Indeed, Tony Blair's justification for the war in Iraq effectively collapsed just cause (*jus ad bellum*) and proportionality and restraint in the exercise of war (*jus in bello*), so that the latter can somehow be justified solely by reference to the good intentions of the former. This is an argument about differentiating not between good and bad wars, but between those deemed to be good, as against those deemed to be bad, or evil (Runciman 2006; Gregory 2004; Chan 2005; Bernstein 2006). More generally, there are further difficult questions, which relate not only to the lead up to these wars, particularly Iraq (Roth 2004; Coates and Krieger 2004; Kiely 2005b), but also to the conduct of these and the earlier wars in the 1990s. These were expressly designed to minimize the risks to combatants, and they therefore increased risks to non-combatant civilians. Indeed, this charge was all the greater in the less controversially 'humanitarian wars' over Kosovo and Afghanistan (Shaw 2005).

More broadly, in terms of the relationship between rights and real politics, US hegemony is closely linked to a neo-liberal agenda which does not necessarily expand liberal rights, and can be positively harmful to the promotion of social and economic rights. Just as neo-liberalism ultimately supports market expansion over substantive democracy (see Chapter 8), US hegemony will ultimately be promoted over the 'international community'. This point applies to the unilateralist Bush administration, but so too did it apply in many respects to the more multilateral Clinton presidency. One weakness of contemporary cosmopolitans is that, like the mainstream globalization theory discussed in the previous chapter, it is too often naive and nostalgic for the 1990s. This is discussed further in the next section through consideration of the World Trade Organization (WTO).

The WTO and Global Economic Governance

In some respects, the World Trade Organization is an international institution that closely conforms to the reality of democratic, multilateral, global governance. Membership is voluntary, and it operates according to the principle of 'one member, one vote'. This is in contrast to the World Bank and IMF, in which voting power is determined by the financial contributions made by each state, which guarantees that the core states and the US in particular have the greatest say in decision-making. This point also applies, albeit through the veto of its permanent members, to the UN Security Council, as we saw above. The principle of equal voting at the WTO gives the developing countries a far greater say in the running of the organization, and this is a major reason why advocates like former Director General Mike Moore (2003: 109; also Legrain 2002) describe it as 'a precious system, the jewel in the crown of multilateralism'.

The WTO (2001) operates according to five principles. These are non-discrimination, transparency, fair trade, special and differential treatment for poorer countries, and progressive trade liberalization. Transparency essentially means clear rules to guide the behaviour of states in the international trading system. Non-discrimination essentially means that any advantage guaranteed to one contracting party (such as lower tariffs) is immediately granted to all contracting parties, which then guarantees fair trade. Trade liberalization means the reduction of tariffs and removal of non-tariff barriers to trade, and it is argued that this will lead to each country developing through the exercise of its respective comparative advantage. Thus, according to the WTO (1999), 'freer trade boosts economic growth and supports development'. Some exceptions are allowed however, particularly for the poorest countries, whose special and differential treatment allows them to liberalize more slowly than other countries.

On the face of it then, the WTO does appear to operate according to democratic principles. There are transparent rules, each member state has an equal vote, and the organization operates a trading system based on non-discrimination. Indeed, special and differential treatment works in favour of the poorest developing countries. However, this section suggests that while the WTO does give some voice to the developing countries, this operates in a distinctly unequal context, and the WTO is committed to the promotion of policies that ultimately exacerbate, rather than alleviate, these global inequalities. In order to develop this argument I will briefly outline some issues that relate to the origins of the WTO, the contentious issues that have dominated discussions at the organization, and the ways in which decisions are taken in practice.

The WTO was a creation of the eighth GATT negotiations, known as the Uruguay Round. These commenced in 1986, in the context of the rise of neo-liberalism and greater pressure for trade and investment liberalization, including in the developing world. The United States was particularly concerned to extract concessions from developing countries over agriculture, services, and intellectual property (Shukla 2002). The developing countries were far from united into a single position, not least because some countries had more to gain from open access to developed countries' markets than others. This was most visible in the early to mid-1990s over bananas, with larger Latin American producers wanting freer access to some markets within the European Union. Britain and France both gave privileged access to smaller producers in the Caribbean and parts of Africa, who produced bananas more expensively than those larger plantation producers in Latin America (Myres 2004). On the whole, the more powerful developing-country producers supported reciprocal liberalization as this would guarantee greater access to developed countries' markets, even if it simultaneously opened up their home markets to developed countries' exports. Developing countries also won some promised concessions on the liberalization of trade in the clothing and textile sectors, two industries in which there had been substantial development in parts of the periphery (see Chapter 7). These promises were important in getting the majority of developing countries to join the WTO, either from its inception in 1995, or in the years that followed. Joining the WTO also held the prospect of developing countries generating a more collective voice, which would not have been possible in case-by-case bilateral agreements, even if this was compromised by the reality of competition between developing countries. But perhaps most important – and significant for the argument that follows – was the fact that developing countries essentially faced a 'Catch 22', in which they either joined the WTO in a subordinate position, or were left out and therefore failed to make the small gains that could be made by being a junior partner within the institution. Nevertheless, there were potentially important gains to be made for developing countries if they joined the WTO. However, by 1999, and especially 2001, it was clear that the promised gains were more limited, and the losses were possibly greater, than initial expectations suggested.

In the case of agriculture, an Agreement on Agriculture was made at the WTO which committed countries to the principle of trade liberalization. However, while developed countries abolished import quotas, these were replaced by 'equivalent tariffs'. These were to be reduced over time, but each country determined its own tariffs, and these were set at very high levels for many goods. Therefore, the commitment to reduction was effectively cancelled out by the initially high starting point. These tariffs reflected not just western domination over the South, but also competition between developed country agricultures, as average tariffs were not necessarily any higher for developing-country imports (although this is the case for particular products). What was – and remains – more significant was the fact that average tariff rates for agriculture were higher than those for manufactured goods, and therefore the promise of trade liberalization had not been fulfilled. This is particularly true for the poorest developing countries, which remain most dependent on the export of agricultural products, in contrast to an increasing number of developing countries who have successfully broken into some (generally lower value) manufacturing, which is discussed in detail in the next chapter. Moreover, subsidies to farmers in developed countries actually *increased* after the founding of the WTO. The overall level of subsidies for agriculture in the developed countries rose from $182 billion in 1995, to $280 billion in 1997 and $318 billion in 2002. The European Union and the US spent between $9 billion and $10 billion more on subsidies after the Agreement on Agriculture was made. According to Oxfam, in 2001, subsidies accounted for 40 per cent of the value of agricultural production in the European Union and 25 per cent in the United States (Oxfam 2002: 12). There is an important debate regarding the beneficial effects of trade liberalization in agriculture by the developed countries, which has dominated the thinking of NGOs like Oxfam, as well as the UN and the British government's Commission for Africa.[7] Even supporters of the WTO are critical of the stance of developed countries in respect of continued protection (Kitching 2001; Legrain 2002). Oxfam (2002: 100; see also Cline 2004) for instance, suggests that trade liberalization and consequent market access could raise the incomes of the poorest least developed countries by between $50 billion and $100 billion.

However, it could well be that the case for trade liberalization in the North over-estimates the benefits for the South. The Oxfam figure only represents about 0.3 to 0.6 per cent of the GDPs of the poorest countries, at least when adjusted to take account of local purchasing power.[8] Moreover, these gains could be outweighed by a rise in the price of non-subsidized food imports from the developed world (Dunkley 2004: 195; Weisbrot and Baker 2002), an issue further addressed in Chapter 9. This point is not made to deny the fact that the developed countries have failed to deliver on the promise of trade liberalization, and this has implications for understanding the reality of global governance. Nor is it made to deny that there is a case for trade liberalization in agriculture by developed countries. But equally it does show that the benefits of free trade policies are limited, an argument we first encountered in Chapter 2 and that we will return to again in due course.

In clothing and textiles, the phasing out of quantitative restrictions was introduced in 1995, with the expected result that 49 per cent of restrictions would be phased out by 2005. However, shorter-term targets were met by the practice of including items that were not previously restricted, thus giving the appearance of liberalization once restrictions were removed from this different starting point. Thus, by 2002 quantitative restrictions had been removed on only a few pre-1995 items. There has been substantial removal of restrictions since then, particularly in 2005. While this can be regarded as a small victory for the developing world, it hardly constitutes a massive shift in international power, not least because it is likely to have contradictory consequences for developing countries competing in a tight and potentially saturated world market. In this respect, while neo-liberals regard China's increasing market share in these sectors as an opportunity for other countries to diversify into new sectors to take advantage of export potential to China (and elsewhere), critics suggest that this account under-estimates the difficulties of simply re-employing labour from one sector to another (Lucas and Shiva 2005). This argument therefore replicates the wider debates around comparative advantage addressed in earlier chapters, and we return to them again, both generally and in terms of the specifics of China, in Chapters 7 and 9.

In the case of intellectual property rights, these actually restrict competition by reinforcing the monopoly power of established technological producers. Patents, for example, guarantee recovery of research and development costs, by allowing the company in question monopoly rights over new inventions. Companies can thus enforce a monopoly by exclusively producing the good, or license it to other companies in exchange for royalty payments. These lead to increased costs for the consumer, but this is justified on the grounds that the product would not have been developed in the first place if there was no guaranteed monopoly to ensure cost recovery and profitability. Before Trade Related Intellectual Property Rights (TRIPS) were introduced at the WTO, the average life-span of patents was anything from 5 to 20 years, depending on both the final product and the processes that were used in making the product. TRIPS attempts to harmonize patent laws, generally extending their duration to twenty years, and extending them to products not previously considered patentable. Most controversially, this includes new plant varieties that may be used in the development of drugs or seeds. This is particularly controversial because the developed countries monopolize expensive research and development, but there is a need for easy access to drugs and food in the developing world. However, patents raise prices by preventing copying by local producers who could make cheap, generic copies of drugs for example, which therefore restricts access to the patented goods to those who can afford the drugs. According to the World Bank, the gains in transfers to developed countries through TRIPS are substantial, amounting to between $5 billion and $7 billion for the US and high sums for other successful pharmaceutical producing nations such as Switzerland, Sweden and Germany. The net transfer out of the developing world has been estimated at $430 million for India, $434 million for South Korea, $481 million for Mexico and $1.7 billion for Brazil. The amount for the poorest developing countries is likely to be lower, which in part reflects the fact that pharmaceutical companies tend to spend most of their research and development budget on studying richer, curative diseases rather than the preventative diseases of the poorest. Having said that, the patents have caused enormous controversy, and South Africa and Brazil have both successfully challenged pharmaceutical companies, arguing that they have the right to use cheap, generic drugs in public health emergencies, which in both cases were related to HIV/AIDS. At Doha in 2001, it was conceded that governments can use public health arguments to sometimes break patent laws, an issue which is likely to remain contentious for many years. It should be noted of course that this victory for developing countries was achieved by resisting, rather than embracing, WTO principles. The case for patents also ignores the high level of public subsidies received by many pharmaceutical companies, and the fact that the initial developer of a new product is likely to build up a substantial lead over followers, due to time-lags in developing imitations, technological know how, and successful marketing of the original product. Certainly, in the nineteenth century, the free-market case was used to argue against the monopoly that patents guarantee (Chang 2002: 54–9; Chang 2003: ch. 8). Finally, the use of patent protection undermines the process of assimilating and adapting technologies to local circumstances, something that was crucial to the growth of all developing countries that followed British industrialization, from the United States right through to the East Asian newly industrializing countries (Chang 2002: 84–7).

The General Agreement on Trade and Services (GATS) is based on the extension of the principle of trade liberalization to services. Some public services, such as defence, central banking and social security, are excluded. More ambiguously, so too are services that are said to be based on the exercise of government authority. However, the agreement also states that if parts of these services are already being delivered commercially, or in competition with the private sector, than they can in principle be counted as part of the agreement. Government is still entitled to regulate but not when this leads to unnecessary barriers to trade. There is thus sufficient ambiguity in GATS regulations to suggest that other than the three services explicitly excluded, any public service may be privatized. If this is not the case, then why are health and education not explicitly excluded, as are defence and central banking? This idea of liberalizing services is closely linked to the neo-liberal idea of the efficiency of privatization, or at least the idea that state services should increasingly be run as if they were private enterprises. This in turn is often linked to the policy of promoting 'public–private partnerships' (PPPs), which essentially guarantee a profit to private shareholders, by guaranteeing that any losses made will be compensated for through taxation. Any notion that public service may motivate the action of workforces operating in the public sector is thereby discounted at the outset.

For all these reasons then, the promises of the WTO for developing countries have not been fulfilled. But in principle, these countries can redress their grievances through the dispute-settlement mechanism that regulates disputes between members, or through the operation of the principle of 'one member, one vote'. However, in practice the reality is again somewhat different from the appearance of multilateral governance. At WTO meetings a vote has never been taken, and delegates from the developing world have constantly expressed their anger at the far from transparent decision-making processes of the institution. The main accusation in terms of procedure is that decisions are taken by powerful countries behind closed doors, through secretive meetings that exclude most delegates from developing countries, a major factor in the collapse of the Seattle Round of WTO talks in late 1999. In terms of dispute settlement, the realities of international inequalities militate against developing countries having real weight. Certainly, developed countries have often lost decisions taken by settlement procedures (and many disputes have been between developed countries), but the time and cost of taking decisions through the settlement process works against developing countries that might have legitimate grievances. Moreover, even if a developing country were to successfully win a dispute against a developed country, the only response to non-compliance with WTO decisions is retaliation by the aggrieved party. For developed countries whose trade with a poorer developing country is a fraction of its total trade, the sanctions are effectively irrelevant. For a developing country that loses a case against a developed country, its heavy dependence on that particular export market is likely to be great. For these reasons, developing countries are more likely to play by the rules than are developed ones.

This point suggests a far bigger problem with the WTO than all of the points so far made, which is that the movement towards free trade is not necessarily in the interest of developing countries. This was an issue briefly addressed in Chapter 2, and is addressed again in detail in the next chapter, but some brief observations are necessary at this point. Established producers – mainly located in the developed countries – have more advanced technologies, skills, infrastructures and markets and this increases the barriers to entry for potential late developers. While special and differential treatment may still give some room for protection (Amsden 2005), this is now implemented less as a strategy to promote ISI development policies (Chapter 3), and more as giving some room for developing countries to adjust to global integration (Singh 2005). Certainly the ongoing NAMA (non-agricultural market access) negotiations at the WTO, aimed at radically cutting industrial tariffs by 2010 and eliminating them altogether by 2015, reflect the broad neo-liberal priorities of the WTO (Chang 2005). The argument then, is that, exemptions notwithstanding, the WTO undermines the kind of development strategies utilized by Third World states in the 1950s and 1960s, and by the developed countries in the late nineteenth century (Whalley 1999; Chang 2002; Toye 2003; Bello 2005: ch. 5).

This is fully discussed through a thorough examination of the global economy in the next chapter. What should be clear by now is that the WTO hardly represents the exercise of genuinely democratic global governance. It was therefore not surprising that the talks at Seattle in 1999, Doha in 2001, and Cancún in 2003 resulted in so much rancour. In particular, the Group of 22 developing countries increasingly resisted pressure from the core states for new liberalization measures in investment and competition, and increasingly argued for liberalization of developed-world agriculture (Henderson 2003). The fact that such pressure occurred at all does suggest that the WTO does not unambiguously express the interests of the dominant powers, and of the US in particular. Indeed, under Bush (and to an extent Clinton), the US became increasingly disillusioned with the dispute-settlement mechanism and increasingly adopted bilateral and regional agreements with other states. But the fact that the US does not always get its way and that policy is contested does not add up to genuinely multilateral and democratic governance. Rather, it suggests that the (market) power of some states is far greater than others, and that this is subversive of any substantive movement towards cosmopolitan democracy.

Civil Society and the State in the International System

Cosmopolitan proponents of global governance are of course not unaware of the limitations to its official institutions. However, they argue that there is further hope for optimism and that this is provided by the existence of a global civil society. Its advocates argue that global civil society represents a 'globalization from below', which challenges the 'globalization from above' associated with some international institutions, dominant states and neo-liberalism (Falk 2000). In the words of Mary Kaldor (2003: 12), global civil society 'is about civilizing or democratizing globalization, about the process through which groups, movements and individuals can demand a global rule of law, global justice and global empowerment'. As we saw above, this concept is linked to the rise of international NGOs and 'transnational social movements', whose concerns are explicitly global and not necessarily focused on particular nation-states. Precisely because these concerns are global, they also represent a movement towards an ostensibly cosmopolitan universalism. These movements thus represent the conscience of the world (Willetts 1996), pressurising nation-states and international institutions to act in more progressive, humanitarian ways, on issues such as human rights, the environment, debt, global poverty and arms reduction.

The activities of international NGOs and transnational social movements should not be dismissed as lightly as some realists and (ex-)Marxists would like. For instance, Chandler's argument that the rise of a so-called global civil society represents a retreat from politics reflects an unwarranted nostalgia for the certainties of the Cold War and a yearning for an outmoded Marxist politics based on Leninist parties capturing nation-states (Chandler 2004a). Similarly, Heartfield's (2005) dismissal of transnational advocacy by 'anti-globalization' movements as the politics of co-option rather than opposition is too black and white, and similarly yearns for a Leninist politics that is no longer relevant to the current era. But on the other hand, these criticisms are suggestive, and they point to the one-sidedness of some of the contentions made for the progressive politics of global civil society. These criticisms reflect four basic problems with the idea of global civil society: first, the question of representation and accountability; second, the question of 'spatial fetishism'; third, the relationship between global civil society and liberalism; and fourth, the question of global civil society and power.

First, there is the question of global civil society and representation. Unlike elected politicians, international NGOs and transnational social movements are not accountable to anyone. This point is often accepted by activists within these movements, but it is then championed as a source of strength. The reasoning here is that unlike career politicians, who have to answer to electorates, transnational movements are not career oriented precisely because they are not answerable in elections. On one level this is acceptable, because it is true that official politics has in many respects become increasingly marginal to electorates in liberal democracies. But it is an odd argument that regards this as inevitable and a source of strength for an alternative politics. Indeed, it could be argued that by ignoring or by-passing official politics, the alternatives represented by global civil society add to this disengagement from politics.[9]

This argument is discussed further below, but for the moment we need to examine a second point about representation. If movements within global civil society are neither self-interested nor accountable, but actually representing the interests of others, how do we know that they represent these interests? This is not simply a question of accountability but one of who speaks for whom. This is a difficult question in a world of inequality and uneven development, and it is one that global civil society theory tends to evade. Put differently, how does inequality affect global civil society, and how does global civil society affect inequality? These issues can be related to precisely those questions that are central to the concerns of transnational movements, such as human rights and the environment. As we have already seen, discourses around human rights are contested, including around 'North–South' issues. Similarly, some Northern environmentalists have been accused of advocating an ecological imperialism against the South, even as movements in the South have espoused different (and not necessarily compatible) interpretations of environmental activism. The issue of universal labour standards is similarly contested, with some trade unions and southern NGOs arguing that attempts to expand minimum labour standards through the World Trade Organization, or indeed through consumer boycotts, undermine the prospects for development in the South. Even the issue of debt relief is contested, with many Northern campaigns advocating an incremental approach, while many Southern campaigns adopt a far more radical position (Kiely 2005a: ch. 8). These points are not made to deny the possibility of universalism, or of genuine solidarity across national boundaries. Neither are they made to suggest that the basic division is between a homogenous North and a homogenous South. But they are made to suggest that, in the context of global inequalities and uneven development, simplistic appeals to global civil society – or indeed Hardt and Negri's 'multitude' – essentially evade such questions.

This evasion is partly a product of the tendency of global civil society theory (and to an extent, cosmopolitanism) to champion the universality of the global at the expense of the particularity of the national or the local. Certainly, global civil society theorists recognize that there are global 'bads' as well as 'goods', but the process of civilizing globalization tends to be advanced through the advocacy of more globalization. Politics that mainly focuses on nation-states is thus too easily dismissed as backward looking or reactionary. But this fails to capture the content or the reality of contemporary politics. First, politics focused on the nation-state may be progressive, reactionary, or even ambiguous. This is also true of global politics, which may involve the advocacy of neo-liberal free trade and 'humanitarian war' on the one hand, or labour internationalism and anti-war solidarity on the other. In focusing on politics through an implicit attempt to quantify the extent of globalization, the specific content of politics tends to be lost. Secondly, the idea that social movements or international NGOs are simply agents of global civil society is too one-sided. Most organizations advocating global issues actually focus their energies on their own nation-states. If it is transnational social movements that make up global civil society, and 'transnational' in this case means movements that organize in ways that are genuinely beyond the nation-state, then it is hard to see which movements are really transnational. In terms of organizational structures at least, most movements are actually international in that they are composed of national branches which then link with national branches in other countries. They may advocate issues of global importance, but they do not transcend nation-states (Laxer and Halperin 2003). On the other hand, the concept of global civil society too easily sets up a false dichotomy between national and global.

The third problem is not so much with the concept of the 'global', but with its account of civil society. The concept of global civil society is closely linked with the revival of the concept of civil society since the collapse of communism. Most contemporary civil society theorists argue that the existence of civil society is fundamental to the existence of human freedom, as it represents a third force against the centralization of the state and the profit motive of the free market. In one respect this is undoubtedly true, and eighteenth- and nineteenth-century theorists of civil society largely saw its emergence as a progressive development in human history. But at the same time, the most convincing theorists regarded it as both social and contradictory, and in doing so, separated themselves from liberal interpretations which regarded civil society as either natural (Kant) or rational (Smith). Summarizing an 'unorthodox' interpretation of Hegel's view in his *Philosophy of Right*, Fine (1997: 21) argues that:

> Civil society . . . is neither a *rational* nor a *natural* order waiting to be set free from external restrictions but a definite *social* order characteristic of our age in which subjective freedom, legal equality and economic wealth coexist with 'dissoluteness, misery, [and] physical and ethical corruption.'[10]

In other words, while it cannot be *reduced* to the capitalist market or sovereign state, neither is civil society autonomous in relation to these institutions. Contemporary civil society theory sets up a dichotomy between progressive civil society on the one hand and the hierarchical state on the other. Similarly, as we have seen, global civil society constructs a dichotomy between progressive global civil society and the particularist nation-state. But this is unconvincing, because civil society is itself composed of particular interests. Thus, to take one example, liberal interpretations of fascism regard it as an example of the triumph of the state over civil society, whereas it is better seen as an example of particular, powerful interests in civil society using the state apparatus to control less powerful agents within that same civil society (Marcuse 1968; Woodiwiss 2005a: ch. 1). Indeed, in championing civil society against the state, contemporary civil society theory (like mainstream globalization theory) comes perilously close to replicating the evasions of classical liberalism.

These points are crucial for understanding the weaknesses of contemporary understandings of global civil society. In advocating global civil society as the main agent of and for contemporary progressive politics, civil society theory evades the question of those forces operating in this space that cannot be regarded as cosmopolitan, and the question of power within this supposedly democratic space. In this respect, advocates of global civil society replicate either the liberal idea that civil society is composed of free and autonomous individuals, or the pluralist view of politics which suggests that essentially neutral institutions make decisions on the basis of arbitration between competing interests in society. Thus, even though the argument is sometimes qualified by reference to different forms of power, civil society organizations are assumed to have substantial influence over the decision making of international institutions such as the IMF, World Bank and WTO (Scholte 1999b; O'Brien et al. 2000). This argument betrays a commitment to a view of power based on its distribution between pre-given, and therefore naturalized, social and political actors, rather than one that sees these actors as constituted by particular social and political relations, and therefore historically specific forms of power (Lipschutz 2005; Lukes 2005a, 2005b). Put differently, we can accept that contestation and conflict do take place both within and beyond 'global civil society'. But in focusing on contestation at the expense of an analysis of power, global civil society theory too easily depoliticizes what precisely is being contested and why. In drawing on the work of Jürgen Habermas (1986), and emphasizing the importance of communication, advocates of global civil society too easily lose sight of the wider context which does not conform to Habermas's endorsement of an ideal speech situation. Indeed, if 'global civil society' actors have the degree of power that is often claimed for it by its advocates, one wonders why there is any need for resistance and contestation in the first place.

It is precisely this need that is often lost sight of by the advocates of global civil society, with the result that at its worst, global civil society is essentially regarded as a filter through which technical decisions can be reached. For example, the *Make Poverty History* campaign in 2005 could be regarded as a classic example of a global civil society campaign that acted as a global conscience, forcing Africa, debt and poverty onto the agenda of the Group of 8 (G8) summit meeting in Scotland that year. In some respects this is undoubtedly true, but for many campaigners and activists, this was at the expense of the sanitization of the politics involved in such campaigns. In particular, some felt it abhorrent that two of the leading politicians at the summit – Tony Blair and George Bush – were still prosecuting a war in Iraq. Indeed, some felt frustrated that Blair was actively courting the protest movement, and felt that this was a classic case of co-opting. Certainly, some forms of protest were actively discouraged by the leadership of the campaign, and anti-war campaigns were marginalized (Hodkinson 2005a). Moreover, while much attention was paid to debt relief, far less attention was paid to the neo-liberal conditions that were attached to debt relief, and openly supported by Blair. Moreover, the actual amounts committed to debt relief and aid were much smaller than some NGOs had demanded – for War on Want, it amounted to just 10 per cent on debt cancellation and 20 per cent on increased aid (Shabi 2005); Christian Aid regarded the summit as a 'grave disappointment'; and a spokesperson for the African Forum on Alternatives explicitly argued that 'people must not be fooled by celebrities: Africa got nothing' (cited in Hodkinson 2005b). Moreover, in linking poverty reduction to increased aid, little attention was paid to the problems associated with aid, including the small amounts (less than a quarter of 1 per cent of total global income), and the ways in which even these are exaggerated by the salaries and administrative fees of the aid dispensers, and the continuing practice of tying aid to buying products from the dispensing country – a practice where the British government has a better record than most. Thus, based on figures from the late 1990s, Sutcliffe (2001: 90) estimates that aid in the form of untied foreign exchange amounts to around one-fiftieth of 1 per cent of total global income. The hype around the good news on increased aid should be seen in this context, but it was one that hardly figured in the pronouncements of the leading figures involved in the campaign, despite some efforts by NGOs (World Development Movement 2004; Oxfam/Action Aid 2005). Moreover, given the (broadly neo-liberal) conditions attached to aid and debt forgiveness, it is highly unlikely that these will result in sustained growth or poverty reduction. Certainly the Commission for Africa's (2005b) call for dedicating greater resources to capacity building was welcome, but it also tended to ignore the ways in which the World Bank and IMF had undermined state capacity in the 1980s and 1990s (Mold 2005).

For all these *political* reasons, some critics regarded the G8 as part of the problem and not the solution, but this was lost in the effective co-opting of the global poverty agenda, in part by various celebrities but above all by a British government for whom celebrity endorsement sometimes appears to be a massive priority (Monbiot 2005; Harris 2005; Jagger 2005).[11] None of these points directly undermine some of the claims made by global civil society theorists, but there is a close parallel between the de-politicizing rhetoric of the (hijacked?) Make Poverty History campaign and some claims made for global civil society (Harris 2006; Colas 2005). In particular, by simply focusing on the existence of various civil society organizations, global civil society theory loses sight of the neo-liberal nature of globalization, and broader questions of power in the global order. Moreover, there is also the issue of the political agendas of organizations operating within global civil society. At the G8 summit in 2005, the issues of global poverty were further marginalized by the brutal atrocities of bombs in London while the G8 summit was taking place, carried out by individuals apparently loosely linked to networks that also operate within the space of global civil society, but who embrace political agendas and methods that are reactionary and completely repellent. These issues also relate closely back to questions of state power and the international state system. What is clear is that demands are placed on nation-states, and that therefore it is difficult to construct a progressive space of 'global civil society' which seeks to by-pass the state system. Too often, advocates of global civil society do precisely this, and in the process come close to embracing a neo-liberal position on the nation-state.

Conclusion

This chapter has challenged some of the more optimistic claims that the international order has made considerable progress towards achieving democratic global governance exercising broadly cosmopolitan principles. It has also by implication suggested that this point has been reinforced by the actions of the more unilateralist Bush administration after 2001, but also that any progress made in the 1990s was very limited. International organizations – both governmental and non-governmental – are not independent of the wider context of capitalist social relations, neo-liberal policies, and unequal state power. This is not to say that such organizations can be *reduced* to capitalist or state power, but it is to say that the conflict over ideas, values and principles cannot be abstracted from this wider social context. In terms of politics then, this chapter has suggested that the mainstream theories of globalization that were discussed and rejected in the previous chapter are wedded to the endorsement of a cosmopolitanism that is too naive about the realities of actually existing global governance. On the other hand, the classical theory of imperialism that was also discussed and rejected in the previous chapter is similarly tied to a weak political approach, that of a one-sided and crude anti-imperialism. This tends towards a functionalist or instrumentalist account of global governance, which does not ignore power relations so much as reify them so that any alternatives seem unconvincing. Insofar as alternatives are suggested, they tend towards a defence of state sovereignty and a romantic vision of anti-imperialist forces, which are deemed to be progressive simply because they are the enemy of the United States and its allies.

The defence of a critical cosmopolitanism in this chapter thus endorses some commitment to social and political movements operating in, for want of a better term, 'global civil society'. However, this is not meant as a replacement for politics, which continue to focus on the nation-state, and neither is it meant to imply that all movements operating in the 'space' of global civil society are progressive. The content as well as the form of politics remains crucial, and cosmopolitanism does have a tendency towards the spatial fetishism which characterizes mainstream globalization theory. In this way, global politics are assumed to be progressive in isolation from the particular forms and programmes that such politics take, and this lies at the heart of an overly naive account of the prospects for global governance. Perhaps above all, cosmopolitan perspectives are too easily guilty of ignoring the uneven development of international capitalism, and therefore the unequal context in which rights, values, ethics and international institutions operate. This is not an argument that rejects universalism, but it is one that suggests that a genuine universalism must not wish away these unequal contexts. And here of course is where the issue of development is so central, because some claims to universalism ignore the specific situations faced by developing countries. Some claims to universalism are simply hypocritical, as the construction of the Security Council and the actual practices of the major powers at the WTO make clear. But even when there are more desirable universal principles, such as those relating to human rights, or 'one member, one vote' at the WTO, these are seriously compromised by the unequal institutional power and uneven contexts in which they operate. Thus, so-called humanitarian intervention is selective, full of double standards, and too easily ignores the complex realities of state formation and capital accumulation in developing countries (we return to the last point in depth in Chapter 8). Similarly, the dispute-settlement mechanisms that exist at the WTO ignore the very different degrees of institutional power enjoyed by different states, so that US defeats mean far less to that state then defeats for a particular developing country. Even the concept of global civil society tends to downplay inequalities in favour of a 'flattened out' politics of resistance which is too easily assumed to operate in similar ways across the world. But questions of environmental regulation, or labour standards, for instance, have very different implications for countries at different levels of development. This is not an argument against these ideas, but one of scepticism towards an overly simplistic liberal universalism (see also Chapter 10).

Rather than questions of inequality and different social and political contexts becoming less important in the age of globalization, I am suggesting that in some respects they have become more important in this age of neo-liberalism. I will suggest why this may be the case in the next chapter, which considers the relationships between neo-liberalism, poverty and inequality, and the global economy.

Chapter 7

Globalization, Poverty and the Contemporary World Economy

This chapter critically examines in more depth the neo-liberal interpretation of, and case for, globalization. It does so by initially focusing on one contemporary debate, that of the link between market friendly or pro-globalization policies, economic growth and poverty reduction. It particularly examines the question of whether poverty has been reduced in recent years, and if so, whether this is a result of neo-liberal policies. It then moves on to examine the relationship between market friendly and poverty-reduction policies and economic performance in developing countries. This discussion questions the claims made for poverty reduction by development agencies such as the World Bank, the Department for International Development, and the US Agency for International Development, and the final section suggests why their claims are mistaken. In this section, I consider in detail the nature of the contemporary global economy, and in examining the evidence concerning capital flows show how, contrary to the claims made by neo-liberals and some globalization theorists, capital is not dispersing throughout the world. Moreover, even when the 'correct policies' are adopted, this is unlikely to happen. I then conclude by suggesting why 'actually existing globalization' does not alleviate, and may indeed intensify, global inequalities, returning to some of the common themes addressed in earlier chapters.

Poverty Reduction?

There have been a number of upbeat assessments which claim that global poverty has declined in recent years, and that the reason for this decline is the adoption of market friendly policies by an increasing number of nation-states. In other words, the adjustment policies that performed so poorly in the 1980s (see Chapter 4), have at last had the desired results. These claims rest on three arguments: first, that poverty (and perhaps inequality) has been reduced; secondly that this is due to market friendly policies; and thirdly, that these favourable outcomes show that the world economy presents opportunities for developing countries, which can be embraced through these correct policies.

Each of these issues will be addressed in detail in this chapter. This section focuses on the first of these contentions. The World Bank has argued that poverty and income inequality have fallen in the last twenty years. In 1980, there were 1.4 billion people living in absolute poverty, and by 1998 this had fallen to 1.2 billion (World Bank 2002b: 30). Bank researchers have since revised this figure, and suggested that the number of people living in absolute poverty has fallen by as much as 400 million (Chen and Ravallion 2004). Elsewhere, it is suggested that the proportion of the world's population living in absolute poverty has fallen from 28 per cent to 24 per cent of the world's population (World Bank 2002). Some researchers, often former Bank employees, are even more upbeat. Bhalla (2002; also Lal 2004: 122–6) suggests that the proportion of people living in absolute poverty has fallen from 46 per cent in 1980 to 29 per cent in 1990 and 18 per cent in 2000, and the latter figure may even be as low as 13 per cent. This amounts to a fall in total numbers (based on the 18 per cent estimate) from 1.58 billion in 1980, to 1.2 billion in 1990, and 899 million in 2000. Sala-i-Martin (2002a and 2000b) reaches broadly similar conclusions. If these assessments are correct, then the most prominent Millennium Development Goal – to reduce the proportion of the world's population living in absolute poverty by 50 per cent[1] – is close to being, or has actually been, fulfilled. Two questions arise from these figures, namely: Are they accurate, and on what basis are they calculated?[2] Absolute or extreme poverty is defined as those people living on an income of less than (approximately) $1 a day. This figure does not refer to a US dollar as such, but is instead based on purchasing power parity (PPP) exchange rates. PPP is based on adjustments that attempt to take account of the fact that the cost of living tends to be lower in poorer countries than in richer ones. As a starting point, the Bank's chosen benchmark figure was US $1 a day in 1985, which was then changed to $32.74 per person a month in the US in 1993. From these two starting points, the Bank then calculates equivalent amounts in currencies of other countries on the basis of purchasing power parity. The Bank then moves from a country's base year and estimates equivalents for other years based on a country's Consumer Price Index (CPI). Through these methods, a national currency poverty line for a country and for a particular year is developed, and the proportion of households living below the poverty line is measured.

This method is the basis for the upbeat arguments cited above, which all suggest that the number of people living below an international poverty line (IPL) of approximately $1 a day has been reduced.[3] But there are problems with this method of calculation, not only because the figures are in some respects arbitrary and not necessarily accurate, but also because they are biased towards presenting an optimistic assessment of the extent of poverty reduction. Sanjay Reddy and Thomas Pogge (2003; also Pogge 2004) have presented a particularly powerful critique of the optimistic scenario, and the following critical account draws heavily on their work.

The first point they make is that the initial benchmark figure – $1 a day in the US – chosen by the Bank is too low. According to the US Department of Agriculture, the lowest cost of home cooking that could meet adequate calorie (and some nutrient) requirements was $5134 for a family of four in 1999. However, the Bank's international poverty line stood at $1812 in 1999 (based on the 1985 figure updated through CPI changes) and $2057 in 2004 (based on the 1993 figure). Thus, the source of the IPL under-estimates total food requirements for the poor in the US, let alone for the rest of the world.

The second point relates to the process by which the Bank measures purchasing power parities. Rather than simply focus on market exchange rates, PPPs attempt to reflect the fact that there are significant price variations in different localities. Price ratios across rich and poor countries tend to be broadly similar for tradeable goods, and quite dissimilar for non-tradeables. The World Bank averages out these price ratios in order to get a more accurate picture of consumption in particular places. As a measure of the consumption of the wealthy in poor countries, this is a reasonable approximation. However, it is not an accurate measure of what the poor consume in a poor country. If we assume a PPP differential of, say, 10, then the Bank will assume that the annual income of a household in a poor country will be 10 times that of a poor household in the US, measured through PPP exchange rates. This differential will lead to similar levels of consumption by both poor households. But the problem is that this average is not calculated by comparing the consumption patterns of the poor in the two countries. Instead, consumption patterns are *averaged* out. This is not a good measure of the consumption of the poor, because the averaging out is based on the consumption patterns of everyone in the poor country, and not just the poor. A likely scenario then is that the PPP differential of 10 is unlikely to generate a figure for buying power that is comparable to that of the poor in the US, but this is 'compensated' (in the PPP calculation) by the fact that the differential of 10 will buy more services in the poor country than in the rich one. This is because services are cheaper in the poor country. But the problem is that services are unlikely to be consumed by the poor. In other words, PPP is not a good measure of poverty because it does not actually measure what the poor are consuming, but instead measures what everybody consumes in a poor country. Based on a sample of 56 countries for the benchmark year of 1985 and 78 countries for 1993, Reddy and Pogge suggest that the prices of all foods and of bread and cereals were higher than general consumption purchasing power parity. For low-income countries (15 of the total in both samples), the price of food was 67 per cent (40 per cent, population weighted) higher, and bread and cereals 111 per cent (34 per cent, population weighted) higher, based on the 1985 benchmark year, and 27 per cent (31 per cent) and 51 per cent (40 per cent) higher for the 1993 benchmark (Reddy and Pogge 2003: 27, 46–7).

This problem of inappropriate measurements is further exacerbated by the fact that these are biased towards showing a downward trend over time. This is because the purchase of food constitutes a falling share in international consumption spending, while services constitute a rising share. In other words, as average incomes rise, so the proportion spent on food declines. In terms of PPP, the result is that the price of food has a diminishing influence on the calculation of PPPs, while services have an increasing influence. The assumption made is that the income of everyone in a country rises equally, which is highly unlikely, since wealthier households are likely to enjoy greater increases in consumption than poorer ones. Moreover, as we have seen, the poor are far less likely to consume services, but the contribution of services to PPP measures will be enhanced as general consumption increases. PPP calculations therefore not only assume a one-to-one increase in consumption for all households, but they also show a bias towards measuring the consumption patterns of households that are not poor.

The even more optimistic accounts of Bhalla (2002) and Sala-i-Martin (2002a and 2002b) replicate and exacerbate these errors. The Bank relies on household surveys in order to calculate poverty, whereas Bhalla and Sala-i-Martin rely on a hybrid mix of household surveys and national income accounts. The latter are the main basis on which they make their calculations, while household surveys are used only to estimate the proportional distribution of each national income total. The problem is that national accounts data usually support higher estimates of aggregate private consumption, which includes the value of housing consumed by owner-occupiers, consumption derived from credit cards and mortgages, and even government spending on military and infrastructural projects that are unlikely to have any impact on the lives of the poor, but which are counted as consumption by the poor.[4] Moreover, both Bhalla and Sala-i-Martin adjust the findings of household surveys to match national accounts data and therefore assume that the poor under-report their consumption as much as richer people in their country. For all these reasons, their wild optimism concerning poverty reduction reflects their fallacious starting point, which is that the poor are not really poor at all (Milanovic 2002). The Bank is not as guilty in this respect, but their methodology still betrays similar fallacious assumptions.

These points become even clearer when we examine the impact of the shift from two different base years. The switch in 2000 from the 1985 to the 1993 base year was particularly significant in generating more optimistic accounts of poverty reduction. Thus, using the 1985 base year, poverty rates in 1993 in sub-Saharan Africa stood at 39 per cent, while for Latin America they were 23 per cent. With the switch to the 1993 base year in 2000, poverty in 1993 in sub-Saharan Africa was calculated as being 49 per cent, while in Latin America, it was 15 per cent. Thus, poverty rates increased from 39 to 49 per cent and decreased from 23 per cent to 15 per cent, as measured for the same year. It was thus not good or bad policies that led to 'poverty reduction', but simply *a change in the way that extreme poverty was calculated*. The World Bank's *World Development Report* on 1999/2000 was thus far more pessimistic than the optimistic assertions cited above, as it used the 1985 base year calculations to argue that absolute poverty had increased from 1.2 billion in 1987 to 1.5 billion in 1999 (World Bank 1999b: 25). The shift from the 1985 count to the 1993 count had the effect of lowering the poverty line in 77 out of 92 countries for which data were available, and these countries contained 82 per cent of the total population of the 92 countries (Reddy and Pogge 2003: 42).

Finally, even if we ignore the problems of counting the poor, and instead accept the Bank's figures, there remains the question of the arbitrary $1.08 headcount. This is all the more problematic given that the 1985 and 1993 base years under-estimate the income needed to purchase food in the US (see above). Thus, even if we accept the Bank's own data, with all its problems, and lift the poverty count to those living on less than $2 a day, then the Bank's own figures suggest that the numbers and proportion of people in this category increased from 1981 to 2001, from 2.45 to 2.74 billion, a 12 per cent increase.[5] Indeed, given that the US Department of Agriculture argues that the 'one dollar a day' starting point is inadequate (see above), then there are strong grounds for using the $2 benchmark. Moreover, on the one-dollar count, poverty numbers have risen by about one-third in Latin America, and one-half in sub-Saharan Africa (Sumner 2004a: 1169), even as most countries have liberalized their economies.

The question of whether world inequality has declined is even more complex. Income distribution can be measured in a variety of ways, as Wade (2004a) points out. Relevant variables include: (i) the use of market or PPP exchange rates; (ii) distribution between countries and within countries; (iii) distribution weighted by population; (iv) distribution measured as an average across the distribution (such as the Gini coefficient), or the ratio of the top to the bottom (say, 20 or 10 per cent). The neo-liberal case is based on measuring PPP incomes, average GDP, population weighting, and average distribution, and the conclusion is that world income inequality fell in the years 1980–2000 (Wade and Wolf 2002). But there are problems with this contention. If China and India are taken out of the equation then the picture is negative. Whether or not they should be taken out is an issue discussed throughout this chapter; but even leaving this debate aside for the moment, there are further problems. First, it leaves out the question of income distribution *within* countries. Secondly, the proportion of the richest to the poorest people is undoubtedly increasing, so inequality as measured by *polarization* is undoubtedly increasing. Thirdly, neo-liberals only focus on relative inequality between countries, while absolute inequality is still increasing. Thus, a growth rate of 10 per cent a year in a country where per capita income is only $500 a year means a closing of the relative gap between that country and a country that has an annual growth rate of 2 per cent a year with a per capita income of $10,000 a year. But the absolute gap continues to rise, as 2 per cent of 10,000 is higher than 10 per cent of 500. The neo-liberal objection to this argument is that this increase in absolute inequality is bound to occur, and can only change over a long period of time (Wade and Wolf 2002). The related argument is then made that growth itself is bound to be uneven and unequal, and that to regret that is to regret growth itself and endorse a situation in which everyone is equally poor (Wade and Wolf 2002).

However, this argument is spurious for two reasons. First, it simply accepts the status quo and ignores the fact both that redistribution can have positive effects on the consumption of the poor (whose extra dollar is far more significant to him or her than the lost dollar of the rich person), and that it is not necessarily incompatible with growth. Secondly, it ignores the fact that the exercise of market friendly policies is supposed to lead to the alleviation of both relative and *absolute* inequality as each country exercises its comparative advantage in the world economy, thus promoting some tendencies towards convergence.

The final problem with the wider neo-liberal case for reduced inequality relates to the issue of PPP versus market exchange rates. As we have seen, PPP rates are important because they attempt to account for local variations in purchasing power. But we can turn the neo-liberal case for globalization on its head and actually make a (limited) case for using market exchange rates, and if these are used, then even neo-liberals accept that inequalities are increasing in the world economy. Market exchange rates are unreliable measures, as currency fluctuations can lead to wild discrepancies in the measurement of global poverty and inequality. This is precisely why PPP rates are generally accepted. But on the other hand, these wild fluctuations – and market exchange rates themselves – are not without significance, not least because *international purchasing power is a reflection of the increased global integration that neo-liberals are otherwise so keen to embrace.* Thus, as Wade (2004b: 166–7) argues, international purchasing power is important 'because this is more relevant than PPP for measuring relative impacts of one part of the world on others, including the ability of one set of people . . . to import, to borrow, to repay loans, and also to participate in international rule-making fora. . . . Creditors have not been lining up to accept debt repayment in PPP-adjusted dollars.'

There are clearly a whole set of problems with the claim that global poverty and inequality has been reduced in recent years. Having said that, over the last twenty years, there *may* have been a decline in absolute poverty. If poverty reduction has occurred, then the reason for the downward trend in the last twenty years is the economic growth and poverty reduction in China and India. If these are excluded, then all the evidence points to an upward trend. But of course on the face of it, there is no good reason to exclude them, especially as these two countries make up a very high proportion of the world's population (Wolf, in Wade and Wolf 2002). On the other hand, if these two countries are the main reasons why poverty has been reduced in recent years, then we need to examine the policies adopted in these two countries, and compare them with policies adopted in other countries (a comparison which does suggest that we should abstract from population-weighted figures and treat each state as one unit). This is the subject of the next section.

Market Friendly Policies, Growth and Poverty Reduction

The second argument made is that the reduction in poverty and inequality has been caused by the best policies for promoting economic growth. These policies are essentially similar to the structural adjustment policies promoted in the 1980s, which are said to be effective because they are 'globalization friendly' and open to market forces. Globalization is thus defined as a progressive force, as is the case for some mainstream accounts of globalization discussed in Chapter 5. However, in the case of the World Bank and neo-liberalism more generally, it is used in the much narrower sense of increased openness and closer integration into the world economy, above all through policies of trade, investment and financial liberalization.

Alongside the work of prominent Bank economists such as David Dollar and Aart Kraay, the 2002 World Bank report *Globalization, Growth and Poverty: Building an Inclusive World Economy* (2002a; also Dollar and Kraay 2002) attempts to establish a causal relationship between structural adjustment and globalization friendly policies, which are said to promote both economic growth and poverty reduction. Although at times the report does make frequent qualifications, which appear to accept that the case for a causal relationship between trade liberalization on the one hand, and growth and poverty reduction on the other, is not proven, the general conclusions and recommendations certainly *do* make this case.

Based on a study of 92 countries over four decades, the report differentiates more and less globalized countries. This is measured by examining trade tariffs from 1985 to 1997 and trade volumes (based on trade/GDP ratios) from 1975 to 1997. The top third of countries are designated as 'more globalized', and the bottom two-thirds as less globalized. The key argument is that the more globalized countries had higher rates of growth then the less globalized, with the former having annual average growth rates of 5 per cent, and the latter, rates of growth of just 1.4 per cent per year. The report therefore reaches the conclusion that growth is good for the poor, and that market friendly, pro-globalization policies are good for growth.

This is similar to the argument of at least one of the mainstream theorists of globalization discussed in Chapter 5. In an argument that combines neo-liberalism and modernization theory, Anthony Giddens (2000: 129) argues that the main problems of the developing world 'don't come from the global economy itself, or from the self-seeking behaviour on the part of the richer nations. They lie mainly in the societies themselves – in authoritarian government, corruption, conflict, over-regulation and the low level of emancipation of women.' It is an argument also repeated by the much trumpeted report of the United Nations Economic Commission for Africa (2004: xi–xii):

> The trade policies of rich countries are clearly only part of the problem. This report takes an introspective look at what reforms Africa needs to undertake in order to benefit from existing and future opportunities in the global trading system. The report underscores that African countries need to make trade liberalization work for them within the context of broad development strategies. . . . Trade liberalization is most likely to bring benefits when accompanied by good macroeconomic policies, institutional reforms and good infrastructure facilities. . . . The continent must urgently improve its supply-side capacities. Only then will exporters be able to compete in global

markets. . . . Successful integration into the world economy will require better-educated and healthier workforces, improved economic and political governance, and better-quality infrastructure.

This quotation shows that the Economic Commission for Africa is clearly concerned with institutional change, something that has also dominated World Bank thinking from the 1990s onwards. But it is also clear that this institutional change is a means to an end, which is closer integration into the world market. It does not represent a shift from the neo-liberal argument that trade and investment liberalization are good for growth and poverty reduction.

These arguments suffer from a number of weaknesses, best illustrated by initially focusing on the contentions of the World Bank and the *Globalization, Growth and Poverty* report. This report suffers from two problems. First, there is the question of how openness is measured, which essentially relies on trade/GDP ratios. Secondly, there is the question of focusing on changes in, rather than amounts of, openness. Trade/GDP ratios measure the volume of trade in a particular economy, but they do not measure trade *policy*. It is quite possible to have high trade/GDP ratios and yet still have relatively closed trade policies. Indeed, this was the point made in the discussion of the rise of East Asia in Chapter 3, which challenged the idea that import substitution and export promotion were mutually exclusive policies. It is therefore not clear how trade/GDP ratios are linked to policies of trade or investment liberalization. Moreover, while there may be countries that experience high rates of economic growth and have high trade/GDP ratios, this correlation does not establish a causal link between the two. For instance, larger countries with huge domestic markets and lots of resources (such as the US) are more likely to have lower trade/GDP ratios than other countries. More relevant to the neo-liberal case is the fact that some of the poorest countries in the world actually have high trade/GDP ratios. Thus, in 1997–8, the trade/GDP ratio for 39 of the poorest, least developed countries averaged 43 per cent, around the same as the world average, but their share of world exports from 1980 to 1999 declined by 47 per cent (UNCTAD 2002a: 103, 112). In the period from 1999 to 2001, the trade/GDP ratios of the least developed countries averaged 51 per cent, which was actually higher than that in the most developed countries (UNCTAD 2002a: 3). If we turn to trade policy, over this same period, least developed countries actually went further than other developing countries in dismantling trade barriers (UNCTAD 2002a: 114), a point I return to below. To an extent, poor growth records may reflect internal factors such as political instability and even civil conflict, but the extent of its generalization across countries suggests that liberalization does not necessarily translate into higher levels of economic growth.

Indeed, if nation-states are weighted on a one-to-one basis, and India and China only count as two countries rather than counting more, according to their higher population, then the growth rate differentials between high and low globalizers is statistically very small (1.5 per cent a year for the former, 1.4 per cent for the latter) (Sumner 2004a: 1174). Of course this again begs the question of whether India and China should be counted in this way, but as was suggested at the end of the last section, the case can be made that given that liberalization is a policy adopted by each individual state, then there should be no population weighting across nation-states. Indeed, as Milanovic (2003: 674) points out:

> Since the catch-up is defined in terms of mean *population*-weighted income of the globalizers, and since China is among these, and since China has had such a remarkable growth record over the last two decades, the authors [Dollar, Kraay and fellow Bank economist Paul Collier – R.K.] should not have even bothered to include other countries. All that is needed to obtain the desired conclusions is that China's growth accelerates.

In fact this argument can be expanded further, and it relates to the second problem with the high globalizer/low globalizer distinction. Even if we leave aside the problem of using trade/GDP ratios as a measure of trade openness, there is a further difficulty, which is that measuring *changes* in the trade/GDP ratio is an even less useful way of measuring trade openness. The most globalized countries tend to be those that initially had a low trade/GDP ratio in 1977, but whose ratios have increased since that time. This measurement therefore excludes countries with high but not rising trade/GDP ratios from the category of more globalized countries, particularly those very poor countries dependent on the export of a few primary commodities, and which have had very low and sometimes negative rates of growth (UNCTAD 2002a: pt 2, ch. 3). The effect of excluding such poor, low-growth countries with high but constant trade/GDP ratios from the 'more globalized' category is to under-estimate the category of constantly high globalizers with low economic growth.

An exaggeration of the relationship between high growth and growing openness also occurs when one critically examines the evidence for China and India, which both make the list of more globalized countries, even though their trade and investment policies remain less open than some of the low-globalizing countries. This is justified by the assertion that 'as they reformed and integrated with the world market, the "more globalized" developing countries started to grow rapidly, accelerating steadily from 2.9 per cent in the 1970s to 5 per cent through the 1990' (World Bank 2002a: 30). But this claim does not conform to the reality of growth in China or India, where the rapid economic expansion of these two countries pre-dated their growing openness; indeed in India, there was little change in growth rates once liberalization measures were implemented in the 1990s (Rodrik 2001: 24; Rodrik and Subramanian 2001). Moreover, despite liberalization, such as the lifting of some restrictions on foreign capital investment, they remain far from open economies. As in the first-tier East Asian NICs, capital controls remain strong, subsidies still exist and there are still relatively high tariffs on selected imports. Average tariff rates in India did decline from 80 per cent at the start of the 1990s to 40 per cent at the end of the decade, while China's declined from 42.4 per cent to 31.2 per cent in the same period, but the latter figures remain higher than the average for developing countries (Rodrik 2000: table 1). Milanovic is not alone in noting the irony that the Bank has used China – a communist country where around one-third of output is produced by state-owned enterprises – as supposed confirmation of the validity of neo-liberal policies (Milanovic 2003: 674–5; Nolan 2004).

For these reasons and others – China is discussed in more detail in Chapter 9 – the idea that growth has been caused by neo-liberal policies should be treated with suspicion, and it is clear that attempts to draw general conclusions from the policies of China and India are misguided. Indeed, when we do attempt to generalize, it is clear that the Bank's own data suggest that if we measure openness not by trade/GDP ratios or changes in these ratios since 1975, but instead by focusing on trade and investment policies in 1997, allegedly high globalizers had higher average tariffs (35 per cent) than low globalizers (20 per cent) (Sumner 2004a: 1174). The IMF index of trade restrictiveness measures trade policy through quantifying average tariff rates and non-tariff barriers, and there is no evidence of greater trade restrictiveness on the part of the poorest countries. Based on an analysis of 46 of the poorest, least developed countries (LDCs), United Nations Conference on Trade and Development found that in 2002, average tariff rates were less than 25 per cent for 42 of these countries, less than 20 per cent for 36 of them, and less than 15 per cent for 23 of them. In 29 of the 46 countries, non-tariff barriers were absent or minor, and in 28 of the 46 countries, there were no significant non-tariff barriers and average tariff rates of less than 25 per cent (UNCTAD 2004a: 16–17). UNCTAD thus concludes that 'most of the LDCs now have more open trade regimes than other developing countries and as open trade regimes as high income OECD countries' (UNCTAD 2004a: 17). This point confirms the argument first made in Chapter 2 of this book, namely that global integration and liberalized trade in themselves do not lead to predictable developmental outcomes, be they benign or malign (Rodriguez and Rodrik 1999).

Finally, the relationship between global integration and poverty reduction is also far from straightforward. The Bank argues that trade liberalization will reduce poverty, as it will increase demand for unskilled labour, and increase growth and therefore government revenue. But, based on an UNCTAD study of 49 LDCs the evidence is ambiguous. It suggests that poverty has actually increased among the LDCs with the most open trade regimes, but at the same time, it has also increased by about the same amount for those with the most closed trade regimes (UNCTAD 2002a: 115–17, esp. chart 33). Between these two extremes are the moderate liberalizers and the more advanced liberalizers, and here the evidence suggests that it is the former that have a better record. No straightforward conclusions can be drawn, beyond the negative ones that trade liberalization neither unambiguously causes an increase or brings about a decline in poverty. In the UNCTAD study, the incidence of poverty fell in 16 LDCs from 1987 to 1999, and only 4 of these saw a decline in their export/GDP ratio. On the other hand, among LDCs in which export orientation increased, there was no general experience of a reduction in poverty – this occurred in 10 out of the 22 countries from 1987 to 1999 (UNCTAD 2002a: 119). In other words, the effects of trade liberalization must be contextualized, and will depend on a whole range of factors. For example, in employment, relevant factors will include job losses in sectors that lose out from trade liberalization, against employment creation in more competitive sectors (Jenkins 2004; 2005). What is clear, however, is that even where there are positive gains in terms of employment and poverty reduction, these tend to be small and are associated with high rates of labour flexibility, long work hours and poor working conditions. These practices could be (somewhat brutally) regarded as instances of competitive advantage that characterize countries at low stages of development, to be shed once development and upgrading occur. In contrast, it will be argued below that there are good reasons to assume that these practices are likely to continue for a very long time to come.

This discussion suggests that on its own, trade liberalization is not necessarily good for growth or poverty reduction. In fairness to neo-liberals, they do argue that market friendly policies need to be accompanied by institutional reforms, as the quotation from the Economic Commission for Africa (above) makes clear. The suggested institutional reforms are considered in the next chapter, but it needs to be stressed here that these reforms are essentially means to an end, and that the reforms are promoted in order to ensure that market forces lead the process of economic growth. The assumption is therefore maintained that market friendly polices are part of the solution to the problems of economic growth and poverty reduction. This in part is because the global economy is something that must be embraced by developing countries, and in this respect, 'globalization' represents an opportunity rather than a constraint. As we have seen, this is the basis for the argument that developing countries suffer from lack of development because of bad policies and because they are insufficiently globalized. But my discussion so far implicitly points in another direction. As a recent UNCTAD (2004a: 35) report concludes:

> The policy problem for the LDCs is not the level of integration with the world economy but rather the form of integration. The current form of integration is not supporting sustained economic growth and poverty reduction.

We therefore need to better understand the current *form* of global integration, and examine possible reasons why this is not conducive to sustained economic growth and poverty reduction. This is the task of the next section.

Neo-liberalism and the Myth of Global Convergence

The arguments that favour liberalization as a means of promoting economic growth and poverty reduction rest on particular assumptions about the world economy. These are similar to those addressed in earlier chapters, such as the nineteenth-century theory of comparative advantage (Chapter 2) and the twentieth-century theory of modernization (Chapter 3). Neo-liberalism rejects the rigid theory of stages outlined by modernization theory, but does accept that growing contact with both 'the West' and the international economy is necessary in order to promote convergence with the advanced economies. For neo-liberals, this will occur through specialization in the production of goods and services in which countries are most efficient – in other words, through the exercise of comparative advantage. However, such efficiency can only be discovered through a process of open competition in which inefficient sectors are out-competed by imports from more effective sectors, and so specialization on producing in efficient sectors will take place as labour moves from uncompetitive to competitive sectors. For this process to occur, policies that promote competition and encourage investment must be carried out – and these are the policies of trade, investment and financial liberalization discussed above.

Earlier chapters also addressed some of the problems of orthodox theories. The most extreme criticism was associated with underdevelopment and dependency theories, which suggested that the world was divided into core and periphery, and that the latter developed by exploiting the former. But this argument suffered from a number of weaknesses, such as the fact that in the nineteenth century most investment and trade took place between the core countries (Chapter 2), and in the second half of the twentieth century some newly industrializing countries developed, in part, through exporting to the developed countries (Chapter 3).

A further criticism of neo-liberalism was that the world economy was structured in such a way as to favour some core regions or countries, and that the form of specialization reinforced this process. In particular, there was the colonial legacy in which poorer countries specialized in producing a few primary products that were exported to the developed countries (Chapter 2). For writers in this structuralist tradition, the solution was a set of policies to promote dynamic economies in the Third World through import-substitution industrialization (Chapter 3). The colonial international division of labour promoted and sustained inequality because primary products suffered from limited demand in the international economy, and had few dynamic spin-offs within the domestic economy. On the other hand, industrialization was associated with high rates of productivity, dynamic linkages to the rest of the domestic economy, and growing demand in the international economy.

How useful, then, are these three approaches to understanding the contemporary international economy? So far in this chapter, I have suggested that global poverty and inequality are not falling as fast as some neo-liberals claim, and that if there has been a fall in poverty, then it is *despite*, and not because of, neo-liberal policies. This undermines the neo-liberal case. On the other hand, those countries that have probably seen a decline in poverty have not done so by delinking from the international economy, but instead have (selectively) embraced it. This undermines the dependency case. What then of the third, structuralist tradition? This section will present an account of the current international economy, and in doing so will implicitly and sometimes explicitly relate this account to the structuralist approach. Briefly, I will suggest that the international division of labour has significantly changed, and in this respect structuralism does not adequately explain these changes. On the other hand, I will also suggest that hierarchies in the international economy persist (and in doing so, challenge neo-liberalism), and that the interests of more powerful states and economies are maintained in this international order. In particular, I will return to a fourth theory, which was briefly introduced in Chapter 2, which suggests that the international economy is based on uneven development and the increased concentration of capital, which enhances accumulation in some regions, and undermines it elsewhere. Indeed, I will also suggest that neo-liberalism and 'actually existing globalization' actually reinforce and intensify these processes. In some respects then, we are witnessing an era of free trade imperialism that has some continuity with a brief period in the mid-nineteenth century (see Chapter 2). This argument will be outlined by examining four issues: (i) the current international division of labour; (ii) the role of transnational companies in the international economy; (iii) commodity chains and capital flows in the world economy; (iv) the role of the state in 'development'.

(i)   The international division of labour

The structuralist argument suggests that global inequalities are reinforced by the patterns of specialization that exist in the international economy. The argument that those specializing in primary goods are less likely to develop remains important. Based on 1985 PPP dollars and weighted for population, the average income gap between the 20 richest countries and 31 least developed countries has increased from 11:1 in 1960 to 19:1 in 1999. The income gap for those LDCs that diversified into manufacturing and services increased from 8:1 to 12:1, but for those countries still most dependent on (non-oil) primary commodities, the increase was from 16:1 to 35:1 (UNCTAD 2002a: 122).

On the other hand, the international division of labour of the nineteenth century has changed enormously. In 1970, 18.5 per cent of the total exports from the developing world were manufactured goods; by 1994, 66.1 per cent of the developing world's exports were manufactured goods. All regions within the developing world have seen an increase in the proportion of their exports that are manufactured: Africa, from 7 per cent in 1970 to 17.8 per cent in 1994; Latin America, from 10.6 per cent in 1970 to 48.7 per cent in 1994; and Asia, from 22.4 per cent in 1970 to 73.4 per cent in 1994 (Baker et al. 1998: 7). Indeed, the share of manufacturing in both GDP and employment is now larger in developing countries than it is in developed countries (Arrighi et al. 2003).

This is clearly a different international division of labour from that in the colonial era. The rise of manufacturing reflects the ISI strategies adopted in the developing world after 1945, but it also represents the increased role of transnational companies (TNCs) in manufacturing investment, including in the developing world. This investment was sometimes associated with ISI strategies, and the desire to gain access to protected markets, and sometimes it was associated with the partial relocation of manufacturing activity to the developing world. The role of TNCs therefore needs to be further addressed.

(ii)   Transnational companies

TNCs are companies that invest in more than one country in the international economy. It is estimated that there are around 61,000 TNCs with over 900,000 foreign affiliates, accounting for around 10 per cent of world output and around one-third of world trade (UNCTAD 2004: 8–9). In contrast, in 1970, there were just 7, 000 TNCs (Robinson 2004: 55). However, despite these large amounts there is considerable concentration of power, and in 2002 the world's top 100 companies accounted for 14 per cent of the sales, 12 per cent of the assets, and 13 per cent of the employment of foreign affiliates worldwide (UNCTAD 2004c: 9). There was a large increase in foreign direct investment (FDI), in the 1990s, from $59 billion in 1982 to $1.2 trillion in 2000, and in annual average rates of growth of FDI from the mid-1980s – 23.6 per cent (1986–90), 20 per cent (1991–5), and 40.1 per cent (1996–2000) (UNCTAD 2002b: 4).

This increase in FDI encouraged a new period of optimism concerning the potential for development in the Third World. The disappointments of structural adjustment in the 1980s were quickly forgotten and the argument was made that provided the right policies were adopted, developing countries could draw on foreign investment and savings in order to develop their economies. This was linked to the idea that globalization had lowered transaction costs and therefore further stimulated the dispersal of production throughout the world, or that it at least had the potential to do so provided the correct market friendly policies were adopted. This in turn was linked to the potential for small-scale businesses to compete effectively in a world economy, adjusting production lines to the new era of flexibility. Moreover, these processes would encourage 'win–win' situations as successful growth and export performance in one country would stimulate growth and exports in other countries, through an increase in import demand in the former (Balassa 1989).

On the face of it, this would appear to be a more convincing argument than that concerning trade liberalization, because clearly some of the most successful developers – above all, China – have encouraged, and received, considerable amounts of foreign investment. This argument is central to the current neo-liberal focus on the importance of direct foreign investment as a major means of promoting development (World Bank 2002a). In particular, it is argued that foreign investment is good for growth, because it leads to an increase in income and employment, and allows developing countries to import advanced technologies that have been developed elsewhere, thus promoting competitiveness. Indeed, neo-liberals claim that the developing countries have a distinct cost advantage over developed countries, and so, provided they have liberal policies that encourage foreign savings and investment to flow to the developing world, they can exercise a competitive advantage, not in primary products, but through *low costs*. As we saw in Chapter 3, for a brief period this was the dominant neo-liberal interpretation of the rise of the East Asian newly industrializing countries (Little 1979; Balassa 1981; Lal 1988).

On the other hand, dependency-oriented analyses had a more critical account, both of TNCs and of the rise of East Asia. The argument was made that the rise of the East Asian NICs was a product of relocation strategies by TNCs, and so constituted only dependent industrialization (Landsberg 1979). This theory never clearly spelt out what an independent industrialization would look like, and neither did it adequately come to terms with either the economic or the social advances made in the East Asian region. But what is more relevant here is how the argument related to the role of TNCs in the rise of East Asia. Essentially, the argument was that TNCs relocated from the core in order to take advantage of lower labour costs in the periphery. Trade unions in the developed world had won substantial wage increases by the 1960s, and so companies increasingly relocated to take advantage of lower wages. The result was the development of a new international division of labour, which encouraged dependent industrialization in the periphery, but which was also based on the 'super-exploitation' of its workforce (Frobel et al. 1980; Frank 1984). This view was often linked to the rise in the number of factories producing goods for the world market, which were granted incentives to invest in areas designated as export-processing zones (Mitter 1986; Klein 2000). It was not very convincing as an explanation for the rise of East Asia, for as we saw in Chapter 3, both the state and local capital played central roles, particularly in South Korea and Taiwan.

More relevant to our concerns here is the argument that TNCs were relocating from core to periphery, and this was promoting a new international division of labour, for there is some common ground between neo-liberals and dependency theorists. Of course, in terms of attitudes to TNCs, the neo-liberal and the dependency accounts are radically different. The former regards TNCs as a mechanism for the development of the Third World, while the latter regards them as agents of exploitation. But despite this difference, there is also a remarkable *similarity* between the two accounts. The neo-liberal position sees potential for development in the comparative advantage in low labour costs, while the dependency position argues that exploitation is derived from low labour costs. Thus, while they may differ in terms of ethical implications, both positions suggest that low labour costs are crucial to determining the investment locations of TNCs. In a sense then, both theories suggest that there is some degree of convergence occurring in the world economy. For the neo-liberals, this is based on a levelling-up in which growth and poverty reduction occur through trade liberalization and foreign investment by TNCs. For the dependency approaches, there is a levelling-down process in which mobile capital moves to areas of low costs, and thereby promotes a race to the bottom, where capital locates in the most attractive investment location (Burbach and Robinson 1999). This argument needs further unpacking.

(iii)   Commodity chains and global capital flows

In the debate on TNCs, both apologists and critics suggest that they are leading agents in the globalization of manufacturing production. In its critical form, this idea of the globalization of production is similar to the theory of transnational capitalism that was examined in Chapter 5. It was suggested in that chapter that this theory usefully pointed to some of the ways in which the international economy had changed since the nineteenth century, but its emphasis on transnationality led to an underestimation of the degree to which some nation-states remain far more powerful than others. Much the same point can be made as regards the location of capital in the world economy, for it will become clear that the globalization of production, insofar as it exists, has not led to anything like convergence in the world economy.

In some respects, it is still fair to say that the world is divided in some ways into core and periphery. This is not to say that the core develops simply through the exploitation of the periphery, but rather that global capital accumulation continues to be associated with uneven and unequal development. This point is to an extent accepted by a variety of globalization theorists, who do not necessarily accept the contentions of dependency theory (Castells 2000a and 200b). For instance, Ankie Hoogvelt (2001: 64-5) has argued that 'the *geographic* core–periphery polarization is being replaced by a *social* core–periphery divide that cuts across territorial boundaries and geographic regions'. In contrast, the argument made here is that the core–periphery divide is both social and geographical. While divisions exist within, and even cut across, territories, it remains the case that some geography remains of crucial significance in understanding global inequalities, and that this reflects increasing inequalities not only *within*, but also *between* countries, an issue discussed below.[6] In other words, while there is no simple 'North–South' divide (and nor has there ever been), neither is such a divide a relic of the past (Silver and Arrighi 2000; Kiely 2003).

How then do we conceptualize uneven development in the context of the globalization of production? A useful starting point is to draw on the concepts of global commodity chains and global production networks (Gereffi and Korzeniewicz 1994; Henderson et al. 2002; Dicken et al. 2001). These theories are similar to the idea of transnational capitalism addressed in Chapter 5. The basic argument is that production processes are no longer confined within national boundaries, but are instead linked through a chain, 'a *transnationally linked sequence of functions in which each stage adds value to the process of production of goods or services*' (Dicken 2003: 14). Of course, this is not necessarily new, and as we saw in Chapter 2, production processes in the past have drawn on the supply of raw materials from overseas producers. What *is* relatively novel however, is that now manufacturing production can be located in different parts of the world, so that final products can be made up of industrial components from different parts of the globe. This is part of the restructuring of capitalism that had its origins in the crisis of the 1970s (Chapter 4), as TNCs entered into a number of organizational relationships, some of which are based on in-house, vertical integration, and some of which are based on collaborative relationships with (supposedly) independent suppliers.

This has led to the development of at least two kinds of commodity chains, those that are producer driven and those that are buyer driven (Gereffi 1994). In the case of the former, rents are still generated by economies of scale (and associated high start-up costs), and control over backward and forward linkages such as supplies and retailing. In the case of buyer-driven chains, barriers to entry are generated at more intangible levels, such as marketing and design (Gereffi 1994; Dicken 2003). Crucially however, those production processes that are contracted out and/or relocated to parts of the periphery tend to be concentrated in low-cost and lower-value production, so that the core recovers most of the value-added at the higher-value end of production, distribution and marketing processes, where rents are generated (see Chapter 1). Therefore, even though these processes encourage the expansion of manufacturing into the periphery, this will still be associated with lower value production. Rents are important because 'the levels of income arising to any producer or country operating in the global economy will depend on the extent of rents which they command. The lower the barriers to entry and the easier it is to copy a particular activity, the lower the associated rents and incomes which are provided' (Kaplinsky 2005a: 64). It remains the case that not only primary products, but increasingly in the manufacturing sector too, production in developing countries is disproportionately concentrated in sectors where barriers to entry are low and therefore rents are far less likely to be generated. This in turn reinforces hierarchical relationships between core firms and suppliers, including in places where fair trade agreements are made.[7]

For example, in recent years there has been a significant concentration of market share in retailing, which has increased buying power for these companies against suppliers (Gibbon and Ponte 2005). The United Kingdom Competition Commission in 2000[8] reported the squeezing of suppliers, not only through the market power of the few retailers forcing down prices to the many suppliers,[9] but through practices that included charging suppliers for supermarket shelf space, compensation paid by suppliers when profits were less than expected, and suppliers part-financing visits by buyers. Similar practices occur in relations between suppliers and final producers in manufacturing, and indeed, this analysis may even apply to supposed success stories such as the Indian software industry, which accounted for as much as 16 per cent of total exports and almost 3 per cent of GDP in 2001–2. However, it is heavily concentrated in the lower-end, labour-intensive sectors of the industry, leaving higher-value production to the more developed countries, which reflects the importance of skills, knowledge and infrastructure further up the production chain (Da Costa 2002; James 2003).

These observations are confirmed if we look closely at data related to international trade and capital flows. The share of Africa and Latin America in world trade has fallen in the era of contemporary globalization: Africa's share declined from 4.1 per cent in 1970 to 1.5 per cent in 1995, and Latin America's from 5.5 per cent to 4.4 per cent over the same period (UNCTAD 1998: 183). The share increased for Asia, from 8.5 per cent to 21.4 per cent, but as we have seen, this was not because of unambiguously open trade policies, still less because of neo-liberal policies. In 1960, Africa's share of total merchandise exports was 5.6 per cent, and Latin America's 7.5 per cent; by 2002, Africa's share had declined to 2.1 per cent and Latin America's to 5.4 per cent (UNCTAD 2004b: 51). In services, concentration was even greater – in 2002, developed countries accounted for 73.2 per cent of the total value of service exports, central and eastern Europe 4.2 per cent, and developing countries just 22.6 per cent. Africa's and Latin America's share have both declined since 1980 (UNCTAD 2004b: 61). These falls have taken place in an era of liberalization and the globalization of production. The continued geographical as well as social hierarchies of the international economy can also be demonstrated by examining the value of manufacturing imports from the developing world to the 'advanced' capitalist countries as a percentage of the latter's total 'consumption' of manufactured goods. For the United States in 1995, the figure was 7 per cent, a strong increase from just 2.5 per cent in 1980, but still very low; for the European Union the figure was 4.5 per cent in 1995 (and 2.5 per cent in 1980); and for Japan the figure was 3.3 per cent in 1995, and 2 per cent in 1980. In other words, in each case over 90 per cent of manufacturing imports came from other 'advanced' countries. Moreover, the category of developing country here includes the East Asian newly industrializing countries, which account for a high proportion of developing countries' manufactured exports to the 'First World'. Indeed, in the late 1990s, just six developing countries (China, South Korea, Taiwan, Mexico, Singapore and Thailand) accounted for around 50 per cent of total developing-country manufacturing exports (Sutcliffe 2001: tables 73 and 74).

In terms of foreign investment, we have already seen that it increased substantially from the mid-1980s and especially the early 1990s, including to parts of the developing world. But this investment also remains very concentrated. Throughout the 1990s, the developed countries received around two-thirds of total direct foreign investment (DFI), while the capital-scarce developing countries (including East Asia) received one-third. Moreover, investment to the developing world is itself highly concentrated, and at the turn of the century just 10 countries received over 70 per cent of it.[10]

These figures do, however, distort the picture in a number of ways. First, mergers and acquisitions between companies can lead to an increase in FDI figures even though they do not involve any new investment. As most mergers and acquisitions take place between 'First World' companies, this has the effect of exaggerating the concentration of FDI in the developed countries. But FDI figures also increase when countries sell off previously state-run enterprises to foreign capital – once again, this is not new, green-field investment, but a simple takeover of existing assets. In some years, mergers and acquisitions have accounted for possibly as much as 85 per cent of new FDI, as was the case in 1997 (Robinson 2004: 59). Thus, in the year 2003, a year in which mergers and acquisitions were not particularly high, FDI inflows were $560 billion. But of this amount, only $440 billion was made up of new, green-field investment. Mergers and acquisitions are more common between developed countries, thus inflating the figures that suggest capital concentration based on FDI flows. Thus, UNCTAD's figures for the year 1999–2000 show that FDI inflows to the developed world constituted 80 per cent of total FDI, and the proportion going to developing countries constituted only 17.9 per cent, but this was a year characterized by a high degree of mergers and acquisitions among companies in the developed world (UNCTAD 2002b: 5). However, this is a point noted by UNCTAD in its annual *World Investment Reports*, and still the evidence points to capital concentration. Moreover, following structural adjustment, there has also been a widespread takeover of locally owned assets in the developing world, especially in Latin America. According to one estimate, since the late 1980s over half of foreign investment in Latin America was actually the purchase of existing enterprises (Petras 2005).

In recent years there has been a slowdown in privatization, with the total sale of state-owned assets falling from $50 billion in 2000 to less than $20 billion in 2003 (UNCTAD 2004a: 6).

Secondly, TNCs may not directly control overseas production but enter into agreements with local capital. This would not count as direct foreign investment even though it is part and parcel of the globalization of production. But on the other hand, the figures for manufacturing imports into the developing world that came from the developing world would in part reflect the use of such subcontracting agreements, and these remain low (see below).

Moreover, DFI figures in some respects under-estimate the concentration of capital flows in the contemporary world economy. The developing countries have a higher proportion of the world's population than developed countries, and so the concentration of DFI is greater than the figures cited above. For the years 1995–9, developed countries received $474 on a *per capita* basis, and for 2001 the figure was $583; for developing countries as a whole, for 1995–9 the figure was $37 and for 2001 $41 (UNCTAD 2002b: 265). Secondly, FDI only makes up a small proportion of total global capital investment. From 1990 to 2003, world FDI flows accounted for only 8 per cent of the world's gross fixed capital formation (UNCTAD 2004b: 4). The share of FDI in the GDP of particular countries varies widely, from (using 1999 figures) 97 per cent in Singapore, 65 per cent in Malaysia, 55 per cent in Chile, 31 per cent in China, 16 per cent in Mexico, almost 8 per cent in South Korea, and 3.6 per cent in India. It then falls rapidly for poorer countries and the average percentage share for developing countries as a whole was 28 per cent in 1999, compared with 14.5 per cent for the developed countries. This is a big leap from the figure of 13.4 per cent for developing countries in 1990 (and 8.4 per cent for developed countries), which reflects the policies of investment liberalization and privatization carried out over that decade.

But despite this sharp increase, the percentage figure only reflects the increasing significance of FDI, and does not reflect a wholesale relocation of investment from core to periphery. Instead, it reflects continued concentration of core activities in the already developed countries, and selected relocation of some lower-value activities. Thus, if we examine the data concerning world manufacturing output, the extent of concentration is striking. In 1996, just 15 countries accounted for almost 84 per cent of total output, and the US, Japan and Germany together accounted for over 55 per cent of the total. The share of the advanced capitalist countries has declined from 95 per cent in 1953 to 77 per cent by 1996, and the developing world's share increased to 23 per cent in the latter year, but there is still considerable concentration in the developed world, and regional variation in the developing world (Dicken 2003: 37). The decline of the developed countries also reflects a shift to services, which now account for as much as 64 per cent of the GDP of the advanced countries (Dicken 2003: 42). Measuring world output of services is not of course particularly useful, as this can include all kinds of low-value-added activity, which is common in both the developed and developing world. It is probably fair to say that higher-value-added services tend to be those that are more likely to be tradable, though of course this too can vary – indeed, it is call centres which have caused so much panic about relocation to the developing world. What is clear however, is that the export of services is also firmly concentrated, with just 15 countries accounting for 63 per cent of the total in 2000 (see also the figures cited above). Of these 15, only 4 are developing countries (Hong Kong, China, South Korea and Singapore) and together they account for only 9 per cent of the total (Dicken 2003: 44).

Where then does this leave the neo-liberal and dependency arguments that suggested that relocation was occurring through the exercise of competitive advantage through, or the exploitation of, cheap labour. Or indeed, where does this leave the argument that capitalism has entered a new period based on the globalization of production? Clearly there has been an important change in the international division of labour, and some shift in the organization and location of manufacturing production and services. But at the same time this has both reinforced some old, and produced some new, hierarchies of international production. The higher-value end of the production of goods and services is still largely concentrated in the older core countries, although the East Asian region has had some success in breaking into these areas of production, albeit less through industrial relocation and more through the role played by the state in directing capital accumulation and industrial production. This means that activities that generate high rents, such as production of (high-value) final product, research and development, design, advertising, marketing and sales, still concentrate in core regions. Some parts of lower-value-added production may then be located in poorer areas – which may be within the core, but also may be in parts of the periphery, where labour and other costs are low. This will of course vary from sector to sector, and it would be a mistake to divide the world into the skilled/high-wage core and unskilled/low-wage periphery (see the next chapter), as in fact much of the expansion of jobs in the core is in low-wage (non-tradable) services (Henwood 2003). But it is true that skilled jobs are overwhelmingly concentrated in the core, while the periphery serves the world market in manufactures (and some services) largely through producing low-cost, labour-intensive goods.

Indeed, it is in these sectors that parts of the developing world have been successful in breaking into developed-country markets, with clothing and footwear produced in the periphery accounting for over 40 per cent of the North American market, compared with less than 10 per cent in the cases of transport equipment, industrial chemicals, and iron and steel, and just over 10 per cent in the case of non-electrical machinery (Sutcliffe 2001: table 73).[11] Having said that, these figures focus exclusively on the question of production, and they do not tell us a great deal about the question of consumption. Indeed, whilst the arguments of this chapter clearly undermine the thesis that at the level of production, workers in the developed world do not benefit from the exploitation of workers in the developing world (Bettelheim 1972), when we turn to the question of consumption the issue is more complex. I return to this issue in Chapter 10.

To return to the main question of this chapter, however: the point concerning the concentration of (productive) capital flows applies equally to financial flows. Neo-liberals argue that the free movement of money allows poorer parts of the world to draw on global savings, and therefore promote economic growth. As well as a substantial increase in direct foreign investment, developing countries did see a substantial increase in flows from international capital markets in the 1990s, particularly in the emerging markets in Latin America and East Asia. This increased from $43.9 billion in 1990 to $299 billion in 1997, falling back to $227 billion in 1998 because of the withdrawal of funds from East Asia (World Bank 1999b: 24). However, portfolio investment to developing countries is still proportionately small – the developing world received 9.7 per cent of total global flows in 1991, 9 per cent in 1994, 6.2 per cent in 1998, and 5.5 per cent in 2000 (Grabel 2003: 327) – and is concentrated in the richer developing countries. Most financial flows, however, concentrate in the developed world, not least the US where it has financed the trade deficit under Clinton and the budget and trade deficits under Bush junior (see Chapter 5).

Moreover, the argument that these flows are necessary to facilitate trade and investment ignores their actual effect in Latin America in the 1990s. In the context of trade liberalization and financial flows into Latin America (which led to over-valued exchange rates, sometimes formalized by currency pegs to the dollar), cheap imports flooded the market, which in turn led to a decline in manufacturing value added. As we saw in Chapter 4, the rationale for financial liberalization was to tap both domestic and foreign savings and thus increase investment rates, but both actually fell in the 1990s: savings, from 22 per cent to 17 per cent of GDP in Argentina from 1989 to 1999, from 28 per cent in 1985 to 20 per cent of GDP in Brazil from 1985 to 2001, and from 30 per cent to 18 per cent of GDP in Mexico from the early 1980s to 2001; investment, from 27 per cent to 20 per cent of GDP in Argentina from the mid-1980s to late 1990s, from 25 per cent to 20 per cent of GDP in Brazil from 1989 to 2001, and from 26 per cent to 21 per cent of GDP in Mexico from 1981 to 2001 (Saad-Filho 2005: 226). The combination of high interest rates and exchange rates, which served to encourage capital inflows, also encouraged cheap imports and undermined both investment and exports. Instead, this combination fuelled consumer-led booms, which were bound to end when deficits became unsustainable and foreign investors were no longer so willing to hold national currencies. This led to financial crashes in Mexico in 1995, Brazil in 1999 and Argentina in 2001. The neo-liberal charge that 'too much government' leads to unproductive rent seeking thus too easily ignores the ways in which deregulated capital can itself be unproductive and costly in the form of its destructive impact on productive investment. As Saad-Filho (2005: 227) points out, 'the neoliberal reforms destabilized the balance of payments and the productive system of most Latin American countries: neoliberalism discarded import substitution and promoted, instead, "production substitution" financed by foreign capital'.

This discussion therefore suggests that developing countries face a problem not because they are insufficiently globalized or integrated into the world economy, but because the form that such integration takes serves to reinforce their (relatively) marginalized position.[12] In contrast to the claims made by neo-liberalism, as well as some radical theories, capital is attracted to areas of established capital accumulation, where increasing returns can be derived from lower relative costs. Once established, accumulation encourages spatial agglomeration through the development of new technology and tacit knowledge, infrastructural development, local linkages and economic diversification, clusters of skilled activities, including research and development, and the development of systems of credit to finance further rounds of accumulation. This does not preclude some industrial activity in poorer regions, but it does not represent anything like convergence between capitalist countries or the end of uneven development (Kiely 1998: chs. 5 and 9; Wade 2003a; Henderson et al. 2002; Arrighi et al. 2003).

Indeed, even the actual investment that does go to the periphery is not necessarily as conducive to growth or poverty reduction as its neo-liberal apologists suggest. For FDI to have positive effects in terms of growth it must lead to an increase in the capital and current accounts, as well as government revenue (Sumner 2005). Thus, a net transfer of income on the capital account will in part depend on whether inflows are greater than outflows in the forms of profit repatriation, royalties, intra-company loans, and tax revenue. Given the high levels of trade between subsidiaries of the same company, a common practice is for TNCs to transfer price, and thus declare profits, in lower-tax countries. Such practices may occur even when states have offered incentives to TNCs such as subsidies financed by national taxpayers. This can have a negative impact on both the capital account and government revenue. Similarly, in terms of the current account, TNCs may export goods but this may be more then outweighed by the high import component of some companies. It is also common practice for TNCs to raise money within the recipient country, which undermines capital inflow levels. Assessing the impact of these issues is not easy, not least because they are likely to vary from sector to sector. Moreover, it is difficult to assess what would happen in the absence of foreign investment – apologists assume that no investment would occur, while critics too easily assume that local capital would behave in more 'socially responsible' ways, when it is likely that it too would rely on imported inputs and indeed would find ways of exporting capital, even if illegal. This suggests that the impact of FDI cannot be separated from the forms of both capital accumulation and state regulation within particular countries – in other words, the impact of such investment is in some respects locally contingent (Jenkins 1987; Kiely 1998: ch. 5). However, what we can say with some confidence is that neo-liberal forms of regulation are likely to reduce the positives and accentuate the negatives of foreign investment. In other words, capital outflows, and tax breaks and avoidance, are more likely to occur in neo-liberal settings, as are limited positive work and environmental regulations (Crotty et al. 1998; Chang 2003: ch. 7). In this sense then, developing countries are caught in a 'Catch 22' in which they receive limited amounts of investment, but, desperate to attract some capital flows, adopt policies which undermine the dynamic developmental potential of that same investment.

However, this investment is unlikely to facilitate upgrading to higher-value production, as it has occurred in the context of the rise of China, a massive global reserve army of labour, falling prices and falling barter terms of trade for low-value manufactures, and therefore stagnant real wages and little growth in employment. These are occurring in the context of excess capacity in many of these sectors, for reasons outlined in Chapter 4. The result is an exacerbation of the 'Catch 22' situation, in which many poor countries cannot find markets for their products, or if they do, they tend to be at the cost of significant reductions in the prices of their products. Indeed, on the basis of wide-ranging studies for the years from 1988 to 2001, using disaggregated data for around 10,000 imports into the European Union, and focusing on products where developing-world exporters were most prominent, Kaplinsky claims that in almost one-third of these sectors the price of Chinese-origin products fell, and for other low-income countries the price fell in one-quarter of the cases. Moreover, the higher the per capita income of a country, the less likely unit prices were to fall (Kaplinsky 2005a: ch. 7; Kaplinsky 2005b; and see Chapter 9 for more discussion of China). Although this applied only to European Union imports, given the wide range of products involved, similar patterns were likely to exist in US and Japanese imports as well.

Above all though, it is the location as well as the nature of capital flows that maintains uneven development in the world economy. Thus, if we examine the mobility of countries in the world economy in recent years it is clear that there has been little change. Drawing on a study of 100 countries from 1960 to 1999, and a three-tier division into core, periphery and semi-periphery, Wade suggests that 72 of the 100 failed to move tiers, and the remaining 28 moved only one zone (Wade 2004a: 167–9; Wade 2004b: 579). Almost as many moved down as up, and there was no significant correlation between such movement and policies related to trade openness. Based on market exchange rates, the per capita GNP of the periphery as a percentage of core-country GNP declined from 1980 to 1999 for most regions: from 4 to 2 per cent for sub-Saharan Africa, from 18 to 12 per cent for Latin America, and from 9 to 7 per cent for West Asia and North Africa. Improvements were made in South Asia, from 8 to 13 per cent, East Asia (excluding China and Japan), from 8 to 13 per cent and China, from 1 to 2 per cent (Wade 2004b: 568). But as we have seen, these are precisely the regions where, despite some liberalization, neo-liberal policies have been limited, at least until recently (see Chapter 9).

Conclusion: States, Neo-liberalism and Globalization

The four main arguments made in this chapter are clear: first, that the claims made that there have been significant reductions in poverty and inequality rest on data that is at least problematic; secondly, that despite these problems, there may have been some reduction in poverty in recent years, but this has not been caused by unambiguously pro-globalization friendly policies of trade, investment and financial liberalization. Thirdly, this is hardly surprising as the nature and direction of capital flows in the world economy suggest a tendency towards concentration, particularly of high-value activities in the developed world. The increase in foreign investment experienced by many developing countries in recent years thus hides this continued concentration, and the fact that much of this foreign investment may not be 'developmental'. Fourthly, policies of liberalization actually hinder the prospects of developing countries successfully upgrading into higher-value activity.

More broadly, this chapter has suggested that the neo-liberal idea that growth, and poverty reduction, will result through a deepening of global integration, which itself will arise from liberalization policies, seriously over-estimates the ease with which developing countries can break into new export markets. But the problem runs deeper than this, and this is where there is some degree of continuity with the free trade imperialism of the mid-nineteenth century. This is because liberalization undermines the capacity of developing countries to develop dynamic comparative advantages through, for example, industrial policy designed to develop industries through protectionist measures. As colonial policy prevented the periphery from adopting such policies (see Chapter 2), so too does the current international context, above all through the WTO rules discussed in the previous chapter. In this sense then, the policies that were implemented by developed countries are precluded in the current neo-liberal international order (Chang 2002; Wade 2003a; Kiely 2005a: ch. 5).

This is of course contested, as we have seen, and this is more likely to occur in an international system of sovereign nation-states. But it is also a highly unequal international state system, and sovereignty does not guarantee anything like autonomy. This point applies to all states, but it applies to some states far more than others. The double standards and protectionism of the developed world – discussed in Chapter 6 – are important means by which states maintain their dominant position in the world economy, but at the same time this chapter has suggested that the movement in the direction of free trade does not constitute an advance for the development of the Third World. This does not mean that the South is simply doomed to stagnate in the global economy, as though the insights of underdevelopment theory applied to the neo-liberal era. But equally neither does it mean that the insights of modernization theory – that integration into the Western dominated international economy will inevitably promote catch-up and development – are correct. Rather, it suggests that neo-liberalism has intensified uneven development.

For there to be sustained and dynamic capital accumulation – development – in the developing world, the state must play a crucial role in the process. This, of course, is true of all processes of capitalist development, but what is being suggested here is that the forms of intervention favoured by neo-liberals have not been conducive to such development. This chapter has therefore rejected the arguments made by neo-liberals. However, there may still be good reasons why neo-liberalism has expanded over the last twenty years, and this is a theme developed further in the next two chapters. On the other hand, a return to the policies of import-substitution industrialization that characterized post-war development could be possible, and this too is discussed in the next chapter. But, in either scenario, one set of technocratic policies (the promotion of market forces) competes with another (the promotion of the developmental state). For neo-liberalism's critics, this begs the question of whether states are always effective developers – the neo-liberal fallacy that state intervention is always inefficient (or only useful to correct market failures) is replaced by the fallacy that state intervention is always efficient. What is required, then, is a better account of the role of institutions in development, and this is also discussed in the next chapter.

Chapter 8

Globalization, Neo-liberalism and the State

This chapter examines the relationship between different nation-states, and how these relate to development in the era of globalization. The chapter starts by outlining the broad debate on the relationship between the state and globalization, challenging the views of both the hyper-globalists and the sceptics. In suggesting that the last twenty to thirty years have seen the restructuring of the nation-state, the first section focuses on state restructuring in the advanced capitalist world, with particular reference to the market imperatives faced by contemporary social democracy, but uses this debate to draw out more global implications for development. The chapter then moves on to the question of restructuring in the developing world, and examines neo-liberal perspectives on the role of the state, and how this has developed since the 1980s, and through to the 'post-Washington consensus' of the 1990s. In the third section, I move on to examine the discourse around notions of failed and rogue states, and discuss how these reflect the close links between development and security since (but also before) 2001. I particularly emphasize how this link is closely related to ideas of neo-liberal restructuring and the expansion of the liberal democratic zone of peace. In the final section, I critique neo-liberal perspectives on the state, both generally and in relation to liberal ideas of reconstructing rogue and failed states. But at the same time, I draw on this discussion to also provide a critique of the concept of the developmental state, and suggest that this idea shares with neo-liberalism a technocratic understanding of (capitalist) development. I argue that in contrast to both these approaches, 'development' is a conflict-ridden process which has enormous implications for understanding not only structural adjustment and poverty reduction, but the emergence of so-called failed and rogue states. This argument is illustrated through brief discussion of a number of regional examples from the developing world. Finally, the chapter concludes by drawing together the argument.

The State and Globalization

The early globalization debate was dominated by two accounts of the state that broadly paralleled the hyper-globalist and sceptical accounts of globalization briefly outlined in Chapter 5. The hyper-globalist position, represented on the neo-liberal right by Ohmae (1995) and the left by Frobel et al. (1980), argued that global flows were now of such a magnitude that the nation-state was in decline. For the neo-liberals this was desirable because it meant that free markets could allocate resources efficiently, which meant that the prospects for development in the former third world were considerably enhanced. A 'left globalization' perspective made a similar case (Kitching 2001; Desai 2002; Harris 2004), arguing that, unencumbered by the restrictive state, capital would move from high- to low-cost areas and thus promote long-term convergence between the developed and developing countries. Others on the left argued that the decline of the nation-state meant that one of the main sources of defence against exploitation had been undermined, as mobile capital had defeated immobile labour (Frobel et al. 1980; Klein 2000). This was because in the absence of state controls, capital could simply shift from one location to the next in search of a cheap and easily exploitable labour. Sceptics challenged this perspective, arguing that the state retained considerable capacity to regulate capital, because the hyper-globalist exaggerated the mobility of the latter (Hirst and Thompson 1999). The argument was thus made that labour could continue to win considerable reforms in the developed countries, and retain some room to actively promote development in the developing world (Weiss 1998). This view suggested that there remained a significant variety of capitalisms in the international order, and these were linked to a variety of institutional structures within particular nation-states. Globalization thus did not promote convergence, either in terms of development outcomes or in terms of state policy (Hay 2005a, 2005b).

Both sides in this debate had their strengths. Clearly there is no absolute convergence on policy between states, and some (developed and developing) states are far more committed to social welfare policies than others (see below). Moreover, specific national histories of resistance have an impact on particular institutional structures in different ways. It is for this reason that some writers advocate a European social model as a progressive alternative to US (and British) neo-liberalism. But at the same time, there have been significant moves towards neo-liberal policies in a wide variety of countries with very different institutional structures, as we saw in Chapters 3 and 4. Moreover, the neo-liberal view of the non-interventionist state is a myth, and it is one that sceptics take too seriously. Clearly, contrary to the views of neo-liberals like Ohmae, states do matter, but equally, contrary to the sceptical view, the fact that they matter does not itself undermine the view that there has been a shift towards neo-liberalism, no matter how nationally specific, uneven and contested. This suggests that what is required is an account of the state and state system that rejects the false dichotomy between globalization and state. Instead, an account of the restructuring of states is needed.[1] As Payne (2005: 33) suggests,

> the changing nature of the state is at the heart of the process of globalization. *The* state is neither transcended nor unaltered in some overarching, all-encompassing fashion: instead, *each* state (whether it is located in the old 'First', 'Second' and 'Third Worlds') is finding that its relationship to key social forces both inside and outside its national space is being restructured as part and parcel of all the other shifts to which globalization as a concept draws attention.

But is this notion of state restructuring satisfactory? Given that it suggests that there has been a universal movement (or convergence) towards neo-liberal states, is this not a version of the hyper-globalization thesis via the back door? Chapter 4 provided a broad account of the rise of neo-liberalism in the 1980s and the consequent restructuring of the nation-state, but does it follow from that particular account that other capitalist models have come to an end? Put differently, is it the case that 'there is no alternative' to neo-liberalism. Or does globalization provide a useful justification for unpalatable (and neo-liberal) policies in the face of political retreat? (Hay and Watson 1999; Kiely 2005a).

To answer these questions some further attention will now be paid to state restructuring, in part by reference to the prospects for social democracy in the developed world. However, what will become clear in this discussion is that there has been a shift away from social democracy towards global competitiveness, and this reflects important material changes in the international economy. And most crucially for our purposes, these material changes undermine not only the prospects for social democracy in the developed world, but the prospects for development in the developing world.

The case for social democratic national alternatives to neo-liberalism is often linked to a body of thought that emphasizes the continued existence of a number of varieties of capitalism in the international order. This school of thought essentially argues that while capitalism is a general feature of the world economy, it is mediated within nation-states (and localities and regions) by different institutional structures. Institutions can be defined as 'socially constituted arrangements that endure over time and play a crucial role as bearers of embedded rules, norms and enforcement practices in regulating social behaviour' (Beeson and Bell 2005: 125; see also North 1990). As well as being created by human action, institutions also influence human behaviour, which leads to a degree of 'path dependency' to social and political activity. The argument is then made that this institutional variation laid the grounds for the post-war distinctiveness of a variety of capitalisms, such as Anglo-American market-led capitalism, progressive North European corporatism (the Rhineland, welfare or Scandinavian models), and the developmental states of East Asia (Berger and Dore 1996; Crouch and Streeck 1997; Hollingsworth and Boyer 1997; Coates 2000; 2005; Hall and Soskice 2001). The first of these is essentially neo-liberal, the third is developmentalist and discussed below, while the second model is said to be associated with high degrees of industrial concentration, intra-firm cooperation, state coordination, high productivity investment, close ties between industry and finance, and a focus on bank-led, long-term investment, as opposed to the short-termism of stock-market led Anglo-American capitalism (Hutton 1994). Perhaps most crucially, the argument has been made that high wages, low unemployment, skills and high-quality social provision give workers a stake in the system, allowing these progressive models to be economically efficient and socially just (Streeck 1992: 32–4). The question that is crucial, however, is the extent to which these distinct varieties continue to exist, and therefore to what extent there can continue to be progressive and competitive alternatives to Anglo-American capitalisms in a post-Bretton Woods, neo-liberal order.

For writers like Jessop (2002) and Cerny (1997) such models have been eroded, and this is said to be linked to the changing structural features of international capitalism. While critical of some of the claims of the varieties of capitalism literature, Hay remains sympathetic to this school of thought's sensitivity to continued institutional divergences across national capitalisms (Hay 2005a and 2005b). It is on this basis that he seeks to rescue social democracy, not least from its growing fatalism in the face of neo-liberalism, above all in the case of the British Labour Party. He rightly points to the continued divergence between advanced capitalist countries, and convincingly shows that the state has actually increased in importance in most developed countries, at least as measured as a proportion of GDP and employment. Thus, in 1960, state spending as a proportion of GDP stood at 32 per cent for (West) Germany, 34.6 per cent for France, 31.1 per cent for Sweden, 32.6 per cent for the UK, and 27.2 per cent for the US; by 1980, the figures were 46.9 per cent (Germany), 46.2 per cent (France), 65.7 per cent (Sweden), 44.6 per cent (UK), and 33.6 per cent (US); and by 2000, the respective figures were 44.5 per cent, 47.5 per cent, 52.2 per cent, 37.7 per cent and (US 1997 figure) 32.7 per cent (Hay 2005a: 246; see also Glyn

2006: ch. 6). He also correctly argues that globalization has not led to a global dispersal of production and that in fact most productive capital stays in the developed world. Moreover, he also argues that in terms of financial liberalization, its effects have been exaggerated. This is because there is little evidence of a global convergence of interest rates, which would occur if capital markets were fully integrated, and there remains a strong correlation between domestic savings and investment rates, which should not occur in a fully integrated global market.

These divergences are used to make the contention that there still can be social democratic routes to global competitiveness. For Hay, globalization is best understood as a discourse that attempts to depoliticize decision-making, used to justify otherwise unpalatable policies because there is supposedly no alternative. But he takes this argument too far, and tends to regard globalization as *just* a discourse, and as a result, he tends towards a voluntarist account of political agency which downplays the structural constraints faced by nation-states. This will be illustrated by examining the prospect for social democratic strategies of progressive competitiveness in today's international order. But before doing so, two more general points need to be made concerning Hay's empirical arguments. The first is that the continued importance of the nation-state certainly challenges crude ideas about its demise, but it does not tell us very much about whether or not there has been a structural shift towards neo-liberalism. While neo-liberal ideology may suggest a minimal state, neo-liberalism requires a highly interventionist state to carry out neo-liberal policies. What is therefore needed is a focus on the importance of different parts of the state, such as the priorities given to government departments and the ways in which welfare policies are carried out. Empirical analysis here would focus on shifts from departments of industry to finance, more regulated systems of welfare provision, taxation priorities, sources of taxation, and so on, rather than state spending *per se* (Perraton and Clift 2004). Secondly, the continued importance of state expenditure may itself be caused by welfare inflation, such as growing unemployment and work-related sickness in an ageing population, which gives rise to highly political questions concerning welfare, health and pensions provision. In other words, insofar as state spending remains central to advanced-economy GDPs, this may come into conflict with neo-liberal priorities (although even this may not necessarily be the case). Thirdly, even if we accept Hay's quantification measures, there has been some decline in state spending since 1990 in those countries (Sweden, Germany) he would regard as being progressive models.

Having said all this, none of these arguments completely undermines Hay's thesis and he is right to point to continued national variation. More problematic is his under-estimation of wider international pressures which do militate against the continuation of social democratic models. Again, my argument is not that national variations have ceased to exist, and by implication comparative political economy no longer serves any purpose, but rather these comparisons and variations should not lose sight of the wider international and global context – a point that applies to both developed and especially developing countries. Strange's (1997: 184) comment is instructive here: 'My quarrel with most comparativists is that they seem to me not to see the wood from the trees, to overlook the common problems while concentrating on the individual differences.'

What then of the prospects for social democratic strategies of progressive competitiveness in the international order, and what implication does this have for understanding development? The starting point for such an argument is the belief that the international economic order does not conform to the neo-liberal utopia of balanced trade, free markets and perfect competition. Indeed, via a process of cumulative causation, competition becomes imperfect as some places and regions develop economies of scale. There is thus a case for a strategic trade policy which can pick winners that can become competitive in the international order. This argument draws heavily on new growth theory, which attempts to incorporate human capital (particularly the utilization of technology by skilled labour) into an understanding of the sources of growth, but which otherwise broadly accepts the efficiency of 'market forces' (Lucas 1988). This is also combined with an upbeat assessment of the restructuring process briefly addressed in Chapter 4, arguing that unemployment in the developed world is a result of purely technological change, which can be reversed by appropriate interventionist policies to upgrade the skills of the labour force, which can thus becoming competitive through flexible specialization (Piore and Sabel 1984). The differences among contemporary social democrats are over the forms of intervention, with the likes of Hutton (1994), Hay (1994) and Hirst and Thompson (1999) arguing for more traditional social democratic interventions. Piore and Sabel even suggest that flexible specialization has the potential to enable small businesses in the developing world to become globally competitive, while more interventionist approaches suggest that just as social democracy can still prosper in the developed world, so too can the developmental state in the developing world.

Despite his convincing criticisms of 'third way' neo-liberalism (Hay 1999), Hay still effectively accepts a key contention of the idea of progressive competitiveness, namely that an interventionist state can deal with market imperfections, and thus increase the market opportunities for both the British state and its competitors, through a process of shaped comparative advantage. This strategy endorses the idea that some countries (the developed world) specialize in skilled production, while others specialize in lower-value production, at least until some kind of development occurs. This argument can even be given a Marxist gloss by suggesting that some countries (where skills, infrastructure and so on are most developed) specialize in sectors where relative surplus value is extracted, while others (where labour is abundant and therefore cheap) focus on absolute surplus value production. In the 'third way' variant of the argument, through specialization, markets can clear effectively and thus promote the traditional win–win situation of neo-liberal theory.

However, a very different implication may actually be drawn, whereby the high-productivity country that has benefited from shaped advantage, and which as a result of its competitiveness runs a trade surplus, will depend on continued market access to exporting countries. If such countries respond with austerity measures or protectionism, then the trade and employment gains for the high-productivity country will be eroded. If we now move the analysis from relations between individual countries to looking at the system as a whole, then there is a more fundamental problem. As Albo (2003: 127–8) argues:

> For individual country strategies, there is every incentive for national competitiveness over unit labour costs to spread from productivity gains to austerity *even* in technologically leading countries as trade imbalances persist. Technological laggards must compete on lower wages to reduce unit costs or face a deteriorating trade deficit (especially as surplus countries may not increase aggregate demand). The sluggish condition for realization, while capacity to produce more output is increasing from productivity advance, makes it imperative that technological leaders eventually follow or lose their surpluses and employment.

This argument is crucial for understanding the wider context of state restructuring, in both developed and developing countries. Indeed, it suggests that there have been important material changes in the character of the international capitalist order, and these have served to undermine both social democracy in the developed world and development in the developing world. National capitalisms need to be located in the wider context of the international capitalist economy, even if specific local, national and regional contexts cannot be read off from this international or global context. More concretely, one does not need to accept the hyper-globalization thesis concerning capital mobility and cost-free capital exit, in order to see that there are significant pressures placed on all states. For example, annual productivity rate comparisons suggest that the US has higher rates of productivity than those in western Europe (Dumenil and Levy 2004; Glyn 2005). However, US workers work an average of around 2000 hours a year, compared with 1500 in France and Germany, a comparison which amounts to around 10 weeks extra work a year in the US. So it may be that the progressive competitive strategy works in terms of productivity per hour, but this is cancelled out by annual productivity in the US, which is based on longer working hours (Harman 2006: 83).

Similar pressures can also be placed on wages. While it is certainly true that rising wages can be financed by rising productivity (and this is a major reason for continued capital concentration in the developed world), given the competitive pressures faced by all states, there remain strong downward pressures on wages throughout the world – indeed, low wage costs in the developing world may be the main source of competitiveness, but in a world of massive unemployment this can actually facilitate even further downward pressure on wages (see Chapter 9). This is further reinforced by the existence of acute trade imbalances in the current world order. Therefore, given that open-economy social democracy relies on export markets to maintain and expand domestic employment, this relies on other countries not protecting themselves from foreign competition or not resolving trade deficits via policies of austerity. But if countries are less competitive, then they will face a trade deficit and such policies are likely to occur. This pressurizes them to compete on the basis of lower labour costs, which at the same time undermines the prospects for the export success of strategies of progressive competitiveness. This strategy therefore tends to repeat the problems associated with neo-liberalism in the 1980s (see Chapter 4), in which each country simultaneously adopts an export strategy and cuts imports, thus leading to a global demand crisis (Albo 1994). The result is that social democratic countries then have to respond by themselves keeping wage costs down, but (as domestic demand is reduced) this may throw more exports onto a world market that cannot absorb them, with the result that surplus capacity exists in a wide variety of sectors, including computers, automobiles, telecommunications, steel, and many others (Brenner 2002; Crotty 2002; Kaplinsky 2005a), a situation aggravated by the rise of China (see Chapters 7 and 9).

Different national models may promote austerity in different ways – as we have seen, Britain has in practice relied on low wage costs in a low-productivity economy, while Sweden has promoted shared austerity from within the working class. But the global context of over-production existing side by side with austerity pressures, has an impact on all 'national capitals'. Indeed, as we will see in the next chapter, this scenario is central to understanding both the character of the current international economy, not least relations between surplus and deficit advanced capitalist countries, and the potential strengths and weaknesses of US hegemony in this order. Finally, it again needs to be stressed that financial capital does constitute an obstacle to any social democratic alternative to neo-liberalism. One need not accept hyper-globalization claims on capital exit and interest-rate convergence, but financialization does involve the restructuring of corporate strategy (see also Chapter 4). As Beeson and Bell (2005: 127) argue,

> in an era when the growth and integration of capital markets have made the idea of distinct national spaces less tenable, both Japan and Germany are facing challenges to their distinctive systems. In Japan, the gradual liberalization of the domestic financial system has opened up new possibilities for domestic firms, simultaneously diminishing the influence of the Japanese government and undermining the integrity of Japan's corporate system. . . . In Germany too, the link between domestic financial institutions, a distinctively national form of capitalism and a constant social accommodation, is not as robust as it once was.

This suggests then that what we are seeing in the international order is continuing institutional variation, existing side by side with patterns of change that point in a distinctly neo-liberal direction – a kind of 'varieties of neo-liberalism' or hybridization approach (Albo 2005; Perraton and Clift 2004). Seen in this way, globalization is less something externally imposed on states and producing uniform convergence, and the end of geography, and more about setting certain global norms and standards that are themselves set by specific localities (and states), and which affect localities and states in an institutionally mediated way. But what is crucial is the fact that these global standards have changed over the last 25 years.

These arguments suggest that not only are neo-liberal claims for the efficiency and equity of the international order problematic, so too are social democratic (and perhaps developmental – see further below) alternatives to neo-liberalism in the context of the current (neo-liberal) international order. But equally important, we need to more explicitly move from changes in the international economy which may have a negative impact on both social democracy and development, and provide more detail on state restructuring in the developing world. The next two sections undertake this task, with a particular focus on how western nation-states and/or western-dominated international institutions play a central role in these processes: first by examining institutional restructuring through the World Bank, the IMF and the shift from the Washington to the post-Washington consensus; and secondly, by examining perhaps the most extreme form of neo-liberal restructuring, that of military intervention. This is followed by a more critical section which challenges the assumptions made by those who lead such interventions, but which also more explicitly focuses on 'internal' processes of state formation within the developing world.

From the Developmental State to Market Friendly Intervention

As we saw in Chapter 3, in the post-war period states in the developing world were highly interventionist. They played a key role in developing domestic industries in order to transcend the colonial legacy of concentrating on primary goods production. This was associated with the 'developmentalist' strategy of import-substitution industrialization, whereby certain incentives were given to the development of industries, including protection from foreign competition, at least in favoured sectors. Sometimes this nationalist strategy was linked to the ideology of socialism, but in practice most approaches aimed to use the state in order to develop productive capacity and promote a vibrant capitalist economy like those associated with the developed countries. The ideology of developmentalism was undermined by the debt crisis of 1982, and the dominant interpretation of the development crisis in the West, which was that this was caused by inefficient intervention and too much government. This interpretation laid the ground for a shift to neo-liberal policies associated with privatization, deregulation and liberalization, and so-called rolling back the state. The results of these policies in the 1980s and early 1990s were poor, not least in the former communist countries, which suffered from shock therapy after the collapse of communism. From the 1990s, there was a shift away from a straightforward embrace of neo-liberalism, to an approach based on promoting institutional change to ensure that neo-liberal policies could work effectively. This was particularly the case with the World Bank and the IMF, who continued to play key roles in regulating economies in the developing world, but now did so through focusing on institutional change. However, this section suggests that this institutional turn did not represent a shift away from the dominance of neo-liberal ideas, but was in many ways an extension of them. In other words, as adjustment in the 1980s undermined ISI and began the shift towards neo-liberal policies, so in the 1990s there also needed to be a shift away from those institutions that supported ISI to those that could facilitate the further expansion of neo-liberal policies.

In particular, from the early 1990s, the ideas of good governance and market friendly intervention were promoted. The former promoted government accountability, the rule of law, and transparent, open government, which included the end of corruption. Aid was increasingly tied to the exercise of practices of good governance, which was regarded as a means to an end. The means – institutional change – would function to promote an efficient, 'free market' economy. Good governance thus means establishing 'the rules that make markets work efficiently' and that 'correct for market failure' (World Bank 1992: 1). Similarly, by 1997, the Bank talked of an enabling state that would 'allow markets to flourish' (World Bank 1997: 1). In other words, the free market agenda was still regarded as the solution to the problem of poverty, but this was increasingly tied to developing institutions which would allow free markets to develop, and deal with situations where market failure took place.

This was not dissimilar to the idea of market friendly intervention. In the 1980s, the World Bank had contrasted the poor record of Latin America and sub-Saharan Africa with the impressive development record in East Asia. The implication was that the latter had adopted the correct, neo-liberal policies and so could be regarded as a model for the rest of the developing world. However, the problem with this argument was that it was quite clear that there were highly interventionist states in East Asia, as Chapter 3 showed. The Bank therefore developed the idea of market friendly intervention to explain the rise of East Asia (World Bank 1993). This argument suggested that the state acted as a substitute for the free market, whereby states intervened in order to either let markets work, or subject interventions to the discipline of domestic and international markets (World Bank 1991). In East Asia, market friendly intervention meant macro-economic stability, selective export-promoting interventions, and efficient, independent institutions, which enabled markets to operate unimpeded by the state.

This idea of market friendly intervention was thus associated with the idea of the enabling state, which was said to be one that enabled markets to work effectively and efficiently (World Bank 1997). The Bank (1997) argued that corruption had hindered development and that this could be overcome through a process of privatization, liberalization and reform of the state. Corruption was said to occur because of state regulation, and therefore the state should be rolled back, while at the same time, those officials still employed by the state should be paid higher wages in order to lower the incentive to continue corrupt practices. Anti-corruption policies were deemed to be important because corrupt practices hindered development, and much was made of the close correlation between low GDP and high rates of corruption (Mauro 1998). The Bank also developed a more comprehensive account of poverty and poverty reduction. But once again, this was largely tied to the idea that market provision is intrinsically more efficient than public provision. Poverty was seen as a condition in which people are poor because they lack access to income-earning activities generated by the market. Market access needed to be expanded, and this was to be carried out through a strategy of deregulating markets (World Bank 1994: 63). The enabling state was thus one that allowed for the so-called free market to lead in the sphere of economic activity, while the state secured the appropriate conditions for this leadership. In practice, the state should therefore promote law and order and deliver public goods, but it should also secure transparent and clear property rights, contracts, bankruptcy laws and financial stability, all of which allow free markets to operate effectively (World Bank 1997). Thus, former Bank President James Wolfensohn (1996) argued that:

> Our new world of open markets raises the stakes for developing countries. Investment is linked to good policies and good governance – liberal trade regimes and high savings rates, combined with sound legal and judicial systems. Simply put, capital goes to those countries that get the fundamentals right. And we are working with our clients on those fundamentals.

Thus, in effect, institutional change was needed so that developing countries could draw on the benefits offered by a more openly integrated global economy. In contrast to the tendencies to concentration outlined in Chapter 7, the Bank and the IMF generally argued that institutional change that embraced market reform would be sufficient to secure development. Insofar as there were disagreements, such as those around the much publicized case of Joseph Stiglitz, these tended to be over the pace of reform, rather than a fundamental challenge to neo-liberal ideas. Cammack (2004: 203) refers to the shift from the Washington to post-Washington consensus as 'institutional shock therapy', which amounts to 'a blueprint for a complete set of social and governmental relations and institutions, founded on macroeconomic discipline and extending across a range of economic and social policies without parallel in depth and intensity of intervention'. The much vaunted national ownership of such policies, part of the Bank's Comprehensive Development Framework, was necessary because of the central need of states to carry out the reform process, even though at the same time there was a need to pass various IMF and Bank assessments.

At the same time, there was now some recognition that markets sometimes fail to work perfectly, and so greater allowance was made for state intervention. Thus, as early as 1991 the Bank stated that 'it is not a question of state or market: each has a large and irreplaceable role' (World Bank 1991: 1). By 2004, the Bank had admitted that privatization had been oversold (World Bank 2004), but this assessment still took place in the context of neo-liberal assumptions that markets are more efficient than states. As Fine and Van Waeyenberge (2005: 151) point out, the Bank's 2004 report 'offers a pecking order of infrastructure targeted for privatization – running from the attractive fields of telecommunications and energy, through transport, to the dead ducks of water and sewerage'. This reflects not only resistance on the part of social movements to privatization, but also the passive resistance of capital when it comes to investing in these less lucrative areas, where there are uncertain returns and poverty stricken customers. The state is therefore assigned a role that supports the private sector, and the Bank has 'taken an apparently more cautious approach to privatization in principle, as the means by which to try and push more of it through in practice, with a focus on sectors where there may be more chance of success'. Thus, at the same time as the Bank has developed a more 'pragmatic' approach, different parts of the World Bank Group have been prioritized in recent years, with the International Financial Corporation (which lends only to the private sector) receiving a four-and-a-half-fold increase in investment from 1980 to 2000, amounting to an increase in its share of total Bank lending from 3.3 per cent in 1980 to 25 per cent by 2000 (Fine and Van Waeyenberge 2005: 165). The Bank also began to look for appropriate frameworks to allow for the development of private sector entrepreneurial activity to take place below the nation-state. In doing so, they have borrowed the concept of social capital (World Bank 1997; Grootaert and van Bastelaer 2001). Associated with the work of Putnam (1993; 2000), the concept refers to the development of networks and associations that exist independently of the state, and it is suggested that these provide the basis for much-needed entrepreneurship in the developing world (World Bank 1998). In this way, the development of social capital helps to facilitate market expansion.

This shift from the structural adjustment of the Washington consensus to the institutionalist turn of the post-Washington consensus is thus not as great as it may first appear (Jomo and Fine 2006). What it ultimately reflects is a shift that recognizes the need for a restructuring of the state if neo-liberal policies are to be implemented. Even the focus on poverty reduction – and the much publicized shift from structural adjustment programmes to poverty reduction strategy papers in 1999 – is compatible with earlier neo-liberal ideas, as the solution to poverty is regarded as being greater access to markets, and thus an increase in the expansion of market provision. The idea that markets may be marginalizing (for some) is thus discounted from the outset. In particular, from 1990 the Bank argued that poverty reduction must focus on 'the productive use of the poor's most abundant asset – labor', which called for 'policies that harness market incentives, social and political institutions, infrastructure and technology to that end' (World Bank 1990: 3).

In the 1990s, aid programmes were increasingly tied – in theory at least – to these institutional changes. The extent to which institutional change has occurred, and an assessment of the results, will be discussed below. Before doing so however, we need to examine another, more extreme, attempt at state reconstruction, associated with the idea of policing rogue and failed states.

Reconstructing Rogue and Failed States

The idea of failed and rogue states can be traced back to the geopolitics of the Cold War, and the shifting alliances made by the two superpowers and their allies and adversaries (Bilgin and Morton 2002). However, their importance has in many ways intensified since the end of the Cold War, and has become increasingly related to the closer link between security and globalization in the era of globalization (Duffield 2001; 2005). This has increased even more since the terrorist attacks on the US in September 2001, and the development of the war on terrorism, re-branded in 2006 as 'the long war' (Department of Defense 2006). Thus, according to the 2002 National Security Strategy, 'the events of September 11, 2001, taught us that weak states, like Afghanistan, can pose as great a danger to our national interests as strong states. Poverty does not make poor people into terrorists and murderers. Yet, poverty, weak institutions, and corruption can make weak states vulnerable to terrorist networks and drug cartels within their borders' (National Security Strategy 2002). Similarly, the Department for International Development in the UK has contrasted strong and weak states, the former 'able to deliver services to their populations, to represent their citizens, to control activities on their territory, and to uphold international norms, treaties and agreements', while the latter 'provide a breeding ground for international crime' (Benn 2004). These views also find considerable support in more academic circles, where the idea of a new form of international governance of 'quasi-states' is mooted, in order to control 'chaos and barbarism from within', leading to a new 'reformation of decolonization' (Jackson 2000: 309–10; also 1990). These ideas are made more explicit elsewhere, with talk of a new 'humanitarian empire' (Fukuyama 2004; Chesterman et al. 2005), while others are more than willing to explicitly embrace a new imperialism, or empire, 'a form of governance that hardly dares speak its name' (Gaddis 1999: 2; 2004; Mallaby 2002). These ideas are linked to the notion of liberal democratic expansion through US hegemony, which will provide both security for the western world, and development (and hence security) for the failed states (see also Chapter 5).

Failed states such as Afghanistan are thus linked to global terrorism and drugs networks.[2] It is precisely because of the existence of such failed states, alongside dictatorships and bankrupt regimes, that there is a need for new development initiatives, in which Tony Blair has played a central role, including the New Partnership for African Development (NEPAD 2002) and the Commission for Africa (2005b). This has increasingly been linked to the reconstruction of rogue states as well. According to former Clinton national security aide Anthony Lake (1994), these are states that undermine the international community or family of nations, the latter of which focus on democratic expansion and the promotion of the free market, and are committed to the peaceful settlement of conflict. For Lake, rogue or outlaw states included Cuba, North Korea, Iran, Iraq and Libya. By 2000, the designation of rogue states was based on three primary criteria: pursuit of weapons of mass destruction; use of international terrorism as an instrument of state policy, and a foreign policy orientation that threatened US interests (Litwak 2000: 49). After 11 September, and the quick removal of the Taliban regime in Afghanistan and the (temporary) dispersal of al Qaeda forces, Bush made his infamous 'axis of evil' speech in January 2002. The terrorist threat was linked to the opposition to rogue states, which were said to back terrorists and undermine international stability. Iran, North Korea and above all Iraq were initially targeted, and Syria and Cuba quickly followed. Libya was also identified but was already developing friendlier relations with the US and Britain, a fact which was then used by the latter in an unconvincing attempt to demonstrate the validity of the force of pre-emption by example. In June 2002 Bush first outlined this strategy of pre-emptive action, which upheld the right of the United States to strike against potential and actual enemies *before* these countries or terrorist groups acquired significant weapons. The unilateralism of the administration was made clear in its National Security Strategy:

> While the United States will constantly strive to enlist the support of the international community, we will not hesitate to act alone, if necessary, to exercise our right of self-defense by acting pre-emptively. (National Security Strategy 2002)

Thus, whatever spurious justifications may have been given for the war in Iraq in 2003, the fact remains that the role of the US and its allies in policing failed and rogue states, no matter how selectively, should be regarded as strategies of state reconstruction. This may not always have been deliberate, and indeed immediately after the terrorist attacks Bush distanced himself from the idea of nation-building in Afghanistan. Moreover, the Pentagon envisaged decapitation of the Saddam regime in Iraq, followed by a takeover of Iraqi state institutions and a reasonably rapid withdrawal from Iraq. This strategy existed alongside longer-term strategies of a managed transition, and the 'democratic imperialist' wing of the neo-conservative movement's hopes for nation-building as part of a wholesale reconstruction of the Middle East (Tripp 2004). In practice the US has adopted a mixture of all three strategies in both Afghanistan and Iraq, but what is also clear is that each of these strategies was premised on the need for state restructuring through the promotion of neo-liberal policies of liberalization and privatization (Dodge 2005). In this regard then, the interventions were a form of neo-liberal adjustment, designed to promote development, and thus security, through the expansion of these countries in the international community, or the liberal zone of peace. As argued in Chapter 5, it is above all this policy, albeit selectively applied and with blatant disregard for consistency in its treatment of non-liberal states, that lies at the heart of the policing role of the US military in the international order. The case for intervention in such cases clearly echoes that of John Stuart Mill's (1973: 409) argument in the mid-nineteenth century that 'the friends of freedom have a right to employ their own thews and sinews to check the onward flow of barbarism and tyranny'. This is closely linked to the idea that commerce and liberal democracy can lead to the end of violence between states, thus promoting the expansion of the liberal zone of peace. Increased commercial links promote a degree of inter-dependence which makes war unlikely, an argument that strongly influenced the most prominent advocate of free trade in nineteenth-century British politics, Richard Cobden. This is reinforced by the argument that liberal democracy is likely to prevent war because leaders are accountable to electorates that know the consequences of war. Liberal economics and politics thus have a pacifying effect on relations between states and individuals. In a contemporary version of this argument, the World Trade Organization (WTO) (1998) argues that 'sales people are usually reluctant to fight their customers . . . if trade flows smoothly and both sides enjoy a healthy commercial relationship, political conflict is less likely. What's more, smoothly flowing trade also helps people all over the world to become better off. People who are more prosperous and contented are also less likely to fight.' This argument has been further reinforced by Thomas Friedman (2005a and 2005b), in a liberal interpretation of globalization that has some parallels with the Marxist theory of transnational capitalism outlined in Chapter 5. His argument is that greater global interdependence – particularly as reflected in the growth of transnational chains of production – is good for world peace. In other words, it is not only trade but the fact that so many products are now sourced from a number of countries, which makes war between liberal market democracies unlikely.

In this approach then, there is a virtuous circle between democratization, liberalization and marketization, all of which mutually reinforce growth, prosperity, security, development and peace. Deviants from this norm must, however, be dealt with – through various forms of pressure from the 'international community', which ultimately can include war. The Bush administration – and to a significant extent the Clinton one before it – has been willing to use military force to do this, and in an increasingly unilateralist way. Thus, while the use of hard power and unilateralism does represent an intensification of the securitization of official development policy (Beeson and Higgott 2005), there remains substantial continuity in terms of assumed causal links between global inter-dependence and liberal democratic expansion (see Chapter 5).

We also saw in Chapter 5 how some other approaches draw on Leninist interpretations of inter-imperialist rivalries and outlets for surplus capital to challenge the liberal peace thesis. However, these theories were criticized, on the grounds that the 'surplus capital' thesis is unconvincing, and for failing to examine questions of state formation and violence within developing countries, preferring instead to read these off from the supposed rivalries between imperialist powers. Chapter 5 also argued that Kautsky's theory of ultra-imperialism was useful in pointing to the ways in which cooperation between capitalist states had increased since 1945, even if this had not, contra Kautsky, led to the end of economic competition or uneven development. This theory of course could potentially mean a kind of Marxist version of the liberal peace thesis. However, I also suggested in Chapter 5 that the relationship between capitalist states, economic competition and military conflict is more contingent than classical theories implied (a point rightly made by Kautsky). This point could also apply to the liberal peace thesis, which rejects the *inevitable war* thesis of Lenin in favour of an *inevitable peace* thesis. The approach suggested here is that neither scenario is inevitable, but what is needed is a better understanding of the relationship between violent conflict on the one hand, and state formation, primitive accumulation, and capitalist development on the other. These questions are integral to understanding the problems of both neo-liberalism specifically, and capitalist development more generally, as we will see in the next section.

Beyond Technocracy: the Limitations of (Neo-)liberal and Statist Perspectives on Development

This section suggests that both the Washington and post-Washington consensus provide unconvincing accounts of development failure and that their alternative strategies are unlikely to provide the basis for sustained development in the former Third World. But it also questions the view that suggests that state-led interventions, on their own, represent a convincing alternative. Indeed, one of the key arguments of this section is that both views are excessively technocratic. This analysis is made through a consideration of both the developmental state and neo-liberal perspectives in general, and is also used to suggest that a similar argument can be applied to the most extreme form of technocratic development: that of military interventions, which share neo-liberalism's optimism about the prospects for liberal peace, a market economy, and economic growth. In challenging these approaches, some potentially more useful alternative perspectives on the varieties of state formation in the developing world are suggested.

As previous chapters have made clear, the idea that increased openness is alone sufficient to promote development is a fallacy. This argument was belatedly recognized with the institutional turn on the late 1980s and early 1990s, but this turn remained committed to the neo-liberalism, as is the Bush administration in the US (Soederberg 2006b). Moreover, the post-Washington-consensus institutional turn was unconvincing, even within its own narrow terms. Thus, indices of institutional quality based on independent bureaucracy, the rule of law and clear property rights and contract suggest that the East Asian NICs scored no higher at take-off than other developing countries (Knack and Keefer 1995). Nor was there any visible sign of (liberal) democracy at take-off. Neither was the practice of corruption any lower in East Asia, even after take-off had occurred (Khan 2002). Indeed, it could be argued that there needs to be greater sensitivity to different forms of corruption, some of which are clearly detrimental to capital accumulation, but some of which are clearly central to helping accumulation to take place (see below).

Alternative accounts to the (neo-)liberal position have suggested that rapid development has most successfully occurred when states have intervened to consciously promote social transformation and industrialization. This has involved, among other things: selective protection for industries so that they are protected from cheap imports from established overseas industries; intervention to secure investment in dynamic sectors; the disciplining of both capital and labour through punitive measures against capital export and workers' rights; and the forcible removal of people from the land in order to secure a labour force (and a potential domestic market) for the new industries. These often authoritarian measures undermine liberal views concerning the efficiency of the limited state, *and* the idea that development is a process based on consensus. These two issues demand further consideration.

The first idea then is that the state is far more interventionist than neo-liberals contend. This is the basis for the idea of the developmental state, which has been defined as a state 'whose politics have concentrated sufficient power, autonomy and capacity at the centre to shape, pursue and encourage the achievement of explicit developmental objectives, whether by establishing and promoting the conditions and direction of economic growth, or by organizing it directly, or a varying combination of both' (Leftwich 1995: 401). Developmental states are thus characterized as having a developmentally oriented elite, relative autonomy from vested interests, a competent bureaucracy, a relatively weak civil society, and a consolidated state prior to the development of powerful economic interests (Leftwich 1995: 405–19). Moreover, the state is seen as vital to the promotion of development in the context of 'late development' (Amsden 2001), for in an era where late developers face the prospect of competition from established producers, there is a need for state protection in an era of unequal competition. This approach has been effectively used to explain the rise of the first-tier East Asian newly industrializing countries (Amsden 1989; Wade 1990), and to some extent the rise of China (Nolan 2004). But it could be argued that such state intervention has characterized *every* process of successful capitalist development (Chang 2002), or at least every one that followed the initial success of British industrial capitalism,[3] a point already made in the context of nineteenth-century imperialism, in the second chapter.

On the other hand, while the literature on the developmental state usefully exposes the weaknesses of the neo-liberal position on development (White 1988; Amsden 1989; Wade 1990), it has its own underlying weaknesses. For now,[4] these can be broken down into two related points. First, it is not entirely clear why some states are, and some are not, developmental. While it is certainly true, contrary to neo-liberalism, that states are not necessarily inefficient, it is also true that they are not necessarily efficient. There is thus a need to break down further the reasons for efficient and inefficient interventions. The standard response has been that some states have sufficient autonomy to exercise power over society and so they can promote development. But this is unconvincing because some states have used this in ways that promote, while others have used such autonomy to hinder, development. The idea of autonomy has then been broken down further to suggest that it is sometimes embedded in society, and is therefore conducive to development (as in East Asia), while sometimes it is dis-embedded and therefore hinders development, as in Mobutu's Zaire (Evans 1995). These attempts to further refine the concept of the developmental state have not been altogether convincing, largely because the reasons why some states have sufficient capacity to promote development while others do not is undertheorized. Even in the best analyses, which at least attempt to link state capacities to wider social forces (Migdal et al. 1994; Kohli 2004; Evans 2005), there is still a tendency to continue to separate state and society, with the state viewed as an external entity that intervenes in society (Cammack 1990; Jayasuriya 2005). This problem can be derived from the concept's reliance on a Weberian theory of the state, in which the state is regarded as a given, and then discussed in terms of the strength or weakness of particular states' capacities to promote social transformation. However, the state is not a thing in itself but a form of social relations, and it is these relations which must first be analysed, in the process discussing the social and historical mechanisms by which the state takes on the (social) form of a 'thing in itself' (Rosenberg 1990). In other words, *sociological* analysis of the developmental state is somewhat limited.

This relates to the second problem with the idea of the developmental state, which is its tendency to reduce development to a technical process, in which neo-liberal technocracy is replaced by statist technocracy. In this way, development policy is regarded as being the product of 'a set of fixed institutional endowments or attributes', and as a result the analysis is 'unable to grasp how these capacities change in response to broader changes in the constellation of social and economic interests' (Jayasuriya 2005: 383). This leads among other things to an ahistorical approach which is unable to account for restructuring in even the most successful developmental states in East Asia, a question discussed in the next chapter. In pointing to continued interventions by states in the developing world, many theorists of the developmental state thus repeat the fallacy that intervention alone is sufficient to disprove the expansion of neo-liberal policies throughout the world (see, for instance, Weiss 2003). In this respect, those that continue to identify the existence of developmental states in, say, South Korea, are essentially upholding the views of the varieties of capitalist literature. But as this chapter has made clear, one needs to pay greater attention to the forms of intervention carried out by states, rather than simply accept by implication the neo-liberal myth of the non-interventionist state, and then disprove this myth by pointing to examples of continuing intervention.

This issue is addressed in relation to East Asia in the next chapter. For the moment, we need to identify a more immediate problem with the idea of the developmental state, and provide a different account of development which challenges *both* the free market technocracy of neo-liberalism *and* the statist technocracy of the developmental state. In other words, the question of development as a process based not on consensus, but on conflict, enters the picture. It is not sufficient for developmental-state theorists to see state formation in terms of pre-conceived capacities for strength and weakness (Migdal 1988), as this is a process that is an intrinsic part of society (Chibber 2003; Fine 2006). Insofar as neo-liberals have an account of conflict, they tend to rely on crude models which suggest that these are caused by rational choices made by individuals who have nothing to lose (and something to gain) by fighting (Collier and Hoeffler 1998; 2002): for example, it is linked to the opportunities presented to young, unemployed men by the easy spoils of civil war (Collier 2000). This methodological individualism thus assumes away any notion that people may be mobilized through collective action, and very real grievances which, under specific conditions, may lead to conflict (Cramer 2002). Indeed, such a sociological understanding is central to an understanding, not only of conflict and development, but of the closely related historical reasons why so-called rogue and failed states have developed. Thus, as Bilgin and Morton (2004: 175–6) suggest, there is the need 'to shift the focus from pathologies of deviancy, or "aberration and breakdown", to understanding the different strategies of accumulation, redistribution and political legitimacy that unfold in zones of conflict, thereby appreciating war as "social transformation"'. In the context of the war on terror, leading development agencies in the US in particular have argued for a more political, even 'transformational' approach to development (Natsios 2006). However, this in effect is simply a repeat of the idea that a liberal model can simply be constructed in developing countries, in isolation from the conflicts that have always occurred in the context of primitive accumulation.

This point brings us back to the question of the limitations of the idea of liberal peace. Without accepting the inevitability of economic competition leading to war, we should reject the idea (shared by neo-liberals and theorists of the developmental state) that transitions to sovereign states, liberal democracies and market economies are smooth processes that exist without violence and conflict. This point applies to earlier transitions in the developed world (Moore 1966; Tilly 1992; Teschke 2003) as well as contemporary transitions that may – or (more likely) may not – follow similar trajectories to that of the developed world. This implies the need for an analysis of the violent ways in which capitalism and the nation-state first establish themselves in countries, and the ways in which the existence of already developed countries may complicate and undermine later transitions (and thus ensure that late developers do not follow similar transitions to that of established capitalist democracies).

Crucial here is an understanding that state formation in parts of the developing world should not be regarded simply as a deviation from a supposed western norm (itself problematic), but that (like earlier western state formation) such a process has been one ridden by conflict and contradiction. Of course, processes of state formation in Africa differ from European experiences, but this cannot be explained by recourse to

African cultural uniqueness, based upon timeless notions of neo-patri-
monialism, corruption or kinship (see, for instance, Bayart 1993; Chabal
and Daloz 1999). Ironically, both Eurocentric and cultural relativist
accounts tend to identify 'Africa' in this way, differing only over the
extent to which judgement can and should be made about such practices.
While some of these practices certainly manifest themselves in some
African societies and polities, these need to be explained rather than
treated as self-evident instances of timeless cultural practices. Mamdani
(1996) characterizes the post-colonial African state as one based on
uneven, hybrid forms that combine elements of modernity and a constructed form of rule based on invented tradition. This bifurcated state
(which of course varied its form from state to state) had its origins in the
colonial period, in which a small colonial minority governed the
majority through indirect rule. Thus, cheap, 'thin' colonial rule occurred
through the use of local states. Colonialism thus combined modern,
impersonal states (albeit characterized by racial classifications) with traditional, personalized forms of rule. At independence, these local despo-
tisms were largely left in place, and patrimonialism served as the link
between the two forms of power. One result was that access to state
office was a major source of power and enrichment, and so the development of a purely political state alongside surplus extraction through a
fully developed capitalist economy did not occur. Thus, for Mamdani
(1996: 16), '(t)he colonial state was a double sided affair. Its one side, the
state that governed a racially defined citizenry, was bounded by the rule
of law and an associated regime of rights. Its other side, the state that
ruled over subjects, was a regime of extra-economic coercion and admin-
istratively driven justice.'

The legacy of such a colonial state had enormous implications for
development in the post-colonial era, because it left a legacy of authoritarian rule, combining elements of high degrees of 'modern' centralization and 'traditional' decentralization. While most post-independence
leaders rejected this legacy, at the same time they also inherited it and
thus found that it was necessary to use it in the process of building, not
only sustained capital accumulation, but a strong nation-state necessary
for such a developed capitalism to be put in place (Young 1994: 1–12).
This was exacerbated in some places by conflicts over territorial boundaries established in the colonial era, which were sometimes used by new
leaders in situations conducive to authoritarian rule to actually increase
their personal power, while doing little to enhance administrative state
power (Herbst 2000: 253). Moreover, the rapid transfer of power in the
colonies, designed at times to prevent the rise of more militant nationalist movements, ensured that clientelist linkages between political
leaders, parties, and sections of the electorate were central in the con-

struction of the new political systems (Allen 1995). Together, and despite the comparatively favourable international context in the Bretton Woods era, these factors all served to undermine the rise of a modern state that could put into effect the process of building developed capitalist economies. In contrast to East Asia, where developmental states were most successfully put in place, the post-colonial era in (parts of) Africa was characterized by conflict-ridden processes of state-building. Idahosa and Shenton (2004: 97–8) argue that:

> Given the compromised modernity of colonialism, post-independence projects of national development contained an unresolved paradox. Regardless of professed political orientation, all such projects were, in reality, examples of state-led economic and social development for the simple reason that no other agency capable of carrying out the developmental task was believed to exist. As such, these projects presumed the existence of a modern state capable of bearing the developmental burden. However, no such state existed. Of necessity, therefore, national development had to be as much about the building of a modern state as about development itself.

Newly independent African states took over colonial state structures that were primarily designed to facilitate the expansion of taxable primary commodities for export. The new post-colonial leaders could not rely on the political support of urban working classes or middle classes, which were too small to ensure a stable political base, and so instead relied on rural elites linked to the state through various networks of patronage. However, it was clear from the 1970s, in the context of slower economic growth and the international economic downturn, that there was simply not enough patronage to buy off sufficient numbers of people in the countryside. Opposition therefore mobilized against political leaders, who responded by further centralizing the state and personalizing presidential rule, backed up by an increasingly powerful army. Despite significant differences, such as political ideology and the treatment of political dissent, this was more or less the process that occurred in Tanzania, Kenya and what was Zaire in the 1970s. Elsewhere, such as in Somalia, Sierra Leone, Nigeria and Ghana, there was less success in centralizing the state, which further encouraged an increasingly out of control system of corruption (Allen 1995).

We should, however, be careful not to over-generalize the extent of state 'failure' in Africa. While there was significant regional variation, despite the unfavourable circumstances, in the Bretton Woods era African states did enjoy relatively high rates of economic growth, led by strategies of import-substitution industrialization. Indeed, the average annual growth rate for sub-Saharan Africa in the development era –

2.3 per cent from 1961 to 1973 – was higher than it has been since (Mkandawire 2001), with the exception of a mid-2000s primary commodities boom, briefly discussed in the next chapter, and which is likely to prove unsustainable and certainly not 'developmental'. If we take these points together – African state weakness, some development in the Bretton Woods era, the need for a strong state to promote capital accumulation – then this has largely negative implications for current attempts at restructuring. The previous chapter showed the problems faced by late developers in the context of the shift to policies that promote the market: there is no guarantee that foreign investment will occur, trade liberalization undermines the prospect for the promotion of dynamic sectors fuelling long-term development, and instead encourages these goods to be imported from overseas competitors, and/or further encourages economic activity in unproductive sectors, which are lucrative for some people but not for the nation-state. At the same time, there was some significant differentiation which reflected the different development experiences that preceded the adjustment years. States which relied on peasant export production tended to fare better, as it was these states that had more successfully built close links with the countryside in the years before adjustment. Those states that relied more heavily on mineral exports, often led by foreign capital, had limited links to, and support in, the countryside. At the same time these lucrative exports were a source of increasing attraction to armed gangs, who were not policed by an increasingly run-down army. Indeed, former soldiers often formed such gangs in response to falling army pay and privileges, and state degeneration due to falling revenues, coups and conflict. When combined with conflict over resources such as oil and diamonds, these developments fuelled warlordism in places like the Congo, Sierra Leone and Angola (Cramer 2006: chs 3 and 4). This is not an argument that suggests simple, one-dimensional explanations for conflict or state failure – resources and adjustment both play their part, but these must be situated in longer histories of state formation, which vary in time and place. But what is also clear, is that adjustment along neo-liberal lines does little to alleviate these problems, and may well exacerbate them.

Moreover, the post-Washington institutional turn may have similarly undesirable effects. For example, the development of civil society is often seen as progressive in that it will provide the basis for a market economy independent of the unproductive state. But as Idahosa and Shenton (2004: 101) argue

> [t]hose who now plea for civil society's renewal in Africa should take note that, if civil society is [erroneously] taken to be synonymous with voluntary associations, then . . . these were ubiquitously thick on the

ground during late colonialism and the early years of independence.
. . . However, and as unpalatable as it may appear to present day proponents of civil society, the dominant forms these associations took
was as societies arising from or created to represent sectional com-
munal interests.

Of course these sectional interests *may* form the basis for a dynamic
capitalist class, but even if they do, they are equally likely to promote
tensions that lead to conflict, which undermines the expectations for
liberal peace. This is not an argument that conflict over state formation
or even primitive accumulation can be reduced to class interests, just as
this was *not* the case in seventeenth-century England. Rather, the argument is that, even leaving aside the question of the state policies required
for such a transition to take place, the (neo-)liberal expectation of a
pacific, conflict-free transition to capitalism is seriously mistaken.

Similarly, in both India and much of Latin America the emergence of
a developmental state along East Asian lines did not occur. However,
rather than regarding such state failure as confirmation of the superi-
ority of markets over states, as neo-liberals contend, we should instead
link the slowdown in growth to the particular social structures of accumulation that existed in these states (and of course their national variations), and how these linked to the wider international economy, particularly with the gradual breakdown of the Bretton Woods era and the
erosion of the space for 'national development'. In particular, in parts of
Latin America and India, state formation has historically been characterized by a class compromise between a nascent bourgeoisie, usually
with close direct links to the state, and landed interests (Corbridge and
Harriss 2000; Anglade and Fortin 1985; 1990). In this context of backward agriculture, productivity remained low and therefore industrial
development has itself been limited (as domestic markets are limited and
import demand on the part of the dominant classes is high). As these
dominant classes would not finance the state spending associated with
ISI through taxation, states ran up large deficits, which had inflationary
consequences that further squeezed the consumption of the poor.
Combined with changes in the international economy in the 1970s and
1980s (economic slowdown, falling demand, increased international
borrowing and increased interest repayments), liberalization became
inevitable. In some respects this undermines the old alliances between
bourgeoisie and landed classes, although in some cases the latter become
more and more like a capitalist class in the context of peasant differentiation, both before and after liberalization. What national capital
increasingly does, however, is to align itself with international capital, in
order to gain access to finance, technology and licensing agreements, or

simply invest money abroad through the export of capital. This brief and overly sketchy account thus shows how the developmental state is not so much autonomous from society, but rather its 'capacities' and 'institutional endowments' are strongly influenced by wider patterns of class formation. Moreover, it also shows how these can change over time (and that ISI was not so much a technical but a social 'failure'), and how there may be domestic sources of support for liberalization – indeed, this point applies all the more strongly to Latin America in the 1990s (see Chapter 7). This argument is developed further and applied to the most successful developmental states in East Asia in the next chapter. But what is perhaps most crucial is the recognition that ISI did come to an end, not because of the intrinsic failings of state-directed development, but because of how particular social structures served to undermine national patterns of accumulation, and how this was reinforced by changes in the global economy, as discussed in Chapter 4.

The relationship between class and state formation can also be usefully applied to the Middle East. This is a particularly useful region to discuss, not only for reasons of topicality, but because it is often regarded as an exceptional region, particularly resistant to democratization. These kinds of arguments reflect earlier accounts of the state and development, strongly influenced by modernization theory. The standard argument of this theory was that democratization would occur via a process of modernization, which would include economic growth, urbanization, rising incomes and increasing literacy (Lerner 1958). But while these processes occurred in the Middle East and its neighbour countries usually considered part of the region, democratization did not occur. This led to culturalist arguments, which suggested that Islam was not conducive to democracy as it rejected the nation-state or the separation of state power and religion (Kedourie 1992). But this argument was guilty of stereotyping and homogenizing Islam,[5] and ignored the diversity of interpretations and changing nature of Islam, and Islamic (and Islamist) movements in the region, as well as the diversity of state formation within the region (Zubaida 1988).

Following the inspiration of Barrington Moore (Moore 1966), who attempted to explain state formation through an analysis of the links between agrarian social structures and political development, Gerber (1987) argued that patterns of political development in the Middle East must be linked to the specificities of class formation. In particular, he contrasted the more democratic politics of Turkey and (for a period) Lebanon, with more authoritarian rule in Egypt, Syria and Iraq. At the start of the formation of a modern nation-state, the 'democratic' regimes were characterized by the absence of a class of urban, absentee landlords living off the produce of peasants in the countryside, while in the latter the social structure was still characterized by the dominance of these 'notable' classes. In order to protect their rule, the notables needed an authoritarian and highly repressive state. On the other hand, these notables were eventually defeated by nationalist mobilizations – in Egypt from 1952, in Iraq from 1958 and in Syria from 1954 – which actually served to keep the state as the central organizer and mobilizer in society. Populist nationalist revolutionaries led these states, and controlled most areas of social life in a highly authoritarian way. This was reinforced by close ties with the Soviet Union, and the borrowing of a number of practices from the Soviet model. In the case of Iraq, the presence of oil rents meant that state revenue and foreign exchange could be heavily sourced from oil sales, and not domestic taxation, thus giving the state further powers over the domestic population. In part because of the highly arbitrary nature of the formation of the Iraqi state, state power took a particularly repressive form in that country. The presence of oil was also central to the character of the state in Iran (before 1979), Saudi Arabia and the Gulf states, where again oil rents played a central role in state domination, though this was slightly different in Iran, where state formation took place in the context of an already independently established clergy and urban classes. The key contrast, however, is that the origins of the Turkish state occurred in a context where there was some independence for civil society organizations from the state, and this did not exist to the same extent in the more authoritarian regimes. Certainly the state was important in Turkey, as ISI strategies were implemented there, but still the control of the state was less prevalent. These developments have shifted over time, with some growing autonomy in Egypt, but less in either Saddam Hussein's Iraq or Saudi Arabia. Bromley (1997: 339–40; see also 1994) summarizes the contrast:

> in those instances where a degree of capitalist development has occurred outside the direct control of the state and has facilitated the beginnings of independent organization by the bourgeoisie and the working class, in short where a civil society has begun to develop, some liberalization and controlled experiments in popular participation have emerged – Turkey most obviously, to a more limited extent Egypt and even Iran. By contrast, where the state has maintained control and has blocked the organization of independent classes and forces, where there has been no opportunity for the emergence of civil society, then the scope for popular initiative has been more limited – the limit cases being Iraq and Saudi Arabia.

This approach is important, as it provides a far more historically grounded, and sociologically sensitive understanding of state formation than the quick-fixes of neo-liberal reconstruction. However, the conclusion – that civil society development is crucial – is, on the face of it, not so far removed from liberal (and neo-liberal) positions on state restructuring to promote market-led development. Indeed, it is also close to the position advocated by some liberal and radical supporters of the war in Iraq in 2003. In this specific case, liberal interventionists contend that while the war was a cause for regret, the outcomes – namely an independent civil society and democracy – may still be progressive. Indeed, for some writers these (potential) consequences were sufficient grounds to support the war in the first place (Ignatieff 2003). This position leads us back to reconsider the claims made for civil society by those otherwise suspicious – though also naive – about neo-liberalism, and indeed, to consider the relationship between capitalism and democracy, for if liberal capitalism opens up spaces in civil society, then these are conducive to a more liberal democratic capitalism. Indeed, one Marxist in development studies in the 1970s went so far as to argue that capitalism and democracy are 'Siamese twins' (Warren 1980).

Certainly it would be wrong to deny that the development of a civil society alongside a functioning liberal democracy does open up potential spaces for, say, a functioning and effective labour movement. However, as already argued in this and earlier chapters, it would be equally mistaken to conflate this space with civil society, which equally involves the presence of all kinds of movements, not all of which are progressive or democratic. Indeed, some of these movements are likely to be extremely hostile to the development of an independent labour movement. The dominant political forces gaining ground in Iraq are clearly hostile to independent trade unions, to women's rights, and so on. But there are also strong grounds for suggesting that the occupying forces have themselves had elections forced on them, as successive plans for post-war Iraq were quickly abandoned in the face of pressure from senior religious figures and the insurgency (Dodge 2005). Certainly, the dominant political forces emerging in Iraq do not leave much room for optimism concerning the future for democracy. US intentions have clearly backfired in Iraq, and the most likely scenario is a semi-authoritarian regime largely hostile to the United States, or a civil war. Having said that, US intentions were themselves hardly committed to a project of substantive, rather than formal, democratic change. This reflects not only the undemocratic way in which the war was carried out, but also the widespread suspicion of democracy associated, not only with the Bush administration, but more generally with both liberal and conservative political thought.

Classical liberalism was always concerned that the politics of democracy may undermine the freedoms of the market, and above all private property, and so concerned itself with ways of restricting the capacity of government (Hayek 1960). Conservatives shared these concerns but were blunter about their fears that democracy could be associated with rule by people unsuitable for government. While liberals saw the market and private property as ways of curtailing the power of democratic governments, conservatives saw the market as being too democratic, leading to the vulgarities of the mass society, and the consequent search for other forms of elite-driven collectivism alongside the market[6] (Polanyi 1944: 256–8). Both liberals and conservatives, however, agree that private property is an important protection against the excesses of democracy (Smith 2005: ch. 1), and scepticism towards democracy has undoubtedly influenced US 'democracy promotion', both at home and overseas (Smith 2002). Democracy thus becomes redefined as something limited to a narrow sphere of politics, while the (naturalized, depoliticized) market extends its influence into more and more areas of public life. This is reflected in the increased power of private property owners over those without property, increasing inequalities alongside inadequate social provision, and increased subordination of nation-states in the periphery to international institutions. This is not to under-estimate the importance of democratization in the developing world in the 1980s and 1990s, which in part was a product of struggles by social and political movements. But at the same time, rather than one-sidedly seeing this as a new democratic revolution (Shaw 2000), we need to be aware of the ways in which these struggles have been successfully subverted by powerful (domestic and international) forces committed to neo-liberal transformation (Gills et al. 1993; Robinson 1996; Evans 2002; Ayers 2006). One of the great ironies of post-Cold War international politics is that the demand for democracy has expanded 'just at that moment when the very efficacy of democracy as a national form of political organization appears open to question' (Held 1992: 31). Moreover, it again needs to be emphasized that the promotion of so-called free markets does not constitute a basis for development, but rather can reinforce subordination in the face of a western-dominated international economy.

This point does not mean that we should accept the claims of underdevelopment theory or those who draw on classical Marxist theories to explain contemporary imperialism. Both these perspectives read off events in the developing world from the 'advanced' capitalist countries, thus reducing agents in the developing world to being passive victims of 'the West'.[7] But nor should we repeat the claims of modernization theory or neo-liberalism, which assume that contact with the advanced countries is automatically benign and beneficial to the development of the poorer countries. And here we again return to an understanding of capitalist development and state formation as conflict-ridden processes. Conflict in the developing world has a diverse set of causes, but it can be exacerbated by struggles over property rights that may involve access to foreign capital, thus provoking nationalist responses. It may also be exacerbated by the ease with which corrupt leaders, local entrepreneurs, and warlords and gangsters may export money to financial institutions in the developed world, rather than investing in long-term, productive and 'developmental' projects in their countries of origin. This can be reinforced by the lucrative benefits that may be derived from exporting particular commodities – such as cocaine from Colombia, heroin from Afghanistan, diamonds from Sierra Leone and coltan from Congo. These exports may occur in times of conflict and indeed may be a major source of conflict in the first place. This is not to say that these raw materials are themselves the single source of conflict, as if certain resources in themselves are a 'curse' for the development prospects of poorer countries (Auty 1995). These resources exist within particular social and political conflicts and these must be identified. But on the other hand, it would be naive to regard them as irrelevant to the causes of conflict (Bush 2004). Thus, just as sixteenth-century enclosures in England were linked to the export of a valuable commodity (wool), so contemporary warlords in conflict-ridden areas are linked to valuable export markets. This involves substantial accumulation that may lead to further productive investment at some point in the future. For this to occur though, there will have to be various institutional mechanisms put in place that promote capitalist development. However, as we have seen, the institutional turn that has occurred at the World Bank and the IMF is counterproductive in this respect as it relies on the fantasy of a limited state allowing development to occur through market forces.

Finally, there is the question of arms exports. Once again there is a tendency among critics of the arms industry to blame exports as the main cause of conflicts in the developing world, as though agents there were simply having their strings pulled by manipulative corporate elites. But at the same time – and especially given the humanitarian rhetoric of many western governments – these arms exports cannot be ignored. In 2003, the G8 countries exported arms to the value of $24 billion, more than half of which went to the developing world. From 1998 to 2001, the US, Britain and France made more from arms sales than they dispensed in aid. Interestingly, given the non-interventionist rhetoric of many western governments, the arms industries enjoy considerable government protection in the form of export credits, which part-finance arms exports, particularly to less credit-worthy countries – which effectively means countries in the developing world. From 1997 to 2001, the arms industry in Britain accounted for around 30 per cent of all export credits. Such credits were also used in the Thatcher era, and arms sales to Saddam Hussein in Iraq were never paid for by his regime, and so British taxpayers met the costs (www.caat.org.uk).

It has been argued by Duffield (2001), Hoogvelt (2001), and Berger and Weber (2006), that states have increasingly collapsed in the developing world because of a change in the nature of development in recent years. This reflects a shift from an expansionary and inclusionary form of development, which effectively characterized the Bretton Woods and Cold War years, to an exclusionary form of development in the years of neo-liberalism. In the former, most states were supported by one of the major powers because of Cold War strategic considerations, and there was significant room for manoeuvre in terms of the space for development to occur. This has been undermined by the ending of the Cold War and increased indifference to poorer countries, and the undermining of the space for development and effective marginalization of some countries from the neo-liberal world order. This view has been challenged by Cramer (2006: ch. 6), who argues that development transitions are themselves ridden with conflict and violence, and this is in part due to the nature of the integration of developing countries into the world economy. However, perhaps these two views are not as mutually exclusive as they first appear. The marginalization of (some) developing countries has intensified in the era of globalization, but this is not absolute. All developing countries are in some respects integrated into the international order – indeed, neo-liberal policies have increased openness and thus integration. But at the same time, as was argued in the previous chapter, the form of integration is one that in some respects marginalizes developing countries in that these same neo-liberal policies undermine the prospects for (capitalist) development in the poorest countries, a point accepted by Cramer. These points do not mean that countries are totally outside the international order, even the poorest developing countries, and they are (unequally) integrated through the exports that may come from war, criminal and other shadow economies, as well as low-value primary products and manufactured goods. Similarly, the post-Cold War order has not led to absolute marginalization of some developing-country states, as the US and other states (including some in the periphery) have their own strategic agendas, which include the close linkage between development and security, which has increased since 2001. But once again, the form of integration is one that undermines the prospects for development and the hoped for incorporation into the so-called liberal zone of peace. In this sense Hoogvelt's (2005) argument that, whatever the specific causes of 'state failure', US-led interventions basically serve to 'manage exclusion', is convincing. While this chapter has recognized that development itself, as a process full of conflict, can create insecurity, neo-liberal policies actually create the worst of both worlds – minimal development and intensified insecurity.

Conclusion: States, Neo-liberalism and Globalization

The argument so far can be summarized by making four main, closely related points:

(i)   There has been some considerable global movement towards neo-liberalism, as states have restructured either voluntarily or through the pressure of adjustment, or indeed a mixture of the two. This has involved institutional readjustment designed to make markets work more effectively, and in some cases, wholesale restructuring through armed intervention, which has included neo-liberal policies as part of a package that makes up post-conflict reconstruction.

(ii)   These neo-liberal policies are naive at best and counter-productive at worst. They ignore the ways in which state intervention is needed to promote a dynamic capitalism, which involves policies that encourage investment in dynamic sectors that simultaneously need well targeted protection from foreign competition. They also ignore the ways in which (capitalist) development is a conflict-ridden process, and thus downplay the fact that violence is intrinsic to the development of a 'purely political' state and 'the market economy'.

(iii)   This has enormous implications for understanding violent conflict, and failed and rogue states in much of the developing world. In this respect development, at least in the short term, is not a guarantor of security, but rather can foster insecurity. Policies designed to create liberal states in the West's perceived self-image are thus unlikely to work, and may actually be counter-productive. Certainly the fact that established powers already exist in the international economy may undermine the prospects for sustained capitalist accumulation, and instead encourage accumulation based on financial flows or specific exports out of the developing world.

(iv)   Finally, irrespective of the consequences and theoretical inconsistencies of neo-liberalism, a restructuring of states has taken place which has in many respects undermined the developmental state.

These four rather pessimistic conclusions lead to two further questions. First, what of the (capitalist) alternatives to neo-liberalism? Are there still significant varieties of capitalism in the international economy, and if so, do these represent a challenge to both (or either) US hegemony and/or neo-liberalism? And how do these varieties relate to the question of the developmental state as a continued and viable alternative in a world dominated by neo-liberal capitalism? Secondly, what of the prospects for alternatives to neo-liberalism 'from below', in the form of social movements that may challenge both (or either) US hegemony and/or neo-liberalism? And how do such movements relate to wider questions of capitalist development, and indeed of anti-capitalist alternatives? These questions are the subject of the next two chapters.

Chapter 9

Globalization, Regionalism and Hegemony

This chapter develops one of the two main themes identified at the end of chapter 8, namely, that of the question of (capitalist) alternatives to neo-liberalism. It does so by linking this issue to the related, though not identical, question of regional and/or national alternatives to US hegemony. In particular it mainly focuses on the question of alternatives from the other two parts of the global triad: East Asia and the European Union. The chapter starts by first briefly outlining current debates over the question of US hegemony, identifying those that see a renewed US hegemony in the neo-liberal era, and those who argue that US hegemony is in decline. The second and third sections then examine these questions in more detail, with specific reference to the rise of East Asia, and particularly Japan and China, in the second section, and the European Union in thew third section. The question of whether either (or both) of these represent a challenge to both US hegemony and neo-liberalism is addressed, although the chapter is careful to link, but not conflate, these two issues. The developmental implications of these questions are particularly addressed, as is the question of whether either of these two regions represents progressive alternatives to US hegemony and/or neo-liberalism. The question of hegemony is then revisited, in order to understand the historical specificity, strengths and weaknesses – and possible futures – of US hegemony, and particularly how this relates to the question of development. Finally, the conclusion brings together the argument by once again examining the question of neo-liberalism and development, with a specific focus on regionalism.

US Hegemony: Strengthening or in Decline?

The US has acted as the hegemonic power in the capitalist world since 1945. In the post-war period, this hegemony was guaranteed by overwhelming military and economic dominance, which left even the most powerful of the other capitalist countries dependent on the US, and this was reinforced by the perceived threat of the communist alternative. There have been two significant changes which have had important implications for US hegemony since then. First, there was the challenge from revived capitalist powers – particularly Japan and Germany – from the late 1960s onwards, which was reinforced by the end of the Bretton Woods agreement and the gradual shift towards neo-liberal policies from the late 1970s. This shift led to the US becoming increasingly reliant on foreign capital inflows, a process which was secured in part by the neo-liberal turn. The second change occurred with the end of communism, which secured the US's dominant, unipolar, position in the global order, albeit in the context of continued concern about revived economic competitors, including China. For some writers (Cox 1981, 1987), these two factors have given rise to the end of US hegemony, even if not the end of US domination. This is because the US is no longer in a position to control the international order, and therefore what has emerged is a transnational hegemony, beyond the control of any single state (Agnew 2005). These issues were addressed in earlier chapters, where it was concluded that the US still has considerable hegemony in the international order, even if it is increasingly reliant on the cooperation of other states and transnational forces, over which it does not have anything like full control.

But this still begs the question of what future there is for US hegemony. Some argue that we are in an era of US super-imperialism, based on the US's dominant military role, the continued strength of US companies in key economic sectors such as information technology, the continued dominance of the US domestic economy and transnational companies, and the continued dominant international role of the dollar (Gowan 1999; Hudson 2003). On the other hand, others argue that US hegemony has weakened, basing this on the comparative decline of the US economy, at least since the 1940s and 1950s, the limitations of military power in a world of sovereign states and capitalist interdependence; the rise of East Asia, increased hostility to the US under Bush II; the US budget and trade deficits; the bubble economy in the US (stock markets in the 1990s, housing in the 2000s); and the possible rise of the euro as an alternative international currency (Arrighi 1994, 2005a and 2005b; Brenner 1998, 2002, 2003; Mann 2003; Wallerstein 2003; Harvey 2003). It has also been argued that the Bush II era is one in which hegemony has declined, if not US domination, as the legitimacy of US leadership in the international order has been increasingly undermined by the unilateralist policies adopted by the United States (Harvey 2003).

Clearly, a fully convincing answer to the question of the fate of US hegemony can only be made if we also examine the rise of potential regional challengers, and the nature of the relationship between these regions and the United States. First however, a little more needs to be said about the question of the relationship between globalization and regionalism. 'Regionalism' can be defined as 'a state-led or states-led project designed to reorganize a particular regional space along defined economic and political lines' (Payne and Gamble 1996: 2). On the face of it, the latter represents a challenge to the former, as it implies a preference for one region over others. Indeed, it could even imply the resurgence of Leninist inter-imperialist rivalries, an argument made by some commentators, as we will see. But – and this point will become clearer as the chapter unfolds – the dichotomy between the regional and the global may be a false one, which closely parallels that between the nation-state and globalization discussed in Chapter 5. The rise of, among others, the European Union, the North American Free Trade Agreement, and Asia-Pacific Economic Cooperation, should be regarded not as a movement towards protectionism (at least for capital, if not for labour), but as part of a process of open regionalism in which 'policy has been directed towards the elimination of obstacles to trade within a region, while at the same time doing nothing to raise external tariff barriers to the rest of the world' (Payne 2004: 16). This is part of a strategic trade policy operated by states in the context of increased international openness. As Payne (2004: 16) explains:

> Instead of insulating the regional economy from foreign competition, the aim has been to expose it to that very competition while at the same time ensuring, via various measures, that regional competitiveness can be achieved and sustained.

The rest of the chapter is concerned less with debates over regionalism *per se*, and more with whether different regions (or nations) constitute potential challengers to US hegemony and/or neo-liberalism. However, implicit in each section is an understanding of the debate over 'open' versus 'resistant' regionalism (Nesadurai 2002), the former of which is an extension of neo-liberal globalization, and the latter of which challenges neo-liberalism.

The East Asian Challenge

The growth of the Asian region in the world economy is one that is undoubtedly under-estimated by globalization sceptics like Hirst and Thompson (see Chapter 5). Rather than 'business as usual', in which Japan is considered to be the only major economy in the East Asian region, one of the most significant changes in recent years has been the growth of Asian economies other than Japan. Thus, the share of global merchandise exports originating from (non-Japan) Asia increased from

9 per cent in 1963 to 18.3 per cent in 2001 – that is, after the crisis of 1997–8. This has included some success in breaking into the export markets in technologically more sophisticated products, such as office and telecommunications equipment, and even some success in automobiles and auto components, as well as some of the more visible labour-intensive sectors like clothing (Gibbon and Ponte 2005: 4; Kaplinsky 2005a: 154). This section therefore examines the rise of East Asia, focusing first on Japan, the country that was initially regarded as the main challenger to US hegemony. It then moves on to briefly examine again the East Asian NICs, with particular attention to South Korea, and the significance of the financial crisis of 1997–8, before finally examining in some detail the rise of China, the country that is now considered by many to lead the East Asian challenge to US hegemony.

Until the early to mid-1990s, Japan was considered to be the main rival to US economic power. Indeed, it was seen by many as embracing a new model of capitalism appropriate to the demands of the third industrial revolution (Lazonick 1991). The Japanese model was said to be based on planned coordination of firms, skilled labour, education, long-term finance of industrial production, close industry–finance links, high degrees of state intervention, and consensual labour relations (Dore 1985; Zysman and Cohen 1986; Lazonick 1991). Particular attention was paid to the role of the state, which was regarded as perhaps the first developmental state, efficiently picking winners and generating dynamic efficiency (Johnson 1995; Weiss 1997). In addition, it was often argued that this efficiency was simultaneously progressive, as employment practices were regarded as less exploitative than those in the US and Britain, though there was a tendency in these analyses to generalize from the life-time-employment practices and seniority-based wages, which actually applied to only 25–30 per cent of the workforce (Ozaki 1991). In focusing on these workers, emphasis was placed on skills and team work, and above all, the capacity of Japanese workers to respond flexibly to the requirements of an increasingly competitive world economy (Womack et al. 1990). Like the European models discussed in the previous chapter (and below), this model was regarded by some as a progressive alternative to neo-liberal American capitalism, the latter of which was not only oppressive but inefficient (Schor 1993: ch. 6; Stanfield 1994). This view downplayed the long hours, the coercive subordination of workers in subcontracted work outside of the core 25–30 per cent, the intensified work routines and the segmented labour market (Kenney and Florida 1993; Kiely 1998: ch. 9; Coates 2000). Indeed, if one can talk of a Japanese model easily transplanted to the rest of the world, then it was this dark-side that was generalized in the context of the expansion of neo-liberalism in the 1990s (see Chapter 4).

Moreover, just as academics and businesses were beginning to discuss the possibilities of (one-sided interpretation of) 'Japanization' beyond Japan, the miracle ran out of steam. And this downturn could only be satisfactorily explained by examining Japan's place in the wider international economy (Brenner 2002: ch. 3). As was briefly outlined in Chapter 5, the Plaza Accord of 1985 devalued the US dollar against competitor currencies in order to try to restore some kind of trade balance between the major economies. In this context of a revalued yen, and thus less competitive exports, the Japanese attempted to stimulate domestic demand to make up for export demand shortfalls. They did this by reducing domestic interest rates. However, this increased demand did not stimulate domestic productive investment so much as domestic speculation. Moreover, the appreciation of the yen created incentives for Japanese firms to increase direct foreign investment abroad, particularly in the rest of East Asia, and increase foreign portfolio investment, above all in foreign shares and bonds. At home, Japanese firms, banks and other financial institutions invested in real estate and capital markets, which fuelled a domestic boom, but this speculative bubble burst in 1990, which led to a loss in asset values of 1000 trillion yen by the mid-1990s. This amounted to 2.4 times Japan's GDP, which was comparable to the US's capital loss of 1.9 times its GDP after the 1929 crash (Itoh 2005: 247). The Japanese response to the recession of the 1990s was to reduce official interest rates so that they were effectively negative by the end of the decade, but this has failed to stimulate the economy. This was because shares and real estate prices continued to contract, exacerbated by falling loans by banks facing a low demand for loans and having to meet international obligations to keep the ratio of their own capital to total assets at a sustainable level. The result was increases in bankruptcies, business failures, the effective end of lifetime-employment commitments, and rising unemployment. The Japanese economy has thus faced a deflationary spiral whereby:

> the bad loans of the Japanese banks have not been cleared up and, instead, they have fed the deflationary spiral of the economy. The result has been a vicious circle, with banks facing difficulties due to their bad loans and shrinking capital base, medium and small firms running into difficulties due to the credit crunch, and the resulting deterioration in workers' employment and income leading to depressed consumer demand and deflating real estate and share prices. (Itoh 2005: 248)

By the mid-1990s then, it was clear that the Japanese miracle had run out of steam.

The first-tier East Asian newly industrializing countries were also briefly seen as potentially progressive models of development. As we saw in Chapter 3, South Korea and Taiwan did not conform to anything like the claims made for neo-liberal, market-led, development. Instead, they developed through highly interventionist states that guided the market (Amsden 1989; Wade 1990). This included policies such as selective credit allocation by nationalized banks, restrictions on foreign investment in certain sectors, restrictions on the export of capital, and rewards (such as further credit allocation or preferential access to the domestic market) to the most successful exporters. Moreover, the first-tier NICs enjoyed relatively progressive records in some respects, reflected in social-development indicators such as a high level of literacy and higher education enrolment rates, a high life expectancy, and low infant mortality rates. For much of the boom period from the 1960s to the 1990s, income distribution was less unequal than in most developing countries, including ones that experienced far lower rates of growth. Given the rise of neo-liberalism, the poor development record of many countries after 1982, and the almost wilful misinterpretation of the East Asian miracles, it was not altogether surprising that some saw these countries as representing a progressive alternative to neo-liberalism (Weiss and Hobson 1995).

This view was undermined by three factors. First, as we saw in the last chapter, the idea that the developmental state represented a model for developing countries ignored the specific historical and social reasons for success in East Asia. Second, it tended to under-estimate negative social and political factors, such as high degrees of state repression, high rates of workplace accidents, and environmental problems (Kiely 1998: ch. 8). But third, by 1997, the East Asian region went into crisis. The region had gradually liberalized controls on finance in the 1990s, which facilitated massive capital inflows. This continued even after 1995, when the US dollar was revalued upwards, and with it other Asian currencies that were effectively tied to the dollar. However, faced with growing international competition (especially from China), and lower rates of global economic growth, returns on the value (though not volume) of exports fell in 1996. South Korea's export growth declined from 31.5 per cent in 1995 to 4.1 per cent in 1996; Thailand's from 24.7 per cent to 0.1 per cent; and Malaysia's from 25.9 per cent to 4 per cent (UNCTAD 1997: 14). However, the speculative boom persisted, driven by the appreciation of dollar-tied currencies. But by 1997, faced with declining competitiveness and falling profits, money began to leave the region in enormous amounts and the downward spiral of currency speculation, falling equity prices, higher interest payments and bankruptcies began. In 1997 alone, East Asia saw a $93 billion inflow become a $12 billion outflow, the equivalent of 11 per cent of combined GDP for the five main countries affected – South Korea, Thailand, the Philippines, Malaysia and

Indonesia (Wade and Veneroso 1998: 20). The region entered a severe recession. South Korea's per capita income fell from $11,380 in 1996 to $6472 in 1998 (Burkett and Hart-Landsberg 2001: 11). Unemployment increased from 2.1 per cent in October 1997 to 8.6 per cent in February 1999 (Crotty and Lee 2002: 669). In Indonesia, unemployment soared from 4.9 per cent to 13.8 per cent and real wages fell by between 40 and 60 per cent (World Bank 2000).

The debate over the causes of the crisis has spilled over into wider debate over the nature of the crisis economies since 1997–8. Broadly, there are two positions in the debate. First, neo-Keynesians argue that the crisis was a result of neo-liberal policies that preceded the crash, and particularly financial liberalization. The fundamentals of the real economy were healthy, as measured by growth rates and employment levels, but these were wrecked by the activities of financial speculators (Wade 1998). On the other hand, neo-liberal commentators argue that crony capitalism existed in the region, and this was caused by inefficient state interventions (Gobat 1998; OECD 1998), which undermined the effective functioning of markets. A third position focuses on the relative economic recovery in the region since the crash and argues that this is a result of the return of the old interventionist policies of the developmental state, which have returned to restore efficiency to East Asian capitalism (Weiss 2003). This position is thus sympathetic to the neo-Keynesian explanation for the crisis, though it differs in terms of the post-crisis scenario, as many in the first camp argue that East Asian – and more specifically, South Korean – capitalism, has moved in a neo-liberal direction. A further position suggests that while the developmental state was central to the East Asian miracle, state restructuring has led to an increasingly neo-liberal state, but this means that South Korea is now trapped in a cycle of low growth, low investment and low-value production (Shin and Chang 2003).

There are problems with all of these positions however (Pirie 2006a), and these can best be illustrated by focusing on the most successful economy that crashed in 1997–8, South Korea. Focusing on crony capitalism and citing many examples to back up this claim ignores the fact that it was the close ties between state, industry and finance, and soft budget constraints that facilitated the miracle in the first place. In a scenario of hard budget constraints, and market coordination, it is unlikely that South Korea would have successfully developed many new industries. It is true that Korean firms generally existed in a state of marginal insolvency (Wade and Veneroso 1998), something emphasized by neo-liberals after the crisis, but this practice was necessary for the miracle to occur in the first place. South Korean firms were always far more dependent on external sources of finance than, say, US firms, but this reflected their weaker competitive position as a late developer. Seen in this way, neo-liberal explanations for the crash are problematic.

But then so too are the neo-Keynesian arguments, for these under-estimate the ways in which domestic capitalist classes and state elites pressurized the state for reforms, and the very real problems faced by the Korean economy, prior to the crash (Chibber 2005). In particular, there was pressure for financial liberalization and labour market reform, both of which met with considerable success. Indeed, these were related to the wider economic problems, as Korean firms faced crises of profitability, limited access to funds, and increasingly resented state controls. On the eve of the crisis, the leading thirty conglomerates (*chaebols*) recorded returns on assets of just 0.23 per cent, and so were effectively not making any significant money at all (Pirie 2006a: 55). Highly dependent on export markets, Korean capital was desperate to access global capital markets, and so, successfully pressurized the state to liberalize financial controls. While this gave capital access to foreign savings, which was increasingly necessary in the context of increasing start-up costs and research and development expenses associated with the growing globalization of capital (see Chapter 5), it also meant that Korea was increasingly subject to speculative flows as well, and thus faced the danger of the abrupt movement of capital that did take place. Nevertheless, while this speculative capital may have exacerbated problems in 1997–8, it was certainly not entirely divorced from shifts in the 'real economy'. What is clear, then, is that the developmental state 'model' relied on high levels of household savings and high rates of corporate debt, precisely because so much finance was committed to industries that were intended to secure dynamic, long-term gains, and which therefore entailed high start-up and running costs (Wade and Veneroso 1998). This worked so long as there was sufficient demand in the world economy, but was undermined by intensified competition in many sectors coinciding with slower rates of economic growth and a profits crisis. In this context, Korea (and the region) was particularly vulnerable to volatile swings in international finance, particularly in those countries with more liberal financial systems.

This brief discussion suggests that the simplistic divide between too much and not enough state intervention is inadequate. Indeed, as the last chapter suggested, too much of the literature that welcomes developmental states concedes too much to neo-liberalism in its understanding of the role of the state, seeing *any* form of intervention as a challenge to neo-liberalism (Radice 2000). Furthermore, in the context of the 'post-Washington consensus', which accepts a significant regulatory role for the state (Stiglitz 2002), much of this debate misses the point. As Pirie (2006a: 54) suggests in relation to the causes of the crash, there is a reasonably broad consensus which only radical free marke-teers and those scholars who are simply opposed to any form of capital account liberalization stand outside, which understands the Korean crisis as being a result of regulatory failures. For the large majority of scholars the crisis stemmed from the failure of the state to discipline domestic firms and financial institutions either directly, or through more market-based controls.

This reflects the post-Washington consensus, but still neo-liberal view of the World Bank (1997: 5) – and Joseph Stiglitz – that advocates 'care-fully sequenced liberalization and the strong market enabling regulatory state'. This point has implications for the view that the region – and Korea in particular – has recovered by reverting to *dirigiste* type, and adopted the older policies of the developmental state. Certainly there were widespread nationalizations in the immediate aftermath of the crisis, but these were necessary to implement a wider process of neo-liberal recomposition, which included takeover of failing financial insti-tutions, restructuring of the chaebols, the selling of firms and banks to foreign capital, and the coordination of debt restructuring and rational-ization. These reforms have led to the death of the developmental state (in South Korea at least), for instance, through: the creation of an inde-pendent central bank, which has disabled the Ministry of Finance from exercising monetary policy, and thereby undermined the state's capacity to coordinate industrial policy; efforts to create accounting standards more in line with US Generally Accepted Accounting Principles; liberal-ization of mergers and acquisitions laws; the speed-up of bankruptcy proceedings; the tightening of capital adequacy and solvency standards (Pirie 2005a, 2006a). It is in this context of restructuring that prof-itability was restored for Korean capital – in manufacturing, it reached 7 per cent by 2004, its highest level since 1968 (Pirie 2006a: 62). These policies clearly reflected a shift towards the shareholder value outlined in Chapter 4.

Clearly then, the notion that South Korea continues to represent a challenge to neo-liberalism is problematic. Like much of the 'progressive competitiveness' and 'varieties of capitalism' approaches discussed in the previous chapter, this view tends to endow states with unchanging capacities, unaffected by the broader social and political context, both domestically and internationally (Jayasuriya 2005). On the other hand, whether or not the Korean national economy will continue to be an important competitive player is an open question, but even if it does, it hardly confirms the claims made by neo-liberal apologists. This is not only because of the centrality of the state in first securing competitive advantages, and the implicit lessons this holds for any developing country, but also because of the related point that Korean neo-liberal competitiveness does not necessarily mean that others at lower levels of development can also become competitive. Moreover, this competitiveness has been achieved through significant costs to labour, including less secure employment, falling living standards in the short term, the redistribution of income from labour to capital, and the intensification of work (Pirie 2006b).

Equally, we should be careful not to reduce the East Asian crisis to one managed by the US in its own interests (see, for instance, Burke 2001). This view is close to that of the 'super-imperialism' and 'inter-imperialist rivalry' positions outlined in Chapter 5. Ironically, in suggesting that regional blocs act in their own interests in isolation from other blocs, it replicates some of the assumptions of those that continue to regard the region as a progressive, developmentalist alternative to US-led neo-liberalism.[1] What the brief account of the crisis suggests, however, is that restructuring had significant domestic as well as international sources, and was not simply imposed by the IMF or the US Treasury, even if these did have important roles to play.

There remains, however, the question of the biggest – and for some, most threatening – East Asian challenger, that of China. The rise of China is particularly important for the concerns of this chapter. For some (neo-liberal) advocates of globalization, China's rise is central to their case that globalization is good for development. Thus, as we saw in Chapter 7, much of the case made by the World Bank for the link between globalization and poverty reduction is based on the fall in the number of people in China living on less than one (PPP) dollar a day. Critics, on the other hand, argue that the massive growth in China cannot be explained simply by the beneficial effects of globalization. Rather, Chinese development fits more closely into the model of the 'developmentalist state', outlined in Chapters 3 and 8. For this reason, and like the other East Asian 'success stories' before it, China may be regarded as offering a possible alternative to that of Anglo-American, neo-liberal capitalism. A third position also recognizes that China is not a neo-liberal model, but is more sceptical about the Chinese 'success story'. This position suggests that China is an example of sustained capitalist accumulation, but (like other capitalist developers) has been undergoing a highly contradictory and conflict-ridden process, even if significant social gains (for some) have been made.

A second debate draws on the rise of China, to examine the broader geopolitical implications. Unlike Japan, South Korea and other East Asian newly industrializing countries, China is not necessarily a clear ally of the United States. Certainly there has been a process of engagement between China and the US since the last years of Mao, in the early to mid-1970s. But tensions have remained, not least over human rights and repression in China (particularly in 1989), and over the issue of relations with Taiwan. These geopolitical questions are made more complex by China's economic rise, and by the increased interdependence between the US and China. This is reflected in growing tensions over trade and investment issues, but also a growing awareness that interdependence has locked both countries into a state of mutual dependence. This has led to a specific debate over US–China relations, which essentially echoes the broader debates over globalization, imperialism and the liberal-democratic peace, which were discussed in Chapters 5 and 8. Will the geopolitical tensions and economic competition give rise to a new era of inter-imperialist competition, with the possibility of war? Or will economic interdependence and, as we will see, some thawing of geopolitical tensions, alongside political reform within China, mean the growth of the liberal zone of peace and/or ultra-imperialist cooperation? Or are these theories too general and abstract, and should the relationship be theorized in a way that allows more room for contingency and specificity (as Kautsky suggested)? These issues will be addressed by first examining the economic rise of China and looking at explanations for this development. The social tensions that have been generated by the Chinese miracle will then be examined, and finally, the question of the rise of China and the international order will be addressed.

China's growth since the late 1970s has undoubtedly been impressive. From 1978 to 2001 its annual average growth rate was 8.1 per cent and its annual rate of industrial growth was 11.5 per cent. Exports grew from $18.1 billion in 1978 to $266 billion in 2001, reflecting an annual average growth rate of 12 per cent. By 2001, manufacturing exports accounted for 90 per cent of total exports (Nolan 2004: 3, 9–10). These impressive figures were part of a deliberate shift away from the Maoist era of central planning, alongside some disastrous experiments in Chinese socialism, such as the Great Leap Forward in the late 1950s and the Cultural Revolution of the 1960s and 1970s. Instead, the policy of the Four Modernizations was introduced, which endorsed the idea of promoting market reforms and some private enterprise. More specifically, it has involved the abolition of the agrarian commune system, allowing more autonomy from the state and party apparatus for individual enterprises; the (controlled) promotion of the private sector; and a greater openness to foreign trade and investment. This included the promotion of special economic zones, and specified priority areas for investment, including by transnational companies (White 1993: 42–50).

These policies did lead to substantial growth in the 1980s, although there was a marked slowdown at the end of that decade. But it was from the early 1990s that the Chinese miracle was most pronounced. This in part reflected the boom in direct foreign investment from the early 1990s, discussed in Chapter 7. Indeed, direct foreign investment in China soared from 1992 onwards. In 1983, inflows were (at constant prices) $636 million; in 1984, $126 million; in 1988, $319 million; in 1991, 436 million; in 1992, $1.1 billion; in 1993, $2.75 billion; in 1993, $3.37 billion; in 1998, $4.55 billion, before falling back to $4.03 billion in 1999 and recovering to $5.27 billion in 2002 (Harvey 2005: 124). Much of this investment came from neighbours such as Hong Kong, where manufacturing employment fell as capital relocated to the mainland. By 2000, Hong Kong capital employed as much as 5 million workers in China (Hore 2004: 10).

But, for all its economic growth, it is difficult to regard China as a neo-liberal miracle. Certainly average tariffs fell substantially in the 1990s, but by the end of the decade they still stood at 25 per cent, and were much higher in some sectors, such as vehicle imports (80 to 100 per cent) and farm products (31 per cent). Moreover, non-tariff barriers (such as technology transfer or joint venture requirements in some sectors) were still in place (Nolan 2001: 18). In the 1990s, 120 large enterprise groups were selected by the State Council, in sectors regarded as being of strategic importance: electricity generation, coal mining, automobiles, electronics, pharmaceuticals, transport and aerospace. These have included the most cutting edge sectors within these industries, such as IT hardware. China's industrial policy has therefore been similar to those of both Japan and South Korea, in that the state has deliberately attempted to foster large companies, or 'national champions'. This strategy has occurred in a different context from that of its East Asian predecessors, who developed (or in the case of Japan, recovered) in the Bretton Woods era, which gave far more room for state-directed development, and who enjoyed a close strategic relationship with the United States which in many ways facilitated further economic development. Certainly some progress has been made, but unlike in Japan and South Korea, not one single company has emerged as a globally competitive player. Indeed, as Nolan (2001: 91) points out, 'in export markets, China's aspiring global giant corporations must content themselves mainly with selling lower end sophisticated products (for example, power stations, steel mills, fighter planes), mainly to other developing countries'. Otherwise, these firms concentrate on the domestic market or export in low-value sectors such as bicycles and motor-bikes. In the *Financial Times* (*FT*) 500 (based on market capitalization), China had just three firms. These were the China National Offshore Oil Company (CNOOC), China Mobile, and China Unicom, each of which operates in a protected domestic market. In one category in the *Fortune 500*, China had six of the top ten firms, but this was in terms of number of employees, and each one of these was mainly state owned and protected – something which is likely to change with WTO membership. For neo-liberals, these failings reflect the inefficiencies of industrial policy, and they contend that growth has occurred despite, rather than because of such a policy. By implication, growth would be even greater if the Chinese state was further liberalized and good governance and market friendly intervention were extended by an enabling state. At the very least, China's growth is attributable to its market conforming policies, while future potential problems are attributable to 'market supplanting' policies (Fan and Woo 1996; World Bank 2002c).

But as we have seen from earlier chapters, this view wrongly assumes that the international economy represents a level playing field, to be embraced through open policies in order to allow development to occur. This ignores the strong tendencies towards capital concentration, and supports the reversal of policies (such as industrial policy) designed to alleviate these tendencies. Thus, if we examine the international context in which China has attempted to promote national champions, we see some movement towards the transnationalization of capital. This was discussed in Chapters 5 and 7, but was also criticized for its failure to adequately describe and account for the growing international concentration of capital. Thus, high-income economies (with 16 per cent of the world's population) account for 91 per cent of stock market capitalization, 95 per cent of the *Fortune 500*, 97 per cent of the *FT 500*, 99 per cent of research and development spending of the top 300 firms, and 99 per cent of top brands. The developing world, including China, with 84 per cent of the population, accounted for just 26 of the *Fortune 500* companies (about 5 per cent), sixteen of the *FT 500* (about 3 per cent), one of the top 100 brands, and none of the Research and Development 300. To get some sort of perspective – and of considerable relevance in discussing US economic hegemony – North America (with 5 per cent of the world's population) makes up 40 per cent of the *Fortune 500*, 50 per cent of the *FT 500*, and 54 per cent of Morgan Stanley Den Witter's 'global competitive edge' firms (compared with 6 per cent for the developing world) (Nolan 2004: 23).

It is in this context that China's industrial policy should be located. Like the East Asian miracles, China has some of the characteristics of a 'high household saving, high corporate debt' development strategy (Lo 2005). Like earlier strategies led by developmental states, this involves a commitment to long-term, industrial upgrading, which in turn relies on high-intensity investment, rather than simply competing in the world economy on the basis of 'static' comparative advantage. Instead, investment is characterized by high start-up costs and slow returns – conditions not conducive to development led by the market. This strategy relies heavily on bank-led finance mediated by states who direct credit into certain potentially dynamic and high-value sectors. As we saw above, in the case of East Asia, this strategy worked so long as there was a favourable external environment, but once this changed, a financial crisis became much more likely, even if financial interests ultimately exacerbated its severity. In the case of China, it is less susceptible to a 1997-style crisis because its foreign debts are low, it has large foreign exchange reserves, and state controls over its capital account still exist. The last of these is likely to change with WTO membership, but of more immediate relevance is the problem of non-performing loans to domestic industries. These constitute anywhere between 25 and 50 per cent of total bank lending, depending on the performance of the economy at any particular time. State-owned enterprises have high debts, but these can be managed in a context of expanding market demand. Contrary to popular perception, state-owned enterprises have actually *increased* their share of output and capital share in recent years, even as employment has fallen in this sector (Lo 2005: 7–8). Average state-owned enterprise debt to asset ratio increased from 19 per cent in 1980 to 79 per cent in 1994, before falling back to 59 per cent in 2002 (Lo 2005: 8), which reflects changing external demand conditions.

In this way, then, China is not unlike the earlier East Asian NICs in that there are high household savings and high corporate debt, which are used to reward good performance through enhanced access to capital. China has had some success in investing in dynamic industries, but this has not been matched by similar success in terms of exports in these sectors. Thus, as Lo (2005: 10–11) points out, 'in the context of steadily expanding market demand, institutions that are infused with rigidities and long-term orientations have the advantage of promoting productivity growth through dynamic increasing returns, particularly collective learning effects. The downside of such institutions though, is their inflexibility in adjusting to cope with demand contraction.' Thus, state-owned enterprises (SOEs) outperformed non-SOEs in the 1980s, but not in the demand-deficient 1990s, before making a substantial recovery at the start of the new century. These issues are lost on neo-liberals and those who regard globalization as a matter of simple opportunity for developing countries. But, in the context of the increasing global dominance of neo-liberal capitalism, such issues are likely to have far-reaching implications for China's future (see below).

It is true, however, that China has undoubtedly been successful in exporting low-value, labour-intensive goods. Thus, in 2003 the US retail company Wal-Mart imported $15 billion worth of products from China, which accounted for as much as 11 per cent of all US imports from China (Kaplinksy 2005a: 176). As earlier chapters have showed, China has also successfully expanded its market share in labour-intensive sectors such as clothing, and this is likely to expand further as the effect of the phasing out of quotas takes hold. Thus, in clothing sectors where there have been quota removals, China's share has increased enormously. For instance, in 2002, the US removed quotas in 29 categories of clothing, and China's share in these sectors rose from 9 per cent to 65 per cent, as prices fell by an average of 48 per cent (Kaplinsky 2005a: 176). Indeed, since 1990, the growth of China's exports in absolute amounts has exceeded that of the rest of the top 10 leading manufacturing exporters from the developing world, and since 2000, the latter nine countries' combined export share has fallen whilst China's has risen (Eichengreen et al. 2004). But it is not necessarily only the case that China has risen while others have fallen. Breslin (2005: 742–4) suggest that China's rise itself may be exaggerated, as its economic miracle cannot be divorced from its role in East Asian production networks. In particular, China specializes in completing the production of low-value, labour-intensive goods, and relies on technologies produced in other East Asian countries, with whom it has a substantial trade deficit. Moreover, the East Asian region provided over 50 per cent of total foreign investment into China for much of the 1990s.

This argument suggests then that while China's rise is in many respects globally significant, it may also be exaggerated, and indeed there are further sources of domestic tension. Thus, while China's balance of trade and payments are healthy, it also has a high level of internal debt. This has come about through budget deficits and the over-extension of bank loans, particularly to state-owned enterprises (see above), with the result that between 25 and 50 per cent of loans made by the biggest four banks are effectively non-performing. Thus, in 2003 central government transferred $45 billion from its foreign exchange reserves to two of the biggest government banks, the third large bail-out in six years (Harvey 2005: 129). While, as we have seen, such financing is characteristic of strategies involving the developmental state, it is also true that this deficit financing is vulnerable to fuller integration into the global financial system, something expected of WTO members after a period of transition. WTO membership was agreed in 1999 and came into effect in 2001, but this has occurred 'at the point at which the degree of unevenness of business capability has never been greater' (Nolan 2001: 187). China was given a five-year adjustment period before fuller implementation of WTO rules, which would include a reduction in average tariff levels from 24.6 per cent to 9.4 per cent, the observation of WTO rules on trade-related investment measures (TRIM), the elimination of local-content requirements for foreign investment, increases in guarantees for intellectual property, and open access for foreign firms to sell to SOEs.

In the automobiles sector tariffs were to be reduced from 80–100 per cent to 25 per cent by 2006, and quotas were to be phased out, chemicals from 15 per cent to 7 per cent by 2005, and steel from 10.3 per cent to 6.1 per cent by the end of 2002 (Nolan 2001: 198–205). Optimists argue that this will allow China to specialize in its most competitive sectors and shed those high-cost industries that constitute a drain on the economy. Upgrading will occur as it did for earlier East Asian miracle economies. Certainly, as we have seen, quota reductions have allowed China to increase its market share in lower-value activities – though this was likely to happen whether or not China joined the WTO. This does not, however, mean that a transition to higher-value production will necessarily occur. Certainly the first-tier NICs upgraded and developed in a very different international environment, which gave far more room for the interventions associated with the developmental state. Based on the arguments in this section – and throughout the book – a more likely scenario over the long term is an increase in the value of its imports compared with its exports, as China has little chance of competing in the most dynamic sectors in the world economy (Nolan 2003). Certainly it is unlikely that the 'high household saving, high corporate debt' model associated with Chinese developmentalism can be sustained in the context of greater global integration. Having said that, the future will in part depend on the processes of liberalization agreed through WTO entry, and as early as 2003 some foreign companies were complaining that China was not meeting its obligations on market access (Breslin 2005: 739–40).

The argument that the rise of China demonstrates that 'globalization' or 'the world economy' somehow represents a level playing field in which all can participate is unconvincing. This certainly means that China does not represent a neo-liberal model for others to follow, but equally it does not necessarily mean that China represents an alternative model to that of neo-liberalism. First, the very rise of China may have enormous implications for any would-be followers. Neo-liberals regard the rise of China as an opportunity for others, as increased exports translate into greater income and therefore increased potential for others to export to the expanding Chinese market. Certainly China's production has tended to rely more on increased imports of inputs, and from 1980 to 1998 the proportion of export revenue that reflected direct imports into production processes rose from 8 to 12 per cent, and the percentage of imports that went into the production of domestically sourced inputs grew from 15 to 23 per cent. Demand for imports has particularly increased in consumer goods, food and metal-based products (Kaplinsky 2005a: 206). Some Latin American countries have expanded their food and raw material exports into China at rapid rates, including Brazil,

Argentina and oil-exporting Venezuela. In 2004 Latin American exports expanded by 37 per cent, much of which was accounted for by rising demand in East Asia, especially China (WTO 2005: 11). The value of iron and steel, ores and minerals and non-ferrous metals increased by between 30 and 45 per cent in 2004, which reflected rising demand from China, which is now the leading importer of many commodities (WTO 2005: 1–2). Some African countries, particularly Sudan and Congo, have also benefited from expansion into the Chinese market, as have East Asian countries.

It is thus mistaken to view the rise of China as a simple zero-sum game, in which China's rise occurs merely at the expense of other developing countries, as some dependency-oriented writers suggest (Burkett and Hart-Landsberg 2004). However, as we have also seen, the question of opportunities for other developing countries to break into new export markets assumes that each country has the capacity to switch production from one sector to another in a relatively painless and costless way (thus preserving Ricardo's full-employment assumption), and that each country has the capacity to compete in sufficient sectors to find a space in these new markets (thus preserving Ricardo's assumption of equal production capacities). In other words, comparative advantage does not necessarily generate competitive advantage, and the result is that dynamic competition between capitalist states leads to uneven development. This is not a zero-sum game, precisely because such competition is dynamic and gives rise to accumulation, but neither does it generate the win–win situation envisaged by neo-liberalism. The 2005–6 global commodities boom fuelled by rising demand in China is significant, but it should be seen in the context of the longer-term tendency for primary commodity prices to fall. Moreover, prices are likely to fall in the future if there is a slowdown in the world economy, probably in the event of adjustments made to redress trade imbalances, particularly between the US and China. Furthermore, increased production in response to increased demand will also mean longer-term price falls, exacerbated by speculators rapidly withdrawing investments in once booming commodities.

In terms of generating competitive capacity, the future is also not as benign as neo-liberals suggest. As we have seen, rather than international competition generating a level playing field, the world economy is better characterized as one in which oligopolistic competition exists, whereby dynamic producers enhance their advantages by generating rents in the most dynamic sectors of the international economy, thus leaving others behind. These others are likely to find some export successes, and direct foreign investment may further encourage this process, but these are likely to be in sectors where there are low barriers to entry and therefore they may be subject to falling prices which are not sufficiently compensated by revenues from increased export sales. In the context of a world economy in which there exists high degrees of capital concentration, a massive reserve army of labour, and over-capacity in many sectors, the prospects for rapid development for all are not great. In this respect the rise of China does not represent a model for the rest of the world, neo-liberal or otherwise, and in some ways it acts as a constraint on the development prospects for others. Indeed, as we saw in Chapter 7, the greater China's participation in global products markets, the more likely it was that these prices would fall, and this had a particularly adverse effect on other low-income countries who faced competition from China (Kaplinsky 2005b: 12). And we have suggested in this chapter that – at a regional level at least – the winners in China's rise have been capital goods exporters and the losers have been those countries specializing in labour-intensive goods. Moreover, this scenario has implications for understanding imbalances in the world economy characterized by both increased interdependence and US hegemony, a point I return to below.

To return to the immediate question however, we should also not lose sight of the fact that Chinese development has come at a great cost to much of the population, even if many of these same people may have also won significant rewards. Thus, for instance, the proportion of people living in absolute poverty in the countryside declined from 31.3 per cent in 1990 to 10.9 per cent in 2002, while undernourishment has declined from 16 per cent of the population in 1990 to 9 per cent in 2000 (Woo et al. 2004). Even if we treat these figures with some scepticism, particularly those relating to poverty reduction (see Chapter 7), the fact remains that there have been significant – and positive – changes for a large section of the population. But at the same time, while poverty has been reduced, inequalities have increased and these reflect very real tensions within the Chinese miracle. About 70 per cent of the population still live in the countryside. However, employment in agriculture has been relatively stagnant despite substantial population increases. While the total population increased by around 16 million a year, and the working age population grew from 679 million in 1990 to 829 million by 1999, employment in agriculture fell slightly, from 333 million in 1995 to 329 million in 1999. It has been estimated that there could be as many as 150 million surplus farm workers. Moreover, employment in township and village enterprises has also stagnated. While the proportion of people living in the countryside has remained more or less constant, the share of the rural population in total consumption has fallen from 60 per cent in the early 1980s to 42 per cent by 2001. This has also occurred in the context of growing inequality: income distribution in the countryside has also increased, with the rural Gini co-efficient moving from 0.21 in 1978 to 0.4 in 1998. Indeed, some estimates suggest that rural poverty is actually increasing (Nolan 2004: 11–13). Thus, Woo et al (2004) argue that the proportion of rural residents with an income of less than 50 cents a day rose from 1.8 per cent to 2.9 per cent between 1996 and 2002, while the proportion of rural residents with a daily income below $1 a day (PPP adjusted) has stagnated at 11 per cent over the same period.

These problems are likely to be exacerbated by the gradual movement towards trade liberalization which will result from China's entry into the WTO, leading to cheap imports from overseas competitors, even if the liberalization processes envisaged from WTO membership have in some respects stalled (see above).

Moreover, the incidence of rural poverty is likely to have adverse effects on wages for unskilled and semi-skilled workers, including in the towns. This is because declining or stagnant rural incomes make migration to the towns more likely, which puts downwards pressure on wages in those sectors. This has been exacerbated by growing unemployment in the towns – employment in state-owned enterprises fell from 76 million in 1995 to 35 million by 2002 (Harvey 2005: 128). Regular employment in the urban, non-state-owned formal sector grew from 21 million in 1995 to 35 million in 1999, but this is nowhere near enough to cope with rural–urban migration and lay-offs in other sectors (Khan and Riskin 2001; Nolan 2004: 14–15; Liu and Wu 2006). For all the talk of the foreign investment boom, employment in that sector has increased from 5.1 million in 1995 to just 7.6 million in 2002 (Harvey 2005: 128). As we saw in Chapter 7, the existence of this reserve army is likely to have adverse consequences, not only for Chinese workers, but also for unskilled workers in other countries dependent on a wage in low-value sectors where there are low barriers to entry. This applies not only to wages, but to work conditions, and China has a very poor record in terms of working hours and safety (www.chinalaborwatch.org).

These low wages and poor conditions contrast sharply with the conditions for a small minority. Indeed, it has been suggested that the new clusters of foreign investment, financial districts and high-tech parks are new versions of the old nineteenth-century Treaty Ports. These areas have high degrees of autonomy, high earnings for a privileged minority, and only highly unequal linkages with the rest of society. Perhaps around 20 million people in the towns have average incomes similar to those for the first-tier NICS, and assuming similar rates of growth for the next decade, this may increase by a further 20 million in 10 years. This is of course a significant number of people, but it amounts to much lower average incomes than are to be found in the high-income countries, and constitutes only 20 per cent of the urban population in China (Nolan 2004: 16–17).

China also faces enormous environmental problems related to its industrialization strategy. While it has limited supplies of oil and gas, China has huge reserves of coal, but these have been mined, transported and used in a highly destructive way. Much of the coal is of a high-sulphur variety, is burned on open fires and using primitive boilers. China's global share of carbon dioxide emissions increased from 10.8 per cent in 1980 to 14.6 per cent by mid-1996, and China is likely to overtake the US as the main producer in the near future (Nolan 2004: 28–9).

These problems and tensions do have implications for understanding China's role in the international sphere. Certainly there may be a tendency to exaggerate the rise of China, and ignore the ways in which domestic conflicts and problems may serve to weaken its international role. Thus in the case of the European Union, China's largest export market, imports from outside the EU only account for 10 per cent of its total goods and services, and China accounts for only 10 per cent of these (Harman 2006: 82). Despite the doubling of the ratio per capita of GDP compared with the US over the past 20 years, China is still as far behind the US as South Korea and Taiwan were before their thirty-year period of rapid development from the 1960s, and is well below the position from which Japan started its rapid growth in the mid-1950s (Glyn 2006: 88–9). This sort of evidence led the late Gerald Segal (2004) to question the view that China really mattered – or at least mattered as much as some people suggested. But at the same time, neither should we deny the rise of China, as if continued domestic poverty and rising inequality somehow negate China's growing domestic economy and enhanced international role. Moreover, focusing on per capita, and PPP adjusted GNP, as Segal does, is not very useful, as it is the combination of high growth and its happening in such a heavily populated country that is most significant (Harris 2004).[2] China's share of world (PPP adjusted[3]) GDP has increased from 5 per cent in 1980 to 14 per cent in 2005, and its share of world trade is close to Japan's peak in the early 1990s of around 9 per cent (Glyn 2005: 16, 20).

The rise of China is particularly important because the United States has at times regarded China less as a strategic partner and more as a strategic competitor, a policy that Segal (2004: 19–20) himself suggested was both necessary and potentially effective – necessary because China was a potential threat, and effective because it was not yet an actual threat. As we saw in Chapter 5, this was a theme in the formation of the neo-conservative *Project for the New American Century* in 1997, and neo-conservatives continue to advocate a far more abrasive policy towards China, and indeed are frustrated by what they see as the weakness of the Bush administration in this regard (Schmitt and Blumenthal

2005). Conservative realists, who accept the neo-conservative position on US primacy but are far more sceptical of the latter's supposed liberal idealism,[4] also tend to suggest that China should be treated as a strategic rival. This is the position of both Henry Kissinger and the US's most prominent realist thinker, John Mearsheimer (see Nolan 2004: Arrighi 2005b). Tensions, such as those that exist over US arms sales to Taiwan, and the redevelopment of the strategic defence initiative, have led some to argue that relations between the US and China are best characterized as being based on (potential or actual) rivalry between major capitalist powers. Thus, arguing from a classical Marxist (Leninist) position, Hore (2004: 24–5) argues that:

> China's rise to being an economic and military threat to US imperialism is both a product of, and an increasingly necessary prop for, US capitalism. As economic ties deepen between the US and China, so too will political and military tensions. It is glaringly obvious that the neoliberals' dream of global economic integration leading to a decrease in military competition is precisely the reverse of reality. We still live in the world of imperialism as Bukharin and Lenin described it almost 100 years ago, where greater economic integration and competition lead to a greater, not a lesser danger of wars.

This position is echoed, albeit with some qualifications, from the conservative right, by John Mearsheimer (2001), and before him Bernstein and Munro (1998). Just before 11 September, Mearsheimer argued that

> China is still far away from the point where it has enough [economic] power to make a run at regional hegemony. So it is not too late for the United States to ... do what it can to slow the rise of China. In fact, the structural imperatives of the international system, which are powerful, will probably force the United States to abandon its policy of constructive engagement in the near future. Indeed, there are signs that the new Bush administration has taken the first steps in this direction. (Mearsheimer 2001: 402)

Although Mearsheimer is far from being a neo-conservative,[5] this point at least echoes Bush's emphasis on using US primacy to pre-empt the rise of *potential* as well as actual hostile powers. Following 11 September, Mearsheimer was even more blunt:

> The United States will go to great lengths ... to contain China and to cut China off at the knees, the way it cut Imperial Germany off at the knees in World War I, the way it cut Imperial Japan at the knees in World War Two, and the way it cut the Soviet Union off at the knees during the Cold War.   (quoted in Arrighi 2005b: 74–5)

The Bush administration was initially determined to break from what it perceived to be Clinton's policy of constructive engagement with China. The extent to which Clinton actually promoted this policy is open to debate, not least as there were ongoing tensions as China increased its military spending after the 1991 Gulf War, the US ordered battleships into the region in response to missile-firing exercises by the Chinese close to Taiwan, and the bombing of the Chinese embassy in Belgrade in 1999 increased tensions. But it seems equally clear that whatever the reality of Clintonite policy, the Bush administration planned to adopt a more abrasive attitude to China, a policy that suited both conservative realists and neo-conservatives.

However, this policy shifted in the context of the war on terror. China supported US policy in Afghanistan and effectively did the same over the decision to go to war in Iraq, albeit in the latter case amidst increased suspicion towards the US. This has not led to the greater hostility that many Bush supporters advocated, and indeed the administration has made the boast that it has enjoyed closer relations with China than any since Mao's rapprochement with Nixon in 1972 (cited in Arrighi 2005b: 75). Now of course the realists and neo-conservatives (and Leninists) may argue that this is only temporary and that, anyway, the war on terror will in the long run exacerbate tensions. The war on terror has led to the expansion of US bases in Central Asia, not so far from the Chinese border. Moreover, the National Security Strategy (2002) argued that the war on terror would have an effect on those countries that were not the US's immediate enemies, deterring them 'from pursuing a military build up in the hope of surpassing, or equaling the power of the United States'. This was similar to statements made by Wolfowitz ten years earlier, when there was some uncertainty as to who these competitors might be, but by 2002 it was clear that the main potential threat was perceived to be China. The Bush administration has also occasionally made criticisms of China's strategic policy, such as implying in June 2005 that China's official defence expenditure was much higher than officially admitted (Jacques 2005). There are also tensions over trade and market access, such as those over access for Chinese textiles to the US (and EU) market, and some have suggested that there is a new scramble for Africa led by competing US and Chinese interests. Certainly China has turned to Africa in search of resources, particularly oil, and has engaged in foreign investment with national petroleum and gas interests in Sudan, Angola, Algeria and Gabon (Alden 2005). China has also invested in Africa to secure preferential access to the EU and US markets for some of the poorest African countries. Clearly then, significant differences exist, and there has been a major debate since the early 1990s in both China and the US over the so-called 'China threat' (Callahan 2005).

But, it could equally be argued that while both economic and military tensions exist, there are simultaneously strong grounds for cooperation. This is not an argument that endorses the liberal-democratic peace thesis, but rather one that suggests that relations between states are more contingent than realists and Leninists contend. Indeed, some have argued that the war on terror has increased US reliance on China (Qingguo 2003). Arrighi (2005b: 76) argues that 'the more the US became entangled in the War on Terror and dependent on cheap foreign credit and commodities, the more successful was China in bringing to bear a different kind of "structural imperative" to those envisaged by Mearsheimer'. The expense of the war on terror, coupled with the ongoing twin deficits in the US (Chapter 5 and below), has meant that the US is increasingly dependent on foreign capital, including Chinese capital. China's trade surplus with the rest of the world apart from the US increased from $32 billion in 2004 to $102 billion in 2005, and its surplus with the US increased from $80 billion in 2004 to $114 billion in 2005[6] (www.bbc.co.uk). This occurred despite the appreciation of the yuan, though (primarily US) critics argue that it has not increased in value enough. This of course leads to tensions with US industries that face competition from Chinese imports, but equally many firms (and consumers) also benefit from such imports. Moreover, the Chinese central bank is one of the main purchasers of US Treasury bills, which allows the US to finance these deficits and at the same time allows Chinese exports to continue to flood into the US market. China is also a growing market and source of investment for US firms. Furthermore, the vulnerabilities of the Chinese economy discussed above may make integration even more of an imperative. If the amount of non-performing loans intensifies in the context of growing integration, then these will again have to be financed from China's trade surpluses, particularly with the United States. As Harvey (2005: 142) argues:

> A peculiar symbiosis emerges, in which China, along with Japan, Taiwan, and other Asian central banks, fund the US debt so that the US can conveniently consume their surplus output. But this renders the US vulnerable to the whims of Asian central bankers. Conversely, Chinese economic dynamism is held hostage to US fiscal and monetary policy.

For these reasons then, and whatever its advocates may think and hope, it is unlikely that the US can prevent the continued growth of China, either through economic or by military means (Bromley 2006). We have also noted, however, that much of the growth that has occurred in China has been in labour-intensive industries, with considerable degrees of state protection. For these reasons the extent of the miracle may be exaggerated, and it most certainly is not one that can be satisfactorily explained by neo-liberalism. The source of tensions with other countries derives from a combination of trade surpluses and growing unemployment in some industrial sectors, and in geopolitical terms from the fact that high growth is combined with the sheer size, and potential military might, of China. However, insofar as China is considered by some to be a geopolitical or economic threat, it is unclear how military power could be effective in changing these developments. Moreover, there are good reasons why cooperation – alongside competition – does occur. We return to reconsider these issues below, after first examining the question of Europe.

Europe: a Progressive Alternative?

The question of a European alternative to US hegemony and/or neo-liberalism is in some respects similar to, and in other respects different from, the East Asian challenge. Europe, and more specifically the European Union, has been championed by some as representing a more humane form than capitalism to American neo-liberalism. This question is closely related to academic debates over the issue of varieties of capitalism (Hall and Soskice 2001; Perraton and Clift 2004), and whether there remain plausible social democratic alternatives to neo-liberal capitalism (Hutton and Giddens 2001; Coates 2000; 2005). Related to these questions of political economy is the more geopolitical question of whether Europe is more committed to a rules-based, multilateral international order, an issue that has become particularly central to debates in international relations since 2001 (Leonard 2003; R. Cooper 2004). These questions are particularly central to political debates in Britain, which is often regarded as a peculiar[7] nation-state which attempts to bridge the gap between the US and Europe (Gamble 2003). How this bridge is supposed to operate – in terms of both political economy and international relations – has been a major debating point in the two main political parties, even if this has not always been made explicit in contemporary political discourse. These two questions are, however, perhaps more closely linked than they are in the case of East Asia, or at least an answer to the two questions can be more closely linked, because the issue of progressive political-economic alternatives and rules-based international governance cuts across the question of whether the European Union adopts 'development friendly' policies towards the developing world. This section thus starts by briefly outlining the first two questions, and then problematizes these, both generally and with specific reference to relations with the developing world.

The argument that the European Union represents a potentially progressive challenge to US hegemony is an old one, but it has been reinvigorated since the US-led invasion of Iraq in 2003. In May 2003, a number of prominent European intellectuals launched their Manifesto for a Renaissance of Europe (Habermas and Derrida 2005). This statement was written by Jürgen Habermas and supported by (among others) Jacques Derrida, Umberto Eco, Gianni Vattimo and the US intellectual Richard Rorty. The immediate rationale for the statement was the increasing unilateralism of the Bush administration, but it also reflected long-standing perceived differences between progressive, collectivist, social democratic Europe, and the neo-liberal, unilateral US and its main European ally, Britain. Habermas argued that the social democratic legacy in Europe reflected the political legacy of labour movements, and had led to a greater emphasis on social security, welfare, and respect for difference, as well as a more inclusive, Kantian world order which focused on human rights, multilateral rule-making, and the peaceful resolution of conflict. Among its proposals were a Common Foreign Security and Defence Policy, based around a core Europe.

The impact of Habermas's manifesto was limited, but it clearly reflects perhaps the dominant tendency in European social democracy, which is to counter-pose a progressive variety of capitalism to that of the US's neo-liberalism, and extend this to the field of international relations. In some respects then, this is a call for Europe to embrace a version of the old, social democratic 'German model' or 'Scandinavian model' within Europe, and to promote this more inclusive approach in the field of international relations, including with the developing world. Implicit in such an approach is an understanding that regionalism is more a challenge to, rather than an extension of, neo-liberal globalization (Nesadurai 2002). Clearly, the strength and comparatively progressive nature of both German and Scandinavian capitalisms should not be under-estimated. But at the same time, as we saw in the previous chapter, there are strong grounds for questioning whether these constitute a European, or any other kind of, model. First, although there are signs of tentative recovery, the record of German capitalism in particular since 1990 is far from convincing. This has in part been caused by the problems of unification with the much weaker eastern region, but it has also been caused by the character of EU policies, which have essentially been neo-liberal in nature. This should give cause for concern for those, like Tony Blair, who advocate a more flexible Europe, embracing neo-liberal globalization through supposedly third way policies, but so too should it give cause for concern to those who tend to regard the EU as a major vehicle for progressive social change, which advocates policies which challenge neo-liberal capitalism. Of course the EU may be such an agent of change, but the evidence to date suggests that in fact it is more an agent of neo-liberal policies. This will become clear below, but before moving on to examine those policies, a brief re-examination of the problems facing the progressive capitalisms of Europe is needed.

For some social democratic European politicians, the European project was at least initially regarded as a challenge to US-led neo-liberalism. This of course has a long tradition not necessarily associated with social democracy, but with Gaullism. However, in the context of growing European integration, former French Prime Minister Lionel Jospin best summed up this position when he argued that 'Europe is much more than a market. It stands for a model of society' (cited in McGrew 2003: 357). This is linked to the collectivism alluded to by Habermas, which in turn is sometimes linked to German and/or Scandinavian 'models' of development, discussed in the previous chapter (Chandler 1990; Hutton 1994). Collectivism and progressive social policy have undoubtedly been important features of North European capitalisms, and their progressive features remain important to this day (Glyn 2006: ch. 7). But at the same time, one need not accept neo-liberal (including Blairite third way) solutions to recognize that these 'models' were in trouble by the 1990s, as the last chapter suggested. This was reflected in lower growth, higher unemployment and the breakdown of the accommodation between capital and labour (Coates 2000: 97–8, 239–40). In many respects, this breakdown was similar to the earlier collapse of the Bretton Woods system in the 1970s and the triumph of neo-liberalism in much of the world in the 1980s. This breakdown was delayed – and continues to be resisted – where social democracy was most firmly entrenched, as the high wages and progressive taxation that financed progressive social democracy were increasingly undermined by falling productivity and a capitalist class no longer prepared to tolerate class compromise (Coates 2000: 101).

Thus the 'sources' of the progressive model have been at least partly undermined. But one can go further, and suggest that one reason that they have been undermined is *because of the European project itself*. This can be linked to a number of important changes in European integration, such as the Single European Act (1986), European Monetary Union (1992, 1999 and 2002), and the Stability and Growth Pact. Together, these Acts expanded Europe as a neo-liberal political project, by removing trade, investment and financial barriers to the movement of capital both within and beyond the European Union, and by prioritizing anti-inflationary policies, at the expense of growth and employment. Thus, for instance, the Stability and Growth Pact (in principle) limits state fiscal deficits to 3 per cent of GDP, though in practice this has been resisted by some states, and by France and Germany in particular. This resistance reflects the uneven implementation of neo-liberal policies, and their resistance by domestic populations, which in turn reflects ongoing disputes within the EU. For instance, the 'no' votes in referenda on further European expansion through adoption of a European Constitution, in 2005, were interpreted by British Prime Minister Tony Blair, who was EU President at the time, as evidence that European populations were eager to reject the failed social democratic models of corporatist Europe and embrace further reform. But evidence was never a particular strong point for Blair. Although nationalist objectives were often involved, the main motivation for rejection of the European constitution was, contrary to the view of both Blair and pro-European social democrats, a rejection of neo-liberal expansion through the European project.

None of this means that there has been a simple neo-liberal convergence between the advanced capitalist countries, and the 'varieties of capitalism' approach is right to point to the strength of entrenched historical and institutional structures, and continued divergence in terms of social and welfare policy (Hay 2004a). But equally, Grahl (2004: 296) is right to make the point that while 'the institutional forms of the European economies are indeed remarkably stable, these views underestimate the deep changes in the priorities and objectives which determine the functioning of institutions'. In this respect we can talk of some degree of policy convergence, while recognizing that this is likely to have divergent outcomes based on differential competitive capacity within the EU. This is not because the EU project is a simple technical reaction to the fact of globalization, as some mainstream globalization theorists imply (see Chapter 5 on Giddens), but rather is part of a process of state-driven, neo-liberal restructuring (Hay 2000, 2004a). And these points are all the more relevant to understanding the relationship between the EU and the developing world, where we can also identify some degree of policy convergence around neo-liberal policies.

In the post-war period, attempts were made to continue to foster close ties between the new states and the former colonial powers, in part through the preferential trade agreements briefly outlined in Chapter 3. In Europe, these were institutionalized through the Yaounde Conventions in the 1960s and, in the context of European expansion after 1973 and specifically of British membership, the four Lomé Conventions, which lasted from 1975 to 2000. These agreements gave preferential access to European markets for a number of African, Caribbean and Pacific (ACP) producers, without these countries having to reciprocate by opening their own markets. Two commodity funds (STABEX and SYSMIN) were also established, under which Europe compensated ACP countries for export-earning shortfalls (Brown 2002). Like other preferential schemes (see Chapter 3), Lomé suffered from a number of limitations related to rules of origin of particular commodities, particularly relating to industrial goods. This had the effect, at least to some extent, of helping to further lock in some countries to older trade patterns, and indeed as a proportion of total EU trade, ACP imports actually fell from (depending on sources) either 8 per cent or 6.7 per cent in 1974–5 to 3.4 per cent or 3 per cent in 1994–5 (Gibbon and Ponte 2005: 212). Despite its limitations, however, Lomé was regarded as important in protecting the poorest producers in the international economy. However, from the 1990s onwards, and with Lomé III and IV, there was a significant shift away from this preferential treatment. Lomé III and especially IV effectively incorporated much of the World Bank agenda, increasingly tying aid to structural adjustment and good governance.

In 2000, Lomé was replaced by the Cotonou agreements, which proposed new Economic Partnership Agreements. On the EU side at least, these agreements increasingly emphasized trade liberalization as one of the most significant policy routes that determined poverty reduction (Hurt 2003). The non-reciprocal trade preferences that existed under Lomé are set to be replaced by a new system in 2007–8, which is said to be compatible with WTO rules. Under this system, the ACP countries are divided into less developed countries on the one hand, and developing countries on the other. Only the former group will continue to receive trade preferences, while the latter group will come under the jurisdiction of the new Economic Partnership Agreements. These developing countries may choose to opt in to another EU preferential system, the Generalized System of Preferences, but this is far more restrictive than even the old Lomé system (Hurt 2003: 168). The least developed countries (39 ACP countries plus others outside the ACP) should in theory benefit from duty free access to the European markets on all goods, except arms. However, there are two likely limitations in terms of development prospects. First, as Chapters 6 and 7 suggested, trade liberalization is likely to benefit some developing-country producers at the expense of others. Secondly, trade liberalization within the EU is still likely to be limited. The WTO talks at Hong Kong in late 2005 showed some commitment in principle to trade liberalization in agriculture. However, this applies only to export subsidies; a small proportion of total subsidies, the change will take place only by 2013; and the commitment is anyway not binding. Clearly then, the EU seems prepared to endorse liberalization for the developing world, but not necessarily for itself.

All in all then, the evidence suggests that far from representing a progressive alternative to neo-liberalism, the European project is effectively expanding it. This does not of course mean that the European project is intrinsically neo-liberal, and neither does it mean that an anti-EU position is intrinsically progressive. What it does mean is that a sceptical position on the EU is not necessarily xenophobic or reactionary (Elliott 2005), and that despite continued variations within national capitalisms in Europe, the dominant tendency in terms of policy is towards neo-liberalism. This point applies both within the EU, and in the EU's relations with the developing world (Rosamond 2000). Neo-liberal expansion is not inevitable, and the EU project remains a contested one. But to project a politics which assumes the progressiveness of the European project not only ignores the evidence to the contrary, but it displays, too, an instance of the spatial fetishism that also characterizes much of the literature on global governance (see Chapter 6). In this case the space of Europe is regarded as a progressive one, somehow challenging the reactionary space of the United States. As we have seen, this ignores Europe's own neo-liberal project as well as somewhat problematically homogenizing US politics. Moreover, it may also be the case that it fails to capture the close links between the EU, the US and neo-liberalism.

Chapter 5 argued that the neo-liberal period has been one in which the US has successfully restored its hegemonic position in the international order. This is a hegemony that is precarious, as the declinists discussed above point out, because of the twin deficits and the limits of military power in a more economically integrated world. We return to this question below, but for our current purposes further discussion of US–EU relations is needed. The first point to make is one that applies to the EU and in many respects East Asia, even if the rise of China clouds the picture somewhat. It is one made by Grahl (2004: 288):

Since 1980, the relative position of the US economy has continuously strengthened while the German and Japanese challenges, at the time so ominous, have faded virtually into insignificance. The excellence of their industrial systems was no match for the range and scale of the dollar-based financial system.

One result in Europe was the undermining of the corporatist model outlined above, with the result that 'the kind of Keynesian intervention attempted by most European countries in the late seventies and early eighties simply could not be financed in a world of depreciating currencies and sky-high interest rates' (Grahl 2004: 288). While interest rates have since declined, the US has continued to successfully use the international role of the dollar to preserve its hegemonic status. The European response to this process has been to follow the US lead, and itself try to build huge financial markets in order to compete with the US.

The euro thus potentially represents an alternative international currency to the dollar, which threatens the US's ability to practise seigniorage[8] through the issuing of dollars, not least within Europe itself as the euro replaces international payments previously carried out in dollars. In practice however, the challenge of the euro to the dollar has been limited, and European states have continued to hold dollars in substantial amounts. In the context of ongoing concerns about the US trade and budget deficits, this may change, but this would itself have negative implications for Europe as well as for the US (see below). Moreover, European monetary union has widened the promotion of shareholder value (see Chapter 4) and thus acted to undermine older social democratic models, and it has constrained the ability of states to address social problems such as unemployment (see above). Thus, even if the euro may potentially challenge the dollar, it has done so through expanding neo-liberal policies, and so hardly represents a progressive challenge to the US. Indeed, after some initial concern about an increasingly protectionist 'fortress Europe', the US has largely welcomed European integration as it has not challenged greater integration with the US through open trade policies and maintaining an open policy towards US foreign investment. Furthermore, to date, the Eurozone has hardly been successful in presenting a regional challenge to US capitalism, and the consequences of a rapid decline in the dollar are by no means positive for a Europe dependent on the US market. Indeed, the implications for European manufacturing exports, international trade and financial assets held by Europeans in dollars suggest that even the European central bank hardly wants a wholesale shift to the Euro. Certainly, since the early 1970s, the three major economic crises in the US (1971–4, 1979–82, and 1987–92) did not lead to a resurgent Europe, but in some respects facilitated a decline as against the US (Grahl 2001: 45–7). The next crisis may of course be different as, on the face of it, the Euro means a united European front, but events in Europe (such as the rejection of the EU constitution by major member states) suggest that this may be exaggerated.

The shared assumptions between those advocating alternative models and those who see the current international order as being based on inter-imperialist rivalries has already been noted in the discussion of East Asia. Thus, as Habermas and Derrida support progressive Europe against the US, so classical Marxists regard the conflict over Iraq as an example of continued inter-imperialist rivalries (Callinicos 2003; 2005). Of course there was conflict in the run up to the war in Iraq (as there has been in the past, particularly between the US and France), but this does not mean that this represents a return of the old rivalries of the pre-1914 era. Indeed, after the invasion, in early 2004, both the German and French governments endorsed the US invasion through the United Nations. Moreover, all the talk of a defence force in Europe genuinely independent of NATO has come to little, and anyway it is unclear how this would challenge US military dominance. Indeed the French defence minister Michelle Alliot-Marie has explicitly stated that such an initiative would complement, and not rival, NATO's role (cited in Panitch and Gindin 2006: 196). As things stand, European powers are happy to form a dependent relationship with the US military. Moreover, too often those who do see an increasingly independent military role for Europe do so in ways that effectively repeat the European colonial practices of old, advocating a 'cosmopolitan imperialism' that supposedly combines universal ideals and imperialist double standards (Cooper 2002).

This section has therefore questioned the nature of a European alternative to US hegemony and neo-liberalism, whether or not this supposed alternative is progressive or not. In terms of political economy, the direction of change has been in a neo-liberal direction, and in terms of geopolitics, there is little evidence of a meaningful challenge to US hegemony. This is not an argument that necessarily dismisses the European Union as an intrinsically neo-liberal project, but it is one that rejects the idea that the EU must represent a social democratic challenge to neo-liberalism. It is not only that the direction of change undermines such an argument, but also that the argument is guilty of a spatial fetishism, reducing politics to geography (good Europe versus bad US). This suggests that we need a better understanding of how different regions are integrated into global capitalism, and how this relates to both neo-liberalism and US hegemony. We thus return to these questions in the next section.

US Hegemony Re-assessed

Up to this point this book has argued that (i) neo-liberal globalization is the (contested) outcome of the break-up of the Bretton Woods agreement, and is closely linked to the restructuring of US hegemony after 1971 and especially after 1980; (ii) the neo-liberal policies that followed this breakdown have increasingly expanded their reach throughout the world; (iii) these policies remain intact, albeit selectively, since 2001 and the unilateralist turn of the Bush administration in the United States; (iv) neo-liberalism does not constitute a way forward to 'developed capitalist status' for most, if not all, of the developing world; (v) despite point iv, there is a growing tendency towards neo-liberal policies throughout the world. What this section tries to do is to further develop the points made in previous parts of the book,[9] and suggest that neo-liberalism is not just a flawed ideology associated with global capitalism, but is in fact a new way of disciplining 'national capitalisms' throughout the globe (Gill 1995; 2003; Harvey 2005: 19). And in focusing on this question, I suggest that we are also in a position to better understand the relationship between (US) hegemony and neo-liberalism in the contemporary world order.

This characterization has implications for understanding the debate introduced above, over whether US hegemony is increasing or is in decline. In certain respects, this debate misses the specificity of the relationship between US hegemony and the neo-liberalism of the last twenty-five years (Albo 2003). In the neo-liberal period, one can point to both (economic) competition between states and (economic and wider) cooperation between them, alongside growing economic inter-penetration ('globalization') and political interdependence. Since the 1980s (or earlier), the world economy has been characterized by uneven and asymmetrical interdependence, particularly between the core capitalist countries, and the more successful developing countries in East Asia (Panitch and Gindin 2003; 2004; 2005a and 2005b; 2006). This is reflected in the US deficits on the one hand, and surpluses among some European and Asian countries. Finance, and particularly the dollar, has played a key role in sustaining these trade imbalances, particularly the US trade deficit, through printing money in the 1970s, high interest rates in the 1980s, and the issuing of government and corporate bonds in the 1990s and beyond. Financial flows have also been important in the developing world, through the recycling of petrodollars in the 1970s, the limited public flows of the IMF and the World Bank in the debt crisis of the 1980s, and the private flows into some developing countries in the 1990s.

But in terms of the centrality of the global economy, while the relationship between the core countries is crucial, these have enormous implications for the developing countries. In particular, since the 1980s, currency adjustments and financial flows have been areas of both cooperation and conflict between the core countries as a result of these ongoing trade asymmetries, which in turn have fuelled the growth of financial flows designed to provide a hedge against currency fluctuations, but which themselves have become sources of instability as they have promoted greater financial speculation. In the 1980s, and against all the expectations of neo-liberal orthodoxies, the US dollar actually increased in value while the trade deficit soared. This led to a coordinated attempt to bring down the dollar, by the key states in the international order, through the Plaza Accord of 1985 and the Louvre Accord of 1987. This met with some success, but the resultant appreciation of the yen and the mark meant that the cost of slower growth in the world economy was met by Germany and Japan, previously regarded as regional challengers to US hegemony. Moreover, the US trade deficit continued to increase. After a recession that hit all the core capitalist countries in the early 1990s, the US recovered in the second half of the 1990s through the so-called new economy boom. Productivity increased, but not at particularly high levels, at least when compared with the stock market boom, which supposedly reflects expectations of future profits. The trade deficit continued, and under Bush Junior the budget deficit again soared, and the stock market boom came to an end. Slower growth has resulted, albeit with spurts of substantial, yet jobless growth. From 2000 to 2006, despite some downturns, the US successfully managed to avoid a sustained recession, as the Federal Reserve (the US central bank) injected more liquidity into the system. However, this has been at the cost of unsustainable asset prices (particularly in housing), soaring debt and continued and worsening imbalances in the international economy.

In terms of understanding US hegemony, this discussion points to an alternative approach: rather than regarding the three core regions of the world economy as being engaged in a zero-sum game whereby the decline of one leads to the advance of another, we should instead focus on the international order as a whole, and how this may have an impact in different regions in different and unpredictable ways.[10] Thus, rather than seeing the US deficits (only) as a sign of weakness, we should instead focus on how resolving the twin deficits may itself have a negative impact, not only on the US, but on the other two regions that depend on the US market. For example, in 2003–4, Asian governments in particular bought up huge amounts of dollars through intervening in foreign exchange markets and selling their own currencies. This reflects an increasing US dependence on foreign capital and governments. But it also reflects the fact that these governments bought the dollars in order to prevent their own currencies from rising in value, which would have undermined their own competitiveness. By the end of 2003, overseas governments held in dollar-based assets the equivalent of 13 per cent of US GDP (Glyn 2006: 85).

These practices demonstrate the 'structural power' of US hegemony (Strange 1987; Gill 2004), which cannot be theorized simply in terms of declining resources or growing deficits. Asymmetrical interdependence does not of course mean that regions converge in any straightforward way, a point made in the previous chapter with regard to states, but it does mean that they are all differentially and unevenly part of this order. This is reflected in the US deficits, and how the trade deficit acts as a market of last resort for the other core regions (and parts of East Asia), who run trade surpluses and export to the US market, while most of the developing world is squeezed to run trade surpluses in order to meet debt obligations (albeit with the broad consent of local elites – see below). These surpluses are met at far lower rates of accumulation than those in the advanced countries. The effect of these interdependencies is to further promote neo-liberalism, not only as an ideology or as government policy, but as *the dominant form of accumulation in the international economy*. Capital throughout the world supports (some variety of) neo-liberalism as the best way to maintain competitiveness and to expand markets in the context of privatization, but perhaps above all to maintain the international circuits of capital that are increasingly important to remain competitive (Burnham 2002). Greg Albo (2003: 109) makes the link most explicit:

> The internationalization of capital has solidified in the imperialist bloc a materialist interest in sustaining the form of uneven development and hierarchical organizational arrangements of the world market today. Neo-liberalism as a social form of power and class relations, and international competitiveness as its externalized expression, is reproduced in national capitalisms, not against a more 'rational' organization of the world market or as an imposition of the 'American model' on 'European' or 'East Asian' models, but as part and parcel of contemporary imperialism. Indeed, even the ruling classes in the dominated bloc can see their interests – both in terms of capital accumulation and the desire to move up the rungs of the imperialist chain – represented in the international circulation of capital, just as colonial and comprador elites of the past did in the old imperialism.

For the *developing world* then, what is being argued is that older, traditional and classical Marxist conceptions of national bourgeoisies, straightforwardly committed to capitalist development in their respective (developmental) states, need to be abandoned. Albo's use of the term 'comprador' is problematic, in that it tends to replicate older notions of dependent classes in the developing world, and thus fails to give dominant classes in the developing world any agency in the context of the post-war expansion of state sovereignty. But his account of contemporary imperialism does undermine the even more outmoded idea of a national bourgeoisie committed to the promotion of national capitalist development (see also Chibber 2004b; Desai 2004). While this argument has some sympathy with the idea of a transnational capitalist class, or at least the idea of an 'interior bourgeoisie' (Jessop 1985: 172), it still needs to recognize hierarchical relations between different states and bourgeoisies, but also that there may still be considerable economic and cultural conflict between these dominant classes. This is reflected not only in conflicts over trade such as those at the WTO, but also in terms of different cultural nationalisms, whereby so-called national capitalist classes and state elites do challenge the dominance of foreign capital and 'the West', while simultaneously entering into alliances with these supposed evils, albeit in the name of localization (Greenfield 2004).[11] This is not a political challenge *against*, but rather one *within* the parameters of both US hegemony and neo-liberalism. We therefore must abandon the idea of domestic capitals in the developing world being committed to a process of national capitalist development. Insofar as such development occurs, this is a secondary issue for domestic capitals committed above all to accessing international circuits of capital accumulation, irrespective of whether or not these may be 'developmental' within particular nation-states. This has enormous implications for anti-imperialist and anti-globalization politics, and we return to it in the next chapter.

Conclusion: Neo-liberalism, Regionalism and Development

The main argument made in this chapter is that in many respects the debate over whether US hegemony is strengthening or weakening misses what is distinctive about US hegemony, namely that it has increasingly – and successfully – promoted neo-liberal expansion throughout the world. This expansion has been supported by dominant elites and ruling classes within many nation-states. This has led to the centrality of the need to promote competitiveness in the global economy. While neo-liberals regard this as desirable, I have suggested in the last three chapters that the results of such competitiveness are bound to be uneven and unequal. Developing countries suffer from competitive disadvantage in the international capitalist economy, as established producers capture markets and undermine potential competitors in liberalized developing countries. Of course this affects developing countries in different ways, and they have of course managed to find some goods to export successfully. This is particularly true for some primary products and for labour-intensive manufacturing goods, but it is these sectors which tend to see rapidly falling prices and so generate limited export revenue and intense competition between developing countries. Dominant political and social agents in the developing world are less concerned with alleviating this subordinate position; rather, their main concern is with securing access to lucrative circuits of capital. This may take a number of forms, such as exporting capital or entering into licensing or subcontracting agreements with foreign capital.

It should be stressed that this is not an argument that necessarily supports the earlier claims made by some cruder versions of dependency theory, which suggested that the exploitation of the South was a major reason for the development of the North. Rather, I am suggesting that the South is in a relatively marginal, subordinate position in the world economy, and neo-liberal globalization intensifies this marginalization, even if a small number of people in the developing world benefit from this process. Put differently, the development gap is an outcome of the uneven development of international capitalism, not its defining feature. But also in contrast to dependency theory, we should be sensitive to regional variation within the developing world. Certainly, parts of East Asia may have developed sufficiently to be able to compete in the international economy on the basis of higher-value production. But I have suggested that, while there has been some technological upgrading in China, this has, to date, been insufficient to suggest that a similar process is occurring there. Instead, China is a successful world leader in exporting the kinds of low-value goods that many other developing countries are also trying to promote. It therefore follows that any success in this process in other parts of Asia, and indeed in Africa and Latin America, is bound to be limited. These points apply all the more in the cases of the poorest, least developed countries, which have limited manufacturing bases and/or rely heavily on the export of a few primary commodities. While, in the mid-2000s, these countries benefited from a primary commodities boom fuelled by the growth of China, I have suggested that this is bound to be short-lived and is anyway insufficient in terms of generating revenue to finance diversification – which, in any case, is undermined by neo-liberal policies of open competition.

Given this exclusion from the core of capitalist development, on the face of it there is a strong case for promoting a different kind of regionalism, which is resistant to neo-liberalism. This could in principle facilitate some protection from competition with cutting-edge producers and thus a return to some form of industrial policy. It could also help to generate larger markets and thus secure the potential to be gained from generating economies of scale. But at the same time, it needs to be recognized that regionalism in the South is not necessarily resistant to neo-liberalism – the New Partnership for Africa's Development (NEPAD), launched in 2001, is basically compatible with the post-Washington consensus (Bond 2005). Moreover, the prospects for a more progressive regionalism are subject to the same problems faced by the new international economic order proposals of the 1970s; that is, they require high rates of cooperation between states in a framework whereby it may make sense for one state to export to the developed world, but not for all states to do the same thing. As we saw in Chapter 7 and in this chapter, many of the successful exports from the developing world are suffering from decreasing returns, but this would not necessarily stop one state from trying to win lucrative export markets at the expense of others. Moreover, though it is true that many indigenous dominant classes in the South support some protection from foreign competition, it is likely that they would also resent the restrictions placed on them by attempts to revive developmental states in a regional context.

Crucially then, as the Albo quote above suggests, the ruling classes in the South may themselves ultimately support the neo-liberal international order, and therefore undermine the prospects for (national and regional) developmentalism. Of course this does not mean that regionalism itself is intrinsically a neo-liberal project, and there may well be some prospects for a resistant regionalism. Interesting in this respect is the Bolivarian Alternative for the Americas (ALBA) initiative of a number of (supposedly) anti-neo-liberal governments in Latin America, led by Venezuela, Bolivia, Argentina, Brazil and Paraguay, which rejects the neo-liberalism of the Free Trade Area for the Americas, and effectively embraces a form of trade based on reciprocity rather than competition. However, this regional challenge has been facilitated by *national* political change, above all in Venezuela (discussed in the next chapter), but which has also met with considerable domestic and international opposition, including capital flight, tacit support by the US for an attempted coup, and ongoing condemnation of the Chavez administration (Lendman 2006). Perhaps most surreal in this regard was the condemnation of Chavez by Tony Blair in early 2006 for the former's supposed rejection of the norms of the international community, only three years after the war in Iraq (Press 2006). This opposition to what is effectively relatively mild, but generally progressive, national-populist opposition to US hegemony and neo-liberalism suggests that for challenges to neo-liberalism to occur, nationally as well as globally, important domestic as well as international, political and social change must occur. These questions are addressed in the next chapter.

Chapter 10

Resisting Globalization?

This chapter provides a critical outline of social and political movements that resist 'actually existing globalization'. This will be done in four sections. The first will refer back to the three political positions on globalization and development outlined in Chapter 1, and discusses the question of politics from within each of these positions. The second section then looks at the so-called Islamic and Islamist challenges to globalization, and will suggest that Islam (and Islamism) cannot be understood as a homogenous force that simply rejects 'the West', even if there are some (reactionary) currents that promote political programmes along these lines. It will also suggest that this has wider implications, and that Islamism cannot be regarded as a political force that is in any straightforward sense anti-imperialist or progressive. The chapter will then move on to examine other social movements – particularly in the South – and the (questionable) claims made that they represent a new era of post-development. The fourth section will then develop this argument by briefly examining some of the debates in the 'global justice movement', and progressive alternatives to (neo-liberal) capitalism, including some further consideration of the return of 'national-developmentalism' to Latin America.

Imperialism and Anti-imperialism in the Era of Globalization

This section revisits the three broad positions on globalization outlined in the opening chapter. It does so by explicitly focusing on questions of imperialism and anti-imperialism. The first position effectively endorses a version of liberal imperialism, or the idea that a benevolent hegemonic power can facilitate both development and security through the promotion of increased international openness, liberal democracy and the expansion of the liberal zone of peace. As we have seen, this view has been associated with the argument that British imperialism, at least from 1846 onwards, was a liberal imperialism, and so too is contemporary

American imperialism. This view is usually linked to the argument that US imperialism is closely related to the expansion of neo-liberalism, and thus it is good for development (Lal 2004). It is particularly good if it is committed to the restructuring or even removal of rogue states that fail to play by the rules of the game (Kagan and Kristol 2000). Some advocates of liberal imperialism are more suspicious of US hegemony, and instead argue either that there needs to be a different hegemonic power – probably the European Union – or that the EU should at least influence the United States to act in accordance with cosmopolitan ideals (Cooper 2004).

The view that supports liberal imperialism is not necessarily incompatible with neo-conservative views in the United States, which, as we have seen, argued that in the post-Cold War world, US power has the capacity to see off other enemies just as it defeated the Soviet Union in the Cold War (Krauthammer 1990; 2002/3). This view has also become prominent since 2001, as previous chapters have demonstrated. However, it is not only neo-conservatives that effectively endorse a new liberal imperialism. This view was closely linked to post-Cold War views that the dominant power could behave in a less self-interested way now that it had seen off its main strategic competitor, and so it could promote a 'new world order'. Again, this view was challenged, above all by the failure of intervention in Somalia and non-intervention in Rwanda in the early 1990s. However, it was effectively revived in the second half of the 1990s in the context of the rise of the discourse of globalization. As we saw in Chapter 5, it was argued that global interconnectedness meant that there was no clear demarcation between national, particular interests, and global, universal interests. It therefore made sense to adopt more interventionist policies in the developing world. This was related to cosmopolitan world views, which revived Kantian ideas and argued that the rights of individuals took precedence over the sovereignty of states (see Chapter 6). Although this was usually linked to the idea that globalization had eroded the power, or at least the particular interests, of nation-states, it was also not incompatible with the idea that the US hegemonic state could be a force for cosmopolitan good in the international order, provided that it too was prepared to endorse international law and multilateral commitments (Kaldor 2004).

This of course changed with the attacks of September 2001. The US adopted an increasingly militaristic and unilateralist policy, in which development and security concerns were more closely intertwined. Contemporary Kantians regretted this turn away from cosmopolitan principles and the Bush administration's endorsement of a 'regressive globalism' (Shaw 2003; Anheier et al. 2003). But interestingly, a number of liberal and radical writers actually (reluctantly) endorsed the policies of the Bush administration (Berman 2004, 2006; Ignatieff 2003; 2005; Hitchens 2003; Kamm 2005; Cushman 2005), on the grounds that Islamo-fascism or Iraqi Baathism constituted a threat to liberal values. Although, as we have seen, these thinkers were far from being open advocates of neo-liberalism or American conservatism, they argued that US hegemony or even empire was 'the lesser evil'.

What is perhaps most interesting about this new advocacy of liberal imperialism is that it at least says something about the nature of so-called anti-imperialist forces in the world today. In contrast, the second position argues that the world remains imperialist in the Lenin–Bukharin sense (see Chapter 5), and that therefore imperialist motives dominate interventions in the developing world. As we have seen, this is based on the argument that inter-imperialist rivalries persist, and that the development of the Third World is hardly a priority of the imperialist powers. More convincingly, this approach also points to the continuities as well as discontinuities of the Bush administration with the 1990s, particularly highlighting Clinton's own unilateralism and double standards, as well as the hierarchies and inequalities associated with neo-liberal capitalism, and the limitations of multilateralism in such an unequal international order.

But equally, as we have seen, this position exaggerates the continuities between the inter-imperialist rivalries of the pre-1914 era and the current era of globalization. In particular, the rise of sovereign states and cooperation between capitalist states is under-estimated. Moreover, enhanced international and global integration – which are closely linked to neo-liberalism – are also not sufficiently considered (see Chapter 5). One of the ironies of this perspective is that it goes to great lengths to link military interventions to economic interests, and particularly argues that such interventions are designed to facilitate foreign investment for its own national capital in such countries. No attempt is made to assess the impact of such investment and certainly it is not clear why such investment should be rejected in favour of local capital investment. This position thus betrays an implicit support for the old fallacies of nationalist versions of dependency theory, which wrongly contrasted the underdevelopment of foreign capital with development by local capital. Such a foreign–local contrast is an odd position for a Marxist, whose main focus is on capital rather than national origin. Moreover, it ignores the fact that underdevelopment is most common in places comparatively starved of foreign capital investment. This of course does not mean endorsement of neo-liberalism, which fails to explain why foreign investment concentrates in some places at the expense of others. Indeed, neo-liberalism suffers from the same fallacies as this position, in that it assumes capital relocation from core to periphery, as Chapter 7 showed.

What this discussion above all shows is that these contradictory positions are derived from a methodology that effectively reduces events in the periphery to the machinations of core countries. In other words, this approach is guilty of reifying the inequalities between different states, organizations, and interests, in the international order, to a point where the weaknesses of some states and movements are such that they can only be regarded as a reaction to those in positions of power. Thus, it is one thing to contextualize the terrorist attacks in 11 September, but quite another to reduce them to the actions of an all-powerful imperialism (Shaw 2002) – indeed, such an approach is guilty of 'hegemonic abstentionism' as it fails to take the question of international solidarity seriously (Halliday 2000: ch. 1). The terrorist attacks in 2001 were made on the day of the 28th anniversary of the US-backed military coup in Chile in 1973. The idea that Chilean socialists or communists would exact their revenge through the brutal attacks that did take place in 2001 was unthinkable. Any convincing analysis of contemporary anti-imperialism thus needs to examine how movements react to imperialism (which, as we have seen, is far from monolithic in any case), and must pay more attention to so-called anti-imperialist movements *in their own right*. This is undoubtedly the great strength of the case made for liberal imperialism by some writers who endorse this position, in contrast, for example, to the dominant positions made by anti-war movements in the US and UK over the war in Iraq in 2003 (Kiely 2005a: ch. 8).

But, as we saw in Chapter 6, this perspective, even when severed from neo-liberalism, ultimately endorses a position where the global good is assumed to derive from (US) power, rather than (US) power being derived from the global good (Chan 2005). It is therefore of little surprise that even the 'radical' liberal imperialists ultimately endorse the neo-conservative position that what(ever) is good for the US must be good for the world. As we saw in Chapter 6, this amounts to an uncritical endorsement of US power in the international arena, effectively unchallenged by any notion of accountability or democracy. This is most clear when the question of double standards arises, because many contemporary liberal imperialists excuse such practices on the grounds that 'better these inconsistencies than the existence of dictatorships like Saddam Hussein's or movements like al Qaeda'. The problem with this perspective is not only that the US has effectively been allies with both of these in the past, but that it continues to align itself with authoritarian regimes in the present. This is not a question of changing the subject, as Wheen (2004: 301–2) contends,[1] as the alliances made in the present are likely to have implications for the future, just as alliances in the past have had implications in the present. Of course, in an imperfect world it is impossible for states to not align themselves in some respects with

authoritarian regimes, but if this is the case, then we should simultaneously take the humanitarian rhetoric of military intervention with something of a pinch of salt, for those prepared to endorse alliances in the
name of compromise in an imperfect world cannot then also claim that
interventions are based on the principle of non-compromise with evil
dictators. When 30 allies were initially named as part of the coalition of
the willing, the US State Department itself suggested that 18 had poor or
very poor human rights records (IPS 2003). Moreover, as we saw in
Chapter 8, invasion can bring with it the collapse of the state or at least
an excessive optimism that liberal democratic states can easily be
created, thus undermining security and administration. This in turn
undermines legitimacy, which further undermines security, which leads
to a downward spiral between the two. Irrespective of whether resistance is progressive or not (and anti-imperialists all too often answer that
question in the affirmative), it is a likely consequence of invasion (and
liberals all too often dismiss it simply as evil, as though there are no
strategic questions to be asked).

Furthermore, the question of collateral damage is itself morally repug-
nant. Just as neo-liberals regard social and environmental costs associated with market transactions as externalities, when in reality they are
external to the theory but internal to reality, so liberal advocates of war
regard collateral damage as an unfortunate consequence of their otherwise good intentions. But collateral damage is not external to war but an
intrinsic part of its operation. This leads to the circular argument, made
again and again by both George Bush and especially Tony Blair, that
restraint is evidence of good intentions and good intentions are evidence
of restraint (Shaw 2005; Runciman 2006: ch. 2). Moreover, if the argument that the promotion of democracy is to be taken seriously, than that
must take place not only within nation-states, but also in terms of relations between nation-states.

These issues point us in the direction of the third perspective, which
attempts to endorse some of the claims made by anti-imperialists, but
which at the same time does take the cosmopolitan issue of solidarity
more seriously. This position is more open-ended, and while it rejects the
excessive focus of cosmopolitans on institutional change, it does not
dismiss this issue altogether. However, unlike the cosmopolitan perspective, it also recognizes that any commitment to universalism cannot
abstract, either from historical and social specificity or from global
inequality. This does not amount to an endorsement of cultural relativism, which, with its silences on oppression within developing countries, has ironically become an effective ally with crude anti-imperialists.
What it does amount to is a recognition that while liberal democracy and
universal standards are desirable, these cannot be imposed as a model.

This book has argued throughout that neo-liberal commitments to liberal democracy and the 'free market', and so-called humanitarian military intervention, do precisely that. The liberal imperialist argument that implementing war is an exercise in solidarity is thus absurd as well as doomed to failure (Shaw 2005). What is instead needed is both a commitment to diplomatic action from above, and closer links between democrats in these societies from below.

Perhaps the most dishonest argument made by liberal pro-war writers in recent times has been that anti-war positions entail effective support for tyrants or Islamo-fascist movements. Certainly, given the political commitments of many anti-imperialists, one can see why such an argument is made, but by this logic liberal imperialists should be calling for war against regimes every week, including against many of their allies in the war on terror. It also has echoes of the Cold War argument that if you criticized western policy, then you were automatically seen as a supporter of the Soviet Union. In this respect, if today's anti-imperialists are yesterday's Stalinists, then the new liberal imperialists of today echo yesterday's McCarthyism.[2] The question of extending democracy (and one should bear in mind the limits of contemporary liberal democracy, as discussed in Chapter 8) is one that deserves the support of all progressives, but this question cannot ignore difficult strategic issues which pro-war liberals ignore. To take another example, there is a strong case for universal labour standards throughout the world, but in a world of uneven and unequal development, such standards can have counter-productive effects, as they could lead to falling investment in parts of the developing world. This is not an argument against labour standards *per se*, nor an argument for neo-liberal capitalism or continued exploitation of cheap labour in parts of the developing world. Rather, it is an argument that recognizes the dilemmas faced by those advocating international labour solidarity, which at the same time may both support the struggles of workers for better wages and conditions while simultaneously opposing a blanket universalism implemented by, say, the WTO or even a strengthened ILO. It is these sorts of dilemmas that are ignored by pro-war liberals.

What this third position suggests then is an ongoing commitment to democratic change, and one that can lay the basis for a more radical social and political transformation in the international order. This certainly means a challenge to neo-liberal globalization and US hegemony, but equally it involves a questioning of the political nature of many states and political and social movements that are committed to so-called 'anti-globalization', 'anti-imperialism' and 'anti-Americanism'. These issues are addressed further in the next three sections, with particular reference to political Islam, post-development, and anti-globalization.

Islam and Islamism

One of the major issues that dominates discussions of international relations in the current era relates to the question of Islam. In particular, the argument that there is a clash of civilizations, and that this is most forceful in relations between the West and Islam, informs much discussion. A different, but paradoxically not unrelated approach, suggests that Islam provides the main challenge to contemporary globalization and US imperialism in the world today. This section will challenge both these claims. It does so by first distinguishing between Islam and Islamisms, and will briefly outline some of the diversity of beliefs and movements within Islam, and within Islamist political movements. This will then be used to challenge the stereotypes associated with both the crude civilizational and anti-imperialist positions.

In the post-Cold War 1990s, Samuel Huntington argued that there was little room for optimism in the new world order. Instead, the old ideological divisions of the Cold War had given way to new cultural clashes, or the clash of civilizations. This involved differences between eight or nine civilizations, divided along cultural lines of identity. These civilizations, primarily based on religion, were characterized as Western, Confucian, Sinic, Japanese, Islamic, Buddhist, Slav-Orthodox, Latin American and African. According to Huntington (1996: 11), '(s)purred by modernization, global politics is being reconfigured along cultural lines. Peoples and countries with similar cultures are coming together. Peoples and cultures with different cultures are coming apart.' Huntington called this process the 'kin country syndrome'. Of most significance was the rise of Confucianist and Islamic civilizations, both of which represented challenges to the dominance of western civilization. There are considerable general problems with this perspective, which above all relate to his use of the concept of culture (see below). For instance, his idea of the West ignores different conceptions of Christianity, secular challenges to religion, and competing ideological positions such as conservatism, liberalism and social democracy, and actually excludes Greece, where the term 'democracy' was first formulated. Similarly, reference to a homogenous African civilization may appeal to the fantasies of both imperialists and Afrocentrics, but flies in the face of conflicts over state formation, cultural identity, and so on.

But whatever the considerable general problems of this perspective, it did enjoy something of a revival after the terrorist attacks of 11 September, 2001. Much has been made, for example, of the so-called incompatibility between Islam and democracy (Scruton 2005). However, both the Bush and Blair administrations were at pains to distance themselves from the crude stereotypes of Huntington's thesis. President Bush (2002: 5) explicitly argued that '(w)hen it comes to the common rights and needs of men and women, there is no clash of civilizations. The requirements of freedom apply fully to Africa and Latin America and the entire Islamic world. The peoples of the Islamic nations want and deserve the same freedoms and opportunities as people in every nation.' Moreover, neo-conservatives claimed a commitment to a universalism in which liberal democracies could be entrenched by US power throughout the globe. Huntington – an opponent of the war in Iraq on the grounds that western societies should co-exist with other cultures – had therefore long ago been dismissed as a conservative pessimist and indeed a right-wing 'anti-American' by most neo-conservatives (Kaplan 1998). On the other hand, a watered down version of the clash of civilizations *was* propagated as part of the war on terror. This amounted to the idea that while there was no straightforward clash of civilizations, there was a clash between good and bad Muslims. This idea was drawn from the work of Bernard Lewis (1990), who actually coined the phrase 'clash of civilizations' before Huntington. 'Good' Muslims are regarded as those who want to become increasingly modern (or western) and embrace liberal democracy and free markets, while 'bad' Muslims are those that have interpreted Islam in a distorted way and have used this to legitimize terrorist actions against the West. In this approach, (bad) Muslim rage and terrorism are rooted in a caricature of Islam which is divorced from specific historical, social and political contexts.

Certainly it is true that there is no one single Islam, or one single Islamist political position. But equally, it is just as stereotypical to divide Muslims into a simplistic binary between good and bad, and by implication to make this division solely on the basis of a supposedly timeless culture, and moreover one that is assumed to exist outside of specific settings. At the same time, such contextualization does not amount to apology for the actions of some Islamist groups, nor indeed does it amount to an argument that such groups are merely reactive to the machinations of a western imperialism that is somehow ultimately responsible for the actions of these individuals and organizations. Certainly, such a contextualization is necessary to challenge not only the certainties of western liberal imperialists and neo-conservatives, but equally some of the spurious assumptions of anti-imperialists.

The idea of a clash of civilizations falsely homogenizes Islam, as if there was only one interpretation of Islamic texts. Moreover, it also falsely conflates Islam with Islamist politics, the latter of which is a political movement that attempts 'to resolve political and social issues by reference to Islam' (Halliday 2003: x). For most Muslims, religion constitutes just one part of their social, cultural and political identity. Islamists, on the other hand, attempt to reduce politics by (selective) reference to Islamic texts, which are themselves the subject of conflicting interpretations. Political and social issues are thus not reducible to a timeless Islamic tradition, because these issues exist in a wider, modern context and are themselves the subject of contesting interpretations. Halliday (2003: xii) thus makes the following distinction: 'Islamic tradition and values may provide an idiom in which these issues are expressed, but do not in themselves make up the argument. For not only is there great diversity of views between Muslims on these questions, and therefore no one "Islam", but the questions themselves are defined by the modern world in which they are located, not by tradition or text.' Thus, ironically, to reduce such issues to timeless cultural difference is actually to take the rhetoric of various Islamist forces at face value. For example, in the western world, much is made of the idea of *jihad*, which is often regarded as being synonymous with holy war and Islamic terrorism. However, *jihad* is subject to a number of interpretations within both Islamic religion and Islamist politics, and it actually means 'effort' (Hayes 2005). Even the Ayatollah Khomeini, perhaps the first recognized fundamentalist in western eyes, distinguished between *jihad-i asghar* (smaller military struggle), *jihad-i akbar* (greater struggle) and *jihad ba nafs* (struggle within the self). Current Islamist movements that advocate *jihad* are far from united in its meaning, both in general, and more specifically in relation to the enemy against whom it is directed. Osama bin Laden, for instance, repeats claims made by earlier Islamist movements that regard it as a personal and permanent obligation, an individual duty for every Muslim, and second only to *iman*, or belief in the key pillars that are said to constitute Islam (see B. Lawrence 2005). On the other hand, more orthodox Islamic scholars argue that profession of faith, prayer, fasting, alms-giving and pilgrimage constitute the five pillars, so bin Laden's argument is hardly part of Islamic orthodoxy. Following Sayyid Qutb, the main inspiration for contemporary Islamists, who was executed in Egypt in 1966, *jihad* is redefined by bin Laden and fellow al-Qaeda leader Ayman al-Zawahari as a permanent revolution against the enemies, both internal and external, that have usurped Islamic authority (Gerges 2005: 4).

On the other hand, there was some popular support in the Muslim and Arab worlds for the terrorist attacks against the United States in September 2001. But there was also considerable condemnation, including from the governments of Syria, Libya and Iran, the last of which is often regarded as the home of the Islamic challenge to the West. Even in Afghanistan, after the invasion there was considerable support for the removal of al-Qaeda forces, particularly from the Northern Alliance and its Iranian allies. Moreover, the sympathy that existed for al-Qaeda and bin Laden related more to issues of western influence in the Middle East, which includes support for autocratic regimes and for Israel in the Israel–Palestine conflict. These points suggest that if we are to employ the language of Huntington, then the various manifestations of contemporary Islamism are better understood in terms of a clash *within*, rather than *between* civilizations. However, even then we need to exercise caution, as this does not mean that such cultures exist in a social and political vacuum. Cultures are not only contested, they are also dynamic and subject to change, not least because they are contested. Moreover, culture must be linked to wider social and political contexts, which in turn show the variety of Islamist movements that exist in the world today. Crucial to this changing context are the colonial legacy, the Cold War and the post-Cold War eras.

The post-colonial era began in the years after the First World War, with the break-up of the Ottoman Empire, and the creation of new states under the tutelage of the victorious colonial powers from World War One (see Chapter 8). The divisions within these contested states were further complicated by the creation of the state of Israel in 1947. This marked the beginnings of secular nationalist regimes, committed to modernization through state-directed, ISI policies that attempted to construct new nations and overturn the colonial legacy (see Chapter 3). However, in practice, there was increasing disappointment with and resentment of the results of secular nationalist regimes, and Islamist movements began to develop in opposition to them. For example, one of the earliest Islamist movements, the Muslim Botherhood, gave support to the Nasserite 'revolution' in Egypt in 1952; it was quickly marginalized, and banned just two years later, although rich exiles continued to finance the movement from Saudi Arabia. There was also considerable opposition to regimes that enjoyed the support of the West, including Saudi Arabia, the Gulf states, Jordan and pre-revolution Iran. Islamism gained some ground with the humiliation of Arab states in the Six Day War with Israel in 1967, which further undermined secular nationalism. Marxist alternatives enjoyed some popularity in the 1970s, particularly among Palestinian movements, but this was short-lived.

Uneven development in the region gave rise to a massive urban poor, and a large number of students, who graduated from higher education institutions in large numbers, and with few resources. Graduate unemployment and underemployment, combined with the highly visible manifestations of urban poverty, provided a potential recruiting base to Islamist movements, both within and beyond the Arab world. This was reinforced with the neo-liberal turn in the 1980s, as states cut back on spending on (among other things) education, and Islamist movements moved in to fill the schooling gap left by the decline in public education.

At the same time, the general processes of marginalization and unemployment were also apparent before the neo-liberal turn, and it was in this context that the 'Islamic revolution' took place in Iran in 1979. This was led by Shia Muslim clerics, who not only challenged westernization in Iran and throughout the region, but also potentially challenged the dominance of Sunni Islam. The minority Shia Islam has it religious origins in the idea that Ali, the cousin and son-in-law of Muhammad, should succeed the Prophet, in contrast to the Sunni majority view that supported the Sultans and Caliphs, who ruled Islamic societies after Muhammad's death. Shi'ite Islam became the majority view in what later became Iran, as a result of the conquests by the Safavid dynasty in the fifteenth and sixteenth centuries. The Iranian revolution of 1979 was thus of great significance in challenging the dominant Sunni Islam in the region, and particularly in Saudi Arabia. It was also of great significance as a challenge to the secular Baathist regime in Iraq, where Sunni Muslims also constituted a majority, but were repressed by a regime that relied heavily on the support of Sunni Muslims, to whom certain privileges were dispensed. So great was the potential threat that Saddam Hussein launched an invasion of Iran in 1980, which led to the Iran–Iraq War of 1980 to 1988. This led to closer ties between the US (and Britain) and Iraq, who saw the new Islamic regime as a threat to its interest and hegemony in the region. At this time, almost all Islamic states also supported Iraq against Iran. Clearly then, these developments fly in the face of any simplistic notion of a clash of civilizations.

The second key issue is that of the Cold War. It is undoubtedly the case that western powers must hold some responsibility for supporting Islamist groups against other movements within the Muslim world. This applied above all to Islamist groups in Afghanistan, who enjoyed considerable support from the United States and its allies in the region including Saudi Arabia and Pakistan. After Soviet withdrawal in 1989, the US continued arming the *mujahidin*, and out of its different factions emerged the Taliban in the early 1990s, actively encouraged by sections of the state in both Pakistan and Saudi Arabia. Current liberal imperialists are quick to make the accusation that Islamists should be held accountable for their actions, as should all responsible moral agents (Geras 2002). It is for this reason that so many former anti-imperialists have moved across to embrace the camp of liberal imperialism. And indeed, it is a perfectly valid point, but it works both ways. For as Fred Halliday (2002: 37), a writer who can hardly be accused of embracing crude anti-imperialist politics, points out, 'there is a striking Western responsibility here too, for stoking up Islamic movements in the cold war period and in helping to promote the kind of autonomous terrorism that culminated in the Taliban and al-Qa'ida'.

This statement is broadly compatible with the idea of blowback (Johnson 2002), an idea that Halliday (2005: 202) elsewhere criticizes, at least by implication. But blowback is best understood not in the sense of absolving the responsibility of terrorists for their actions, but rather in the sense of not absolving the West from the historical amnesia with regard to past actions that are likely to have consequences in the present – and, one might add, for present actions that are likely to have consequences for the future (Gregory 2004; Kiely 2005b: ch. 6; Saull 2006). More immediately, in terms of relations within the Islamic world, the war in Afghanistan remained crucial in securing continued support for the Saudi regime's Wahhabist Islam, a strand of conservative Islam associated with the eighteenth-century thinker Muhammad ibn 'Abd al-Wahhab'. In particular, Wahhabi Islam now developed an activist, Islamist wing.

However, Saudi standing in the Muslim and Arab worlds was seriously undermined by the consequences of the Gulf War that followed Saddam Hussein's invasion of Kuwait in 1990. While this enjoyed considerable support by many Muslims and Arabs, as it challenged a conservative autocratic regime, it was opposed by many regimes that saw Saddam as a threat. The Saudi regime in particular welcomed US forces and the defeat of Iraq in 1991, but the growing US military presence in the region led to opposition to the Saudi regime, reinforced over the next few years by declining oil revenues and unemployment and underemployment in what was increasingly regarded as being a corrupt regime. Among the opponents of the US presence was Osama bin Laden, who had initially welcomed the US expulsion of Iraqi forces from Kuwait, but who also became increasingly opposed to an ongoing US presence in the form of military bases in Saudi Arabia. Support for both al-Qaeda and the Taliban grew on the Afghan–Pakistan border, and then in Afghanistan when the Taliban took power in 1996, although this remained small among Islamist movements as a whole (see below).

This brief historical survey of the rise of different strands of Islamism suggests a very different interpretation from that espoused by Huntington, and by Islamist movements themselves. These movements are less the product of a true, authentic civilization of Islam, and more the product of particular historical developments. These can be rooted in the legacies of colonialism, the Cold War and the post-Cold War world, but perhaps the most striking are two closely related factors. First, there are a wide variety of Islamist movements, which have their own political agendas and which are likely to conflict with the agendas of other movements. Secondly, while these agendas may be linked to regional and global questions, and so include the Israel–Palestine conflict, the question of oil, and foreign influence in the region, each movement is the outcome of specific, local and national circumstances and thus has its own local and national agenda. What this suggests then, is that Islamism and Islamist terrorism are closely linked to clashes within civilizations, and in particular 'between those who want to reform and secularize and those whose power is threatened or who want to take power in the name of fundamentalism' (Halliday 2002: 46).

This approach undermines the orientalist assumptions of many Middle East scholars, as Edward Said (1978) long ago pointed out. Huntington's work stands in a long line of political and other work on the Middle East, which assumes a homogenous region essentially determined by a culture of Islam. This of course ignores the existence of other religions in the region, the fact that Islam and the Middle East cannot be equated in this way (not least because so many non-Arabs are Muslims), different and contesting interpretations of Islam, and indeed different traditions of political thought (including within Islamist political thought). But this emphasis on heterogeneity equally undermines the assumptions of crude anti-imperialists who, by dividing the world into imperialist and anti-imperialist 'camps', implicitly or explicitly suggest that Islam or Islamism is simply the latest version of anti-imperialist politics (Chitty 2002; Petras and Veltmeyer 2005: 108–11, 124–6). Indeed, this approach is a kind of mirror image of the Huntington thesis, as it assesses Islamism solely in relation to the West, albeit this time the latter is regarded as the source of all the problems in the Islamic world. This reverse orientalism thus denies any agency to the developing world, or assesses this solely in relation to western imperialism, thus ignoring local and national sources of conflict, and the particular forms that these may take. These are of course internationalized, as the discussion above makes clear, but they are not reducible to western imperialism, or indeed the presence of the state of Israel, notwithstanding the policies of that particular state. Indeed, from the 1970s until the mid-1990s, Islamist movements paid little attention to the question of the West and imperialism, and instead focused on the removal of regimes within the Middle East.

It was events in Afghanistan that paved the way for a change in direction for some Islamist movements, but even then, the initial intention was to remove the Soviet-backed regime, and provide a haven for Islamist movements to prepare for the overthrow of a variety of regimes across the Middle East and West Asia. Indeed, this appeared to be the main motivation for the likes of bin Laden and al-Zawahari, who were both happy to be part of the marriage of convenience with the US in Afghanistan (Gerges 2005). It was only in the 1990s that bin Laden's version of 'jihad' was globalized, partly in response to the events that followed the Gulf War of 1990–1, but also in response to the failure of Islamism to achieve its goals. This failure reflected political incoherence and divisions, and the success of states in the region in marginalizing these movements, through both ideological and repressive means. But the result was an intensification of divisions, not only between mainstream and 'radical' Islamists, but also within the radical, jihadist wing itself. As Gerges (2005: 24) argues, 'In this sense, the United States was a secondary, not a primary target of jihadis' military escalation, and the bulk of jihadis [religious nationalists] remained on the sidelines and did not join the onslaught by their transnationalist counterparts.' The declarations of bin Laden and al-Zawahari against the 'far enemy', the United States and its allies, from the mid-1990s were thus part of a desperate attempt to revive a movement in decline. Indeed, many jihadist movements condemned al-Qaeda, largely on strategic grounds but sometimes by reference to Islamic law. This was most pronounced among senior figures within the largest Arab jihadist organization, *Al-Jama'a al-Islamiya*, or the Islamic Group. From among its leading figures came condemnations of bin Laden, rejections of inevitable confrontations between the West and Islam (a direct reference to an Islamic Group document of 1980 which, in a mirror image of Huntington, stressed 'the inevitability of confrontation'), and the assertion that Qutb was not an Islamic scholar of any note. These condemnations of bin Laden and al-Qaeda were well publicized in the Islamic and Arab worlds, though they received little attention in the West (Gerges 2005: 246). What they suggest is that al Qaeda was a seriously marginalized movement.

On the other hand, the Iraq war was a reprieve for the hopes and aspirations of the organization, as it hoped to develop a new movement of resistance to foreign occupation, as occurred in Afghanistan in the 1980s. Although this is unlikely to occur, the questionable grounds for invasion, and disastrous occupation, have provided fertile recruiting ground for people attracted to al-Qaeda, which, since 2001, exists less as an organization and more as a symbol of resistance against foreign occupation (Burke 2004). Seen in this light, the US and British war in Iraq was a spectacular own goal in the so-called war on terror, as the Joint Intelligence Committee, Foreign Affairs Committee and some influential think-tanks argued both before and after the invasion (Norton Taylor 2005; Royal Institute of International Affairs 2005). But equally, the divisions within these movements demonstrate the analytical bankruptcy of those anti-imperialist approaches which assume that such movements can be regarded as unproblematic representations of Islamic or Islamist resistance to imperialism. Certainly, the current insurgency in Iraq is united only in its hostility to the occupation, a hostility that goes way beyond the activities of the insurgents themselves. Moreover, there are all kinds of factions, including different varieties of Islamist and non-Islamist movements, many of which include reactionary political agendas as well as brutal methods of resistance, and perpetrated more on Iraqis than on the occupying forces (Hashim 2006). This point suggests that it is a question not only of recognizing these differences but also of understanding what these movements aspire to create. Because, for all their differences, Islamist movements generally aspire to authoritarian, backward-looking, and anti-democratic politics, with hostility directed towards democratic socialism as much as western imperialism. Certainly there is every reason to examine how and why such movements have developed, and the role of western imperialism in facilitating the emergence of such movements,[3] but there is no reason whatsoever for sympathy with their politics even if they are anti-imperialist (Levine 2005).

Social Movements: Agents of Post-development?

The idea of post-development represents a wider theoretical challenge than that of political Islam. At its core lies a critique and rejection of the idea of development. This academic debate focuses on the idea that development is intrinsically related to domination, is Eurocentric, technocratic and rejects the views and aspirations of local, grassroots, movements (Escobar 1995: 215). Post-development is championed as a subversive, radical, and people-centred alternative (Rahnema 1997). This section briefly outlines the broad contentions of post-development theory, and subjects them to a critical assessment. This implies the need for some theoretical discussion, but this is also related to post-development theory's contention that social movements in the developing world are agents of post-development, an issue taken up in more detail in the next section.

Post-development theory argues that development is a discourse invented after 1945. In this approach, 'discourse' means a particular way of viewing the world, an epistemological construction which closes off other ways of seeing the world (Sachs 1992). In closing off these alternatives, development becomes implicated in certain relations of power. Thus, for example, poverty is regarded as a problem to be resolved by 'development', which essentially means the use of technology, western knowledge, and growth, to overcome lack of income. The 'Third World' is thus defined by what it lacks when compared with the West. The Third World is poor because it does not have as high a 'standard of living', or is not as 'efficient', as the West. Post-development writers question the neutrality of concepts like 'standard of living' and 'efficiency', and suggest that these are inseparable from the construction of the discourse of development. Living standards are thus measured by the supposed norm of high Gross National Product (GNP), which ignores non-com-modified sources of livelihood, as well as wider questions such as environmental destruction and whether increased consumption actually leads to happiness (Hamilton 2004). In this way, the development discourse ultimately conflates difference with backwardness.

This approach is usually linked to Foucault's use of the concept of discourse, something explicitly acknowledged by many post-development thinkers (DuBois 1991; Escobar 1995). On the other hand, while Foucault tended to emphasize breaks and discontinuities, post-development theory tends to portray development as a monolithic idea (Ziai 2004). Moreover, while post-development writers undoubtedly draw on Foucault's earlier work (Foucault 1979), but end up with a notion of power from which there is no escape, Foucault attempted to reconstruct his ideas on the relationship between power and freedom, in later works (Foucault 1982, 1991). The question of how these works related to his earlier views on the relationship between discourse and power are, to say the least, problematic, not least because the latter works point in the direction of both a foundationalism and a universalism that Foucault was previously keen to reject (Dews 1987).

But more important for our purposes is the question of how post-development theory addresses these questions. In particular, if the development discourse is so pervasive and so tied to the question of power, then it is not clear how this can be evaded. Post-development writers are far from united on the question of alternatives (Ziai 2004), but these tend to fall into one of two categories, which are not necessarily mutually exclusive. The first is to embrace a politics of the grassroots, which itself is linked to the valorization of local communities as against the homogenizing influence of the development discourse. This in turn is linked to the rejection of development and modernity (Rahnema 1997; Esteva and Prakash 1998). It can be argued that this approach also constructs a rigid blueprint for the future, and thus is guilty of the same crime with which it charges the discourse of development (Cowen and Shenton 1996). Moreover, it is one that, despite some qualifications (Rahnema 1997: 381), tends to downplay the oppressive nature of 'vernacular societies' (Kiely 1999). Indeed, at times the hierarchies of these societies are celebrated in ways that closely resemble the conservative wing of US neo-conservatives (see, for example, Rahnema 1997). Related to this point, it is also a position that focuses excessively on the downside of development rather than on progressive features, such as improvements in health and other life chances, as well as the potential for participation in democratic societies (Corbridge 1998).

Of course, as the discussion in Chapter 7 made clear, these things are unevenly and unequally distributed, but this can hardly be blamed on the prevalence of a so-called homogenizing discourse of development.

Rather, such inequalities must be likened to capitalist development, which is intrinsically uneven and unequal, and is even more so in the era of neo-liberal globalization. The utility of post-developmental, cultural understandings of development, thus cannot be at the expense of critical political-economy approaches (Kiely 1999). When post-development writers draw on political economy, they tend to repeat the fallacies of 1960s underdevelopment theory, thus paving the way for anti-development blueprints based on the celebration of 'the local', delinked from the hierarchies of the world economy (Shiva 2005). But as we have argued throughout this book, these hierarchies cannot be explained through a simplistic core–periphery model in which the former develops simply by exploiting the latter. Certainly these hierarchies exist, but in many ways they are a product of the marginalization of some localities, countries and regions in the international order. Unfortunately, the localist wing of post-development theory adopts a position that effectively endorses such marginalization. Post-development writers regard this marginalization as an opportunity to construct alternatives to development, but in doing so they ignore the questions of inequalities and oppressions both within and between localities.

A second alternative is to embrace a more open-ended approach. This is potentially more fruitful, but it also has its problems. The argument in this case is that universal blueprints or models based on philosophies of history or essentialist objective interests must be rejected in favour of a more radical, democratic contingency. This is linked to Laclau and Mouffe's (2001: 191) claim that 'there is no radical and plural democracy without renouncing the discourse of the universal and its implicit assumption of a privileged point of access to 'truth''. Thus, Escobar (1995) endorses open-endedness through rejection of the idea of concretizing alternatives to development, on the grounds that such alternatives would constitute the very closure that characterizes the development discourse which he rejects. But, while open-endedness and a rejection of models and blueprints is welcome, contrary to Ziai (2004: 1057–8), this must not be through an endorsement of absolute open-endedness or contingency. This is so, not least because the idea of radical democracy that Ziai, and Laclau and Mouffe, endorse ultimately involves the closing off of anti-democratic alternatives and thus some universal principles, even if these face radically different social and political contexts that liberal universalists ignore (see Chapter 8 and earlier in this chapter). In other words, political engagement of any kind requires some forms of closure, a point well made by Derrida among others (see Parfitt 2002: ch. 4). In ignoring this uncomfortable reality, post-development theorists easily endorse an escape from, rather than engagement in, politics (Kiely 1999; 2005a: ch. 7; Parfitt 2002).

These abstract points are best illustrated by now turning our attention to the so-called anti-globalization 'movement of movements' (Klein 2002).

Global Justice and Anti-globalization

Anti-globalization and anti-capitalist politics broke into the mainstream after the protests at the WTO talks at Seattle in late 1999. Delegates from the WTO faced massive protests from a bewildering variety of activists. Although talks broke down owing to conflicts within the WTO meeting, the impact of the new anti-capitalist politics was still considerable. Protests continued, but what was less clear was the politics of the protestors. They were against something called 'globalization', but it was less clear what they were *for*.

Activists in the movement have debated this question since at least 1999, and some of the concrete proposals are discussed below. However, in some respects this objection to the open-endedness of the 'movement of movements' is misplaced, because it actually reflects a commitment to a different way of carrying out political practice. Rather than adopt an orthodox politics based on rigid political programmes, organizational hierarchies, and blueprints for the future, it is suggested that what is crucial is a commitment to open-endedness, lack of organization and hierarchy (not only internally, but also including a strategy of by-passing nation-states), and a rejection of blueprints. This argument is made on the not unwarranted grounds that a commitment to such closure helped to lay the basis for the 'authoritarian socialisms' of the twentieth century. It is made most strongly by autonomists and anarchists in the global justice movement, who reject any notion of closure and hierarchy on the grounds that these lead to new forms of domination (Holloway 2002). It is also of course very similar to the arguments made by post-development theorists, as discussed above. But this is also precisely where the weaknesses of this approach are most evident. For a commitment to absolute open-endedness, and a total rejection of any forms of political organization, carry their own dangers. As we saw above, the complete rejection of closure leads to an evasion from, rather than an engagement with politics, which must by its nature close off particular (oppressive and exploitative) forms of politics. Similarly, rejecting organization *per se* leads to new forms of hierarchies (or 'vanguards') based on the principle that the most daring or committed activists win the day, without any accountability to anyone else (Ross 2002). Organization is needed to ensure democratic accountability, and so, once again, politics cannot be evaded (Kiely 2005a: ch. 7). This does not mean that particular forms of hierarchical organization are needed, such as self-styled Leninist vanguard parties, but it does mean that some forms of organization are necessary. This is not only because of the question of accountability, but also because of the question of political *effectiveness*. Certainly, if the global justice movement is to have a future, then it must move beyond the simplistic celebration of resistance that can be found in concepts such as Hardt and Negri's multitude. This idea does nothing to take us beyond the 'market forces' shaping our world and the populist reactions to them (Bull 2005). Having said that, there remain important progressive, political and social movements throughout the world, and contrary to the claims made by many anarchists and autonomists, many of these movements in the South are not particularly influenced by autonomist ideas. Indeed, most have some form of political organization and, rather than by-pass them, these movements place concrete demands on local and national states.

What this suggests then is that many movements are more open-ended and flexible than the socialist and communist movements of old, but they are still committed to concrete political goals. Struggles over land, water, housing, employment, trade union rights, the environment, and so on are part and parcel of struggles against neo-liberalism. These are usually captured by the idea of 'reclaiming the commons', of reversing the increasing privatization of the world, and rejecting the idea that neo-liberal economics and the market can dominate public politics and citizenship (IFG 2002). The idea that the commons can be reclaimed is not without its problems, and it can lead to endorsement of a localist rejection of globalization. This principle is based on 'increased control of the economy by communities and nations, creating greater social cohesion, reduced poverty and inequality, improved livelihoods, social infrastructure and environmental protection, and with these a marked enhancement of the all-important sense of security' (Hines and Lang 2001: 290). A key principle is that of subsidiarity, which means that 'all decisions should be made at the lowest level of governing authority competent to deal with them' (IFG 2002: 107). International trade will only occur in cases that promote the reconstruction, rather than destruction, of local economies (Hines 2000). Localization therefore advocates the autonomy of localities from malign global processes. The precise boundaries of such localities are not very well defined, but it appears that they may refer to spaces below and above the nation-state, and to the nation-state itself (Hines and Lang 2001: 290). This principle applies throughout the globe, to countries of North and South alike. It is closely linked to eco-feminism, which champions 'an ecologically sound, non-exploitative, just, non-patriarchal, self-sustaining society' (Mies and Shiva 1993: 297). But equally, it can be linked to the populist critiques of capitalism that propose reactionary, backward-looking alternatives. In the late twentieth and early twenty-first centuries, these demands have often taken explicitly religious as well as localist forms, including political Islam, Hindu nationalism and Pentecostal Christianity (Hansen 2001; Davis 2004). While religious allegiance, even when combined with politics, is not necessarily reactionary, the fact is that many contemporary movements do take reactionary forms. Given that many of these have replaced the older, traditional left, this does represent an important strategic challenge for progressives (Roberts 2002). Simplistic celebrations of resistance, the multitude, the local and even the commons do not help in this regard.

Localism is also compatible with (some) ecological critiques of capitalist, industrial and consumer societies. This perspective refers to a radically different kind of society, in which economic growth is problematized or even rejected. This argument is part of a much broader critique of industrial (and post-industrial) society, which is based on the premise that such societies regard growth *per se* as a sign of progress, but this is not actually the case as it has led to all kinds of environmental problems. For orthodox economics, if there is environmental destruction this is because we do not sufficiently value the environment, and we express this fact through our purchases in the marketplace. The problem with this valuation is that the price of commodities only expresses their individual, and not their social, costs. The price mechanism therefore fails to take account of externalities, where the cost is external to the individual product and consumer. Thus, in the case of diminishing resources or pollution, those people that cause the problem are not the only ones affected by it. Orthodox theory's proposed solution to this problem is to make individuals accountable through an extension of the price mechanism. Thus, if a forest is rapidly depleted the solution is to privatize the forest, and the owner could then charge loggers a fee. The forest owner would have an interest in protecting the forest as his or her source of income would be undermined if all the trees were destroyed. But this does not guarantee that the owner will preserve the forest in an environmentally friendly way. If it is more profitable to cut down all the trees and build something else, or lease or sell the land, then the owner may well do so. This will have the effect of intensifying the environmental problem, and will not eliminate the problem of externalities caused by the destruction of the forest.

Green perspectives therefore reject both the over-emphasis on growth and the idea that the market can effectively regulate the problem of environmental destruction. However, what is less clear is how the issue of localism in itself could resolve these problems. Certainly, localist Greens can point to environmental problems associated with increased international trade (Wall 2005: ch. 4). But what is less clear is how localization in itself could resolve this problem. The principle of subsidiarity is based on the notion that self-determination is achieved by allowing political decisions to be devolved downwards as much as possible. But what if one locality wants to pollute? This is not a purely hypothetical question, as the European Union principle of subsidiarity allowed a Conservative government in Britain to embark on a road building programme that included the destruction of Twyford Down, an area that ecologists were particularly keen to preserve (Pepper 1996: 308). This suggests that localism in itself is not *necessarily* conducive to Green politics, or at least that such politics cannot be reduced to a question of scale.

This question relates to wider problems with the localist perspective, for it fails to deal with the question of inequality within, and between, localities. As it stands, the localist perspective tends to simply celebrate the local at the expense of the global, or in the case of Shiva's eco-feminism (hierarchical and unequally gendered), tradition at the expense of modernity. Localism can also lead to reactionary forms of politics, based on the principle of locals first. These points return us to the definitions of globalization addressed in Chapter 5, which suggested that much of the debate on the politics of globalization has focused on space rather than social relations. While contemporary advocates of globalization celebrate a progressive global against a backward local, localists tend to simply reverse the equation and celebrate the local at the expense of the global. However, local, national and global 'spaces' are not the issue – rather, the issue is about the social relations (and politics) within and between these spaces.

This is not to say that local or national struggles should be dismissed. Rather, like global struggles, they should be assessed on the basis of the ways in which they open up and extend rather than close off and restrict democratic principles and practices. The argument then is less about reclaiming the commons and more one of using the commons in new and radically democratic ways. In this way democracy is not simply a means to elect a government once every few years, and a government that has little power in the face of the power of global capital. Rather, democracy is regarded as a genuinely participatory process, operating at global, international, national and local levels (de Sousa Santos 2006). Democratic alternatives to neo-liberal capitalism thus challenge the domination of the market, the hierarchies of the state and the international nation-state system, and the inequalities between rich and poor, both within and between countries.

This book has demonstrated that these questions are closely linked. For example, a radical-democratic alternative to neo-liberal capitalism is, at one and the same time, a challenge to the dominance of consumer capitalism. As the great nineteenth-century theorists of modernity showed, modern society is in many respects a progressive society, but it is also one that has its downside, including questions not only of inequality and poverty, but also of alienation, disenchantment and anomie (Marx 1977; Durkheim 1984; Weber 1978). These themes continue to be developed in the present context of neo-liberal consumer capitalism, which has sometimes drawn on previously radical, alternative ideas as the basis for a new, dynamic capitalism (Frank 1997; Boltanski and Chiapello 2005). The contradictions of this new spirit of capitalism have been scrutinized by those (increasingly few) critical sociologists who remain committed to a critical analysis of a discipline which itself has become increasingly rationalized, technocratized and McDonaldized (Ritzer 1993; 2004; Bauman 1999; Woodiwiss 1997; 2005b; see also Adorno and Horkheimer 1979). For our purposes, we should also emphasize how the sociology of the developed capitalist societies is closely linked to the political economy of North–South relations. One of the main themes of this book has been to challenge the idea that there is a convergence between North and South based on increases in capital flows from core to periphery. This argument has also been used to challenge the crude anti-imperialist argument that the global North develops simply by exploiting the global South through capital relocation from core to periphery.

The evidence in Chapter 7 in particular demonstrated the fallacies of these arguments. However, neither is it the case that there are no links between the two, and if we shift our focus from production to consumption, then we can see these links in a different way. As Chapter 7 argued, there has been a substantial increase in manufacturing production in the periphery. This tends to be in labour-intensive sectors with low barriers to entry and which therefore are prone to competitive price pressures that lead to substantial price falls. The benefits to producers are therefore not as great as the benefits for those operating in higher-value sectors where barriers to entry remain high – and, which remain concentrated in the developed world. Hence, we have the high levels of concentration of capital in the international order discussed in Chapter 7. But at the same time, we also have substantial imports of lower-value consumer goods into the developed world from the developing world. These are crucial to the ongoing reproduction of consumer capitalism, particularly in the context of state policies that have relocated income from lower to higher wage earners, and from labour to capital, since the neo-liberal turn of the 1970s. In this context of falling real wages, falling consumer prices for these developing-world imports play a significant ideological role in the reproduction of consumer capitalism. But at the same time of course, the pressures of neo-liberal capitalism intensify the alienation and disenchantment associated with capitalist modernity. In this respect, neo-liberal capitalism produces alienation in the core countries, but at the same time, it relies (among other things) on increasing consumption as the new opium for the people. As well as relying on increased debt and asset (especially housing and share prices), this consumption draws heavily on imports from (parts of) the developing world.

These questions, then, relate to other proposed alternatives made by the global justice movements, particularly since the development of local, national, regional and global social forums since 2001. Among the proposals are increased controls on capital, increased aid and debt relief without neo-liberal conditions, increased democratization of some international forums and abolition of others, increased investment and democratization of public spheres, and increases in environmental regulation (Kiely 2005a: chs. 6 and 9; Wall 2005). The question of the feasibility of these issues (and how they might be put into practice) is a difficult one, but is it any less so than the claims made by those advocates – the neo-liberal imperialists addressed in this book – of the current order? In other words, challenging the feasibility of alternatives would be more acceptable if the current international order worked in the ways that its current advocates envisaged, but clearly it does not. Moreover, the question of 'what works' is not the same question as what is democratic, and the current order is clearly not democratic, not least because it 'only works' for some people. Of course there are difficult strategic questions for those committed to radical democracy to address, and which autonomists and anarchists fail to recognize. But what is clear is that democratic alternatives must be made on the basis of challenging, not expanding, the rule of the market, and the unquestioned logic of competitiveness as the way forward for all countries (and people). This would include some version of localization, but not as an end in itself, but rather as a means towards a more democratic end, drawing on collectivist strategies of work redistribution, planned international trade (including social protectionism), and greater regulation of the environment. In contrast, neo-liberal globalization, free trade and progressive competitiveness are all guilty of the charge commonly made against protectionism, namely that it is against internationalism and therefore should be rejected by progressives. A country that is promoting competitiveness at the expense of others, is attempting to export unemployment to other countries. Moreover, as we have seen, this is a self-defeating strategy that encourages a process of competitive austerity, while simultaneously dumping goods onto international markets already suffering from surplus capacity. The result is a greater intensification of work for some, lack of income for others, and limits on global demand while poverty and inequality persist at enormous levels.

The neo-liberal world is in this respect highly inefficient. It is also undemocratic as it involves the increased domination of the market over the lives of people throughout the world. Certainly, democratic expansion must be part of the alternative, but this certainly involves more participatory approaches to democracy than those envisaged by neo-liberalism. Furthermore, in a world increasingly urbanized but not necessarily proletarianized, at least in the sense that most cities are numerically dominated by the unemployed and underemployed, social and political change will rest on wider notions of class-led social transformation – or at least, wider than those envisaged by traditional, classical Marxism (Davis 2006). For all the populist (and even potentially authoritarian) weaknesses of the current opposition to neo-liberalism in Latin America, there may well be important lessons to be learnt for future political directions (Gibbs 2006). This is particularly true of the case of Venezuela, where Hugo Chavez has emerged as the champion of a renewed 'developmentalist' challenge to neo-liberalism (Gott 2000; Ellner and Hellinger 2003). Indeed, the left is on the rise in Latin America once again, with election victories in recent years in Brazil, Argentina, Peru and Bolivia, though the extent to which all of these have actually challenged neo-liberalism is questionable (for example, on Brazil, see Mollo and Saad-Filho 2006).

Nevertheless, important challenges are occurring, and the rise of Chavez is significant. He was elected in 1998, as leader of the *Movimiento Quinta República* (MVR). Over the next few years, Chavez set about establishing a new constitution and a new nationalist (and, he claims, socialist) alternative development strategy. This is in response to the failures of neo-liberalism in Venezuela, and the Latin American region as a whole (Adelman 2002), and has been opposed by old economic elites, third way social democrats who effectively support neo-liberalism, and the US states, especially during the Bush II presidency. This opposition has included a failed military coup in 2002, carried out with the full knowledge of the Bush administration, a lock-out and strike led by senior management in late 2002 and early 2003, and a referendum called to challenge Chavez's presidency (allowed for as part of Chavez's constitutional changes, whereby petitions signed by 20 per cent of the electorate can lead to a referendum). Given the fact that Chavez and the MVR have won numerous elections upheld as fair by international observers, this does put the current US commitment to democracy promotion, as well as Blair's calling on Chavez to uphold international law, into some kind of perspective. But what is crucial here is the kind of democracy being promoted by Chavez, and how this differs from the neo-liberal, low-intensity democracy supported by Blair and Bush.

In particular, the policies of the Chavez regime have aroused opposition in three key areas: oil, land, and urban slums. Venezuela has large quantities of oil and has benefited in recent years from high oil prices. In contrast to many of Bush's oil producing allies, Chavez has attempted to use this income to fund social programmes designed to reach the poor. In particular, he has challenged the formally nationalized state oil company, the PDVSA. This was taken over by the state in 1976, but was effectively run as a 'state within a state' by a senior management hostile to OPEC and national developmentalism, and broadly supportive of privatization. Successive presidents of the PDVSA used the company's overseas investments to transfer price, thus declaring profits outside of Venezuela and limiting royalties paid to the Venezuelan state. Chavez responded by limiting the amount of foreign investment in joint ventures, and by doubling the fixed royalties that the company had to pay to the state (Mommer 2003). This was strongly opposed by the oil company and led to a first attempt at a national strike in late 2001, as well as a further, stronger attempt a year later, as well as heavy involvement in the coup attempt in April 2002.

In the area of land, the regime has committed itself to an agrarian reform. Although Venezuela is an overwhelmingly urbanized country, and agriculture contributes only relatively small amounts to GDP, land reform was regarded as important in the context of a society where 5 per cent of the population owned 75 per cent of the land, and 75 per cent of landowners owned just 6 per cent of land, and where most producers worked land with no legal entitlement (Wilpert 2003: 108). The land reform that was introduced was actually hardly radical, although some important levies and restrictions were placed on large amounts of land that remained idle. Insofar as expropriation occurred, this was for large amounts of idle land, or smaller (but still quite large) amounts of high-quality and idle land. Landowners were still, however, compensated. Even this limited reform was too much for the main landowner federation, FEDECAMARAS, which was also active in the opposition that started with the lock-outs in late 2001.

Finally, and perhaps most important, there were developments in the shanty towns, or *barrios*. Protests against neo-liberalism were brutally suppressed in 1989, under President Carlos Andrés Pérez, but this led to the formation of the *asamblea de barrios*, which involved essentially social movements representing shanty-town dwellers, and that were key supporters of Chavez. These movements particularly demanded legal recognition of their homes, something taken up by opposition to Chavez in Congress, led by the movement *Primero Justicia*. Drawing on the idea of a Peruvian maverick neo-liberal populist, Hernando de Soto (2001), they promoted a draft law transferring land titles to slum dwellers where the state was the landowner, or where they had occupied the land for more than ten years. In Februrary 2002, Chavez issued a decree transferring legal ownership of the *barrios* to their inhabitants. This effectively meant a privatization of land, initially at least, as only public land could be transferred in this way. Private land could only be transferred once new legislation was passed through Congress. For some left-wing critics of the Chavez administration (Petras 2004), this 'privatization' is evidence not only of how moderate the Chavez regime is, but also of its continued commitment to neo-liberalism. But this argument misses the rationale for the shift in ownership, for as Wilpert (2003: 113) points out, 'where De Soto and Primera Justicia view urban land reform as essentially a means to encourage the accumulation of capital in the *barrios*, Chavez's supporters see it as a path to [participatory] democracy and self-help in the communities'.

This alternative perspective can be seen most clearly in the health programmes of the Barrio Adentro Mission, launched in April 2003, which is a health programme involving doctors, health workers and physical trainers (many from Cuba), and involves active local participation through local neighbourhood health committees (*Comités de Salud*), which manage the clinics. Subsidized drugs have also been made widely available. This extension of health care, to 17 million poor Venezuelans in its first eighteen months, has been praised by the Director of the Pan American Health Organization, and contrasts sharply with the pre-1998 era when around 70 per cent of the population were largely excluded from health care (Gibbs 2006: 271–2). Similar policies have also been adopted in education, where basic literacy campaigns and the upgrading of schools has occurred (Gibbs 2006: 274).

Chavez's vision is thus in some respects socialist, but he is also clear that '(w)e must reclaim socialism as a thesis, a project, and a path, but a new type of socialism, a humanist one which puts humans and not machines or the state ahead of everything' (cited in Albo 2006: 3). It is this commitment to a participatory, democratic means which has so confused both neo-liberals and traditional Marxists. For it is true that in some respects, Chavez's reforms have been quite moderate, in many ways compatible with older traditions of social democracy, which are clearly not to the tastes of the current neo-liberal leader of the British Labour Party. But equally, the classical Marxist condemnation of Chavez as a reformist misses important aspects of the Venezuelan experience. This book has argued that domestic capital in the developing world is largely committed to neo-liberalism, and that therefore any challenge to neo-liberalism is bound to have wider implications. This point has led at least one classical Marxist to invoke the spectre of the Chilean coup in 1973, and ask the question: 'Could socialism, the transfer of power from one class to another, actually be achieved within the framework of bour-geois democracy, even if the left were in government?' (Gonzalez 2004: 86; see also Ali 2004b; Petras 2004). This is a valid question, and any strategy of socialist transformation does have to address such questions. On the other hand, there is an implicit assumption that strategic prob-lems, contradictions and tensions simply disappear provided that the 'correct strategy' – the seizure of state power and nationalization of the commanding heights of the economy – is implemented. This ignores the likelihood of continued domestic and international resistance, and the question of avoiding authoritarian outcomes, which, as the history of socialism tells us, are all the more likely when such opposition arises. Above all, strategy must reflect on the tendency of socialists to separate means from ends, with the dire consequences for democracy that this has entailed. And this must mean rejecting simplistic models, either those associated with neo-liberalism and the market, or the one-dimensional classical Marxist understandings of revolution. Indeed, it is ironic that this Marxist purity has been used to attack a reasonably progressive (if far from flawless) government in Venezuela, whilst adopting a carelessly opportunistic policy of effective support for Islamism, all in the name of a simplistic anti-imperialism. Surely there is a far greater argument for more critical responses to Islamism, where anti-imperialism combines with reactionary politics, than to Chavez, where anti-imperialism com-bines with reasonably progressive politics.

Of course, none of this means that the events in Venezuela, or pos-sible future events in Bolivia, represent fully developed alternatives to neo-liberalism. There are some questions concerning some authori-tarian practices relating to the MVR's internal structure and some heavy-handed treatment of dissent within the country. Moreover, there are question marks over the extent to which progressive changes have relied on the fortuitous circumstances of high oil prices, and how this might change in the future. But these questions would not disappear if a Marxist 'revolutionary model' was implemented. It is also clear that the opposition to Chavez – including from the United States – is at least partly designed to wear down the Venezuelan population, in much the same way that this occurred in Nicaragua in the 1980s, culminating in the 1990 election defeat of the Sandinistas. What this brief discussion suggests then, is that the processes of social change in Venezuela, or indeed elsewhere, can only be understood in terms of processes, and not models, of social change. These processes are contingent, though not of course completely contingent, and they still require the asking of impor-tant strategic questions. But these must be asked in ways which do not discount these contingencies, and replace them with simplistically easy answers.

This brings us back to more general questions of alternatives, for it is also the case that for those advocating alternatives, perhaps most difficult is the question of recognizing the often unexpected or at least unintended consequences of certain reforms in the context of existing global inequalities. For instance, debt relief on its own could lead to later shortages of financial funds for countries now considered to be financial pariahs, and so the question of alternative sources of funds must be addressed. Similarly, consumer boycotts or universal labour standards could, if only operating as single issues, lead to increased unemployment in already poor countries. Universal environmental standards could have adverse consequences for poor countries and peoples for similar reasons (Kiely 2005a: ch. 8). Even the Tobin tax on international financial transactions is unlikely to present a convincing challenge to speculative finance, and indeed may further encourage the concentration of capital in the United States, as it would undermine the liquidity of less developed financial systems (Grahl and Lysandrou 2003). However, allusions to the contradictory consequences of certain proposed reforms are too often made by those who want to hang on to ways of justifying the status quo, and therefore amount to undemocratic rationalizations for an unequal and unjust international order. Or they are made by traditional Marxists who reject reformism in the name of simplistic calls for world revolution. We thus arrive back at the liberal-imperialist and anti-imperialist positions outlined – and rejected – throughout the book.

Conclusion

This chapter has provided an overview of alternatives to actually existing globalization, and done so by returning to the three political positions introduced in the opening chapter. It re-emphasized the point that liberal imperialism suffers from a naive view of the relationship between US hegemony, imperialism and globalization on the one hand, and development on the other. In doing so, it effectively endorses all kinds of double standards in support of US hegemony, in ways which contravene its own supposed commitment to universal human rights. It also has very little to say about issues of political economy, and development, and at worst effectively endorses (neo-)liberal fallacies concerning development, particularly concerning the issues of failed and rogue states. Anti-imperialists, on the other hand, offer essentially a mirror image of this view, supporting movements solely on the basis of opposition to US and western imperialism. Although this does not necessarily lead to an endorsement of underdevelopment theory, whereby the West develops by exploiting the developing world, this is the position effectively taken by many anti-imperialists. At the very least, they share the assumption with underdevelopment theory that agency in the developing world can only be assessed in terms of how it reacts to the fact of western domination, which leads to the politics of 'my enemy's enemy is my friend'. Finally, the third position takes a critical approach to US hegemony and imperialism, and rejects the idea that neo-liberal globalization represents the best route to development. But it accepts that some development may occur, albeit in an uneven and unequal context, and this leads to a complex position in terms of political alternatives. In short, this is a position that supports a progressive, democratic and cosmopolitan anti-imperialism, but which also recognizes the difficulties, contradictions and tensions in finding ways forward in the achievement of these goals. It was briefly argued that some quick-fix rejectionist positions, such as post-development theory, do not offer valuable ways forward, and indeed, too easily fall back on a position closer to crude anti-imperialism, albeit through a position that endorses cultural relativism. Important ways forward include the forging of alternatives designed to challenge the rule of the market, but done in ways which do not rigidly separate means from end, and which thus remain committed to democratic, participatory ways of presenting such a challenge.

Chapter 11

Conclusions

As the introduction suggested, all the chapters in this book can be read as stand-alone chapters, but they are also united by some common themes and a common theoretical approach, which were broadly identified in that introduction. This brief conclusion attempts to bring together the argument. It does so by returning to the four concepts identified in the introduction, and summarizing the general contentions made through the specific issues addressed in Chapters 2 through to 10.

Revisiting Globalization

This book has challenged many of the claims made about globalization, both generally and with specific reference to development. It has challenged the idea that globalization is a causal factor that can explain anything, and suggested that globalization can only refer to a set of processes that are caused by other factors. This argument laid the basis for an understanding of globalization that recognized the continued reality of the nation-state system, the hierarchical nature of this system, and the continued inequalities and unevenness associated with capitalist development. This is reflected in unequal voting power at the UN Security Council, the World Bank and the IMF, unequal bargaining power at the WTO, and the overwhelming capacity of some states to make (and break) international rules without fear of recrimination. It is also reflected in the power of some states to attract capital investment, and to bargain the terms on which such investment takes place. And it has intensified the power of capital to extract profits and to move money from one location to another, with limited developmental effects (see below). For these reasons, the idea that 'globalization' – defined more specifically as trade, investment and financial liberalization – is good for development is equally problematic.

On the other hand, globalization remains a useful concept for clarifying and understanding important recent changes in the international political economy. Essentially, the book has suggested that 'globalization' refers to a specific period of capitalist development that has some continuity, and some differences, with previous periods. The current era of globalization can be linked to the neo-liberal turn in the international economy from the 1970s onwards. This turn can itself be related to the post-war settlement, which provided some space for more consciously directed development in the periphery, and the generalization of import-substitution industrialization strategies. Despite the uneven and contested nature of the turn to neo-liberal globalization, this era of development through ISI is largely over. East Asia remains the one region that has challenged neo-liberal hegemony, and it continues to do so to some extent, particularly in China. However, the financial crisis in much of the region in 1997 consolidated a longer process of change in the direction of neo-liberalism, something that has occurred even in China since its 2001 entry into the WTO. Crucial to understanding these developments is not only the neo-liberal turn, but the growing globalization of production, which is discussed further in the context of development, below.

Revisiting Imperialism

Neo-liberals welcome the shift away from state-directed capitalist development on the grounds that markets can most efficiently allocate resources in the world economy. This contention has been challenged throughout this book, but relevant here is one of the historical arguments made to back up this claim. Much is made by this approach of the parallels between the current era of globalization and an earlier era of globalization, in the period before 1914, which was characterized by high growth in world trade and output (see Chapters 2 and 5). Interestingly, this is not so far removed from another comparison made between the two eras, by those Marxists advocating the continued relevance of classical Marxist theories of imperialism to understanding both the pre-1914 period and the current era of globalization. This view also draws parallels between the two eras, to suggest a renewal of inter-imperialist rivalries and the (neo-)colonial domination that characterized the pre-1914 (or pre-1945) period.

However, this book has suggested that much of the material in both the globalization and imperialism literature misunderstands the pre-1914 period, and makes fallacious comparisons with the current era. On the one hand there is the neo-liberal globalization position, which argues that the period before 1914 was one of increased openness and substantial growth, interrupted by the closed inter-war period. This perspective therefore sees contemporary globalization as desirable. On the other hand there is the classical imperialist position, which argues that the pre-1914 era was based on inter-imperialist rivalry, in which economic competition had given way to military competition. This occurred in the context of the export of (some) capital to the periphery and a new era of colonial annexation. These theorists condemn the current era for replicating the run-up to 1914. Alternatively, it could be argued that there are substantial differences between the two eras, and insofar as similarities exist, neither the liberal imperialist nor the classical Marxist positions get to grips with what these are. In terms of differences, there is a far greater degree of integration in the current era, based on openness in dealing with trade, but crucially in foreign investment. Contrary to the liberal view, the pre-1914 era was not one based on an open international economy – it was an era, as Hilferding pointed out, of protectionist tariffs at home, and monopoly trade with the colonies (see Chapters 2 and 5). Britain was an exception in that it attempted to continue its free trade policies, at least until the 1930s, but then free trade was the policy that had promoted British interests when it was the most powerful economy in the world. Other major powers responded by protecting themselves from foreign competition – a policy not available to the colonies who had open trade policies with their respective colonial power – and ultimately, despite two world wars, undermining British hegemony (Chapter 2).

In the current era of globalization, greater openness has been encouraged, particularly since the neo-liberal resurgence of the 1980s and 1990s (Chapter 4). This has led to greater international and transnational integration and cooperation (Chapters 6 and 9) – something that more critical theories of globalization have, sometimes clumsily, tried to capture. Moreover, this has occurred in the context of the universalization of state sovereignty, rather than the earlier period of colonialism, a phenomenon that is not adequately theorized by classical Marxists or many theorists of contemporary globalization.

These criticisms suggest that classical theories of imperialism are strictly limited in their usefulness for understanding the contemporary era of globalization. Does this mean that we live in a post-imperialist era? I have suggested not, and have linked this to the hierarchies that characterize actually existing globalization, such as the capacity of some states to determine, or strongly influence, the actions of others, and the unevenness and inequality of international capitalist accumulation. I return to the former issue in discussing US hegemony, and the latter issue in examining development.

Revisiting Hegemony

In the post-war period, US hegemony in the advanced capitalist world was secured through reliance on the US economy (particularly aid and foreign investment), and the US military as a shield against the potential communist challenge. It has been suggested by some that with the rise of new economic competitors, neo-liberalism, and the end of the Cold War, US hegemony has come under considerable challenge. For this approach, the US remains dominant but not hegemonic (R. Cox 1987).

This book has partially challenged this perspective, and suggested that in many (if not all) respects, the US remains the hegemonic power in the international order, even if this has partially been undermined by the more naked displays of unilateralism and militarism since 2001. The predominant direction of change in the international order is in a neo-liberal direction, even in the East Asian region, which until recently most successfully resisted neo-liberal ascendancy. The reasons for such changes cannot be reduced to the fact of US primacy, simply imposing its will on all nations. There are good reasons why dominant actors and states in the developing world choose to opt in to the US-led, neo-liberal order (Chapters 5, 8 and 9), even if this has sometimes taken a more overtly disciplinary form (Chapters 4 and 8), and even given rise to (economic) conflict (Chapter 6). Thus, contrary to R. Cox's (1987: 299) claim that US hegemony has given way to US domination, we can still talk of the existence of US hegemony.

This hegemony has relied on the extension of the concept of state sovereignty, and so has ruled through the existence of other states. This always carries the risk that these states will not ally themselves with the US, even if (as argued above) dominant actors may increasingly support neo-liberal capitalism. Given its commitment to the extension of state sovereignty, as opposed to formal colonialism, can the US be described as an empire (M. Cox 2004)? The answer to this question in part depends on what is meant by 'empire', which throughout history has usually meant formal control of other territories. In this respect at least, describing the US as an empire fails to capture the distinctiveness of US hegemony in an international *capitalist* order, in which political–territorial control has become increasingly separated from the control of economic power (Rosenberg 1994; Saull 2004).

As has already been made clear, we can still talk of imperialism, albeit in a changed context of globalization, as this reflects the structural power of the US in the world economy. But it is also an imperialism based on sovereign states and high degrees of interdependence between these states, particularly (but not exclusively) in the developed capitalist countries. Indeed, it could be argued that R. Cox's (1981: 146) theory of the internationalization of the state reflects an *increase* in US hegemony, as dominant actors in capitalist states increasingly accept and actively promote the neo-liberal international order. Insofar as we can draw on the concept, the current international order is characterized by an *imperialism of free trade*, ultimately policed, but not totally controlled, by the US state. The US state is the dominant and hegemonic state in this order, not only because of its military role or political power, but also because of the structural power of the US economy and its privileged position in terms of international finance (which in turn has facilitated considerable productive leadership in cutting-edge sectors since the early 1980s).

But clearly there have been some important changes since 2001. Rather than regarding these as completely novel, this book has suggested that they should be located in the context of the primary position of the US in a capitalist world of sovereign nation-states. Since 1945, there has been a tension between the role of the US state as the leader of the empire of civil society, and the US state as the state of exception, claiming 'the power to decree national and international rules, laws and norms, whilst reserving "exceptional power" for themselves' (Gill 2004; see also, Agamben 1998; 2005). What this suggests is that since 2001 and perhaps before then, the US state has attempted to use hard military power to 'Americanize'[1] (parts of) the world. Thus, paradoxically, R. Cox's distinction between hegemony and domination may be more appropriate, after 2001, rather than using a comparison of the 'domination' of the 1980s and 1990s with the 'hegemony' of the 1950s and 1960s. Seen in this way, it may well be the case that 'Bill Clinton was actually a much more effective imperialist than George W. Bush' (Johnson 2004: 255).

Much of the literature on US 'empire' reflects the shifts in US foreign policy under Bush, and especially the unilateralist and militarist trends in current US politics. However, this book has suggested that the use of hard and unilateral power is unlikely to work, and in some respects it is not a rational response to the realities of the international order – even from the viewpoint of the most powerful agents in that order. But equally, the overt unilateralism of the Bush administration is in retreat, and we should remember that all US administrations since 1945 have contained elements of unilateral and multilateral practices. It is certainly true that most of the US's European allies regarded the war against Iraq as an imperial adventure that had little to do with the war on terror. But this disagreement is hardly evidence of a new era of inter-imperialist rivalries. These same allies have, with the exception of Iraq, given their support to post-Cold War military adventures, and even in this case, they effectively legitimized the US-led occupation after the invasion through the United Nations. Nevertheless, it remains the case that US military power does not guarantee its economic supremacy, despite the fantasies of US neo-conservatives and their Leninist critics. We should not conflate the existence of limitations on US power with the idea that a new hegemonic region is likely to emerge, at least in the foreseeable future. Current regional 'challengers' to the US have too much stake in the current international order, are themselves moving in neo-liberal directions, and so are unlikely to constitute a challenge, either to US or to neo-liberal hegemony (Chapter 9).

The shift after 2001 to a more openly unilateral position reflects two probably incompatible trends: (i) impatience with the slow pace of extension of liberal states and/or US allies in the international order; (ii) a 'realist' commitment to US primacy in that order. There is a tension between these two goals, but also it is far from clear that US military power alone is sufficient to promote liberal expansion in the periphery (Chapter 5). This is not only because of the methods used, or the double standards in which some non-liberal states are allies in the war on terror, but perhaps above all because the idea that the promotion of a liberal state represents a model for others to follow ignores the conflicts – over property, accumulation, state legitimacy, national identity - that have taken place in the current liberal states in the past (Chapter 8). But perhaps above all, the US state's commitment to a neo-liberal international order, backed up by most states in the current international order, will not resolve important contradictions and tensions in the international capitalist order, and these are most acute in the developing world.

Revisiting Development

This book has argued that there has been a significant change in the international and global context in which development is occurring. Particularly important has been the shift from a neo-Keynesian to a neo-liberal world. The case made by neo-liberals and mainstream globalization theorists is that provided the correct policies and institutions are in place, developing countries can reap the fruits of the opportunities presented by globalization. In contrast, this book has argued that greater openness has effectively undermined the development prospects for the (former) 'Third World' by reversing those protectionist and industrial policies that led to the rise of the newly industrializing countries (Chapter 3), and before that, those nineteenth-century economies that protected themselves from British competition. Seen in this way, developed countries have literally 'kicked away the ladder' on which they climbed, through protectionist industrial policies, but which they increasingly disallow for current developing countries (Chang 2002).

This can be seen in the ways in which free trade is increasingly promoted, which undermines the potential for protectionist measures that could be used to promote upgrading. Instead, developing countries continue to specialize in lower-value activities, importing higher-value goods that accrue significant rents, mainly from the already developed world (and parts of East Asia). And at the same time, developed countries continue to protect these rents, not least through various agreements made at the WTO (see Chapter 6), the very organization which is supposedly committed to the expansion of free trade. While not always and everywhere harmful, liberalization policies still have negative developmental consequences: trade liberalization can undermine the prospects for industrial upgrading; investment liberalization can too easily increase bargaining power for foreign capital against states; and financial liberalization can promote speculative activity and generally influence corporate behaviour in ways less conducive to long-term development and more for short-term profit-making. For these reasons, contemporary globalization can be associated with the return of an era of free trade imperialism (Chapters 2, 5, 6 and 7). In this era, not only do late developers suffer, in that their ability to adopt dynamic comparative advantage is undermined, but so, too, is there a concentration of capital in established areas of accumulation (Chapter 7). This is not so different from the pre-1914 era, when most capital flowed to other developed countries, rather than to the periphery – an argument that undermines both neo-liberalism and Leninist theories of imperialism (Chapter 2).

On the other hand, while neo-liberal ideologues are clearly wrong in their claims made for the international economy, it is the case that neo-liberalism is increasingly becoming the dominant form of capitalist accumulation throughout the world, and this must be linked to the liberalization of finance and its effect on corporate behaviour in general (Chapters 4 and 8). This has not led to convergence in terms of outcomes, or indeed policy, and a considerable variety of national capitalisms continue to exist. Moreover, global restructuring since the 1970s has facilitated a growing concentration of power for capital as against other social groups. Capital has partially relocated some activities to the developing world, but has simultaneously concentrated high-value activity in the developed world. Developing countries may have increased their levels of industrial output and activity, but this has generally been at the lower end of value chains. Indeed, while investment liberalization has in some ways encouraged foreign investment in parts of the developing world, trade and investment liberalization has also ensured that this has simultaneously undermined the capacity of developmental states to upgrade and develop higher-value activity in developing countries.

This of course begs the question of the rise of China, which is often used to support the idea that globalization can be development friendly and can lead to high rates of poverty reduction. However, this book has questioned the extent to which China has been more 'globalization friendly' than other countries. It has also pointed to some real contradictions in Chinese development strategy, and while it has accepted that industrial policy's success has been limited on its own terms, this in itself does not undermine the case for industrial policy or confirm the case for neo-liberalism. Neo-liberalism is found wanting in that it either ignores the forms of intervention that run counter to its arguments, or fails to see the rationale for such intervention in a world of unequal competition. Insofar as the claim is made that industrial policy is irrelevant to China's rise, this fails to analyse the limits of Chinese industrial development convincingly. More specifically, I have argued that Chinese development must in part be analysed in terms of the restructuring of global capitalism, and the success of China in attracting investment and subcontracting agreements with foreign capital. But on the whole, this has not led to the kinds of significant technological upgrading and domestic linkages that have characterized the shift to 'developed' country status or indeed the upgrading that characterized the first-tier East Asian newly industrializing countries. Moreover, Chinese development in the context of a massive global reserve army of labour and global over-capacity means that the prospects for other developing countries are limited, and therefore so too is the potential for substantive reductions in global inequality. This final point relates to the wider limits of pro-globalization policies, which essentially advocate a process of competitive austerity in which everyone is expected to attempt to increase exports and cut imports, or one of progressive competitiveness, which in the context of global over-capacity and uneven development, eventually leads back to a process of competitive austerity (Chapters 8 and 9).

Alternatives to neo-liberal development may include the revival of the developmental state, and a return to a Bretton Woods-type system of nationally directed capitalism. Thus, many of those who decry the kicking away of the ladder by developed countries have called for a revival of the developmental state (Gallagher 2005). Certainly, in some respects this may be more desirable than a neo-liberal world of increasing inequalities, environmental destruction and growing uncertainties associated with the fall-out from competitiveness. But we need to remember that there were good reasons why Bretton Woods was first put into place, in response to brutal struggles, world wars and the rise of Nazism and Stalinism. We should also remember that Bretton Woods was a compromise that reflected the existence, no matter how undesirable in many other respects, of the Soviet alternative. We also must remember that development in this era was also a brutal, conflict-ridden process, as is always the case with capitalist (or any?) development. And perhaps above all, in the current era of neo-liberal globalization, where 'national capitals' in the developing world benefit from access to the free movement and globalization of the circuits of capital, entering into joint ventures and licensing agreements with foreign capital, and easily moving money from one location (and/or currency) to another, we must question the capacity and commitment of domestic capitalists to a process of renewed national capitalist development in the developing world. In this regard, while it may be true that a developmentalist national *capitalism* is in some respects progressive (if also contradictory), when compared to relatively weak, underdeveloped or backward capitalisms, it does not follow that national *capitalists* are progressive agents, committed to such a task of national development. Indeed, this point increasingly applies even to East Asia, where there have been significant processes of neo-liberal restructuring which pre-date the 1997 financial crisis. For these reasons, simplistic attempts to revive the concept of the developmental state in opposition to neo-liberalism look naive at best, and counter-productive at worst. Certainly, domestic opposition by capital to current experiments in Latin America is instructive in this regard.

Thus, insofar as the developmental state is to be revived, it must be recognized that this will be in a radically changed domestic and international context, which is likely to involve important challenges, not only to the dominance of the market, but to those social agents that have increasingly come to support the rule of the market. As the last chapter suggested, this is not an endorsement of an old-fashioned socialist revolution based on a state takeover of power and immediate nationalization of the commanding heights of the economy. Political strategies committed to progressive social change have to be committed to democratic methods, and in doing so, learn from the mistakes of the past. But at the same time, they also need to be aware of how strategies can both challenge and transcend existing power relations.

The question of development is central to such understandings. One of the key arguments of the book has been that neo-liberalism is not a strategy that is likely to promote convergence with the developed countries through ongoing processes of capital accumulation, but at the same time local capital in the developing world is increasingly committed to neo-liberalism as it sustains access to global circuits of capital. This argument should not be mis-interpreted. In particular, I am not advocating a return to older theories of dependency, and especially underdevelopment theory, which argued that capitalist development was impossible in the periphery, so long as nation-states remained integrated into the world economy (for a critique, see Kiely 1995: ch. 3). Nor am I advocating a return to the old Soviet Marxist analysis of the 1930s, which suggested that imperialism held back development and so what was needed was an anti-imperialist alliance led by national bourgeoisies in the colonial world (for a survey, see Brewer 1990: 133–4). Delinking from the world economy represents a dead end as an alternative strategy, and of course some capitalist development has occurred, and is still occurring in the developing world (albeit at slower rates than in the ISI era).

But on the other hand, I have also suggested that growing openness in the international economy does not represent a way forward, as it undermines the prospects for upgrading and developing more dynamic sectors in a very unevenly developed and unequal world economy. Thus, while development of the productive forces continues to occur in a capitalist-dominated world, this does not lead to convergence and in many ways undermines it. Modernization, neo-liberal and even some Marxist approaches such as that associated with Bill Warren (1980) are therefore also wrong, in that they assume some processes of convergence simply through the diffusion of capitalism throughout the globe. Selective delinking through industrial policy, alongside other protectionist policies, is thus important, in part to develop the productive forces (but also for other reasons which would include environmental considerations). In this way it is not a case of either integration or openness, but of changing the terms on which integration takes place – and, contrary to the claims of the post-Washington consensus, this would involve policies designed to limit, rather than extend, the rules of the market. But ultimately, development should not be defined in such a narrowly technocratic way, and the case for alternatives does not just rely on the 'developmentalist' potential of alternatives to neo-liberalism. Instead, development also means the extension and expansion of people's capacities and capabilities, and this must mean transcending the narrow limits of liberal democracies, both generally, and in the specific contexts of neo-liberal rule, particularly, but not exclusively, in the developing world (Wood 1995; Boron 2005; de Sousa Santos 2006). In a world in which liberal democracy is everywhere in crisis, development is thus a major issue for all nation-states, and indeed for relations between these states.

More generally, we would also do well to remember that many of the supposed alternatives to 'actually existing globalization' in the current period are far from progressive, and thus warn against the anti-imperialist principle of 'my enemy's enemy is my friend'. Any search for alternatives must therefore be committed to democratic and internationalist principles, which must challenge the rule of the market, and therefore must transcend the view that there is no alternative to actually existing globalization.

Notes

Notes to Chapter 2: Capitalist Expansion and Imperialism

1 For fuller explanations, see Teschke (2003), and Kiely (forthcoming).
2 See Chapters 3 and 9.
3 This is the main flaw in the work of Gallagher and Robinson on the imperialism of free trade. They argue that there was a substantial continuity in the nature of imperialism throughout the nineteenth century, pointing out that '(b)etween 1841 and 1851 Great Britain occupied or annexed New Zealand, the Gold Coast, Labuan, Natal, the Punjab, Sind and Hong Kong. In the next twenty years British control was asserted over Berar, Oudh, Lower Burma and Kowloon, over Lagos and the neighbourhood of Sierra Lerone, over Basutoland, Griqualand and the Transvaal: and new colonies were established in Queensland and British Colombia.' (Gallagher and R. Robinson 1953: 3–4). They argue that annexation was largely a response to anti-colonial revolt in the 'colonies'. This view is rightly associated with the idea that formal political domination is not necessary for imperial domination (though this view is compatible with Lenin), and that there was substantial continuity (that is, the promotion of free trade policies) within the *British* Empire. However, the expansion of so many powers reflected a changed context, and therefore considerable discontinuity with the situation before the 1880s.
4 This is not to say that this legacy has *determined* post-colonial politics irrespective of time and place, but it is to say that it has helped to shape the character of post-colonial politics, albeit in historically and socially specific ways in particular locations. See also, note 6.
5 It is also associated with some Marxists, such as Bill Warren, and enjoyed a revival by Marxist-inspired work, as we will see in later chapters. For a Marxist-influenced critique of this work, which discusses in detail Marx's dual legacy on colonialism, transitions to capitalism, and the international division of labour, see Kiely (1995: ch. 2).
6 This is a favourite argument of Niall Ferguson, who compares postcolonial developmental performance with economic growth and living standards in the colonial era. But his own contentions hardly present a favourable account of the colonial era. For instance, he accepts that the 'average Indian had not got much richer under British rule', and cites evidence that per capita income in India increased by just 14 per cent from 1757 to 1947, compared with 347 per cent for Britain (see Ferguson 2003: 216). His argu-

ment that the colonial legacy is irrelevant to understanding postcolonial states and economic development is, for a historian, breathtakingly ahistorical.

7 Fieldhouse's (1973; 1999) case for liberal Empire rests largely on the myth of underdevelopment, and the recognition that there was some growth in the colonies. His case for liberal Empire – a far more subtle one than Ferguson's – is marred, however, by setting up the argument in terms of the 'either/or' of underdevelopment or modernization. Instead, a case could be made for uneven development, as has been made in this chapter. For a critique of this either/or approach, albeit applied to post-1945 development, see Kiely (1995: ch. 3).

Notes to Chapter 5: Globalization and Contemporary Imperialism

1 For three works influenced by Marxism but which welcome the decline of the nation-state on the grounds that this will promote convergence between capitalist countries, see Harris (2003), Desai (2002), Kitching (2001). For a critique of these arguments see Kiely (2005a: chs. 2 and 9). See also the argument in Chapter 2 of this book.

2 In response to the critiques by Rosenberg (2000; 2005), Scholte (2005b) has partially retreated on this dichotomy, but only at the cost of further retreat from his own stronger claims about the novelty and distinctiveness of globalization theory.

3 Cooper makes the charge against A. Appadurai, *Modernity at Large: Cultural Dimensions of Globalization* (1996).

4 In this respect his work differs from neo-Gramscians like Gill, who more closely links this transnationalization process to US state strategy. See Gill (2003: especially chs 5 and 7); and Gill (2004).

5 For state capitalist analyses of the former Soviet Union and of the Cold War, see Cliff (1988) and Harman (1988). For critiques of this approach, applied both to the Soviet Union and to understanding the Cold War, see Bellis (1988) and Saull (2001).

6 In fairness to Harvey, his analysis does not assume that such a strategy will work, while other theorists such as Callinicos, Gowan and Tariq Ali assume that there is a relatively straightforward functional connection between US military and US economic dominance.

7 The question of regionalist challenges to US hegemony is discussed in Chapter 9.

8 The best account of contemporary economic imperialism is Albo (2003). For similar if not entirely compatible analyses, see Panitch and Gindin (2003; 2004; 2005a), Kiely (2005b; 2005c) and Bromley (2006).

9 There are of course significant differences, not least the fact that such cooperation is organized by a hegemonic US power. Kautsky also under-esti-

mated the significance of uneven development. Nevertheless, given the degree of cooperation between core capitalist states and the fact that continued competition does not *necessarily* give rise to inter-imperialist rivalry, the international order is best described as ultra-imperialist.

10 This account of the links between US hegemony, neo-liberalism and financial capital owes something to Gowan (1999), even if this work is marred by a tendency to exaggerate the coherence of US policy from 1971 onwards.

11 See www.globalissues.org/Geopolitics/ArmsTrade.

12 Much the same point was made in Chapter 2 about classical imperialism. A similar point is made in J. Nederveen Pieterse (2004: 270).

13 These points are developed further in Kiely (2005b: chs 4 and 6); Bromley (2006); and from a liberal position by Nye (2004); and from a constructivist position by Reus-Smit (2004).

14 Thus, some neo-conservatives outside the Bush administration criticized its foreign policy for not being sufficiently belligerent. Lawrence Kaplan and William Kristol for instance were unconvinced that the administration, including allies such as Rumsfeld, Cheney and Wolfowitz, had the stomach for a long-term occupation or invasion of other 'enemy states', arguing for overwhelming military force instead of the policy of 'Iraqification'. Similarly, Max Boot argued that further 'blowback' against US primacy could only be avoided by a massive expansion of US overseas commitments. This amounts to a call for massive expansion of US overseas commitments, but it is difficult to see how this can be compatible with the preservation of a system of state sovereignty, or any idea of liberal or perpetual peace. Instead, it is a programme for absolute domination – and even that provokes 'blowback'. Certainly it is a world away from the idea that US power can be justified by the idea that it represents the global good. See Kaplan and Kristol (2003); Kristol and Kagan (2003); Boot (2003). On blowback – the idea that US foreign policy and alliance building in one period will have dire consequences for the US in another period – see Johnson (2002; 2004).

15 In fairness to Duffield and Waddell, they do qualify the extent of the break.

16 One prominent US neo-conservative, Charles Krauthammer (2004), distinguishes between the 'democratic globalist' and 'democratic realist' wings of the neo-conservative movement in the US. The former are more committed to liberal democratic expansion, the latter to more traditional power politics. In practice, in promoting unilateralism, military power and alliances with undemocratic countries, all neo-conservatives mix the two positions.

17 Risk is a concept associated with the prominent sociologist Ulrich Beck (2005), but Blair's usage is quite different, at least when applied to contemporary international relations. Briefly, the former suggests that politicians talk down the language of risk to give the appearance of managing risk (and therefore being in control), while the latter talks up risk to suggest the potentially catastrophic consequences of future possibilities – in this case, of the coming together of terrorists and Weapons of Mass Destruction.

18 See www.mca.org

Notes to Chapter 6: Cosmopolitanism, Globalization and Global Governance

1 There is now a massive literature on the concept of global civil society. See, for example, the annual global civil society yearbooks, edited by Anheier et al. More sceptical accounts can be found in Colas (2002) and Kiely (2005d), while Chandler (2004a) represents a hostile rejection of the idea that global civil society constitutes a new space, in which progressive politics operate. A useful collection with views from all sides, albeit rather too many distinctly odd ones, can be found in Chandler and Baker (2005).

2 United Nations, *Universal Declaration of Human Rights* (at www.un.org/rights).

3 This sociological account of human rights has a long tradition, usefully surveyed in Woodiwiss (2005a).

4 For an argument along these lines, specifically applied to the war in Iraq in 2003, see Kiely (2004b).

5 The use of the terms 'positive' and 'negative' is not, however, a value judgement. Berlin (1969) remains the standard account of positive and negative rights, and he comes down on the side of the latter. For a position more sympathetic to positive rights, see Shue (1980).

6 On the role of civil society organizations and the global media in promoting global awareness of humanitarian crises, see Shaw (1996). For a more negative view, focusing much more explicitly on development NGOs working in humanitarian crises, see de Waal (1997).

7 See Commission for Africa (2005a).

8 Purchasing Power Parity is defined and discussed in more depth in the next chapter.

9 This is the basic argument made by Chandler (2004a). While one can certainly see the strength of the argument, it is taken too far by Chandler, and is contradicted by his later criticisms of global civil society's advocacy role, which essentially means putting pressure on representatives from within official politics.

10 The quote within the quote is from G. Hegel's *Philosophy of Right*. See also Fine (2001: chs 1 and 2).

11 Geldof (2005) defends the achievements of the campaign. Interestingly, in an earlier defence (see Burkeman, 2005), the promise was made that in the absence of breakthrough talks at the WTO meeting in Hong Kong, the campaign would heighten its demands for trade justice. Beyond a vague and non-binding commitment to trade liberalization in agriculture by 2012, no breakthrough of significance did occur, but no campaign was forthcoming.

Notes to Chapter 7: Globalization, Poverty and the Contemporary World Economy

1 See www.un.org/millenniumgoals. The proposed reduction has been back-

dated, so that it starts from 1990, and not when the goals were adopted in 2000.

2 A third, and wider question also arises, which is the extent to which income itself is a useful measure of poverty. See, for example, the use of wider development indicators in annual United Nations Development Programme (UNDP) *Human Development Reports*, which was strongly influenced by the work of Amartya Sen – see Nussbaum and Sen (1993) and Sen (1999). This is an important debate, but is not the main concern of this chapter. Briefly, it is fair to say that income is not a sufficient measure, but it remains a central factor in any adequate measurement of poverty and inequality, and there is some correlation between economic growth and wider social development indicators, even if this is not as straightforward as neo-liberals claim. See the discussion in Kiely (1998: ch. 2). Also, the principal focus on income measurements in this chapter is justified by the fact that it takes issue with neo-liberal claims about poverty and inequality *on their terms*. Moreover, one of the ironies of using the less economistic Human Development Index (HDI) is that this is bound to show considerable evidence of convergence, and therefore – despite the UNDP's intentions – could be used to support the neo-liberal case. This is because two of the components of the HDI (education, and life expectancy, the other is purchasing power parity (PPP) per capita income) are bound to slow down the higher the gain in education and life expectancy. For example, one cannot have a literacy rate beyond 100 per cent and gains in life expectancy are bound to be slower once the average reaches a level above 70, at least compared with countries where life expectancy may only be in the forties. Any gains made by poorer countries therefore register as a movement towards convergence.

3 The precise figure is $1.08 a day, based on PPP, but the $1 a day figure is still drawn on as a headline figure.

4 Sala-i-Martin has revised his figures so that state spending is broken down into areas that are relevant to the poor, which has led to slightly more cautious findings than his previous assertions. See recent papers at www.columbia.edu/~xs23/home/html. However, this still assumes that the poor can benefit as much from certain state measures as wealthier households, which is not necessarily the case – not least in welfare states in richer countries, let alone states in poor countries where benefits for the poor are likely to be much smaller.

5 See http://research.worldbank.org/povcal/Net/jsp/index.jsp

6 A point that Hoogvelt – and Castells – appear to accept in their focus on the politics of exclusion.

7 The question of fair trade is briefly examined in Chapter 6.

8 While this report did not find supermarkets guilty of abusing their market position, the findings like those of the Hutton inquiry over the death of David Kelly, are more interesting than the final report. Moreover, the Chair of the report, John Bridgeman, has since said that there is a need for another report as market share becomes ever more concentrated in the retail sector (F. Lawrence 2005). In early 2006, a new inquiry was announced by the Competition Commission.

9 Out of 2,600 suppliers, Tesco had only 8 whose share of total intake exceeded 1 per cent and only 230 with a share higher than 0.1 per cent (Gibbon and Ponte 2005: 20).

10 The top 10 countries in 2000 were Hong Kong (still counted separately from China), China, Brazil, Mexico, Singapore, Argentina, Indonesia, Malaysia, Chile, and South Korea. See UNCTAD (2002b) and UNCTAD (2001: annex table B3).

11 The figures are for the mid-1990s.

12 This is an all too common misunderstanding made, not only by globalization theorists such as Giddens, but by some international relations theorists. See, for example, Brown and Ainley (2005: ch. 8, especially pp. 160–1).

Notes to Chapter 8: Globalization, Neo-liberalism and the State

1 In this respect the position adopted here is closer to the transformationalist position outlined in Chapter 5. However, as was pointed out in that chapter, global transfomationalists do not offer a convincing *explanation* of the various processes of globalization, but rather a *description* of globalizing processes. When clarification is attempted these add spatial rather than social explanation to this description.

2 Though of course drug exports to the West have increased enormously since the fall of the Taliban regime. This is yet another example of the idea of globalization being used to make over-generalizations, be it about 'global bads' such as terrorists and drugs or 'global goods' such as market expansion.

3 Even in this case, the state played a developmentalist role. See, for instance, Patnaik (2006), on state protection of British textiles against potential competition from India.

4 The question of the developmental state is revisited, with specific reference to East Asia, in Chapter 9.

5 See further discussion of this point in Chapter 10.

6 These have included the nation, family, race and religion. This mixture of neo-liberal economic and cultural conservatism was particularly prominent in the ideology of Thatcherism, and in contemporary US neo-conservatism, where religion at home and US strength abroad are particularly important (see Kiely 2005b). The non-conservative third way, which is happy with neo-liberal economics and cultural liberalism, has still attempted to foster some forms of solidarity and collectivism, via the concepts of communitarianism and social capital. Both ideas – at least in their 'third way' form – under-estimate the ways in which neo-liberal economics subverts their possibilities, and indeed social capital is used in such a way as to individualize – and thus depoliticize – structurally unequal social relations.

7 A similar point could be applied to realist theories of international relations, which assume and de-historicize the existence of sovereign nation-states. But

equally, this point applies to some critics of 'IR theory', who suggest that because unproblematic sovereign states do not exist in parts of the periphery, then 'IR theory' cannot apply there (see, for instance, Dunn and Shaw 2001). The problem with this position is that it assumes that 'IR theory' and realism are one and the same, and that realism at least applies to the core states. On the one hand, this assumes away the historical and social realities of state formation in these core states, and on the other, the processes of state formation in the developing world (which, in part at least, involve conflict over the nature of statehood), and the fact that these peripheral states are still part of an international order (see Brown 2006). While certainly this order is one where core states have more power, it is also the case that peripheral states have had agency, not least in the (contested) processes of state formation.

Notes to Chapter 9: Globalization, Regionalism and Hegemony

1 Compare Wade (2003b) and Gowan (1999: 78–100).
2 Indeed, given the enormous size of its agricultural sector, and continued rural–urban migration (as outlined in the text), this is likely to have a globally depressing effect on wages for unskilled and semi-skilled workers, thus exacerbating the tendencies towards global inequality outlined in Chapter 7. See further, Kaplinsky (2005a).
3 Segal expresses reservations about using PPP figures, but does not say why. Certainly, as we have seen, they are problematic as measures of the consumption of the poor (Chapter 7), but less so as a measurement of average local purchasing power.
4 Some neo-conservatives, such as Charles Krauthammer, distinguish between two wings of neo-conservatism on this basis, and ultimately opt for primacy over liberal expansion. See Krauthammer (2004).
5 Arguing from a realist position, Mearsheimer (2005) has made one of the strongest arguments against the war in Iraq.
6 These figures need to be treated with some caution however, as China acts as an East Asian, regional exporter for goods that end up in the US and EU. China remains technologically dependent in many areas on other East Asian nations. The US's trade deficit with China in some respects is actually a regional deficit, reflecting the use of East Asian production networks and China's role as a finished-goods producer. See Breslin (2005: 743).
7 This question of peculiarity can be traced back to the origins and development of English (and later British) capitalism and capitalist imperialism, and how this relates to the later question of commitments to 'free market capitalism' and Atlanticism. Briefly, Britain is regarded as having a backward capitalism which developed on the back of a pre-capitalist 'superstructure'. On this debate, see Anderson (1993), Cain and Hopkins (1993), Gamble (1994), Nairn (1964a; 1964b), Thompson (1965), Corrigan and Sayer

(1986), Barratt-Brown (1988) and Wood (1991). My own position is closer to that of the last four sources, which suggest that there are in fact no (ahistorical) models of capitalism, just historically differentiated processes of capitalist development. Moreover, the supposedly archaic nature of English capitalism was in some respects a major reason for its initial advance, as the 'absences' of a modern state and political culture 'signalled the presence of a well-developed capitalism and a state that was evolving in tandem with the capitalist economy' (Wood 1991: 19), even if these same absences undermined Britain's capacity to respond to competitive pressures from later developers in Europe and the US. The first set of sources is therefore right to point to certain questions of peculiarity, but these are theorized in an unconvincing way. See further, Kiely (forthcoming).

8 Seigniorage is the practice of profiting from the issuing of money. This occurs at the international level as the US issues its national currency, which is also the main international means of payment. This also gives the US considerable – though far from absolute – autonomy in financing its external deficits. See Gowan (1999).

9 In particular the last section in both Chapters 4 and 5, and all of Chapter 8.

10 Though of course, given the failure in stimulating growth and trade balances across all the major regions, in this one respect we can regard the relationship as a zero-sum game.

11 This is perhaps most starkly seen in the case of India from the 1990s, particularly under the Hindu nationalist Bharatiya Janata Party (BJP). An anecdotal example is also illustrative of the point being made here. In 1990, while waiting to interview representatives from the Council for Progressive Trade Unions, the radical trade union federation in Trinidad in 1990, I observed a poster extolling the virtues of Trinidadian ownership of the 'national economy'. My interviews were concerned with trade union strategies in the context of retrenchment and IMF and World Bank adjustment. It struck me that the leaders of retrenchment programmes were precisely those companies highlighted in the poster – and indeed that these same companies had increasingly entered into joint-venture agreements with foreign capital. See Kiely (1996).

Notes to Chapter 10: Resisting Globalization?

1 Though, of course, this point is valid to the extent that it applies to the crude anti-imperialist left, and above all, as Wheen points out, to the work of Noam Chomsky.

2 For illustrative examples, see the responses by leading neo-conservative William Kristol and liberal imperialist Christopher Hitchens, to Francis Fukuyama's (2006) break from neo-conservatism, which essentially accuses the latter of being soft on Islamist terrorism in Iraq (see Cornwell 2006).

3 Liberal imperialists are thus quite right to make this point, but equally they tend to conflate explanations for the emergence of such political forces as

evidence of sympathy for those same forces. Indeed, in de-contextualizing the rise of what they describe as Islamo-fascism, liberal imperialists come perilously close to rejecting the argument that political Islam is an ideological phenomenon. This can only lead them to a Huntington-style, civilizational critique. In drawing some parallels with the popularity of some right-wing ideas among the US working class, Levine (2005) does an excellent job at balancing explanation and critique. This is in marked contrast to the views of Norman Geras (2005), who suggests that contextualization (in this case the July 2005 London bombings) can easily become apology. This is of course true, and is too often the case for those on the so-called anti-imperialist left. But this does not mean that contextualization must lead to apology. As Geras is more than aware, historians have contextualized the rise of the Nazis without collapsing into David Irving apologetics, and sociologists have similarly contextualized the rise of white racism without lapsing into apology. If Geras wants to draw parallels along these lines, then, given Geras's uncritical support for the war in Iraq, I would suggest the following: a series of racist attacks leading to multiple murders would surely deserve total condemnation. But it would not deserve a police operation in response, in which innocent people were killed, all in the name of collateral damage and/or the good intentions of liberal anti-racists, or the police use of allies that were guilty of similar crimes to those undertaken by the original racist murderer. Of course Geras is right to point to the shabby rush to contextualize by many 'anti-imperialists', but his own liberal-imperialist position is itself full of evasions.

Note to Chapter 11: Conclusions

1 'Americanize' here refers to the perception made by dominant actors in the US, and so means expanding US allies through 'liberal democracy' and 'free markets'. Whether or not this represents 'authentic Americanization' is another issue, not only because of the selectivity of this commitment in terms of foreign policy, but also because, like all cultural forms, 'Americanization' is contested within the US itself.

Further Reading

Chapter 1 Introduction

There are a great number of international political economy texts. The most useful in terms of their attention to globalization and development, are Anthony Payne, *The Global Politics of Unequal Development* (2005), Nicola Phillips (ed.), *Globalizing International Political Economy* (2005), Richard O'Brien and Marc Williams, *Global Political Economy* (2004), and John Ravenhill (ed.), *Global Political Economy* (2005), and Ankie Hooogvelt, *Globalization and the Postcolonial World* (2nd edn, 2001). See also the special issue of *Third World Quarterly* 25:1, (2004) on international political economy and the 'Third World'. The best political economy of globalization can be found in the work of a geographer, Peter Dicken, *Global Shift* (3rd edn, 2003).

Two earlier works that bear some similarity in relation to the three positions outlined in the first chapter are Teddy Brett, *International Money and Capitalist Crisis* (1983), and Chris Edwards, *The Fragmented World* (1985). The three-fold division in the latter is, however, not the same as the division in the opening chapter of this book, though there is some important crossover.

Trade theory is well covered in Anwar Shaikh, 'Foreign Trade and the Law of Value', parts 1 and 2 (1979 and 1979–80), two outstanding articles. See also the three perspectives in Sheila Smith and John Toye, 'Trade and Poor Economies' (1979).

For the classics, see Adam Smith, *The Wealth of Nations* (1998; first published 1776), and David Ricardo, *Principles of Political Economy* (1981; first published in 1819). See also Bertil Ohlin, *Inter-Regional and International Trade* (1933), and Nicholas Kaldor, 'The Irrelevance of Equilibrium Economics' (1972), the latter of which has influenced some of the arguments made in this book. Although less cited these days, Karl Marx, *Capital*, volumes 1 (1976; first published 1867) and 3 (1981, first published 1884) also have much relevant material, particularly concerning capital accumulation, concentration and the international division of labour.

Readings from classics by the likes of Ricardo, List and Hilferding, can be found in Chris Brown, Terry Nardin and Nicholas Rengger (eds), *International Relations in Political Thought* (2002).

Chapter 2 Capitalist Expansion and Imperialism

Useful histories of capitalist development can be found in Eric Hobsbawm's *Industry and Empire* (1968), *Age of Revolution* (1973), *Age of Capital* (1975), and *Age of Empire* (1987). On the origins of capitalism, see in particular the work of Robert Brenner, 'Agrarian Class Structure and Economic Development in Pre-Industrial Europe' (1976), 'The Origins of Capitalist Development: a Critique of Neo-Smithian Marxism' (1977), and 'The Agrarian Roots of European Capitalism' (1982).

From a very different, radical perspective, see Immanuel Wallerstein, *The Modern World System* (1974) and *The Capitalist World Economy* (1979). See also Andre Gunder Frank, *Capitalism and Underdevelopment in Latin America* (1969) and *Latin America: Underdevelopment or Revolution?* (1969), and Walter Rodney, *How Europe Underdeveloped Africa* (1972). These debates relate back to those over the origins of capitalism, and Rodney Hilton (ed.), *The Transition from Feudalism to Capitalism* (1976) remains essential. Also useful, if rather thin empirically, is Ellen Meiksins Wood, *The Origins of Capitalism* (2002), a work sympathetic to Brenner's arguments. Also part of this Brenner tradition is Benno Teschke's impressive work, *The Myth of 1648* (2003). The recent turn to global history replicates some of these earlier debates, even if these are not always explicitly referenced. See Kenneth Pomeranz, *The Great Divergence* (2000), Andre Gunder Frank, *Re-Orient* (1998) and Jim Blaut, *The Colonizer's Model of the World* (1993). My own view is that much of this work suffers from the same problems as the trade-centric analyses criticized by Brenner.

On liberal imperialism, both generally and as applied to the nineteenth century, see Niall Ferguson, *Empire* (2003) and *Colossus* (2004). Much better then these over-hyped works are David Fieldhouse, *The Economics of Empire* (1973) and *The West and the Third World* (1999). Classical Marxist theories of imperialism are very well surveyed in Anthony Brewer, *Marxist Theories of Imperialism* (1990) and in the much neglected Charles Barone, *Marxist Thought on Imperialism* (1985), both of which update and discuss classical theories in the light of changes in the international order since 1914. Although old, Michael Barratt-Brown's, *After Imperialism* (1970) remains indispensable. Also useful are Bob Sutcliffe and Roger Owen (eds), *Studies in the Theory of Imperialism* (1972), which includes one of Barratt-Brown's outstanding essays. Lenin's *Imperialism: The Highest Stage of Capitalism* (1975) and Bukharin's, *Imperialism and World Economy* (1973) are still easy to obtain. Less easy to find is Rudolf Hilferding, *Finance Capital* (1981; first published 1910), and extracts from Karl Kautsky, *Ultra-Imperialism* (1970 and 2002; first published 1914). Bob Sutcliffe's forthcoming *After Imperialism* discusses the classics and assesses them in relation to the current international order – it is therefore relevant to the concerns of this chapter, but to later chapters too.

Chapter 3   Post-1945 Capitalism and Development

The Bretton Woods era, the 'Golden Age' of capitalism, is discussed in Andrew Glyn et al., *The Golden Age of Capitalism* (1990). See also Andrew Glyn and

Bob Sutcliffe, *British Capitalism, Workers and the Profit Squeeze* (1972). More mainstream international relations and international political economy accounts can be found in Robert Gilpin, *Global Political Economy* (2001), Joan Spero and Jeffrey Hart, *The Politics of International Economic Relations* (6th edn, 2003). The collection edited by Richard Stubbs and Geoffrey Underhill, *Political Economy and the Changing Global Order* (1999), has some useful material on the post-war international order and its demise.

Among Marxists, Michael Webber and David Rigby, *The Golden Age Illusion: Rethinking Postwar Capitalism* (1996), partly challenges the Golden Age thesis. Ben Fine and Laurence Harris, *Re-reading Capital* (1979), is a readable and informative use of Marxist concepts to illustrate specific periods of capitalist development, as is Ernest Mandel's, *Late Capitalism* (1975), which draws on a very different account of the history of capitalist development. Less useful is Simon Clarke, *Keynesianism, Monetarism and the Crisis of the State* (1988), largely because of its reluctance to concretize specific periods of capitalist development, instead reading off specificities from the general laws of motion of capitalist development. A useful edited collection drawing on a variety of Marxist understandings of the post-war boom, recession and globalization, can be found in Robert Albritton et al. (eds), *Phases of Capitalist Development* (2001). Fred Block's, *The Origins of International Economic Disorder* (1977) is more specifically on the rise and fall of the Bretton Woods order, as is Teddy Brett's, *The World Economy since the War* (1985). This latter work is particularly good, but is even more useful when read in conjunction with his 1983 work, recommended among the readings for Chapter 1.

Very few books relate the post-war boom to the question of development, but see Giovanni Arrighi, *The Long Twentieth Century* (1994) and Giovanni Arrighi et al., *Chaos and Governance in the Modern World System* (1999), both impressive works, even if marred by a theorization of systemic cycles of accumulation. Ray Kiely, *The Clash of Globalisations* (2005), ch. 3, is more explicit in relating the Golden Age to the era of development.

Development theory is the subject of a wide range of books, most of which do not situate theory in the wider political and economic context of the post-war boom, and also do not distinguish between mainstream and critical approaches to development. They do, however, often present very coherent and constructive assessments of theories of development. See among others, Jorge Larrain, *Theories of Development* (1989), Ray Kiely, *Sociology and Development* (1995) and Peter Preston, *Development Theory* (1996). These three books are more useful than most in contextualizing as well as critically assessing development theory. The best work however is Colin Leys, *The Rise and Fall of Development Theory* (1996), particularly the extended introductory essay.

Chapter 4   The End of the Post-war Boom and Capitalist Restructuring

The end of the post-war boom is discussed in many of the works recommended for Chapter 3. See also Robert Brenner, 'The Economics of Global Turbulence'

(1998), Ernest Mandel, *The Second Slump* (1980), Andrew Glyn, *Capitalism Unleashed* (2006) and Leo Panitch and Sam Gindin, 'Finance and American Empire' (2004).

The rise of neo-liberalism is discussed in Gerard Dumenil and Dominique Levy, *Capital Resurgent* (2004), and in David Harvey, *Neo-liberalism: A Short History* (2005), as well as the books cited for Chapter 3. Alfredo Saad-Filho and Deborah Johnston (eds), *Neo-liberalism: A Critical Reader* (2005) is an excellent edited collection, including chapters on the rise of neo-liberalism, its development into the era of globalization, and case studies of particular themes and regions, including developing countries.

On financialization, see Eric Helleiner, *States and the Re-Emergence of Global Finance* (1994), Peter Gowan, *The Global Gamble* (1999) and Giovanni Arrighi, *The Long Twentieth Century* (1994). Despite their very different arguments and, in the case of the latter two at least, conclusions, all three of these works usefully stress the centrality of finance to contemporary US hegemony, even if they disagree on whether or not this is in decline. On shareholder value, see the special issue of *Economy and Society* 29:1 (2000).

On the debt crisis, see Stuart Corbridge, *Debt and Development* (1993). This book has very usefully divided interpretations of the crisis into three. For representatives from each of these positions, see Peter Bauer, *The Development Frontier* (1991) and Deepak Lal, *The Poverty of 'Development Economics'* (1984) (neo-liberal); Willy Brandt, *Common Crisis, North–South* (1983) (neo-Keynesian); and Susan George, *A Fate Worse than Debt* (1989) (radical/neo-dependency). Marxist positions tend to situate the debt crisis in the context of the wider accumulation of capital and uneven development, and so focus on the fall and rise of Bretton Woods, of which the 1982 debt crisis was one outcome.

On structural adjustment, see Poul Engberg-Pedersen et al., *Limits of Adjustment in Africa* (1996), David Simon et al., *Structurally Adjusted Africa* (1995), Tony Killick, *IMF Programmes in Developing Countries* (1995) and Paul Mosley et al., *Aid and Power*, 2 volumes (1991).

On restructuring in general, see David Harvey, *The Condition of Postmodernity* (1989). Perhaps the best book is the already mentioned Peter Dicken, *Global Shift* (2003), marketed as a text, and certainly student friendly, but also so much more than this. On post-Fordism, neo-Fordism, flexible specialization, Toyotaism, and various other designations, see Ash Amin (ed.), *Post-Fordism: A Critical Reader* (1994), which has positions representative of all sides in this debate. For a dense theoretical and empirical account, see Winfried Ruigrok and Rob van Tulder, *The Logic of International Restructuring* (1996). See also the material on the state, discussed in the reading for Chapter 8.

Chapter 5   Globalization and Contemporary Imperialism

On globalization, see David Held et al., *Global Transformations* (1999) and David Held and Anthony McGrew (eds), *The Global Transformations Reader*

(2002). See also Jan Art Scholte, *Globalization: A Critical Introduction* (2nd edn; 2005), which has some very useful empirical and political discussion, even if (as I argue in the chapter) it is theoretically unconvincing. See also, Anthony Giddens, *Runaway World* (1999), a popular, if highly superficial, account of globalization. Charles Leadbeater, *Living on Thin Air* (1999) and Geoff Mulgan, *Connexity* (1998) both actually manage to surpass *Runaway World*'s high levels of superficiality, an achievement of sorts. Much more rigorous, if deeply flawed, is Manuel Castells's 3-volume study, *The Rise of the Network Society* (1996), *The Power of Identity* (1997) and *End of Millennium* (2000). On debates over measures of globalization, see the sceptical positions outlined by Paul Hirst and Graham Thompson, *Globalization in Question* (1999), Colin Hay and David Marsh (eds), *Demystifying Globalization* (2001), Suzanne Berger and Ronald Dore (eds), *National Diversity and Global Capitalism* (1996). A good, historically sensitive account of the economics of globalization can be found in Jonathan Michie (ed.), *The Handbook of Globalization* (2004).

For critiques of globalization theory, see Justin Rosenberg, *The Follies of Globalisation Theory* (2000) and his 'Globalization: a Postmortem', in *International Politics* 42:1 (2005). Critical responses to this article can be found in *International Politics* 42:3, including one by Scholte entitled 'Premature Obituaries: a Response to Justin Rosenberg'. The most convincing response, to my mind, is Andrew Gamble, 'Globalization: Getting the "Big Picture" Right, a Comment on Justin Rosenberg' (2005). For other critiques which more explicitly relate globalization to the question of imperialism, see Ray Kiely, *Empire in the Age of Globalisation* (2005) and, more implicitly, J. Nederveen Pieterse, *Globalization or Empire* (2004).

For theories of transnational capitalism, see Leslie Sklair, *The Transnational Capitalist Class* (2001) and *Globalization* (2002). Much better however is Bill Robinson, *A Theory of Transnational Capitalism* (2004). See also Jerry Harris's work, such as his 'Transnational Competition and the End of US Hegemony (2003). This theory owes something to neo-Gramscian theories, such as those of Robert Cox. See his 'Social Forces, States and World Orders: Beyond International Relations Theory' (1981) and *Production, Power and World Order* (1987). Although also a neo-Gramscian, Stephen Gill more explicitly links neo-liberalism and globalization to continued US hegemony. Amongst a wide body of work, see particularly his *Power and Resistance in the New World Order* (2003) and his recent essay 'The Contradictions of US Supremacy' (2004). A forthcoming collection of debates between open Marxism and neo-Gramscian theories can be found in Andreas Bieler et al., *Global Restructuring: State, Capital and Labour* (2006).

Also relevant are the influential books by Michael Hardt and Toni Negri, *Empire* (2000) and *Multitude* (2004). A much more interesting theorization can be found in Jon Agnew, *Hegemony* (2005).

On classical Marxist understandings of 'the new imperialism', see Alex Callinicos, *The New Mandarins of American Power* (2003), and David Harvey, *The New Imperialism* (2003), as well as Peter Gowan, *Global Gamble* (1999), an overly conspiratorial, but still very useful, account of the relationship between US hegemony and global finance.

The approach adopted in this chapter is closest to Leo Panitch and Sam Gindin, 'Global Capitalism and American Empire' (2003), 'Finance and American Empire' (2004), and 'Superintending Global Capital' (2005). Despite my sympathies with these and other works by Panitch and Gindin (cited in the text and full bibliography), it is still probably fair to say that they over-estimate the extent of US power (and by implication under-estimate the contradictions in the international order), an issue discussed from a radical Weberian perspective by Michael Mann, *Incoherent Empire* (2003). My own position is also very close to that of Simon Bromley, 'The Logic of American Power in the International Capitalist Order' (2006), and Greg Albo, 'The Old and New Economics of Imperialism' (2003). Also useful, if perhaps still too soft on Lenin, is Neil Smith, *The Endgame of Globalization* (2005).

On the Bush administration, see www.whitehouse.gov, as well as the links to the Pentagon (www.defenselink.mil) and National Security Strategy (www.whitehouse.gov/nsc/nss.html) sites, for a wide variety of very useful material. On neo-conservatism, see the *Weekly Standard* newspaper, and the Project for the New American Century website (www.newamericancentury.org). See the collection *Neoconservatism* (2005), edited by Irving Seltzer. For more critical accounts of the neo-conservative project and its relationship to the Bush administration, see Garry Dorrien, *Imperial Designs* (2004). Peter Singer, 'The President of Good and Evil' (2004), is a useful deconstruction of George Bush's public statements.

Chapter 6   Cosmopolitanism, Globalization and Global Governance

The literature on global governance tends to be quite descriptive and not well related to the question of power. Better than most is Marc O'Brien et al., *Contesting Global Governance* (2000), though unfortunately it remains stuck within an overly institutionalist, distributive view of power. For a classic example of such thinking see United Nations, *Our Global Neighbourhood* (2005). Anne-Marie Slaughter, *A New World Order* (2004) is more interesting. David Held and Tony McGrew (eds), *Governing Globalization* (2002) is an excellent collection of articles. Global economic governance is critically discussed in Suzanne Soederberg, *Global Governance in Question* (2006).

On the UN, see Paul Taylor, *International Organization in the Modern World* (1993), and David Malone (ed.), *The UN Security Council: From the Cold War to the Twenty-First Century* (2004).

On humanitarian intervention, see James Mayall (ed.), *The New Interventionism, 1991–94* (1996), Nicholas Wheeler, *Saving Strangers* (2000), Simon Chesterman, *Just War or Just Peace* (2001), Jennifer Walsh (ed.), *Humanitarian Intervention in International Relations Theory* (2004). Noam Chomsky, *The New Military Humanism* (1999) and David Chandler, *From Kosovo to Kabul* (2004) dismiss humanitarianism as simply a justification for western power, but tend towards a view that whatever 'the West' does is malevolent, which puts them both firmly in the crude anti-imperialist camp discussed throughout the book.

On war post-9-11, particularly the war in Iraq, see Christopher Hitchens, *Regime Change* (2003), and Thomas Cushman (ed.), *A Matter of Principle* (2005). These liberal arguments for the war in Iraq are challenged by a number of anti-imperialist positions on US hegemony, such as those by Callinicos and Chandler (see previous writings cited). David Coates and Joel Kreiger, *Blair's War* (2004), Amy Bartholomew (ed.) *Empire's Law* (2006) challenges the war from a position that is critical of both liberal imperialism and one-dimensional anti-imperialism. The war in Iraq, and the changing but equally spurious justifications for it, figure prominently in David Runciman's outstanding deconstruction of Tony Blair, *The Politics of Good Intentions* (2006). The best right-wing realist case against the war came from John Mearsheimer, 'Hans Morgenthou and the Iraq War' (2005). And useful official sources on the war on terrorism and 'the long war' can be found at www.cia.gov/terrorism. Critical accounts, usually incorporating a long-term perspective, include Dilip Hiro, *War without End* (2004), John Cooley, *Unholy Wars* (2002), Mahmoud Mamdani, *Good Muslim, Bad Muslim* (2004). While some of these works tend to conflate context with full explanation, effectively granting Islamist movements only a reactive agency, they all usefully provide much needed context.

On the WTO, see Amrita Narlikar, *International Trade and Developing Countries: Bargaining Coalitions in the GATT and WTO* (2003). Graham Dunkley, *The Free Trade Adventure* (2000) and *Free Trade: Myth, Reality and Alternatives* (2004) has relevant chapters on the WTO and locates them in the context of wider, classical debates about free trade. See the official WTO website at www.wto.org, and the spoof (and now sadly dated) site at www.gatt.org.

On global civil society, see David Chandler and Gideon Baker (eds), *Global Civil Society* (2005), a collection marred by some very odd critical chapters. See also David Chandler, *Constructing Global Civil Society* (2005), a book less about global civil society and the contemporary international order, and more one about the author's nostalgia for the (false) certainties of an older era. A more balanced critique can be found in Alejandro Colas (2002) *International Civil Society*. The idea of global civil society is embraced in various ways by John Keane, *Global Civil Society?* (2003), Mary Kaldor, *Global Civil Society: An Answer to War* (2003) and Richard Falk, 'Resisting "Globalization from Above" through "Globalization from Below"' (2000). See also the annual Global Civil Society yearbooks, edited by Helmut Anheier, Marlies Glasius and Mary Kaldor.

On cosmopolitanism, see Immanuel Kant, *Perpetual Peace and Other essays on Politics, History and Morals* (1983), David Held, *Global Covenant* (2004), Andrew Linklater, *The Transformation of Political Community* (1998), and the very good collection, Daniele Archibugi (ed.), *Debating Cosmopolitics* (2004). Discussions of human rights, and how they relate to the international order and debates over cosmopolitanism, can be found in Tim Dunne and Nicholas Wheeler (eds), *Human Rights and Global Politics* (1999), Simon Caney, *Justice beyond Borders* (2005), Anthony Woodiwiss, *Human Rights* (2005), and Chris Brown, *Sovereignty, Rights and Justice* (2002).

Chapter 7 Globalization, Poverty and the Contemporary World Economy

The debate on global poverty and inequality is addressed by Robert Wade and Martin Wolf, 'Are Global Poverty and Inequality Getting Worse?' (2002). On the optimist side, which links the decline in global poverty to neo-liberal, globalization friendly policies, as well as Wolf see World Bank, *Globalization, Growth and Poverty* (2002), D. Dollar and A. Kraay, 'Growth is Good for the Poor' (2002), Xavier Sala-i-Martin, 'The Disturbing "Rise" of Global Income Inequality' (2002), and 'The World Distribution of Income (estimated from Individual Country Contributions)' (2002), and Surjit Bhalla, *Imagine There's No Country* (2002). Some of these views are criticized by Robert Wade, 'On the Causes of Increasing World Poverty and Inequality, or Why the Matthew Effect Prevails' (2004), and 'Is Globalization Reducing Poverty and Inequality?' (2004), and especially, Branko Milanovic, 'The two faces of globalisation: against globalisation as we know it' (2004), and *The Ricardian Vice: Why Sala-i-Martin's Calculations of World Income Inequality are Wrong* (2002). See also Sanjay Reddy and Thomas Pogge, 'How *Not* to Count the Poor' (2003), and Thomas Pogge, 'The First UN Millennium Development Goal: a Cause for Celebration?' (2004).

On capital flows and inequality, see the annual *World Investment Reports* published by UNCTAD, and their annual *Least Developed Countries Reports*. On explaining the concentration of capital flows, see Ray Kiely, *Industrialization and Development* (1998) chs. 5, 8 and 9, Robert Wade, 'What strategies are viable for developing countries today? The World Trade Organization and the Shrinking of "Development Space"' (2003), and 'On the Causes of Increasing World Poverty and Inequality, or Why the Matthew Effect Prevails' (2004). See also the classics cited in the reading for Chapter 1.

On commodity chains and inequality, see among many others, Raphael Kaplinsky, *Globalization, Poverty and Inequality* (2005) and Peter Gibbon and Stefano Ponte, *Trading Down* (2005). Kaplinsky is particularly useful for problematizing the rise of China. See also (once again) Peter Dicken, *Global Shift* (2003) and Gary Gereffi and Miguel Korzeniewicz (eds), *Commodity Chains and Global Capitalism* (1994). On foreign investment more generally, see the older but still valuable work of Rhys Jenkins, *Transnational Corporations and Uneven Development* (1987) and *Transnational Corporations and the Industrial Transformation of Latin America* (1984). Although the latter is more region specific, it is actually better, and has more general implications, which are very well discussed.

Chapter 8 Globalization, Neo-liberalism and the State

The debate on globalization and the state is addressed in Nicola Phillips (ed.), *Globalizing International Political Economy* (2005), especially chapter 4, and in

Anthony Payne *The Global Politics of Unequal Development* (2005). These debates relate to older globalization debates which can be found in the hyper-globalization versus sceptics debate, references of which are cited in Chapter 5.

On models of capitalism and institutionalism, see Suzanne Berger and Ronald Dore (eds), *National Diversity and Global Capitalism* (1996), Colin Crouch and Wolfgang Streeck (eds.), *Political Economy of Modern Capitalism* (1997), Peter Hall and David Soskice (eds.), *Varieties of Capitalism* (2001), David Coates, *Models of Capitalism* (2000), and his edited work *Varieties of Capitalism, Varieties of Approaches* (2005).

Gordon White (ed.), *Developmental States in East Asia* (1988) is the original text on the developmental state. See also Linda Weiss and John Hobson, *States and Economic Development* (1995), Linda Weiss, *The Myth of the Powerless State* (1998), Atul Kohli, *State Directed Development: Political Power and Industrialisation in the Global Periphery* (2004). The two most famous case-study approaches are Alice Amsden, *Asia's Next Giant* (1989) and Robert Wade, *Governing the Market* (1990), the latter of which was recently published in a new edition.

The post-Washington consensus is associated with World Bank, *World Development Report 1997: The State in a Changing World* (1997). See also World Bank, *Governance and Development* (1992), World Bank, *World Development Report 1999/2000* (1999) and World Bank, *World Development Report 2000/01* (2000). One of the most influential proponents of the post-Washington consensus was ultimately marginalized by the World Bank. His views are represented in Joseph Stiglitz, *Globalization and its Discontents* (2002).

More critical accounts – of both the post-Washington consensus and the developmental state – can be found in Ben Fine et al., *Development Policy in the Twenty First Century* (2001), and K. S. Jomo and Ben Fine (eds), *The New Development Economics* (2006).

Neo-liberal restructuring through military intervention is addressed in Chris Cramer, *Civil War is Not a Stupid Thing* (2006), and more implicitly in Tarak Barkawi, *Globalization and War* (2006). This material is also important – if only by implication – for understanding the issue of failed and rogue states, and how these relate to both development and security. This is addressed by Edward Litwak, *Rogue States and US Foreign Policy* (2000), Anthony Lake, 'Confronting Backlash States' (1994), Robert Cooper, *The Breaking of Nations: Order and Chaos in the 21st Century* (2004) and Thomas Barnett, 'The Pentagon's New Map' (2003). More academic works on failed states include Robert Jackson, *Quasi-States: Sovereignty, International Relations and the Third World* (1990) and *The Global Covenant: Human Conduct in a World of States* (2000). The relationship between development and security is more criti-cally discussed in Mark Duffield, *Global Governance and the New Wars* (2001). See also the special issue of *Third World Quarterly*, 27:1, on reconstructing and policing rogue and failed states. To my mind, much greater understandings of state failure can be gained by looking at historical sociologies of state formation, such as those by Barrington Moore, *Social Origins of Dictatorship and Democracy* (1966), Charles Tilly, *Coercion, Capital and European States* (1992) and Benno Teschke, *The Myth of 1648* (2003). This also relates to the 'democratic peace' thesis, for which see Bruce Russet, *Grasping the Democratic Peace* (1993). For a critique, see Tarak Barkawi and Mark Laffey (eds), *Democracy, Liberalism and War* (2001).

On Iraq, see the special issue of *Third World Quarterly* 26:4/5 (2005), which discusses 'post-war' restructuring and so usefully focuses on the question of 'development'. The war itself is covered in an ever-increasing literature, some of which is recommended in the reading for Chapter 6. A valuable account based on a weekly interpretation of events as they unfolded, can be found in Paul Rogers, *A War Too Far: Iraq, Iran and the New American Century* (2006).

On the tensions between liberalism and democracy, see John Stuart Mill *On Liberty* (1973; first published 1869), Jacob Talmon, *On the Origins of Totalitarian Democracy* (1955), Frederick Hayek, *The Constitution of Liberty* (1960). See the very useful survey of democracy in David Beetham, *Democracy: A Beginner's Guide* (2005), and on democracy in the developing world see Barry Gills et al., *Low Intensity Democracy* (1993) and Bill Robinson, *Promoting Polyarchy* (1996). On US foreign policy and democracy promotion, see Michael Cox et al. (eds), *American Democracy Promotion* (2002). And on British democracy and the Iraq war, see Steven Kettell, *Dirty Politics? New Labour, British Politics and the Invasion of Iraq* (2006).

Chapter 9 Globalization, Regionalism and Hegemony

Hegemony is of course associated mainly with the work of Antonio Gramsci, *Selections from the Prison Notebooks* (1971). In international relations theory, it is generally associated with both neo-realist and neo-Gramscian theory. For discussions, see Robert Keohane, *After Hegemony* (1984), Duncan Snidal, 'The Limits of Hegemonic Stability Theory' (1985), Susan Strange, 'The Persistent Myth of Lost Hegemony' (1987), and the neo-Gramscian work cited in the reading for Chapter 5.

The rise of East Asia is discussed in Mark Berger, *The Battle for Asia* (2004), Giovanni Arrighi, 'Hegemony Unravelling – II', and the aforementioned Alice Amsden, *Asia's Next Giant* (1989) and Robert Wade, *Governing the Market* (1990). On the financial crisis of the late 1990s, there is now a vast literature. Particularly useful are the special issues of *Cambridge Journal of Economics* 22:6, (1999), and *Journal of Development Studies* 34:6, (1998), which cover a variety of (generally critical) positions (though not necessarily the one taken in this chapter), and have lots of relevant empirical material. See also K. S. Jomo, (ed.), *After the Storm* (2004).

On China as a development miracle, the best discussion in the English language is by Peter Nolan, *China and the Global Business Revolution* (2001) and *China at the Crossroads* (2004). On China–US relations, see Giovanni Arrighi, 'Hegemony Unravelling – II' (2004), and Barry Buzan and Rosemary Foot (eds), *Does China Matter?* (2004). See also the special issue of *Review of International Studies* 31:4, (2005).

On the EU, see Ben Rosamond, *Theories of European Integration* (2000). On the EU and the developing world, see Martin Holland, *The European Union and the Third World* (2002), and especially Will Brown, *The European Union and Africa* (2002), which is empirically rich and theoretically rigorous.

On European social democracy, see the literature on models of capitalism in the readings for Chapter 8.

On regionalism, see Andrew Gamble and Anthony Payne (eds), *Regionalism and World Order* (1996), and Anthony Payne (ed.), *The New Regional Politics of Development* (2004), Mary Farrell et al. (eds), *Global Politics of Regionalism* (2005), William Coleman and Geoffrey Underhill (eds), *Regionalism and Global Economic Integration* (1998). Most of these books also contain useful case-study material of particular regions and/or nation-states.

US hegemony in the era of globalization is discussed by many writers cited in the readings for Chapter 5.

Chapter 10   Resisting Globalization?

On liberal imperialism, see Michael Ignatieff, *Empire Life* (2003), Christopher Hitchens, *Regime Change* (2003), and Thomas Cushman (ed.), *A Matter of Principle* (2005). The last of these is characteristic of the liberal interventionist position – it champions the right of liberal democratic states to intervene, while simultaneously absolving them of any negative responsibilities if things go wrong after the invasion (though, of course, credit will be taken for any progress). It seems that the liberal imperialist charge that anti-imperialists do not take responsibility for the actions of terrorists can also be applied to the former. See also the already cited David Runciman, *The Politics of Good Intentions* (2006) for a biting critique. More openly neo-liberal and neo-conservative views can be found in Lawrence Kaplan and William Kristol, *The War over Iraq* (2003), Deepak Lal, *In Praise of Empires* (2004) and Niall Ferguson, *Colossus* (2004).

On anti-imperialism, see Andrew Chitty, 'Moralism, Terrorism and War – response to Shaw' (2002), which even the most one-dimensional anti-imperialist may find embarrassing.

On 'cosmopolitan anti-imperialism' see Martin Shaw, '10 Challenges to Anti-War Politics' (2002), Mark Levine, *Why They Don't Hate Us* (2005), Amy Bartholomew (ed.), *Empire's Law* (2006), and the editors' introduction to Alejandro Colas and Rick Saull (eds), *The War on Terrorism and American "Empire" after the Cold War* (2006).

On Islamism, see Roger Scruton, *The West and the Rest* (2005), Samuel Huntington, *The Clash of Civilisations and the Remaking of World Order* (1996), and Bernard Lewis, *What went Wrong?* (2003). Less culturalist explanations can be found in Fred Halliday, *Nation and Religion in the Middle East* (2000), *Two Hours that Shook the World* (2002) and *Islam and the Myth of Confrontation* (2003) and Olivier Roy, *The Failure of Political Islam* (1994) and *Globalized Islam* (2004). Many writers have pointed to the tensions between different Islamists, and Fawaz Gerges, *The Far Enemy* (2005) takes this furthest, by pointing to the tensions within the most violent organizations and networks. There are a vast number of journalistic accounts of al-Qaeda, of which the best is probably Jason Burke, *Al-Qaeda* (2004), which draws out the changes in al-Qaeda since 2001, and suggests that it is less an organization today than a symbol of the most violent forms of resistance among Islamists. Bruce Lawrence (ed.), *A Message to the World: The Statements of Osama bin Laden* (2005) is very useful.

On post-development, see Arturo Escobar, *Encountering Development* (1995), Victoria Bawtree and Majid Rahnema (eds), *The Post-Development Reader* (1997), Gustavo Esteva and Madhu Prakash, *Grassroots Postmodernism* (1998) and Vandana Shiva, *Earth Democracy* (2005). A critical but sympathetic analysis of some strands of post-development thinking can be found in Aran Ziai, 'The ambivalence of post-development: between reactionary populism and radical democracy' (2004). More critical analyses, but still not without their sympathies, can be found in Stuart Corbridge, 'Beyond the Pavement only Soil' (1998) and Ray Kiely, 'The Last Refuge of the Noble Savage' (1999).

On environmentalism, see the excellent David Pepper, *Modern Environmentalisms: An Introduction* (1996), and also the very readable Andrew Dobson, *Green Political Thought* (2000).

On Latin America, Costas Lapavitsas (ed.), *Beyond Market Driven Development* (2005) and Duncan Green, *Silent Revolution: The Rise and Crisis of Market Economies in Latin America* (2003) both have very useful critiques of neo-liberalism, while Steve Ellner and Daniel Hellinger (eds), *Venezuelan Politics in the Chavez Era* (2003) provides a useful account of the challenge to neo-liberalism in that particular country.

On anti-globalization politics, see Ray Kiely, *The Clash of Globalisations* (2005), chapters 6–9, Derek Wall, *The Economics of Anti-Capitalism* (2005), Naomi Klein, *No Logo* (2000) and *Fences and Windows* (2002), Simon Tormey, *Anti-Capitalism: A Beginner's Guide* (2005) and Kevin McDonald, *Global Movements* (2006). There are also a bewildering number of websites.

References

Abu-Lughold, J. (1989) *Before European Hegemony: The World System AD 1250–1350* (New York: Oxford University Press).

Adelman, J. (2002) 'Andean Impasses', *New Left Review* 2:18, pp. 41–72.

Adorno, T. and M. Horkheimer (1979) *Dialectic of Enlightenment* (London: Allen Lane; first published 1944).

Agamben, G. (1998) *Homo Sacer: Sovereign Power and Bare Life* (Stanford, CA: Stanford University Press).

Agamben, G. (2005) *State of Exception* (Chicago: University of Chicago Press).

Agnew, J. (2005) *Hegemony* (Philadelphia: Temple University Press).

Albo, G. (1994) '"Competitive Austerity" and the Impasse of Capitalist Employment Policy', in R. Miliband and L. Panitch (eds) (1994) *The Socialist Register 1994* (London: Merlin), pp. 144–70.

Albo, G. (2003) 'The Old and New Economics of Imperialism', *The Socialist Register 2004* (London: Merlin), pp. 88–113.

Albo, G. (2004) 'A World Market of Opportunities? Capitalist Obstacles and Left Economic Policy', in L. Panitch, C. Leys, A. Zuege and M. Konings (eds) (2004) *The Globalization Decade* (London: Merlin), pp. 111–52.

Albo, G. (2005) 'Contesting the "New Capitalism"', in D. Coates (ed.) (2005) *Varieties of Capitalism, Varieties of Approaches* (Basingstoke: Palgrave Macmillan), pp. 63–82.

Albo, G. (2006) 'The Unexpected Revolution: Venezuela Confronts Neoliberalism' (Toronto, University of York paper).

Albritton, R., M. Itoh, R. Westra and A. Zuege (eds) (2001) *Phases of Capitalist Development* (Basingstoke: Palgrave Macmillan).

Alden, C. (2005) 'China in Africa', *Survival* 47:3, pp. 147–64.

Ali, T. (2004a) *Bush in Babylon* (London: Verso).

Ali, T. (2004b) 'Why He Crushed the Oligarchs: The Importance of Hugo Chavez', *Counterpunch*, 16 August.

Allen, C. (1995) 'Understanding African Politics', *Review of African Political Economy* no. 65, pp. 301–20.

Allen, R. (1992) *Enclosure and the Yeoman: The Agricultural Development of the South Midlands, 1450–1850* (Oxford: Clarendon Press).

Amin, A. (ed.) (1994) *Post-Fordism* (Oxford: Blackwell).

Amin, S. (1975) *Accumulation on a World Scale* (New York: Monthly Review Press).

Amin, S., G. Arrighi, A. Gunder Frank and I. Wallerstein (1982) *Dynamics of Global Crisis* (New York: Monthly Review Press).

Amsden, A. (1989) *Asia's Next Giant* (Oxford: Oxford University Press).

Amsden, A. (2001) *The Rise of 'the Rest': Challenges from Late Industrializing Economies* (Oxford: Oxford University Press).

Amsden, A. (2005) 'Promoting Industry under WTO Law', in K. Gallagher (ed.) (2005) *Putting Development First* (London: Zed), pp. 216–32.

Anderson, P. (1993) *English Questions* (London: Verso).

Anderson, P. (2003) 'Casuistries of Peace and War', *London Review of Books* 25:5 (6 March), pp. 3–9.

Anglade, C. and C. Fortin (1985) *The State and Capital Accumulation in Latin America* (Pittsburgh: Pittsburgh University Press), vol. 1.

Anglade, C. and C. Fortin (1990) *The State and Capital Accumulation in Latin America* (Pittsburgh: Pittsburgh University Press), vol. 2.

Anheier, H., M. Glasius and M. Kaldor (eds) (2001) *Global Civil Society Yearbook 2001* (London: Sage).

Anheier, H., M. Glasius and M. Kaldor (2003) 'Global Civil Society in an Era of Regressive Globalisation', in M. Kaldor, M. Glasaius and H. Anheier (eds) *Global Civil Society Yearbook 2003* (London: Sage), pp. 3–17.

Anheier, H., M. Glasius and M. Kaldor (eds) (2004) *Global Civil Society Yearbook 2004/5* (London: Sage).

Anheier, H., M. Glasius and M. Kaldor (eds) (2005) *Global Civil Society Yearbook 2005/6* (London: Sage).

Appadurai, A. (1996) *Modernity at Large: Cultural Dimensions of Globalization* (Minneapolis: University of Minnesota Press).

Appelbaum, R. and B. Robinson (eds) (2005) *Critical Globalization Studies* (London: Routledge).

Archibugi, D. (2005), 'Cosmopolitan Democracy and its Critics: a Review', *European Journal of International Relations* 10:3, pp. 437–73.

Archibugi, D. (ed.) (2003) *Debating Cosmopolitics* (London: Verso).

Archibugi, D., D. Held and M. Kohler (1995) 'Introduction', in D. Archibugi, D. Held and M. Kohler (eds), *Re-imagining Political Community* (Cambridge: Polity), pp. 1–14.

Arend, A. and R. Beck (1993) *International Law and the Use of Force* (London: Routledge).

Arrighi, G. (1994) *The Long Twentieth Century* (London: Verso).

Arrighi, G. (2003) 'The Social and Political Economy of Global Turbulence', *New Left Review* II:20, pp. 5–71.

Arrighi, G. (2005a) 'Hegemony Unravelling – I', *New Left Review* II:32, pp. 23–80.

Arrighi, G. (2005b) 'Hegemony Unravelling – II', *New Left Review* II:33, pp. 83–116.

Arrighi, G. and B. Silver (1999) *Chaos and Governance in the Modern World System* (Minneapolis: University of Minnesota Press).

Arrighi, G., B. Silver and B. Brewer (2003) 'Industrial Convergence, Globalization, and the Persistence of the North–South Divide', *Studies in Comparative International Development* 38:1, pp. 3–31.

Auty, R. (1995) *Patterns of Development: Resources, Policy and Economic Growth* (London: Edward Arnold).

Ayers, A. (2006) 'Demystifying Democratisation: the Global Constitution of

(Neo)liberal Polities in Africa', *Third World Quarterly* 27:2, pp. 321–38.

Bairoch, P. (1993) *Economics and World History* (London: Harvester Wheatsheaf).

Bairoch, P. and R. Kozul-Wright (1996) *Globalization Myths: Some Historical Reflections on Integration, Industrialization and Growth in the World Economy* (Geneva: UNCTAD, Discussion Paper no. 113).

Baker, D., G. Epstein and R. Pollin (1998) 'Introduction', in D. Baker, G. Epstein and R. Pollin (eds), *Globalization and Progressive Economic Policy* (Cambridge: Cambridge University Press, 1998), pp. 1–34.

Balassa, B. (1981) *The Newly Industrializing Countries and the World Economy* (New York: Pergamon).

Balassa, B. (1989) *New Directions in the World Economy* (New York: New York University Press).

Baran, P. (1967) *The Political Economy of Growth* (New York: Monthly Review Press, first published 1959).

Barkawi, T. (2006) *Globalization and War* (Lanham, MD: Rowman and Littlefield).

Barkawi, T. and M. Laffey (eds) (2001) *Democracy, Liberalism and War* (Boulder: Lynne Rienner).

Barnett, T. (2003) 'The Pentagon's New Map', *Esquire*, 1 March.

Barone, C. (1985) *Marxist Thought on Imperialism* (London: Macmillan).

Barratt-Brown, M. (1970) *After Imperialism* (London: Merlin, second edition).

Barratt-Brown, M. (1988) 'Away with all Great Arches: Anderson's History of British Capitalism', *New Left Review* I:167, pp. 22–51.

Bartholomew, A. (ed.) (2006) *Empire's Law* (London: Pluto).

Bauer, P. (1971) *Dissent on Development* (London: Weidenfeld & Nicolson).

Bauer, P. (1991) *The Development Frontier* (London: Harvester Wheatsheaf).

Bauman, Z. (1999) *In Search of Politics* (Cambridge: Polity).

Bawtree, V. and M. Rahnema (eds) (1997) *The Post-Development Reader* (London: Zed Books).

Bayart, J-F. (1993) *The State in Africa: The Politics of the Belly* (London: Longman).

Beck, U. (2000) *What is Globalization?* (Cambridge: Polity).

Beck, U. (2004) 'Cosmopolitan Realism: on the Distinction between Cosmopolitanism in Philosophy and the Social Sciences', *Global Networks* 4:2, pp. 131–56.

Beck, U. (2005) *Power in the Global Age* (Cambridge: Polity).

Beck, U. (2006) *Cosmopolitan Vision* (Cambridge: Polity).

Becker, D. and R. Sklar (1987) 'Why Postimperialism?', in D. Becker, J. Frieden, S. Schatz and R. Sklar, *Postimperialism: International Capitalism and Development in the Late Twentieth Century* (Boulder: Lynne Rienner), pp. 1–18.

Becker, D., J. Frieden, S. Schatz and R. Sklar (1987) *Postimperialism* (Boulder, CO: Lynne Rienner).

Beeson, M. and S. Bell (2005) 'Structures, Institutions and Agency in the Models of Capitalism Debate', in N. Phillips (ed.) *Globalizing International Political Economy* (Basingstoke: Palgrave Macmillan), pp. 116–40.

Beeson, M. and R. Higott (2005) 'Hegemony, Institutionalism and US Foreign

Policy: Theory and Practice in Comparative Historical Perspective', *Third World Quarterly* 26:7, pp. 1173–88.

Beetham, D. (2005) *Democracy: A Beginner's Guide* (Oxford: One World).

Bellis, P. (1988) *Marxism and the Soviet Union* (London: Macmillan).

Bello, W. (2003) *Deglobalization* (London: Zed Books).

Bello, W. (2005) *Dilemmas of Domination* (New York: Metropolitan).

Benn, H. (2004) 'The Development Challenge in Crisis States' (at www.dfid.gov.uk).

Berger, M. (2004) *The Battle for Asia* (London: Routledge).

Berger, M. (2006) 'From Nation-Building to State-Building: the Geopolitics of Development, the Nation-State System and the Changing Global Order', *Third World Quarterly* 27:1, pp. 5–35.

Berger, M. and H. Weber (2006) 'Beyond State-building: Global Governance and the Crisis of the Nation-State System in the 21st Century', *Third World Quarterly* 27:1, pp. 201–08.

Berger, S. and R. Dore (eds) (1996) *National Diversity and Global Capitalism* (Ithaca, NY: Cornell University Press).

Berlin, I. (1969) *Four Essays on Liberty* (Oxford: Oxford University Press).

Berman, P. (2004) *Terror and Liberalism* (New York: W. W. Norton).

Berman, P. (2006) *Power and the Idealists* (Boston, MA: Soft Skull Press).

Bernstein, R. (2006) *The Abuse of Evil* (Cambridge: Polity).

Bernstein, R. and R. Munro (1998) *The Coming Conflict with China* (New York: Vintage).

Bettelheim, C. (1972) 'Appendix I: Theoretical Comments', in A. Emmanuel *Unequal Exchange* (London: New Left Books), pp. 271–322.

Bhagwati, J. (2004) *In Defence of Globalization* (Oxford: Oxford University Press).

Bhalla, S. (2002) *Imagine There's No Country* (Washington: Institute of International Economics).

Bieler, A., and A. D. Morton (2004) 'A Critical Theory Route to Hegemony, World Order and Historical Change: Neo-Gramscian Perspectives in International Relations', *Capital and Class* 82, pp. 85–113.

Bieler, A., W. Bonefeld, P. Burnham and A. D. Morton (2006) *Global Restructuring: State, Capital and Labour* (London: Palgrave Macmillan).

Bilgin, P. and A. D. Morton (2002) 'Historicising Representations of "Failed States": Beyond the Cold War Annexation of the Social Sciences', *Third World Quarterly* 23:1, pp. 55–80.

Bilgin, P. and A. D. Morton (2004) 'From "Rogue" to "Failed" States? The Fallacy of "Short-Termism"', *Politics* 24:3, pp. 169–80.

Blaut, J. (1993) *The Colonizer's Model of the World* (New York: Guilford).

Block, F. (1977) *The Origins of International Economic Disorder* (Berkeley: University of California Press).

Boltanski, L. and E. Chiapello (2005) *The New Spirit of Capitalism* (London: Verso).

Bond, P. (2005) 'Neoliberalism in Sub-Saharan Africa: from Structural Adjustment to NEPAD', in A. Saad-Filho and D. Johnston (eds), *Neoliberalism: A Critical Reader* (London: Pluto), pp. 230–6.

Bonefeld, W. (ed.) (1991) *Post-Fordism and Social Form* (London: Macmillan).

Boot, M. (2003) 'The Case for American Empire', *Weekly Standard*, 15 October.

Boron, A. (2005) 'The Truth about Capitalist Democracy', in L. Panitch and C. Leys (eds), *The Socialist Register 2006* (London: Merlin), pp. 28–58.

Brandt, W. (1980) *North–South: A Programme of Survival* (London: Pan).

Brandt, W. (1983) *Common Crisis, North–South* (London: Pan).

Brenner, R. (1976) 'Agrarian Class Structure and Economic Development in Pre-Industrial Europe', *Past and Present* 70, pp. 30–75.

Brenner, R. (1977) 'The Origins of Capitalist Development: a Critique of Neo-Smithian Marxism', *New Left Review* 104, pp. 25–92.

Brenner, R. (1982) 'The Agrarian Roots of European Capitalism', *Past and Present* 97, pp. 16–113.

Brenner, R. (1998) 'The Economics of Global Turbulence', *New Left Review* I:229, pp. 1–265.

Brenner, R. (2002) *The Boom and the Bubble* (London: Verso).

Brenner, R. (2003) 'Towards the Precipice', *London Review of Books* 25:3 (at www.lrb.co.uk), pp. 12–18.

Breslin, S. (2005) 'Power and Production: Rethinking China's Global Economic Role', *Review of International Studies* 31, pp. 735–53.

Brett, E. (1983) *International Money and Capitalist Crisis* (London: Heinemann).

Brett, E. (1985) *The World Economy since the War* (London: Macmillan).

Brewer, A. (1990) *Marxist Theories of Imperialism* (London: Routledge, 2nd edition).

Bromley, S. (1994) *Rethinking Middle East Politics* (Cambridge: Polity).

Bromley, S. (1997) 'Middle East Exceptionalism – Myth or Reality?', in D. Potter, D. Goldblatt, M. Kiloh and P. Lewis (eds) (1997) *Democratization* (Cambridge: Polity), pp. 321–44.

Bromley, S. (2005) 'Oil and United States Hegemony', *Government and Opposition* 40:2, pp. 225–55.

Bromley, S. (2006) 'The Logic of American Power in the International Capitalist Order', in A. Colas and R. Saull (eds), *The War on Terror and American Empire* (London: Routledge), pp. 44–64.

Brown, C. (2002) *Sovereignty, Rights and Justice* (Cambridge: Polity).

Brown, C., T. Nardin and N. Rengger (eds) (2002) *International Relations in Political Thought* (Cambridge: Cambridge University Press).

Brown, C. and K. Ainley (2005) *Understanding International Relations* (Basingstoke: Palgrave Macmillan).

Brown, W. (2002) *The European Union and Africa* (London: I. B. Tauris).

Brown, W. (2006) 'Africa and International Relations: a Comment on IR Theory, Anarchy and Statehood', *Review of International Studies* 32:1, pp. 119–43.

Bukharin, N. (1973) *Imperialism and World Economy* (London: Merlin, first published 1914).

Bull, M. (2005) 'Limits of Multitude', *New Left Review* II:35, pp. 19–39.

Burawoy, M. (1983) 'Factory Regimes under Advanced Capitalism', *American Sociological Review* 48:5, pp. 587–605.

Burbach, R. (2004) *Imperial Overstretch* (London: Zed Books).

Burbach, R. and B. Robinson (1999) 'The Fin-de-Siècle Debate: Globalisation as Epochal Shift', *Science and Society* 63:1, pp. 10–39.

Burke, J. (2004) *Al-Qaeda* (London: Penguin).

Burke, M. (2001) 'The Changing Nature of Imperialism: the US as Author of the Asian Crisis', *Historical Materialism* 8, pp. 49–87.

Burkeman, O. (2005) 'Three months ago Bob Geldof declared Live 8 had reached its aim. But what really happened next?', *Guardian*, 12 September.

Burkett, P. and M. Hart-Landsberg (2001) 'Crisis and Recovery in East Asia: the Limits of Capitalist Development', *Historical Materialism* 8: pp. 3–47.

Burkett, P. and M. Hart-Landsberg (2004) 'China and Socialism', *Monthly Review* 56:3, pp. 13–123.

Burnham, P. (1999) 'The Politics of Economic Management in the 1990s', *New Political Economy* 4:1, pp. 37–54.

Burnham, P. (2002) 'Class, States and Global Circuits of Capital', in M. Rupert and H. Smith (eds), *Historical Materialism and Globalization* (London: Routledge), pp. 1134–28.

Bush, G. (2002) 'Remarks by the President at 2002 Graduation Exercise of the US Military Academy, West Point, New York', www.whitehouse.gov/news/releases/2002/06/20020601-3.html

Bush, R. (2004) 'Undermining Africa', *Historical Materialism* 12:4, pp. 173–201.

Cain, P. and A. Hopkins (1993) *British Imperialism* (London: Longman), 2 volumes.

Callahan, W. (2005) 'How to Understand China: the Dangers and Opportunities of Being a Rising Power', *Review of International Studies* 31:4, pp. 701–14.

Callinicos, A. (2002a) 'Marxism and Global Governance', in D. Held and A. McGrew (eds), *Governing Globalization* (Cambridge: Polity), pp. 249–66.

Callinicos, A. (2002b) 'The Grand Strategy of the American Empire', *International Socialism* 97, pp. 3–38.

Callinicos, A. (2003) *The New Mandarins of American Power* (Cambridge: Polity).

Callinicos, A. (2005) 'Imperialism and Global Political Economy', *International Socialism* 108, pp. 109–27.

Cameron, A. and R. Palan (2004) *The Imagined Economies of Globalization* (London: Sage).

Cammack, P. (1990) 'Statism, New Institutionalism and Marxism', in R. Miliband and L. Panitch (eds) (1990) *The Socialist Register 1990* (London: Merlin), pp. 147–70.

Cammack, P. (2004) 'What the World Bank Means by Poverty Reduction, and Why it Matters', *New Political Economy* 9:2, pp. 189–211.

Campbell, A. (2005) 'The Birth of Neoliberalism in the United States: a Reorganisation of Capitalism', in A. Saad-Filho (ed.), *Neoliberalism: A Critical Reader* (London: Pluto), pp. 187–98.

Caney, S. (2005) *Justice Beyond Borders* (Cambridge: Cambridge University Press).

Castells, M. (1996) *The Rise of the Network Society* (Oxford: Blackwell, 1st edition).

Castells, M. (1997) *The Power of Identity* (Oxford: Blackwell, 1st edition).

Castells, M. (2000a) *End of Millennium* (Oxford: Blackwell, 2nd edition).

Castells, M. (2000b) *The Rise of the Network Society* (Oxford: Blackwell, 2nd edition).

Cerny, P. (1997) 'Paradoxes of the Competition State: the Dynamics of Political Globalisation', *Government and Opposition* 32:1, pp. 251–74.

Chabal, P. and J.-P. Daloz (1999) *Africa Works: Disorder as a Political Instrument* (London: James Currey).

Chan, S. (2005) *Out of Evil* (London: I. B. Tauris).

Chandler, A. (1990) *Scale and Scope* (Boston, MA: Harvard University Press).

Chandler, D. (2004a) *Constructing Global Civil Society* (Basingstoke: Palgrave Macmillan).

Chandler, D. (2004b) *From Kosovo to Kabul* (London: Pluto).

Chandler, D. and G. Baker (eds) (2005) *Global Civil Society: Contested Futures* (London: Routledge).

Chang, H. J. (2002) *Kicking Away the Ladder* (London: Anthem).

Chang, H. J. (2003) *Globalisation and the Economic Role of the State* (London: Zed Books).

Chang, H. J. (2005) *Why Developing Countries Need Tariffs* (Geneva: South Centre).

Chen, S. and M. Ravallion (2004), 'How Have the World's Poorest Fared since the Early 1980s', *World Bank Policy Research Working Paper* no. 3341 (at http//econ.worldbank.org).

Chesterman, S., M. Ignatieff and R. Thakur (eds) (2005) *Making States Work: State Failure and the Crisis of Governance* (New York: United Nations University Press).

Chibber, V. (2003) *Locked in Place* (Princeton: Princeton University Press).

Chibber, V. (2004a) 'The Return of Imperialism to the Social Sciences', *European Journal of Sociology* 45:3, pp. 427–41.

Chibber, V. (2004b) 'Reviving the Developmental State? The Myth of the "National Bourgeoisie"', in L. Panitch and C. Leys (eds), *The Socialist Register 2005* (London: Merlin), pp. 144–65.

Chibber, V. (2005) 'The Politics of a Miracle: Class Interests and State Power in Korean Developmentalism', in D. Coates (ed.), *Varieties of Capitalism, Varieties of Approaches* (Basingstoke: Palgrave Macmillan), pp. 122–38.

Chitty, A. (2002) 'Moralism, Terrorism and War – Response to Shaw', *Radical Philosophy* 111, pp. 16–19.

Chomsky, N. (1999) *The New Military Humanism* (London: Pluto).

Clarke, S. (1988) *Keynesianism, Monetarism and the Crisis of the State* (London: Edward Elgar).

Cliff, T. (1988) *State Capitalism in Russia* (London: Bookmarks).

Cline, W. (2004) *Trade Policy and Global Poverty* (Washington: Institute of International Economics).

Coates, D. (2000) *Models of Capitalism* (Cambridge: Polity).

Coates, D. (ed.) (2005) *Varieties of Capitalism, Varieties of Approaches* (Basingstok: Palgrave Macmillan).

Coates, D. and J. Krieger (2004) *Blair's War* (Cambridge: Polity).

Cobden, R. (1903) *Speeches on Free Trade* (London: Macmillan, speeches from 1840s).

Cohen, B. (1973) *The Question of Imperialism* (New York: Basic Books).

Cohen, R. (2006) *Migration and its Enemies* (Aldershot: Ashgate).

Colas, A. (2002) *International Civil Society* (Cambridge: Polity).

Colas, A. (2005) 'Global Civil Society: Analytical Category or Normative Concept?', in D. Chandler and G. Baker (eds), *Global Civil Society: Contested Futures* (London: Routledge), pp. 17–33.

Coleman, W. and G. Underhill (eds) (1998) *Regionalism and Global Economic Integration* (London: Routledge).

Collier, P. (2000) 'Doing Well Out of War: an Economic Perspective', in M. Berdal and D. Malone (eds), *Greed and Grievance: Economic Agendas in Civil Wars* (Boulder, CO: Lynne Rienner), pp. 91–111.

Collier, P. and A. Hoeffler (1998) 'On Economic Causes of Civil War', *Oxford Economic Papers* vol. 50, pp. 563–73.

Collier, P. and A. Hoeffler (2002) 'Greed and Grievance in Civil War', Oxford Centre for the Study of African Economies, Working Paper 2002–01.

Commission for Africa (2005a) Commission for Africa Report: Our Common Future (at www.commissionforafrica.org).

Commission for Africa (2005b) *Our Common Interest* (London: Penguin).

Cooley, J. (2002) *Unholy Wars* (London: Pluto).

Cooper, F. (2004) 'Empire Multiplied: a Review Essay', *Comparative Studies in Society and History* 46:2, pp. 247–72.

Cooper, R. (2002) 'Why We Still Need Empires', *Observer* 7 April.

Cooper, R. (2004) *The Breaking of Nations: Order and Chaos in the 21st Century* (London: Atlantic).

Corbridge, S. (1993) *Debt and Development* (Oxford: Blackwell).

Corbridge, S. (1998) 'Beneath the Pavement Only Soil?', *Journal of Development Studies* 34:6, pp. 138–49.

Corbridge, S. and J. Harriss (2000) *Reinventing India* (Cambridge: Polity).

Cornwell, R. (2006) 'Warmongers Admit they were Wrong – and Deliver a Dangerous Message to Bush', *The Independent*, 9 March.

Corrigan, P. and D. Sayer (1986) *The Great Arch* (Oxford: Blackwell).

Cowen, M. and R. Shenton (1996) *Doctrines of Development* (London: Routledge).

Cox, M. (2004) 'Empire, Imperialism and the Bush Doctrine', *Review of International Studies* 30:3, pp. 585–608.

Cox, M., J. Ikenberry and T. Inoguchi (eds) (2002) *American Democracy Promotion* (Oxford: Oxford University Press).

Cox, R. (1981) 'Social Forces, States and World Orders: Beyond International Relations Theory', *Millennium* 10:2, pp. 126–55.

Cox, R. (1987) *Production, Power and World Order* (New York: Columbia University Press).

Cox, R. (1993) 'Structural Issues of Global Governance: Implications for Europe', in S. Gill (ed.), *Gramsci, Historical Materialism and International Relations* (Cambridge: Cambridge University Press), pp. 259–89.

Cramer, C. (2002) 'Homo Economicus Goes to War: Methodological Individualism, Rational Choice, and the Political Economy of War', *World Development* 30:11, pp. 1845–64.

Cramer, C. (2006) *Civil War is Not a Stupid Thing* (London: Hurst).

Crotty, J. (2002) 'Why There is Chronic Excess Capacity', *Challenge* 45:4, pp. 21–44.

Crotty, J. (2003) 'The Neoliberal Paradox: the Impact of Destructive Product Market Competition and Impatient Finance on Nonfinancial Corporations in the Neoliberal Era', *Review of Radical Political Economics* 35:3, pp. 271–9.

Crotty, J. and C. Lee (2002) 'A Political Economy Analysis of the Failure of Neo-liberal Restructuring in Post-crisis Korea', *Cambridge Journal of Economics* 26:5, pp. 667–78.

Crotty, J., G. Epstein and P. Kelly (1998) 'Multinational Corporations in the Neo-liberal Regime', in D. Baker, G. Epstein and R. Pollin (eds), *Globalization and Progressive Economic Policy* (Cambridge: Cambridge University Press), pp. 117–43.

Crouch, C. and W. Streeck (eds) (1997) *Political Economy of Modern Capitalism* (London: Sage).

Cumings, B. (1987) 'The Origins and Development of the North-East Asian Political Economy: Industrial Sectors, Product Cycles and Political Consequences', in F. Deyo (ed.), *The Political Economy of the New Asian Industrialism* (Ithaca, NY: Cornell University Press).

Cumings, B. (1999) 'Still the American Century', in M. Cox, K. Booth and T. Dunne (eds) (1999), *The Interregnum: Controversies in World Politics* (Cambridge: Cambridge University Press), pp. 271–99.

Cushman, T. (ed.) (2005) *A Matter of Principle* (Berkeley: University of California Press).

Da Costa, A. (2002) 'Uneven and Combined Development: Understanding India's Software Exports', *World Development* 31:1, pp. 211–26.

Darity, W. and L. Davis (2005) 'Growth, Trade and Uneven Development', *Cambridge Journal of Economics* 25:6, pp. 141–70.

Davis, M. (1985) 'Reaganomics Magical Mystery Tour', *New Left Review* 149 pp. 45–65.

Davis, M. (2004) 'Planet of Slums', *New Left Review* II:26, pp. 5–34.

Davis, M. (2006) *Planet of Slums* (London: Verso).

Department of Defense (2006) Quadrennial Defense Review Report (at http://www.defense.link.mil).

Desai, M. (2002) *Marx's Revenge* (London: Verso).

Desai, R. (2004) 'From National Bourgeoisie to Rogues, Failures and Bullies: 21st Century Imperialism and the Unraveling of the Third World', *Third World Quarterly* 25:1, pp. 169–85.

Dews, P. (1987) *Logics of Disintegration* (London: Verso).

de Soto, H. (2001) *The Mystery of Capital* (London: Black Swan).

de Sousa Santos, B. (ed.) (2006) *Democratizing Democracy* (London: Verso).

de Waal, A. (1997) *Famine Crimes* (London: James Currey).

Dicken, P. (2003) *Global Shift* (London: Sage, 3rd edition).

Dicken, P., P. Kelly, P. Olds and H. Wai-Chung Yeng (2001) 'Chains and Networks, Territories and Scales: Towards a Relational Framework for Analyzing the World Economy', *Global Networks* 1:2, pp. 89–112.

Dobson, A. (2000) *Green Political Thought* (London: Routledge).

Dodge, T. (2005) 'Iraqi Transitions: from Regime Change to State Collapse', *Third World Quarterly* 26:4/5, pp. 705–21.

Dollar, D. and A. Kraay (2002) 'Growth is Good for the Poor', *Journal of Economic Growth* 7, pp. 195–225.

Dore, R. (1985) 'Authority or Benevolence: the Confucian Recipe for Industrial Success', *Government and Opposition* 20:2, pp. 196–217.

Dorrien, G. (2004) *Imperial Designs* (New York: Routledge).

Doyle, M. (1983) 'Kant, Liberal Legacies and Foreign Affairs: Part One', *Philosophy and Public Affairs* 12:3, pp. 205–35.

DuBois, M. (1991) 'The Governance of the Third World: a Foucauldian Perspective on Power Relations in Development', *Alternatives* 16, pp. 1–30.

Duchesne, R. (2001/2) 'Between Sinocentrism and Eurocentrism: Debating Andre Gunder Frank's *Re-Orient: Global Economy in the Asian Age*', *Science and Society* 65:4, pp. 428–63.

Duffield, M. (2001) *Global Governance and the New Wars* (London: Zed Books).

Duffield, M. (2005) 'Getting Savages to Fight Barbarians', *Conflict, Security and Development* 5:2, pp. 141–59.

Duffield, M. and N. Waddell (2004) *Human Security and Global Danger*, Department of Politics, University of Lancaster.

Dumenil, G. and D. Levy (2004) *Capital Resurgent* (Cambridge, MA: Harvard University Press).

Dunkley, G. (2000) *The Free Trade Adventure* (London: Zed).

Dunkley, G. (2004) *Free Trade: Myth, Reality and Alternatives* (London: Zed Books).

Dunn, K. and T. Shaw (eds) (2001) *Africa's Challenge to International Relations Theory* (Basingstoke: Palgrave Macmillan).

Dunne, T. and N. Wheeler (eds) (1999) *Human Rights and Global Politics* (Cambridge: Cambridge University Press).

Durkheim, E. (1984) *The Division of Labour in Society* (London: Macmillan, first published 1893).

Edwards, C. (1985) *The Fragmented World* (London: Methuen).

Eichengreen, B., Y. Rhee and H. Tong (2004) 'The Impact of China on the Exports of Other Asian Countries' (NBER Working Paper no. 10768).

Elliott, L. (2005) 'Rich Spend 25 Times More on Defence than Aid', *Guardian*, 6 July, 2005.

Ellner, S. and D. Hellinger (eds) (2003) *Venezuelan Politics in the Chavez Era* (Boulder, CO: Lynne Rienner).

Elson, D. (1995) 'Gender Awareness in Modeling Structural Adjustment', *World Development* 23:11, pp. 1851–68.

Engberg-Pedersen, P., P. Gibbon, P. Raikes, and L. Udsholdt (1996) *Limits of Adjustment in Africa* (London: James Currey).

Engerman, S. (1994) 'Mercantilism and Overseas Trade, 1700–1800', in R. Floud and D. McCloskey (eds), *The Economic History of Britain since 1700*, vol. 1: *1700–1860* (Cambridge: Cambridge University Press), pp. 165–80.

Escobar, A. (1995) *Encountering Development* (Princeton, NJ: Princeton University Press).

Esteva, G. and M. Prakash (1998) *Grassroots Postmodernism* (London: Zed Books).

Etherington, N. (1984) *Theories of Imperialism: War, Conquest and Capital* (London: Croom Helm).

Evans, P. (1995) *Embedded Autonomy* (Princeton, NJ: Princeton University Press).

Evans, P. (2005) 'Harnessing the State: Rebalancing Strategies for Monitoring and Motivation', in M. Lange and D. Rueschemeyer (eds), *States and Development* (Basingstoke: Palgrave macmillan), pp. 26–47.

Evans, T. (2002) 'If Democracy, Then Human Rights?', *Third World Quarterly* 22:4, pp. 623–42.

Falk, R. (2000) 'Resisting "Globalization from Above" through "Globalization from Below"', in B. Gills (ed.), *Globalization and the Politics of Resistance* (Basingstoke: Palgrave Macmillan), pp. 46–56.

Fan, G. and W. Woo (1996) 'State Enterprise Reform as a Source of Macroeconomic Instability: the Case of China', *Asian Economic Journal* 10:3, pp. 207–24.

Farrell, M., B. Hettne and L. Van Langenhove (eds) (2005) *Global Politics of Regionalism* (London: Pluto).

Ferguson, N. (2003) *Empire* (London: Penguin).

Ferguson, N. (2004) *Colossus* (London: Allen Lane).

Fieldhouse, D. (1973) *The Economics of Empire* (London: Weidenfeld and Nicolson).

Fieldhouse, D. (1999) *The West and the Third World* (Oxford: Blackwell).

Fine, B. (2006) 'The Developmental State and the Political Economy of Development', in K. S. Jomo and B. Fine (eds), (2006) *The New Development Economics* (London: Zed Books), pp. 101–22.

Fine, B. and L. Harris (1979) *Re-reading Capital* (New York: Columbia University Press).

Fine, B. and E. Van Waeyenberge (2005) 'Correcting Stiglitz: from information to power in the world of development', in L. Panitch and C. Leys (eds), *The Socialist Register 2006* (London: Merlin), pp. 146–68.

Fine, R. (1997) 'Civil Society, Enlightenment and Critique', in R. Fine and S. Rai (eds), *Civil Society: Democratic Perspectives* (London: Frank Cass), pp. 7–28.

Fine, R. (2001) *Political Investigations* (London: Routledge).

Foucault, M. (1991) 'Governmentality', in G. Burchell (ed.), *The Foucault Effect* (Chicago: University of Chicago Press), pp. 87–104.

Foucault, M. (1982) 'The Subject and Power', in H. Dreyfus and P. Rabinow (eds), *Michel Foucault: Beyond Structuralism and Hermeneutics* (New York: Pantheon), pp. 201–28.

Frank, A. G. (1969a) *Capitalism and Underdevelopment in Latin America* (New York: Monthly Review Press).

Frank, A. G. (1969b) *Latin America: Underdevelopment or Revolution* (New York: Monthly Review Press).

Frank, A. G. (1984) 'Asia's Exclusive Models', *Far Eastern Economic Review*, June 25, pp. 22–3.

Frank, A. G. (1998) *ReOrient: Global Economy in the Asian Age* (Berkeley: University of California Press).

Frank, T. (1997) *The Conquest of Cool* (Chicago: University of Chicago Press).

Frank, T. (2004) *What's Wrong with America?* (London: Secker and Warburg).

Friedman, T. (2005a) *The World is Flat* (New York: Allen Lane).

Friedman, T. (2005b) 'Global is Good', *Guardian*, 21 April.

Frobel, F., J. Heinrichs and O. Kreye (1980) *The New International Division of Labour* (Cambridge: Cambridge University Press).

Fukuyama, F. (2004) *State Building* (Ithaca, NY: Cornell University Press).

Fukuyama, F. (2006) *America at the Crossroads* (New Haven, CT: Yale University Press).

Gaddis, J. L. (1999) 'Living in a Candlestick Park', *Atlantic Monthly* 283:4, pp. 70–82.

Gaddis, J. L. (2004) *Surprise, Security and the American Experience* (Cambridge, MA: Harvard University Press).

Gallagher, J. and R. Robinson (1953) 'The Imperialism of Free Trade', *Economic History Review* 6:1, pp. 1–18.

Gallagher, K. (ed.) (2005) *Putting Development First* (London: Zed Books).

Gamble, A. (1994) *Britain in Decline* (London: Macmillan, 3rd edition).

Gamble, A. (2003) *Between Europe and America* (Basingstoke: Palgrave Macmillan).

Gamble, A. (2005) 'Globalization: Getting the "Big Picture" Right, a Comment on Justin Rosenberg', *International Politics* 42:3, pp. 364–71.

Gamble, A. and A. Payne (eds) (1996) *Regionalism and World Order* (Basingstoke: Palgrave Macmillan).

Geldof, B. (2005) 'Geldof's Year', *Guardian*, 28 December.

George, S. (1989) *A Fate Worse than Debt* (London: Penguin).

Geras, N. (2002) 'Marxism, the Holocaust and September 11th', *Imprints* 6:3 (at http://eis.bris.ac.uk/~plcdib/imprints.html).

Geras, N. (2005) 'There are Apologists Amongst Us', *Guardian*, 21 July.

Gerber, H. (1987) *The Social Origins of the Middle East* (Boulder, CO: Lynne Rienner).

Gereffi, G. (1994) 'Capitalism, Development and Global Commodity Chains', in L. Sklair (ed.) (1994) *Capitalism and Development* (London: Routledge), pp. 211–31.

Gereffi, G. and M. Korzeniewicz (eds) (1994) *Commodity Chains and Global Capitalism* (Westport, CT: Praeger).

Gerges, F. (2005) *The Far Enemy* (Cambridge: Cambridge University Press).

Gibbon, P. and S. Ponte (2005) *Trading Down* (Philadelphia: Temple University Press).

Gibbs, T. (2006) 'Business as Usual: What the Chavez Era Tells Us about Democracy under Globalisation', *Third World Quarterly* 27:2, pp. 265–79.

Gibson-Graham, J. K. (1996) *The End of Capitalism (as we knew it)* (Oxford: Blackwell).

Giddens, A. (1991) *The Consequences of Modernity* (Cambridge: Polity).

Giddens, A. (1999) *Runaway World* (Cambridge: Polity).

Giddens, A. (2000) *The Third Way and its Critics* (Cambridge: Polity).

Gill, S. (1990) *American Hegemony and the Trilateral Commission* (Cambridge: Cambridge University Press).

Gill, S. (1995) 'Globalisation, Market Civilisation and Disciplinary Neoliberalism', *Millennium* 24:3, pp. 399–423.

Gill, S. (2003) *Power and Resistance in the New World Order* (London: Routledge).

Gill, S. (2004) 'The Contradictions of US Supremacy', in L. Panitch and C. Leys (eds), *The Socialist Register 2005* (London: Merlin), pp. 23–45.

Gills, B. and W. Thompson (eds) (2006) *Globalization and Global History* (London: Routledge).

Gills, B., J. Rocamora and R. Wilson (1993) *Low Intensity Democracy* (London: Pluto).

Gilpin, R. (1987) *The Political Economy of International Relations* (Princeton, NJ: Princeton University Press).

Gilpin, R. (2001) *Global Political Economy* (Princeton, NJ: Princeton University Press).

Glyn, A. (2005) 'Global Imbalances', *New Left Review* II:34, pp. 5–37.

Glyn, A. (2006) *Capitalism Unleashed* (Oxford: Oxford University Press).

Glyn, A., A. Hughes, A. Lipietz and A. Singh (1990) 'The Rise and Fall of the Golden Age', in S. Marglin and J. Schor (eds), *The Golden Age of Capitalism* (Oxford: Clarendon), pp. 39–125.

Gobat, J. (1998) 'Republic of Korea', *IMF Country Issues* 98:74 (Washington, DC: IMF).

Godley, W., D. Papadimitriou, C. dos Santos and G. Zezza (2005) *The United States and her Creditors: Can the Symbiosis Last* (New York: Levy Economics Institute Strategic Analysis).

Golding, P. (2000) 'Forthcoming Features: Information and Communications Technologies and the Sociology of the Future', *Sociology* 34:1, pp. 165–84.

Gonzalez, M. (2004) 'Venezuela: Many Steps to Come', *International Socialism* 104, pp. 65–94.

Gott, R. (2000) *In the Shadow of the Liberator* (London: Verso).

Gowan, P. (1999) *The Global Gamble* (London: Verso).

Gowan, P. (2001) 'Neoliberal Cosmopolitanism', *New Left Review* 11, pp. 79–93.

Gowan, P. (2002), 'The American Campaign for Global Sovereignty', *The Socialist Register 2003* (London: Merlin), pp. 1–27.

Grabel, I. (2003) 'International Private Capital Flows and Developing Countries', in H. J. Chang (ed.), *Rethinking Development Economics* (London: Anthem), pp. 325–46.

Grahl, J. (2001) 'Globalized Finance', *New Left Review* 8 (2nd series), pp. 23–46.

Grahl, J. (2004) 'The European Union and American Power', in L. Panitch and C. Leys (eds), *The Socialist Register 2005* (London: Merlin), pp. 280–96.

Grahl, J. (2005) 'Financial Markets and Globalization', *Soundings* 29, pp. 110–27.

Grahl, J. and P. Lysandrou (2003) 'Sand in the Wheels or Spanner in the Works? The Tobin Tax and Global Finance', *Cambridge Journal of Economics* 27:4, pp. 597–621.

Gramsci, A. (1971) *Selections from the Prison Notebooks* (London: Lawrence & Wishart).

Green, D. (2003) *The Silent Revolution: The Rise and Crisis of Market Economies in Latin America* (London: Latin America Bureau).

Green, P. (2002) '"The Passage from Imperialism to Empire": a Commentary on *Empire* by Michael Hardt and Antonio Negri', *Historical Materialism* 10:1, pp. 29–77.

Green, F. and B. Sutcliffe (1987) *The Profit System* (Harmondsworth: Penguin).

Greenfield, G. (2004) 'Bandung *redux*: Anti-Globalization Nationalisms in South-East Asia', in L. Panitch and C. Leys (eds) (2004) *The Socialist Register 2005* (London: Merlin), pp. 166–96.

Gregory, D. (2004) *The Colonial Present* (Oxford: Blackwell).

Grooteart, C. and T. van Bastelaer (2001) *Understanding and Measuring Social Capital: A Synthesis of Findings and Recommendations from the Social Capital Initiative* (Washington, DC: World Bank, Social Capital Initiative Working Paper no. 24), pp. 1–31.

Habermas, J. (1986) *The Theory of Communicative Action*, vol. 1 (Cambridge: Polity).

Habermas, J. and J. Derrida (2005) 'February 15, or, What Binds Europeans Together', in D. Levy, M. Pensky and J. Torpey (eds), *Old Europe, New Europe, Core Europe* (London: Verso), pp. 3–13.

Hall, P. and D. Soskice (eds) (2001) *Varieties of Capitalism* (Oxford: Oxford University Press).

Halliday, F. (1983) *The Making of the Second Cold War* (London: Verso).

Halliday, F. (1989) *Cold War, Third World* (London: Hutchinson Radius).

Halliday, F. (2000) *Nation and Religion in the Middle East* (London: Saqi).

Halliday, F. (2002) *Two Hours that Shook the World* (London: Saqi).

Halliday, F. (2003) *Islam and the Myth of Confrontation* (London: I. B. Tauris, 2nd edition).

Halliday, F. (2005) *100 Myths about the Middle East* (London: Saqi).

Hamilton, C. (2004) *Growth Fetish* (London: Pluto).

Hansen, T. (2001) *Wages of Violence: Naming and Identity in Postcolonial Bombay* (Princeton, NJ: Princeton University Press).

Hardt, M. and A. Negri (2000) *Empire* (Cambridge, MA: Harvard University Press).

Hardt, M. and A. Negri (2004) *Multitude* (New York: Penguin).

Harman, C. (1988) *Class Struggles in Eastern Europe* (London: Bookmarks).

Harman, C. (2006) 'The Dragon's Fire: China's Economy and Europe's Crisis', *International Socialism* 109, pp. 69–90.

Harris, Jerry (1998/9), 'Globalization and the Technological Transformation of Capitalism', *Race and Class* 40:2/3, pp. 21–36.

Harris, Jerry (2003) 'Transnational Competition and the End of US Economic Hegemony', *Science and Society* 67:1, pp. 68–80.

Harris, John (2005) 'What do we want? History! When do we want it? Now!', *The Independent on Sunday*, 3 July.

Harris, John (2006) 'Essay', *New Statesman*, 23 January.

Harris, N. (2003) *The Return of Cosmopolitan Capital* (London: I. B. Tauris).

Harris, S. (2004) 'China in the Global Economy', in B. Buzan and R. Foot (eds), *Does China Matter? A Re-assessment* (London: Routledge), pp. 54–70.

Hart-Landsberg, M. (1993) *The Rush to Development* (New York: Monthly Review Press).

Harvey, D. (1989) *The Condition of Postmodernity* (Oxford: Blackwell).

Harvey, D. (2003) *The New Imperialism* (Oxford: Oxford University Press).

Harvey, D. (2005) *A Brief History of Neoliberalism* (Oxford: Oxford University Press).

Hashim, A. (2006) *Insurgency and Counter-Insurgency in Iraq* (London: Hurst).

Hay, C. (1994) 'Labour's Thatcherite Revisionism: Playing the Politics of "Catch Up"', *Political Studies* 42:4, pp. 700–7.

Hay, C. (1999) *The Political Economy of New Labour* (Manchester: Manchester University Press).

Hay, C. (2000) 'Contemporary Capitalism, Globalization, Regionalization and the Persistence of National Variation', *Review of International Studies* 26:4, pp. 509–31.

Hay, C. (2004a) 'Common Trajectories, Variable Paces, Divergent Outcomes? Models of European Capitalism under Conditions of Complex Economic Interdependence', *Review of International Political Economy* 11:2, pp. 231–62.

Hay, C. (2004b) 'Re-stating Politics, Re-politicising the State: Neo-liberalism, Economic Imperatives and the Rise of the Competition State', *Political Quarterly* 75 (supplement), pp. 38–50.

Hay, C. (2005a) 'Globalization's Impact on States', in J. Ravenhill (ed.), *Global Political Economy* (Oxford: Oxford University Press), pp. 235–62.

Hay, C. (2005b) 'Two Can Play at That Game . . . Or Can They? Varieties of Capitalism, Varieties of Institutionalism', in D. Coates (ed.), *Varieties of Capitalism, Varieties of Approaches* (Basingstoke: Palgrave Macmillan), pp. 106–21.

Hay, C. and D. Marsh (eds) (2001) *Demystifying Globalisation* (Basingstoke: Palgrave Macmillan).

Hay, C. and M. Watson (1999) 'Globalisation: "Sceptical" Notes on the 1999 Reith Lectures', *Political Quarterly* 70:4, pp. 418–25.

Hay, C. and M. Watson (2003) 'The Discourse of Globalisation and the Logic of No Alternative: Rendering the Contingent Necessary in the Political Economy of New Labour', *Policy and Politics* 31:3, pp. 289–305.

Hayek, F. (1960) *The Constitution of Liberty* (London: Routledge and Kegan Paul).

Hayes, E. (2005) '*Jihad*: How a Word Became a Weapon' (at www.open-democracy.net).

Hayter, T. (1971) *Aid as Imperialism* (London: Penguin).

Heartfield, J. (2005) 'Contextualizing the "anti-capitalist" movement in global civil society', in G. Baker and D. Chandler (eds), *Global Civil Society and Contested Futures*, pp. 155–70.

Hegel, G. (2005) *Philosophy of Right* (New York: Dover, first published 1821).

Held, D. (1992) 'Democracy: From City-State to Cosmopolitan Order', *Political Studies* vol. 40 (special issue), pp. 10–39.

Held, D. (2004) *Global Covenant* (Cambridge: Polity).

Held, D. and A. McGrew (2002) 'Introduction', in D. Held and A. McGrew (eds), *Governing Globalization* (Cambridge: Polity), pp. 1–21.

Held, D. and A. McGrew (2003), 'The Great Globalization Debate: an Introduction', in D. Held and A. McGrew (eds), *The Global Transformations Reader* (Cambridge: Polity).

Held, D., A. McGrew, D. Goldblatt and J. Perraton (1999) *Global Transformations* (Cambridge: Polity).

Helleiner, E. (1994) *States and the Re-emergence of Global Finance* (Ithaca, NY: Cornell University Press).

Henderson, C. (2003), 'Cancunblog: from Mexico to the world' (at www.openDemocracy.net).

Henderson, J., P. Dicken, M. Hess, N. Coe and H. Wai-Chung Yeung (2002), 'Global Production Networks and the Analysis of Economic Development', *Review of International Political Economy* 9:3, pp. 436–64.

Henwood, D. (2003) *After the New Economy* (London: New Press).

Herbst, J. (2000) *States and Power in Africa* (Princeton, NJ: Princeton University Press).

Hewitt, T. (2000) 'Half a Century of Development', in T. Allan and A. Thomas (eds), *Poverty and Development into the Twenty First Century* (Oxford: Oxford University Press), pp. 289–308.

Higott, R. (2003) 'American Unilateralism, Foreign Economic Policy and the "Securitisation" of Globalisation', *Centre for the Study of Globalisation and Regionalisation*, University of Warwick, Working Paper no. 124/03.

Hilferding, R. (1981) *Finance Capital* (London: Routledge, first published 1910).

Hines, C. (2000) *Localization: A Global Manifesto* (London: Zed Books).

Hines, C. and T. Lang (2001) 'The New Protectionism of "Localization"', in E. Goldsmith and J. Mander (eds), *The Case Against the Global Economy* (London: Earthscan), pp. 289–95.

Hiro, D. (2004) *War without End* (London: Routledge, 2nd edition).

Hirst, P. and G. Thompson (1999) *Globalization in Question* (Cambridge: Polity, 2nd edition).

Hitchens, C. (2003) *Regime Change* (London: Penguin).

Hobsbawm, E. (1968) *Industry and Empire* (London: Weidenfeld and Nicolson).

Hobsbawm, E. (1973) *The Age of Revolution* (London: Abacus).

Hobsbawm, E. (1975) *The Age of Capital* (London: Weidenfeld and Nicolson).

Hobsbawm, E. (1987) *The Age of Empire* (London: Weidenfeld and Nicolson).

Hobson, J. (2004) *The Eastern Origins of Western Civilization* (Cambridge: Cambridge University Press).

Hodkinson, S. (2005a) 'Make the G8 History', *Red Pepper* 132 (June).

Hodkinson, S. (2005b) 'G8 – Africa Nil', *Red Pepper* 137 (November).

Holland, M. (2002) *The European Union and the Third World* (Basingstoke: Palgrave Macmillan).

Hollingsworth, J. and R. Boyer (eds) (1997) *Contemporary Capitalism: The Embeddedness of Institutions* (Cambridge: Cambridge University Press).

Holloway, J. (2002) *Change the World without Taking Power* (London: Pluto).

Hoogvelt, A. (1982) *The Third World in Global Development* (Basingstoke: Macmillan).

Hoogvelt, A. (2001) *Globalization and the Postcolonial World* (Basingstoke: Palgrave Macmillan).

Hoogvelt, A. (2005) 'Globalisation and Imperialism: Wars and Humanitarian Intervention', in Open University, *War, Intervention and Development* (forthcoming).

Hore, C. (2004) 'China's Century?', *International Socialism* 103, pp. 3–48.

Hudson, M. (2003) *Super-Imperialism* (London: Pluto, 2nd edition).

Huntington, S. (1996) *The Clash of Civilisations and the Remaking of World Order* (New York: Simon and Schuster).

Hurt, S. (2003) 'Co-operation and Coercion? The Cotonou Agreement between the European Union and ACP States and the End of the Lomé Convention', *Third World Quarterly* 24:1, pp. 161–76.

Hutton, W. (1994) *The State We're In* (London: Cape).

Hutton, W. and A. Giddens (2001) 'In Conversation', in W. Hutton and A. Giddens (eds), *On the Edge* (London: Vintage), pp. 1–51.

ICISS (2001) *The Responsibility to Protect* (Ottawa: ICISS).

Idahosa, P. and R. Shenton (2004) 'The Africanist's "New" Clothes', *Historical Materialism* 12:4, pp. 67–113.

IFG (2002) *Alternatives to Economic Globalization* (San Francisco, CA: Berrett Kohler).

Ignatieff, M. (2003) *Empire Lite* (New York: Vintage).

Ignatieff, M. (2005) *The Lesser Evil* (Princeton, NJ: Princeton University Press).

IPS (2003) *Coalition of the Willing, or Coalition of the Coerced? – Part II* (Washington, DC: Institute of Policy Studies).

Itoh, M. (1990) *The World Economic Crisis and Japanese Capitalism* (Basingstoke: Macmillan).

Itoh, M. (2005) 'Assessing Neoliberalism in Japan', in A. Saad-Filho (ed.), *Neoliberalism: A Critical Reader* (London: Pluto), pp. 244–50.

Jackson, R. (1990) *Quasi-States: Sovereignty, International Relations and the Third World* (Cambridge: Cambridge University Press).

Jackson, R. (2000) *The Global Covenant: Human Conduct in a World of States* (Oxford: Oxford University Press).

Jacques, M. (2005) 'Relying on China', *Guardian*, 20 June.

Jagger, B. (2005) 'Real People Power or Pernicious Platitudes?', *New Statesman*, 11 July.

James, J. (2003) 'Information Technology, Cumulative Causation and Patterns of Globalization in the Third World', *Review of International Political Economy* 8:1, pp. 147–62.

Jayasuriya, K. (2005) 'Beyond Institutional Fetishism: From the Developmental to the Regulatory State', *New Political Economy* 10:3, pp. 381–7.

Jenkins, R. (1984) *Transnational Corporations and the Industrial Transformation of Latin America* (Basingstoke: Macmillan).

Jenkins, R. (1987) *Transnational Corporations and Uneven Development* (London: Methuen).

Jenkins, R. (2004) 'Globalization, Production, Employment and Poverty: Debates and Evidence', *Journal of International Development* 16:1, pp. 1–12.

Jenkins, R. (2005) 'Globalisation of Production, Employment and Poverty:

Three Macro-Meso-Micro Studies', *European Journal of Development Research* 17:4, pp. 601–25.

Jessop, B. (1985) *Nicos Poulantzas: Marxist Theory and Political Strategy* (Basingstoke: Macmillan).

Jessop, B. (2002) *The Future of the Capitalist State* (Cambridge: Polity).

Johnson, C. (1995) *Japan: Who Governs? The Rise of the Developmental State* (New York: W. W. Norton).

Johnson, C. (2002) *Blowback* (London: Time Warner).

Johnson, C. (2004) *Empire of Sorrow* (London: Verso).

Jomo, K. S. (ed.) (2004) *After the Storm* (Singapore: Singapore University Press).

Jomo, K. S. and B. Fine (eds) (2006) *The New Development Economics* (London: Zed Books).

Journal of Development Studies (1998), 'Special Issue on the Asian Financial Crisis', 34:6.

Kagan, R. and W. Kristol (2000) 'American Power – for What?', *Commentary,* January, pp. 30–2, 35–6.

Kaldor, M. (2003) *Global Civil Society* (Cambridge: Polity).

Kaldor, M. (2004) 'American Power: from "Compellance" to Cosmopolitanism?', *International Affairs* 79:1, pp. 1–22.

Kaldor, N. (1972) 'The Irrelevance of Equilibrium Economics', *Economic Journal* 82:328, pp. 1237–55.

Kambhampati, U. (2004) *Development and the Developing World* (Cambridge: Polity).

Kamm, O. (2005) *Anti-Totalitarianism: The Left-Wing Case for a Neoconservative Foreign Policy* (London: Social Affairs Unit).

Kant, I. (1983) *Perpetual Peace and Other Essays on Politics, History and Morals* (Indianapolis: Hackett, first published 1795).

Kaplan, L. (1998) 'Leftism on the Right: Conservatives Learn to Blame America First', *Weekly Standard*, 9 February.

Kaplan, L. and W. Kristol (2003) *The War over Iraq: Saddam's Tyranny and America's Mission* (San Francisco, CA: Encounter Books).

Kaplinsky, R. (2005a) *Globalization, Poverty and Inequality* (Cambridge: Polity).

Kaplinksy, R. (2005b) 'Revisiting the Revisited Terms of Trade: Will China Make a Difference?', mimeo.

Kautsky, K. (1970) 'Ultra-Imperialism', *New Left Review* I:59, pp. 41–6.

Kautsky, K. (2002) 'Ultra-Imperialism', *Workers' Liberty* 2:3, pp. 73–9 (first published 1914).

Keane, J. (2003) *Global Civil Society?* (Cambridge: Cambridge University Press).

Kedourie, E. (1992) *Politics in the Middle East* (Oxford: Oxford University Press).

Kennedy, P. (1988) *The Rise and Fall of Great Powers* (London: Unwin Hyman).

Kenney, M. and R. Florida (1993) *Beyond Mass Production: The Japanese System and its Transfer to the US* (Oxford: Oxford University Press).

Keohane, R. (1984) *After Hegemony* (Princeton, NJ: Princeton University Press).

Keohane, R. and J. Nye (1977) *Power and Interdependence* (Boston, MA: Little Brown).

Kettell, S. (2006) *Dirty Politics? New Labour, British Politics and the Invasion of Iraq* (London: Zed Books).

Khan, A. and C. Riskin (2001) *Inequality and Poverty in China in the Age of Globalization* (Oxford: Oxford University Press).

Khan, M. (2002) 'Corruption and Governance in Early Capitalism: World Bank Strategies and their Limitations', in J. Pincus and J. Winters (eds), *Reinventing the World Bank* (Ithaca, NY: Cornell University Press), pp. 76–100.

Kiely, R. (1995) *Sociology and Development: The Impasse and Beyond* (London: University College London Press).

Kiely, R. (1996) *The Politics of Labour and Development in Trinidad* (Kingston, Jamaica: University of West Indies Press).

Kiely, R. (1998) *Industrialization and Development: A Comparative Analysis* (London: University College London Press).

Kiely, R. (1999) 'The Last Refuge of the Noble Savage?', *European Journal of Development Research* 11:1, pp. 30–55.

Kiely, R. (2003) 'The Race to the Bottom and International Labour Solidarity', *Review: A Journal of the Fernand Braudel Center* 26:1, pp. 67–88.

Kiely, R. (2004a) 'The World Bank and "Global Poverty Reduction": Good Policies or Bad Data?', *Journal of Contemporary Asia* 34:1, pp. 3–20.

Kiely, R. (2004b) 'What Difference does Difference Make? Reflections on Neo-conservatism as a Cosmopolitan Project', *Contemporary Politics* 10:3/4, pp. 185–202.

Kiely, R. (2005a) *The Clash of Globalisations: Neo-liberalism, the Third Way and 'Anti-globalisation'* (Leiden: Brill).

Kiely, R. (2005b) *Empire in the Age of Globalisation* (London: Pluto).

Kiely, R. (2005c) 'Capitalist Expansion and the Imperialism–Globalisation Debate', *Journal of International Relations and Development* 8:1, pp. 27–56.

Kiely, R. (2005d) 'Global Civil Society and "Spaces of Resistance"', in J. Eade and D. O'Byrne (eds), *Global Ethics and Civil Society* (Aldershot: Ashgate), pp. 138–53.

Kiely, R. (2005e) 'Globalisation and Poverty and the Poverty of Globalisation Theory', *Current Sociology* 53:6, pp. 897–916.

Kiely, R. (forthcoming) *States–Imperialism–Globalisation*.

Killick, T. (1995) *IMF Programmes in Developing Countries* (London: Routledge).

Kitching, G. (1982) *Development and Underdevelopment in Historical Perspective* (London: Methuen).

Kitching, G. (2001) *Seeking Social Justice through Globalization* (Philadelphia: Pennsylvania State University Press).

Klare, M. (2002) *Resource Wars* (Basingstoke: Palgrave Macmillan).

Klare, M. (2004) *Blood and Oil* (London: Hamish Hamilton).

Klein, N. (2000) *No Logo* (London: Flamingo).

Klein, N. (2002) *Fences and Windows* (London: Flamingo).

Knack, S. and P. Keefer (1995) 'Institutions and Economic Performance: Cross Country Tests Using Alternative Institutional Measures', *Economics and Politics* 7:3, pp. 207–27.

Kohli, A. (2004) *State Directed Development: Political Power and Industrialisation in the Global Periphery* (Cambridge: Cambridge University Press).

Konings, M. (2005) 'The United States in the Post-War Global Political Economy: Another Look at the Brenner Debate', in D. Coates (ed.), *Varieties of Capitalism, Varieties of Approaches* (Basingstoke: Palgrave Macmillan), pp. 189–210.

Korten, D. (1995) *When Corporations Rule the World* (London: Earthscan).

Krasner, S. (1982) 'Structural Causes and Regime Consequences: Regimes as Intervening Variables', *International Organization* 36, pp. 185–205.

Krauthammer, C. (1990) 'The Unipolar Moment', *Foreign Affairs* 70:1, pp. 23–33.

Krauthammer, C. (2002/3) 'The Unipolar Moment Revisited', *The National Interest* 70, pp. 5–17.

Krauthammer, C. (2004) 'In Defense of Democratic Realism', *The National Interest* 77, pp. 15–25.

Kristol, W. and R. Kagan (2003) 'Exit Strategy or Victory Strategy', *Weekly Standard*, 17 November.

Krugman, P. (1986) *Strategic Trade Policy and the New International Economics* (Cambridge: MIT Press).

Lacher, H. (2003) 'Putting the State in its Place? The Critique of State-centrism and its Limits', *Review of International Studies* 29:4, pp. 521–41.

Lacher, H. (2005), 'International Transformation and the Persistence of Territoriality: Toward a New Political Geography of Capitalism', *Review of International Political Economy* 12:1, pp. 26–52.

Laclau, E. and C. Mouffe (2001) *Hegemony and Socialist Strategy* (London: Verso).

Lake, A. (1994) 'Confronting Backlash States', *Foreign Affairs* 73:2, pp. 72–80.

Lal, D. (1984) *The Poverty of 'Development Economics'* (London: Institute of Economic Affairs).

Lal, D. (1988) 'Ideology and Industrialization in India and East Asia', in H. Hughes (ed.), *Achieving Industrialization in East Asia* (Cambridge: Cambridge University Press), pp. 195–240.

Lal, D. (2004) *In Praise of Empires* (Basingstoke: Palgrave Macmillan).

Landes, D. (1998) *The Wealth and Poverty of Nations: Why are Some so Rich and Others so Poor* (New York: W. W. Norton).

Landsberg, M. (1979) 'Export-led Industrialization in the Third World', *Review of Radical Political Economics* 11:4, pp. 50–63.

Lapavitsas, C. (ed.) (2005) *Beyond Market Driven Development: Drawing on the Experience of Asia and Latin America* (London: Routledge).

Larrain, J. (1989) *Theories of Development* (Cambridge: Polity).

Lawrence, B. (ed.) (2005) *Messages to the World: The Statements of Osama bin Laden* (London: Verso).

Lawrence, F. (2005) 'Former OFT Chief Urges Inquiry into "Abuse" of Market Position by Supermarkets', *Guardian*, 10 November.

Laxer, G. and S. Halperin (eds) (2003), *Global Civil Society and its Limits* (Basingstoke: Palgrave Macmillan).

Lazonick, P. (1991) *Business Organisation and the Myth of the Market Economy* (Cambridge: Cambridge University Press).

Leadbeater, C. (1999) *Living on Thin Air* (London: Viking).

Leftwich, A. (1995) 'Bringing Politics Back In: Towards a Model of the Developmental State', *Journal of Development Studies* 25:4 pp. 363–86.

Legrain, P. (2002) *One World: The Truth about Globalization* (London: Abacus).

Lendman, P. (2006) 'Venezuela's Bolivarian Moment' (www.zmag.org).

Lenin, V. (1975) *Imperialism: The Highest Stage of Capitalism* (Moscow: Progress, first published 1916).

Levine, M. (2005) *Why They Don't Hate Us* (Oxford: One World).

Leonard, M. (ed.) (2003) *Why Europe will Run the 21st Century* (London: Fourth Estate).

Lerner, D. (1958) *The Passing of Traditional Society* (New York: Free Press).

Lewis, B. (1990) 'The Roots of Muslim Rage', *The Atlantic*, September 1990 (www.theatlantic.com/issues/90Sep).

Lewis, B. (2003) *What Went Wrong?* (New York: Perennial).

Lewis, W. A. (1954) 'Economic Development with Unlimited Supplies of Labour', *The Manchester School of Economic and Social Studies* 22:2, pp. 139–91.

Leys, C. (1996) *The Rise and Fall of Development Theory* (London: James Currey).

Lindert, P. and J. Williamson (2001) 'Does Globalization Make the World More Unequal?', National Bureau of Economic Research Working Paper no. 8228 (Cambridge, MA: NBER).

Lipschutz, R. (2004) *Global Environmental Politics* (Washington, DC: CQ Press).

Lipschutz, R. (2005) 'Power, Politics and Global Civil Society', *Millennium* 33:3, pp. 747–69.

List, F. (1966) *The National System of Political Economy* (New York: Augustus Kelley, first published in English 1885).

Little, I. (1979), 'The Experience and Causes of Rapid Labour-intensive Development in Korea, Taiwan Province, Hong Kong and Singapore, and the Possibilities of Emulation', in E. Lee (ed.), *Export Led Industrialization and Development* (Geneva: ILO), pp. 23–45.

Litwak, E. (2000) *Rogue States and US Foreign Policy* (Washington, DC: Woodrow Wilson Center Press).

Liu, Y. and F. Wu (2006) 'The State, Institutional Transition and the Creation of New Urban Poverty in China', *Social Policy and Administration* 40:2, pp. 121–37.

Lo, D. (2005) 'China, the "East Asian Model" and Late Development', paper to International Political Economy of Globalization conference, SOAS, University of London.

Locke, J. (1994) *The Second Treatise on Civil Government* (New York: Amherst, first published 1690).

Lucas, C. and V. Shiva (2005) 'G8's Free Trade Project is Here to Stay – Along with World Poverty', *Guardian*, 4 July.

Lucas, R. (1988) 'On the Mechanics of Economic Development', *Journal of Monetary Economics* 22:1, pp. 3–42.

Lukes, S. (2005a) 'Power and the Battle for Hearts and Minds', *Millennium* 33:3, pp. 477–93.

Lukes, S. (2005b) *Power: A Radical View* (Basingstoke: Palgrave Macmillan, 2nd edition).

Lysandrou, P. (2005) 'Globalisation as Commodification', *Cambridge Journal of Economics* 29:5, pp. 769–97.

Mallaby, S. (2002) 'The Reluctant Imperialist: Terrorism, Failed States and the Case for American Empire', *Foreign Affairs* 81:2, pp. 2–7.

Malone, D. (ed.) (2004) *The UN Security Council: From the Cold War to the Twenty-first Century* (Boulder, CO: Lynne Rienner).

Mamdani, M. (1996) *Citizen and Subject: Contemporary Africa and the Legacy of Late Colonialism* (Princeton, NJ: Princeton University Press).

Mamdani, M. (2001) *When Victims Become Killers: Colonialism, Nativism and Genocide in Rwanda* (Princeton, NJ: Princeton University Press).

Mamdani, M. (2004) *Good Muslim, Bad Muslim* (New York: Pantheon).

Mandel, E. (1975) *Late Capitalism* (London: New Left Books).

Mandel, E. (1980) *The Second Slump* (London: Verso).

Mann, M. (2003) *Incoherent Empire* (London: Verso).

Marcuse, H. (1968) *Reason and Revolution* (London: Routledge & Kegan Paul).

Marx, K. (1973) *Grundrisse* (London: Penguin, written in 1857–8).

Marx, K. (1976) *Capital*, vol. I (Harmondsworth: Penguin, first published 1867).

Marx, K. (1977) *Economic and Philosophical Manuscripts 1844* (London: Lawrence & Wishart).

Marx, K. (1978) *Critique of the Gotha Programme* (Moscow: Progress, first published 1875).

Marx, K. (1981) *Capital*, vol. III (Harmondsworth: Penguin, first published 1884).

Mauro, P. (1998) 'Corruption: Causes, Consequences and Agenda for Further Research', *Finance and Development*, May, pp. 11–14.

Mayall, J. (ed.) (1996) *The New Interventionism, 1991–94* (Cambridge: Cambridge University Press).

McCauley, J. (2001) 'The Trouble with Capitalism in One Country', *Against the Current* 94, pp. 42–8.

McDonald, K. (2006) *Global Movements* (Oxford: Blackwell).

McGrew, T. (2003) 'Between Two Worlds: Europe in a Globalising Era', *Government and Opposition* 39:3, pp. 343–58.

McKinnon, R. (1973) *Money and Capital in Economic Development* (Washington, DC: Brookings Institute).

Mearsheimer, J. (2001) *The Tragedy of Great Power Politics* (New York: W. W. Norton).

Mearsheimer, J. (2005) 'Hans Morgenthau and the Iraq War: Realism versus Neoconservatism' (at www.opendemocracy.net).

Michie, J. (ed.) (2004) *A Handbook of Globalisation* (Cheltenham: Edward Elgar).

Mies, M. and V. Shiva (1993) *Ecofeminism* (London: Zed Books).

Migdal, J. (1988) *Strong States and Weak Societies* (Princeton, NJ: Princeton University Press).

Migdal, J., A. Kohli and V. Shue (eds) (1994) *State Power and Social Forces* (Princeton, NJ: Princeton University Press).

Milanovic, B. (2002) *The Ricardian Vice: Why Sala-i-Martin's Calculations of World Income Inequality are Wrong* (at http://ideas.repec.org).

Milanovic, B. (2003) 'The Two Faces of Globalisation: Against Globalisation as We Know It', *World Development* 31:4, pp. 667–83.

Mill, J. S. (1973) *On Liberty* (London: Penguin, first published 1869).

Mitter, S. (1986) *Common Fate, Common Bond* (London: Pluto).

Mkandawire, T. (2001) 'Thinking about Developmental States in Africa', *Cambridge Journal of Economics* 25:3, pp. 289–313.

Mold, A. (2005) 'Africa's "Last Chance"? Reflections on the Commission for Africa and the Millennium Project Reports', *Real Instituto Elcano*, Working Paper 42, pp. 1–23.

Mollo, M. and A. Saad-Filho (2006) 'Neoliberal Economic Policies in Brazil (1994–2005): Cardoso, Lula and the Need for a Democratic Alternative', *New Left Review* 11:1, pp. 99–123.

Mommer, B. (2003) 'Subversive Oil', in S. Ellner and D. Hellinger (eds), *Venezuelan Politics in the Chavez Era* (Boulder, CO: Lynne Rienner), pp. 61–75.

Monbiot, G. (2005) 'Bards of the Powerful', *Guardian*, 21 June.

Monthly Review (2003), 'Editorial: What Recovery?', *Monthly Review* 54:11, pp. 1–11.

Moore, B. (1966) *Social Origins of Dictatorship and Democracy* (Boston, MA: Beacon).

Moore, M. (2003) *A World without Walls* (Cambridge: Cambridge University Press).

Morgan, P. (2003) 'Iraq', in F. Reza (ed.), *Anti-Imperialism: A Guide for the Movement* (London: Bookmarks), pp. 107–16.

Morton, A. D. (2005) 'The "Failed State" of International Relations', *New Political Economy* 10:3, pp. 371–9.

Mosley, P., J. Harrigan and J. Toye (1991) *Aid and Power*, 2 vols (London: Routledge).

Mulgan, G. (1998) *Connexity* (London: Vintage).

Murray, R. (1989) 'Fordism and Post-Fordism' in S. Hall and M. Jacques (eds), *New Times* (London: Lawrence & Wishart), pp. 38–52.

Myres, G. (2004) *Banana Wars: The Price of Free Trade* (London: Zed Books).

Nairn, T. (1964a) 'The British Political Elite', *New Left Review* I:23, pp. 19–25.

Nairn, T. (1964b) 'The English Working Class', *New Left Review* II:24, pp. 43–57.

Narlikar, A. (2003) *International Trade and Developing Countries* (London: Routledge).

National Security Strategy (2002) 'The National Security Strategy of the United States of America' (at www.whitehouse.gov/nsc/nss.html).

Natsios, A. (2006) 'Five Debates on International Development: the US Perspective', *Development Policy Review* 24:2, pp. 131–9.

Nederveen Pieterse, J. (2004) *Globalization or Empire?* (New York: Routledge).

NEPAD (2002) New Partnership for Africa's Development (at www.nepad.org).

Nesadurai, H. (2002) *Globalization and Economic Regionalism: A Survey and Critique of the Literature*, University of Warwick: CSGR Working Paper 108/02.

Nolan, P. (2001) *China and the Global Economy* (Basingstoke: Palgrave Macmillan).

Nolan, P. (2003) 'Industrial Policy in the Early 21st Century: The Challenge of the Global Business Revolution', in H. J. Chang (ed.), *Rethinking Development Economics* (London: Anthem), pp. 299–321.

Nolan, P. (2004) *China at the Crossroads* (Cambridge: Polity).

North, D. (1990) *Institutions, Institutional Change and Economic Performance* (Cambridge: Cambridge University Press).

Norton Taylor, R. (2005) 'Use and Abuse of Intelligence', *Guardian*, 19 July.

Nussbaum, M. and A. Sen (eds) (1993) *The Quality of Life* (Oxford: Oxford University Press).

Nye, J. (2004) *The Paradox of American Power* (Oxford: Oxford University Press).

Nye, J. (2005) *Soft Power* (New York: Public Affairs).

Nzula, A., I. Potekhin and A. Zusmanovich (1979) *Forced Labour in Colonial Africa* (London: Zed Books).

O'Brien, P. (1991) 'The Foundations of European Industrialization: From the Perspective of the World', *Journal of Historical Sociology* 4:3, p. 302.

O'Brien, P. (1997) 'Intercontinental Trade and the Development of the Third World since the Industrial Revolution', *Journal of World History* 8:1, pp. 75–133.

O'Brien, P. (1999) 'Imperialism and the Rise and Decline of the British Economy, 1688–1989', *New Left Review* 238, pp. 48–79.

O' Brien, P. (2003) 'The Myth of Anglophone Succession', *New Left Review* II:24, pp. 113–34.

O' Brien, P. (2006) 'Colonies in a Globalizing Economy, 1815–1948', in B. Gills and W. Thompson (eds), *Globalization and Global History* (London: Routledge), pp. 248–91.

O'Brien, R. and M. Williams (2004) *Global Political Economy* (Basingstoke: Palgrave Macmillan).

O'Brien, R., A. M. Goetz, J. Aart Scholte and M. Williams (2000) *Contesting Global Governance* (Cambridge: Cambridge University Press).

OECD (1998) *Economic Survey of Korea* (Paris: OECD).

Ohlin, B. (1933) *Inter-Regional and International Trade* (Cambridge, MA: Harvard University Press).

Ohmae, K. (1995) *Borderless World* (London: Fontana).

Ohmae, K. (1998) *The End of the Nation State* (London: Diane Publishers).

Olle, W. and W. Schoeller (1982) 'Direct Investment and Monopoly Theories of Imperialism', *Capital and Class* 16, pp. 41–60.

Overton, M. (1996) *Agricultural Revolution in England: The Transformation of the Agrarian Economy 1500–1800* (Cambridge: Cambridge University Press).

Oxfam (2002) *Rigged Rules and Double Standards* (Oxford: Oxfam).

Oxfam/Action Aid (2005) *Millstone or Milestone: What Rich Countries Must Do to Make Aid Work for Poor People* (Oxford: Oxfam International).

Ozaki, R. (1991) *Human Capitalism: The Japanese Enterprise System as World Model* (London: Penguin).

Panitch, L. (1981) 'Trade Unions and the Capitalist State', *New Left Review* 125, pp. 21–43.

Panitch, L. (1994) 'Globalisation and the State', in *The Socialist Register 1994* (London: Merlin), pp. 60–93.

Panitch, L. and S. Gindin (2003) 'Global Capitalism and American Empire', in L. Panitch and C. Leys (eds), *The Socialist Register 2004* (London: Merlin), pp. 1–42.

Panitch, L. and S. Gindin (2004) 'Finance and American Empire', in L. Panitch and C. Leys (eds), *The Socialist Register 2005* (London: Merlin), pp. 46–81.

Panitch, L. and S. Gindin (2005a) 'Euro-Capitalism and American Empire', in D. Coates (ed.), *Varieties of Capitalism, Varieties of Approaches* (Basingstoke: Palgrave Macmillan), pp. 139–59.

Panitch, L. and S. Gindin (2005b) 'Superintending Global Capital', *New Left Review* II:35, pp. 101–23.

Panitch, L. and S. Gindin (2006) 'Imperialism: a Reply to Callinicos', *International Socialism* 109, pp. 194–9.

Parekh, B. (1997) 'Dilemmas of a Multicultural Theory of Citizenship', *Constellations* 4:1, pp. 54–62.

Parfitt, T. (2002) *The End of Development* (London: Pluto).

Patnaik, U. (2006) 'Ricardo's Fallacy: Mutual Benefits from Trade Based on Comparative Costs and Specialization?', in K. S. Jomo (ed.), *The Pioneers of Development Economics* (London: Zed Books), pp. 31–41.

Payne, A. (2004) 'Rethinking Development inside International Political Economy', in A. Payne (ed.), *The New Regional Politics of Development* (Basingstoke: Palgrave Macmillan), pp. 1–28.

Payne, A. (2005) *The Global Politics of Unequal Development* (Basingstoke: Palgrave Macmillan).

Payne, A. and A. Gamble (1996) 'Introduction: the Political Economy of Regionalism and World Order', in A. Gamble and A. Payne (eds), *Regionalism and World Order* (Basingstoke: Palgrave Macmillan), pp. 1–20.

Pepper, D. (1996) *Modern Environmentalisms: An Introduction* (London: Routledge).

Perraton, J. and B. Clift (2004) 'So Where are National Capitalisms Now?', in J. Perraton and B. Clift (eds), *Where are National Capitalisms Now?* (Basingstoke: Palgrave Macmillan), pp. 195–261.

Petras, J. (2004) 'Myths and Realities: President Chavez and the Referendum' (at www.counterpunch.org/petras09022004.html).

Petras, J. (2005) 'Six Myths about the Benefits of Foreign Investment' (at www.counterpunch.org/petras07022005.html).

Petras, J. and H. Veltmeyer (2005) *Empire with Imperialism* (London: Zed Books).

Phillips, A. (1987) *The Enigma of Colonialism* (London: James Currey).

Phillips, N. (2005) '"Globalizing" the Study of International Political Economy', in N. Phillips (ed.), *Globalizing International Political Economy* (Basingstoke: Palgrave Macmillan), pp. 1–19.

Piore, M. and C. Sabel (1984) *The Second Industrial Divide* (London: Basic Books).

Pirie, I. (2005a) 'Better by Design: Korea's Neoliberal Eeconomy', *Pacific Review* 18:3, pp. 1–20.

Pirie, I. (2005b) 'The New Korean State', *New Political Economy* 10:1, pp. 27–44.

Pirie, I. (2006a) 'Economic Crisis and the Construction of a Neo-liberal Regulatory Regime in Korea', *Competition and Change* 10:1, pp. 49–71.

Pirie, I. (2006b) 'Social Injustice and Economic Dynamism in Contemporary Korea', *Critical Asian Studies* (forthcoming).

Pogge, T. (2002) *World Poverty and Human Rights* (Cambridge: Polity).

Pogge, T. (2004) 'The First UN Millennium Development Goal: a Cause for Celebration?' (at www.socialanalysis.org).

Polanyi, K. (1944) *The Great Transformation* (New York: Beacon).

Pomeranz, K. (2000) *The Great Divergence: China, Europe and the Making of the Modern World Economy* (Princeton, NJ: Princeton University Press).

Prebisch, R. (1959) 'Commercial Policy in the Underdeveloped Countries', *American Economic Review* vol. 44, pp. 251–73.

Press, C. (2006) 'Chavez Calls Blair "Pawn of Imperialism"', *Associated Press*, 8 February.

Preston, P. (1996) *Development Theory* (Oxford: Blackwell).

Project for the New American Century (1997) *Statement of Principles* (www.newamericancentury.org).

Project for the New American Century (1998) *Letter to President Clinton on Iraq* (www.newamericancentury.org).

Putnam, R. (1993) *Making Democracy Work: Civic Traditions in Modern Italy* (Princeton, NJ: Princeton University Press).

Putnam, R. (2000) *Bowling Alone* (New York: Simon & Schuster).

Qingguo, J. (2003) 'The Impact of 9–11 on Sino-US Relations: a Preliminary Assessment', *International Relations of the Asia-Pacific* 3:2, pp. 159–77.

Radice, H. (2000) 'Responses to Globalisation: a Critique of Progressive Nationalism', *New Political Economy* 5:1, pp. 5–19.

Rahnema, M. (1997) 'Towards Post-Development: Searching for Signposts, a New Language and New Paradigms', in M. Rahnema and V. Bawtree (eds), *The Post-Development Reader* (London: Zed Books), pp. 377–403.

Rao, R. (2004) 'The Empire Writes Back (to Michael Ignatieff)', *Millennium* 33:1, pp. 145–66.

Ravenhill, J. (ed.) (2005) *Global Political Economy* (Oxford: Oxford University Press).

Reddy, S. and T. Pogge (2003) 'How *Not* to Count the Poor' (at www.socialanalysis.org).

Rees, J. (2000) 'Oil, Gas and NATO's New Frontier', *New Political Economy* 5:1, pp. 100–4.

Rees, J. (2001) 'Imperialism: Globalization, the State and War', *International Socialism* 93, pp. 3–34.

Reus-Smit, C. (2004) *American Power and World Order* (Cambridge: Polity).

Review of International Studies (2005), 'Special Issue on China', 31:4.

Ricardo, D. (1981) *Principles of Political Economy* (Cambridge: Cambridge University Press, first published 1819).

Ritzer, G. (1993) *The McDonaldization of Society* (London: Sage).

Ritzer, G. (2004) *The Globalization of Nothing* (London: Sage).

Roberts, H. (2002) 'The Left and the Algerian Catastrophe', in L. Panitch and C. Leys (eds), *Socialist Register 2003* (London: Merlin), pp. 152–71.

Robinson, B. (1996) *Promoting Polyarchy* (Cambridge: Cambridge University Press).

Robinson, B. (2002) 'Capitalist Globalization and the Transnationalization of the State', in M. Rupert and H. Smith (eds), *Historical Materialism and Globalization* (London: Routledge), pp. 210–29.

Robinson, B. (2004) *A Theory of Global Capitalism* (Baltimore, MA: Johns Hopkins University Press).

Robinson, B. and J. Harris (2000) 'Towards a Global Ruling Class? Globalization and the Transnational Capitalist Class', *Science and Society* 64:1, pp. 11–54.

Rodney, W. (1972) *How Europe Underdeveloped Africa* (London: Bogle L'Ouverture).

Rodriguez, F. and D. Rodrik (1999) *Trade Policy and Economic Growth: A Skeptics Guide to Cross National Evidence* (Washington, DC: NBER Working Paper no. 7081), pp. 1–90.

Rodrik, D. (2000), 'Comments on "Trade, Growth and Poverty" by D. Dollar and A. Kraay' (at http://ksghome.harvard.edu/~drodrik/Rodrik%20on%20 Dollar-Kraay).

Rodrik, D. (2001) *The Global Governance of Trade as if Development Really Mattered* (Geneva: United Nations Development Programme).

Rodrik, D. and A. Subramanian (2001) 'From "Hindu Growth" to Productivity Surge: The Mystery of the Indian Growth Transition', *IMF Working Papers* 04/77 (2001).

Rogers, P. (2006) *A War Too Far: Iraq, Iran and the New American Century* (London: Pluto).

Rosamond, B. (2000) *Theories of European Integration* (Basingstoke: Macmillan).

Rosenau, J. (1997) *Along the Domestic–Foreign Frontier* (Cambridge: Cambridge University Press).

Rosenberg, J. (1990) 'A Non-Realist Theory of Sovereignty? Giddens' *The Nation State and Violence*', *Millennium* 19:2, pp. 240–54.

Rosenberg, J. (1994) *The Empire of Civil Society* (London: Verso).

Rosenberg, J. (2000) *The Follies of Globalization Theory* (London: Verso).

Rosenberg, J. (2005) 'Globalization Theory: a Postmortem', *International Politics* 42:1, pp. 2–74.

Ross, S. (2002) 'Is This what Democracy Looks Like: the Anti-Globalization Movement in North America', in L. Panitch and C. Leys (eds), *Socialist Register 2003* (London: Merlin), pp. 281–304.

Rostow, W. (1960) *The Stages of Economic Growth* (Cambridge: Cambridge University Press).

Roth, K. (2004) 'War in Iraq: Not a Humanitarian Intervention', *Human Rights Watch* (at www.hrw.org).

Roy, O. (1994) *The Failure of Political Islam* (London: I. B. Tauris).

Roy, O. (2004) *Globalized Islam* (New York: Columbia University Press).

Royal Institute of International Affairs (2005) *Security, Terrorism and the UK* (London: Chatham House).

Ruggie, J. (1982) 'International Regimes, Transactions and Change: Embedded Liberalism in the Post-war Economic Order', *International Organisation* 36:3, pp. 379–96.

Ruigrok, W. and R. van Tulder (1996) *The Logic of International Restructuring* (London: Routledge).

Runciman, D. (2006) *The Politics of Good Intentions* (Princeton, NJ: Princeton University Press).

Russett, B. (1990) *Controlling the Sword* (Cambridge, MA: Harvard University Press).

Russett, B. (1993) *Grasping the Democratic Peace* (Princeton, NJ: Princeton University Press).

Saad-Filho, A. (2005) 'The Political Economy of Neoliberalism in Latin America', in A. Saad-Filho and D. Johnston (eds), *Neoliberalism: A Critical Reader* (London: Pluto), pp. 222–9.

A. Saad-Filho and D. Johnston (eds), *Neoliberalism: A Critical Reader* (London: Pluto).

Sachs, J. and A. Warner (1995) *Economic Reform and the Process of Global Integration* (Washington, DC: Brookings Papers on Economic Activity, no. 1).

Sachs, W. (1992), 'Introduction', in W. Sachs (ed.), *The Development Dictionary* (London: Zed Books), pp. 1–12.

Said, E. (1978) *Orientalism* (London: Penguin).

Sala-i-Martin, X. (2002a) 'The Disturbing "Rise" of Global Income Inequality', NBER Working Papers no. 8904 (Cambridge: National Bureau of Economic Research).

Sala-i-Martin, X. (2002b) 'The World Distribution of Income (estimated from Individual Country Contributions)', NBER Working Papers no. 8933 (Cambridge: National Bureau of Economic Research).

Saull, R. (2001) *Rethinking Theory and History in the Cold War* (London: Frank Cass).

Saull, R. (2004) 'On the "New" American "Empire"', *Security Dialogue* 35:2, pp. 250–3.

Saull, R. (2006) 'Reactionary Blowback: the Uneven Ends of the Cold War and the Origins of Contemporary Conflict in World Politics', in A. Colas and R. Saull (eds), *The War on Terrorism and American "Empire" after the Cold War* (London: Routledge), pp. 65–90.

Schmitt, G. and D. Blumenthal (2005) 'Wishful Thinking in Our Time', *Weekly Standard*, 8 August.

Scholte, J. A. (1999a) 'Globalization: Prospects for a Paradigm shift', in M. Shaw (ed.), *Politics and Globalization* (London: Routledge), pp. 90–107.

Scholte, J. A. (1999b), '"In the Foothills": Relations between the IMF and Civil Society', in R. Higott and A. Bieler (eds), *Non-State Actors and Authority in the Global System* (London: Routledge), pp. 256–73.

Scholte, J. A. (2000) *Globalization: A Critical Introduction* (Basingstoke: Palgrave Macmillan, 1st edition).

Scholte, J. A. (2005a) *Globalization: A Critical Introduction* (Basingstoke: Palgrave Macmillan, 2nd edition).

Scholte, J. A. (2005b) 'Premature Obituaries: a Response to Justin Rosenberg', *International Politics* 42:3, pp. 390–9.

Schor, J. (2003) *The Overworked American* (New York: Basic Books).

Scruton, R. (2005) *The West and the Rest* (London: Continuum).

Segal, G. (2004) 'Does China Matter', in B. Buzan and R. Foot (eds) (2004) *Does China Matter? A Re-assessment* (London: Routledge), pp. 11–20.

Seltzer, I. (ed.) (2005) *Neo-Conservatism* (New York: Atlantic).

Semmel, B. (1970) *The Rise of Free Trade Imperialism* (Cambridge: Cambridge University Press).

Sen, A. (1999) *Development as Freedom* (Oxford: Oxford University Press).

Shabi, R. (2005) 'Was Africa Short Changed?', *Guardian* 13 July.

Shaikh, A. (1979–80) 'Foreign Trade and the Law of Value – Part Two', *Science and Society* 44, pp. 27–57.

Shaikh, A. (2005) 'The Economic Mythology of Neoliberalism', in A. Saad-Filho (ed.), *Neoliberalism: A Critical Reader* (London: Pluto), pp. 41–9.

Shaw, E. (1973) *Financial Deepening in Economic Development* (New York: Oxford University Press).

Shaw, M. (1996) *Civil Society and the Media in Global Crises* (London: Pinter).

Shaw, M. (2000) *Theory of the Global State* (Cambridge: Cambridge University Press).

Shaw, M. (2002) '10 Challenges to Anti-War Politics', *Radical Philosophy*, pp. 11–19.

Shaw, M. (2003) 'The Global Transformation of the Social Sciences', in M. Kaldor, H. Anheier and M. Glasius (eds), *Global Civil Society* (Oxford: Oxford University Press), pp. 35–44.

Shaw, M. (2005) *The New Western Way of War* (Cambridge: Polity).

Shin, J. S. and H. J. Chang (2003) *Restructuring Korea Inc.* (London: Routledge).

Shiva, V. (2005) *Earth Democracy* (London: Zed Books).

Shue, H., (1980) *Basic Rights: Subsistence, Affluence and US Foreign Policy* (Princeton, NJ: Princeton University Press, 1980).

Shukla, S. (2002) 'From the GATT to the WTO and Beyond', in D. Nayar (ed.), *Governing Globalization* (Oxford: Oxford University Press), pp. 254–83.

Silver, B. and G. Arrighi (2000) 'Workers North and South', in *The Socialist Register 2001* (London: Merlin), pp. 53–76.

Simon, D. (ed.) (1995) *Structurally Adjusted Africa* (London: Pluto).

Singer, H. (1950) 'The Distribution of Gains from Trade between Investing and Borrowing Countries', *American Economic Review* vol. 40, pp. 473–85.

Singer, P. (2004) *The President of Good and Evil* (London: Granta Books).

Singh, A. (2005) 'Special and Differential Treatment: the Multilateral Trading System and Economic Development in the Twenty-First Century', in K. Gallagher (ed.), *Putting Development First* (London: Zed Books), pp. 233–63.

Sklair, L. (2001) *The Transnational Capitalist Class* (Oxford: Blackwell).

Sklair, L. (2002) *Globalization: Capitalism and its Alternatives* (Oxford: Oxford University Press).

Slater, D. (2004) *The Geopolitics of Social Theory* (Oxford: Blackwell).

Slaughter, A. M. (2004) *A New World Order* (Princeton, NJ: Princeton University Press).

Smith, A. (1998) *The Wealth of Nations* (Oxford: Oxford Paperbacks, first published 1776).

Smith, N. (2005) *The Endgame of Globalization* (New York: Routledge).

Smith, S. (2002) 'US Democracy Promotion: Critical Questions', in M. Cox, J. Ikenberry and T. Inoguchi (eds), *American Democracy Promotion* (Oxford: Oxford University Press), pp. 63–82.

Smith, S. and J. Toye (1979) 'Trade and Poor Economies', *Journal of Development Studies* 15:1, pp. 1–18.

Snidal, D. (1985) 'The Limits of Hegemonic Stability Theory', *International Organisation* 39:4, pp. 579–614.

Soederberg, S. (2006a) 'The War on Terror and American Empire: Emerging Development Agendas', in A. Colas and R. Saull (eds), *The War on Terrorism and the American "Empire" after the Cold War'* (London: Routledge), pp. 155–79.

Soederberg, S. (2006b) *Global Governance in Question: Empire and the New Common Sense in Managing North–South Relations* (London: Pluto).

Solow, B. and S. Engerman (1987) 'British Capitalism and Caribbean Slavery: the Legacy of Eric Williams: an Introduction', in B. Solow and S. Engerman (eds), *British Capitalism and Caribbean Slavery: The Legacy of Eric Williams* (Cambridge: Cambridge University Press), pp. 1–35.

Spero, J. and J. Hart (2003) *The Politics of International Economic Relations* (Belmont, CA: Wadsworth).

Stanfield, J. (1994) 'Learning from Japan about the Nurturance Gap in America', *Review of Social Economy* 52:1, pp. 2–19.

Starr, H. (1997) 'Democracy and Integration: Why Democracies Don't Fight Each Other', *Journal of Peace Research* 32:2, pp. 153–62.

Stiglitz, J. (2002) *Globalization and its Discontents* (London: Penguin).

Stokes, D. (2005) 'The Heart of Empire? Theorising US Empire in the Era of Transnational Capitalism', *Third World Quarterly* 26:2, pp. 217–36.

Strange, S. (1987) 'The Persistent Myth of Lost Hegemony', *International Organisation* 41:4, pp. 551–74.

Strange, S. (1997) 'The Future of Global Capitalism: or, Will Divergence Persist for Ever?', in C. Crouch and W. Streeck (eds), *Political Economy of Modern Capitalism* (London: Sage), pp. 182–91.

Streeck, W. (1992) *Social Institutions and Economic Performance* (London: Sage).

Sumner, A. (2004) 'Epistemology and "Evidence" in Development Studies: a Review of Dollar and Kraay', *Third World Quarterly* 25:6, pp. 1167–77.

Sumner, A. (2005) 'Is Foreign Direct Investment Good for the Poor: a Review and Stocktake', *Development in Practice* 15:3/4), pp. 1–14.

Sutcliffe, B. (2001) *100 Ways of Seeing an Unequal World* (London: Zed Books).

Sutcliffe, B. and R. Owen (eds) (1972) *Studies in the Theory of Imperialism* (London: Longman).

Sweezy, P. (1976) 'A Critique', in R. Hilton (ed.), *The Transition from Feudalism to Capitalism* (London: Verso), pp. 35–56.

Talmon, J. (1955) *On the Origins of Totalitarian Democracy* (New York: Secker and Warburg).

Taylor, I. (2005) 'Globalisation Studies and the Developing World: Making International Political Economy Truly Global', *Third World Quarterly* 26:7, pp. 1025–42.

Taylor, P. (1993) *International Organization in the Modern World* (London: Pinter).

Teschke, B. (2003) *The Myth of 1648* (London: Verso).

Third World Quarterly (2004) 'Special Issue – IPE and the "Third World"', 25:1.

Third World Quarterly (2005) 'Special Issue – Reconstructing Iraq', 26:4/5).

Third World Quarterly (2006) 'Special Issue – Nation and State Building', 27:1.

Thompson, E. (1965) 'The Peculiarities of the English', in R. Miliband and J. Saville (eds), *The Socialist Register 1965* (London: Merlin), pp. 311–62.

Thrift, N. (1996) 'A Hyperactive World', in R. Johnston, P. Taylor and M. Watts (eds), *Geographies of Global Change* (Oxford: Blackwell), pp. 18–35.

Tilly, C. (1992) *Coercion, Capital and European States* (Oxford: Blackwell).

Todaro, M. (1989) *Economic Development in the Third World* (London: Longman).

Tomaney, J. (1994) 'A New Paradigm of Work Organizations and Technology', in A. Amin (ed.), *Post-Fordism* (Oxford: Blackwell), pp. 157–94.

Tomlinson, J. (1999) *Globalization and Culture* (Cambridge: Polity).

Tormey, S. (2005) *Anti-Capitalism: A Beginner's Guide* (Oxford: One World).

Toye, J. (1987) *Dilemmas of Development* (Oxford: Blackwell).

Toye, J. (2003) 'Order and Justice in the International Trade System', in R. Foot, J. Lewis Gaddis and A. Hurrell (eds), *Order and Justice in International Relations* (Oxford: Oxford University Press), pp. 103–24.

Tripp, C. (2004) 'The United States and State-building in Iraq', *Review of International Studies* 30:3, pp. 545–58.

UNCTAD (1997) *World Investment Report 1998* (Geneva: UNCTAD).

UNCTAD (1998) *World Investment Report 1998* (Geneva: UNCTAD).

UNCTAD (2001) *World Investment Report 2001* (Geneva: UNCTAD).

UNCTAD (2002a) *The Least Developed Countries Report 2002* (Geneva: UNCTAD).

UNCTAD (2002b) *World Investment Report 2002* (Geneva: UNCTAD).

UNCTAD (2004a) *Development and Globalization: Facts and Figures* (Geneva: United Nations).

UNCTAD (2004b) *The Least Developed Countries Report 2004* (Geneva: UNCTAD).

UNCTAD (2004c) *World Investment Report 2004* (Geneva: UNCTAD).

UNDP (1995) *Human Development Report* (New York: United Nations Development Program).

United Nations (1948) *Universal Declaration of Human Rights* (at www.un.org/rights.html).

United Nations (1995) *Our Global Neighbourhood* (London: Earthscan).

United Nations Economic Commission for Africa (2004) *Economic Report on Africa 2004: Unlocking Africa's Trade Potential* (Addis Ababa: UN Economic Commission for Africa).

Urry, J. (2002) *Global Complexity* (Cambridge: Polity).

van der Pijl, K. (1998) *Transnational Classes and International Relations* (London: Routledge).

Vanaik, A. (1990) *The Peaceful Transition* (London: Verso).

Wade, R. (1990) *Governing the Market* (Princeton: Princeton University Press).

Wade, R. (1998) 'The Asian Debt and Development Crisis of 1997: Causes and Consequences', *World Development* 26:8, pp. 1535–53.

Wade, R. (2003a) 'What Strategies are Viable for Developing Countries Today? The World Trade Organization and the Shrinking of "Development Space"', *Review of International Political Economy* 10, pp. 621–44.

Wade, R. (2003b) 'The Invisible Hand of the American Empire', *Ethics and International Affairs* 17:2, pp. 77–88.

Wade, R. (2004a) 'On the Causes of Increasing World Poverty and Inequality, or Why the Matthew Effect Prevails', *New Political Economy* 9:2, pp. 163–88.

Wade, R. (2004b) 'Is Globalization Reducing Poverty and Inequality?', *World Development* 32:4, pp. 567–89.

Wade, R. and F. Veneroso (1998), 'The Gathering World Slump and the Battle over Capital Controls', *New Left Review* II:23, pp. 13–42.

Wade, R. and M. Wolf (2002) 'Are Global Poverty and Inequality Getting Worse?', *Prospect,* March, pp. 16–21.

Wall, D. (2005) *Babylon and Beyond* (London: Pluto).

Wallerstein, I. (1974) *The Modern World System*, 2 vols (New York: Academic Press).

Wallerstein, I. (1979) *The Capitalist World Economy* (Cambridge: Cambridge University Press).

Wallerstein, I. (2003) *The Decline of American Power* (New York: New Press).

Waltz, K. (1979) *Theory of International Politics* (New York: Random House).

Walzer, M. (1992) *Just and Unjust Wars* (New York: Basic Books, 2nd edn).

Ward, J. (1983) *The British Economists and the Empire* (London: Routledge).

Warren, B. (1973) 'Imperialism and Capitalist Industrialization', *New Left Review* 81, pp. 9–44.

Warren, B. (1980) *Imperialism: Pioneer of Capitalism* (London: Verso).

Webber, M. and D. Rigby (1996) *The Golden Age Illusion* (New York: Guilford).

Weber, M. (1978) *Economy and Society* (London: Routledge, first published 1921).

Weisbrot, M. and D. Baker (2002) 'The Relative Impact of Trade Liberalization on Developing Countries' (at www.cepr.net).

Weiss, L. (1997) 'Globalization and the Myth of the Powerless State', *New Left Review* I:225, pp. 3–27.

Weiss, L. (1998) *The Myth of the Powerless State* (Cambridge: Polity).

Weiss, L. (2003) 'Guiding Globalisation in East Asia: New Roles for Old

Developmental States', in L. Weiss (ed.), *States in the Global Economy: Bringing Domestic Institutions Back In* (Cambridge: Cambridge University Press), pp. 245–70.

Weiss, L. and J. Hobson (1995) *States and Economic Development* (Cambridge: Polity).

Welsh, J. (ed.) (2004) *Humanitarian Intervention in International Relations Theory* (Oxford: Oxford University Press).

Went, R. (2002) 'Globalization in the Perspective of Imperialism', *Science and Society* 66:4, pp. 473–97.

Whalley, J. (1999) 'Special and Differential Treatment in the Millennium Round', CSGR Working Paper no. 30 (Coventry: University of Warwick).

Wheeler, N. (2000) *Saving Strangers* (Oxford: Oxford University Press).

Wheeler, N. and A. Bellamy (2005) 'Humanitarian Intervention and World Politics', in C. Baylis and S. Smith, *Globalization and World Politics* (Oxford: Oxford University Press), pp. 555–78.

Wheen, F. (2004) *How Mumbo-Jumbo Conquered the World* (London: Fourth Estate).

White, G. (1993) *Riding the Tiger* (Basingstoke: Macmillan).

White, G. (ed.) (1988) *Developmental States in East Asia* (Basingstoke: Macmillan).

Willetts, P. (ed.) (1996) *The Conscience of the World* (London: Hurst).

Williams, E. (1987) *Capitalism and Slavery* (London: André Deutsch, first published 1942).

Williams, K. (2000) 'From Shareholder Value to Present-day Capitalism', *Economy and Society* 29:1, pp. 1–12.

Wilpert, G. (2003) 'Collision in Venezuela', *New Left Review* II:21, pp. 101–16.

Wolfensohn, J. (1996) 'People and Development', in IMF, *Summary Proceedings of the 51st Annual Meeting of the Board of the IMF* (Washington: IMF), pp. 24–8.

Womack, J., D. Jones and D. Roos (1990) *The Machine that Changed the World* (New York: Rawson Associates).

Woo, W., L. Shi, Y. Ximing, H. Xiaoying and X. Xingpeng (2004) *The Poverty Challenge for China in the New Millennium* (New York: UN Millennium Development Goals Project).

Wood, E. M. (1991) *The Pristine Culture of Capitalism* (London: Verso).

Wood, E. M. (1995) *Democracy against Capitalism* (Cambridge: Cambridge University Press).

Wood, E. M. (2002) *The Origins of Capitalism* (London: Verso).

Wood, E. M. (2003) *Empire of Capital* (London: Verso).

Woodiwiss, A. (1997) 'Against Modernity: a Dissident Rant', *Economy and Society* 26:1, pp. 1–21.

Woodiwiss, A. (2005a) *Human Rights* (London: Routledge).

Woodiwiss, A. (2005b) *Scoping Social Theory* (Maidenhead: Open University Press).

World Bank (1981) *Accelerated Development in Sub-Saharan Africa* (Washington, DC: World Bank).

World Bank (1990) *World Development Report* (Washington, DC: World Bank).

World Bank (1991) *World Development Report* (Washington, DC: World Bank).
World Bank (1992) *Governance and Development* (Washington, DC: World Bank).
World Bank (1993) *The East Asian Miracle* (Oxford: Oxford University Press).
World Bank (1994) *Adjustment in Africa* (Oxford: Oxford University Press).
World Bank (1997) *World Development Report* (Oxford: Oxford University Press).
World Bank (1998) *The Initiative on Defining, Measuring and Monitoring Social Capital* (at www.worldbank.org/socialcapital).
World Bank (1999a) *Global Economic Prospects and the Developing Countries* (Washington, DC: World Bank).
World Bank (1999b) *World Development Report 1999/2000* (Oxford: Oxford University Press).
World Bank (2000) *World Development Report 2000/01* (Oxford: Oxford University Press).
World Bank (2002a) *Globalization, Growth and Poverty: Building an Inclusive World Economy* (Oxford: Oxford University Press).
World Bank (2002b) *Global Economic Prospects and Developing Countries – Making Trade Work for the Poor* (Washington, DC: World Bank).
World Bank (2002c) *Transition – The First Ten Years: Analysis and Lessons for Eastern Europe and the Former Soviet Union* (Washington, DC: World Bank).
World Bank (2004) *Reforming Infrastructure: Privatization, Regulation and Competition* (Washington, DC: World Bank).
World Development Movement (2004) 'Media Briefing: UK Government's Commission for Africa' (at www.wdm.org.uk).
Worsley, P. (1964) *The Three Worlds* (Chicago: University of Chicago Press).
Wrigley, E. (1994) 'The Classical Economists, the Stationary State and the Industrial Revolution', in G. Snooks (ed.), *Was the Industrial Revolution Necessary?* (London: Routledge), pp. 27–42.
WTO (1998) *Draft Report of Committee on Trade and Development* (at www.wto.org).
WTO (1999) 'Ten Common Misunderstandings about the WTO' (at www.wto.org).
WTO (2001) *Trading into the Future* (Geneva: WTO).
WTO (2005) *International Trade Statistics* (Geneva: WTO).
www.caat.org.uk.
www.cia.gov/terrorism.
www.defenselink/mil/pentagon.
www.gatt.org.
www.globalissues.org/Geopolitics/ArmsTrade.
www.mca.org.
www.newamericancentury.org.
www.un.org/millenniumgoals.
www.worldbank.org/research/povmonitor.
Young, C. (1994) *The African Colonial State in Comparative Perspective* (New Haven, CT: Yale University Press).

Ziai, A. (2004) 'The Ambivalence of Post-development: Between Reactionary Populism and Radical Democracy', *Third World Quarterly* 25:6, pp. 1045–60.

Zubaida, S. (1988) *Islam, the People and the State* (London: Routledge).

Zysman, J. and S. Cohen (1986) 'The International Experience', in D. Obey and P. Sarbanes (eds), *The Changing American Economy* (Oxford: Blackwell), pp. 41–55.

Index